Brutality in an Age of Human Rights

Brutality in an Age of Human Rights

Activism and Counterinsurgency at the End of the British Empire

BRIAN DROHAN

Cornell University Press

Ithaca and London

First published 2017 by Cornell University Press

Printed in the United States of America

Library of Congress Cataloging-in-Publication Data

Names: Drohan, Brian, 1983– author.
Title: Brutality in an age of human rights : activism and
    counterinsurgency at the end of the British empire / Brian Drohan.
Description: Ithaca : Cornell University Press, 2017. | Includes
    bibliographical references and index.
Identifiers: LCCN 2017024006 (print) | LCCN 2017026166 (ebook) |
    ISBN 9781501714672 (pdf) | ISBN 9781501714665 (ret) |
    ISBN 9781501714658 (cloth : alk. paper)
Subjects: LCSH: Counterinsurgency—Cyprus. |
    Counterinsurgency—Yemen (Republic)—Aden. |
    Counterinsurgency—Northern Ireland. | Human rights—Cyprus. |
    Human rights—Yemen (Republic)—Aden. | Human rights—
    Northern Ireland. | Cyprus—History—War for Union with Greece,
    1955–1959. | Yemen (Arab Republic)—History—1962–1970. |
    Northern Ireland—History—1968–1998. | Postcolonialism—Great
    Britain.
Classification: LCC U241 (ebook) | LCC U241 .D76 2017 (print) |
    DDC 355.02/1809171209045—dc23
LC record available at https://lccn.loc.gov/2017024006

For

Mark Daily, Second Lieutenant, U.S. Army

David Schultz, First Lieutenant, U.S. Army

Clinton Ruiz, Sergeant, U.S. Army

Mike Gilotti, First Lieutenant, U.S. Army

and the loved ones they left behind

Contents

Acknowledgments

The inspiration for this book came from my personal experiences as a U.S. Army officer and my academic studies in history at the University of North Carolina at Chapel Hill, but the project would never have come to fruition without help from a long list of mentors and colleagues. While I was an undergraduate at the University of Pennsylvania, Walter McDougall, Ronald Granieri, and Jeffrey Engel steered me toward international and military history. During my operational assignments in the army, I have been fortunate to work with talented military and foreign service officers such as Jeff Anderson, John Craven, Valerie Fowler, Chris Gunning, Patrick Hu, Kelly Jones, John Nagl, Amos Oh, Tom Ryno, Chris Teal, and Diem Vo. Glen Davis encouraged me to choose history as my graduate school discipline. At UNC-Chapel Hill, Susan Pennybacker and Wayne Lee helped me develop this project from its early stages to completion. I also benefited from a wide-ranging faculty in the global and military history subfields, particularly Mike Morgan, Cemil Aydin, Klaus Larres, and Joe Glatthaar. For my friends and colleagues Jessica Auer, Ansev Demirhan, Joel Hebert, Erika Huckestein, Mark Reeves, Jordan Smith, Larissa Stiglich, and Mary Elizabeth Walters: thank you for helping me navigate life as a graduate student. Joel helped me articulate what exactly I wanted to study and how to approach the topic and helped sharpen my arguments by commenting on several chapters. Mark read every word of the entire manuscript and posed several probing questions in addition to catching numerous typographical errors.

I finished this book while teaching in the history department at the U.S. Military Academy, West Point, which was a phenomenal intellectual environment in which to work. I owe many thanks to Colonels Ty Seidule and

Gail Yoshitani, as well as senior faculty members Greta Bucher, David Frey, Randy Roberts, Cliff Rogers, John Stapleton, Sam Watson, and Steve Waddell. I am also thankful for the fellowship and support of my colleagues Amanda Boczar, Casey Baker, Matt Cohen, Logan Collins, Andy Forney, Jason Halub, Rich Hutton, Nate Jennings, Rory McGovern, Peggy O'Donnell, John "Rocky" Rhodes, and Nick Sambaluk. The greatest part of teaching at West Point, however, is the student body. I have been amazed by the dedication, excitement, and intelligence of the cadets whom I have taught, especially Simone Askew, Gabriel Beck, Erin Colburn, Lindsay Gabow, Mitchell Magill, and Curtis Valencia.

Research for this book benefited from financial support provided by the Omar N. Bradley Foundation, the UK Society for Army Historical Research, and the Raymond Faherty Research Grant awarded by UNC-Chapel Hill. The professional staff members at numerous archives were a tremendous resource, helping to sift through the available evidence. In Chapel Hill, Evdokia Glekas kindly translated several Greek-language sources for me and Gabe Moss did a great job creating maps for the book. In 2015, I was privileged to participate in the Global Humanitarianism Research Academy in Mainz, Germany, and Geneva, Switzerland, where Johannes Paulmann, Fabian Klose, Jean-Luc Blondel, and Michael Geyer fostered a stimulating environment for the study of humanitarianism and human rights in history. Friends from the program helped encourage this project, particularly Tehila Sasson, Boyd van Dijk, and Mie Vestergaard.

Several scholars also contributed to the development of this project. David Anderson took an interest from the moment I met him and provided insightful guidance and support throughout the writing process. His help has been indispensable. On two separate occasions, Huw Bennett asked penetrating questions that honed my thinking about the Cyprus and Aden campaigns. Kim Wagner has been an excellent sounding board for ideas. In 2014, Martin Thomas and Gareth Curless organized a conference at the University of Exeter that allowed me to air some of my early ideas. At the University of Exeter, Stacey Hynd, Marc-William Palen, Gajendra Singh, and Andrew Thompson encouraged this project and brought me into the fold of their wonderful community of scholars in imperial and global history. At Cornell University Press, my editor, Roger Haydon, has been a joy to work with. He offered incisive comments and expertly guided me through the process of turning this manuscript into a book. Two anonymous reviewers also provided useful feedback for which I am very grateful.

Beyond academia, David Copley, Mike Kirkman, and Matt Klapper have always provided friendship and perspective. Matt Gallagher, who pursued his own path as a writer, was always an inspiration for me to keep writing. My greatest thanks, however, go to my family—my father, Tom; mother, Madeline; sister, Laura; and especially Kirsten Cooper, who despite having

to read every draft of this book in its multitude of forms and listen to count-
less hours of my thinking out loud, has remained my travel buddy, intellectual colleague, editor in chief, and partner in all that life has to offer.

Finally, a note to put this book in perspective: The topics discussed in the
following pages remain relevant to contemporary debates concerning human rights and warfare, particularly in my country. Americans like to see
themselves as a people who aspire to grand ideals such as liberty and justice. These ideals have meant many things to many people throughout our
history, and we have often failed to live up to them, but they are nonetheless enshrined in our founding documents and in our sense of national
identity. I am of the opinion that if we lose our moral compass in war, we
lose ourselves. This opinion brings me to my next point—although I work
for the United States government, this is my book. Consequently, I should
make it clear that *the views expressed herein do not necessarily represent the
views of the U.S. Military Academy, the U.S. Army, or the Department of
Defense.*

Maps

Map of Cyprus

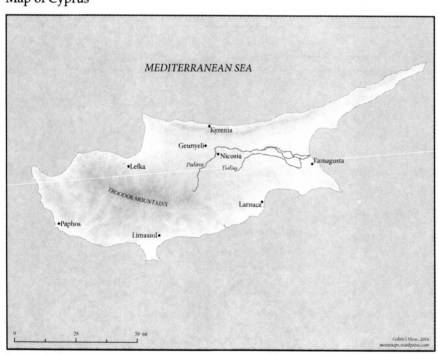

Map of Aden and South Arabia

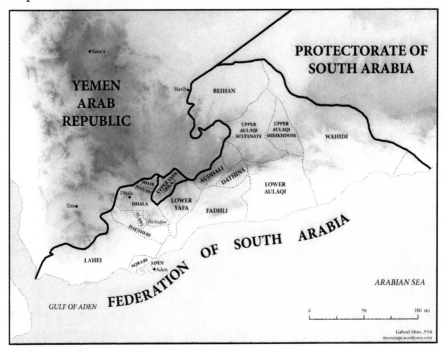

Map of Northern Ireland

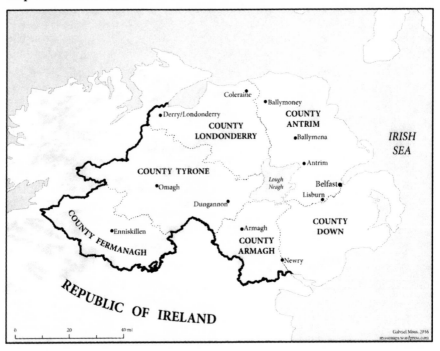

Brutality in an Age of Human Rights

Counterinsurgency and Human Rights in the Post-1945 World

During the 2003 invasion of Iraq, the United States military expected a quick, "surgical" victory. Instead, it soon encountered what General John Abizaid described as a "classical guerrilla-type campaign," much to the chagrin of Defense Secretary Donald Rumsfeld.[1] A similar situation emerged in Afghanistan as the Taliban and Al Qaeda regrouped within Pakistani sanctuaries after 2001. Military practitioners and policymakers in the United States began to grope for answers to these unexpected wartime challenges. In their search for solutions, analysts turned to "successful" European counterinsurgency campaigns—especially Britain's wars of decolonization.

Embedded within the narratives of these post–World War II campaigns were a series of assumptions about British counterinsurgency practices and cultural values. These assumptions coalesced around the notion that Britain was more successful at waging counterinsurgency than France and other imperial powers. During the 1946–54 war in Indochina and the 1954–62 Algerian War, France suffered ignominious defeats. In both conflicts, French forces embraced torture to obtain intelligence on insurgent activities and terror to cow civilian populations into submission.[2] Likewise, many supporters of the "British approach" to counterinsurgency viewed the American defeat in Vietnam as the result of the United States' reliance on overwhelming firepower and technological panaceas. This contrast contributed to a sense of British "exceptionalism" in which Britain had succeeded where others had failed. Proponents of this view claimed that British forces' counterinsurgency prowess derived from the British army's military culture, including the flexibility to adapt to changing circumstances and effectively operate in a decentralized manner. Furthermore, those who supported this notion of exceptionalism insisted that Britain succeeded by using methods that aligned with liberal democratic values.

1

According to this view, British forces succeeded because they achieved a kind of moral legitimacy. They won the "hearts and minds" of civilian populations by obeying the "rule of law" and using the minimum amount of force necessary against insurgents.[3]

This idealized image of past British victories proved particularly compelling for American policymakers because it appeared to offer a solution that not only was effective but also aligned with American liberal democratic ideals and contemporary international human rights norms. In December 2006, the United States military released *Field Manual 3–24: Counterinsurgency*, which wholeheartedly embraced the idea that Britain's counterinsurgency approach was both effective and moral. The manual generated instant fanfare and unprecedented attention. Pundits immediately hailed the new manual as "groundbreaking" and "paradigm-shattering."[4] Initially issued as a government document, the manual was downloaded 1.5 million times in the first month after public release. Within a year, the University of Chicago Press published an edition that included an introduction written by the Harvard University human rights professor Sarah Sewall. Sewall wrote that the new manual "heartily embraces a traditional . . . British method of fighting insurgency" and was "based on principles learned during Britain's early period of imperial policing and relearned during responses to twentieth-century independence struggles in Malaya and Kenya."[5] The manual was also the subject of a glowing *New York Times* book review written by the prominent human rights advocate and later U.S. ambassador to the United Nations Samantha Power. Scholars, security analysts, and policymakers across the political spectrum believed that the new field manual offered a viable alternative approach to the intractable problems facing American policymakers in Iraq and Afghanistan.[6] Counterinsurgency—or "COIN"—became a fashionable policy buzzword in Washington as the idea of British exceptionalism gained favor within both defense and human rights policy circles.[7]

In actuality, Britain's post-1945 counterinsurgency campaigns involved a heavy dose of brutality and coercion against combatants and noncombatants alike.[8] Torture, forced relocation, collective punishment, and other forms of coercion also occurred during other colonial conflicts between 1945 and 1967, including those in Palestine, Malaya, Cyprus, Nyasaland, and Aden.[9] Malaya's communist-inspired insurgency began in 1948 as poor, landless ethnic Chinese fought against the colonial government and ethnic Malays. In response, British forces hunted insurgents in the jungle, forcibly resettled dispersed rural populations into "new villages," and employed a series of punishments and rewards to convince ethnic Chinese to support the government. The conflict lasted until 1960 and led to the creation of an independent, but pro-British, republic in which ethnic Malays remained politically dominant.[10]

As the Malayan insurgency dragged on, other colonized peoples rose in resistance to empire. In Kenya, the colonial government had long backed the interests of expatriate British settlers who had seized the best farmland in Kenya's Central Highlands from the Kikuyu people. Land disputes and a lack of political representation for the Kikuyu and other groups led to conflict between the government and militant nationalist Kenyans. In 1952, a group calling itself the Land Freedom Army but known to the British as "Mau Mau" began to attack white settlers, government forces, and conservative Kenyans who supported the colonial state. The colonial government responded by approving strict legislation that empowered police and military officials with wide-ranging powers of arrest and detention. British forces detained almost the entire Kikuyu population in a "gulag" system. Torture and beatings were frequent in the camps and during operations against Mau Mau insurgent groups. When the International Committee of the Red Cross (ICRC) attempted to intervene, the colonial government refused to admit Red Cross delegates into the colony until the tide of the war turned decisively in favor of the British in 1957. Colonial authorities also manipulated the judicial system by changing rules of evidence and expanding the range of crimes that qualified for capital punishment. Ultimately, the government executed 1,090 Kenyans for emergency-related offenses during the conflict, often with little evidence of guilt. Reports that British forces summarily executed many captured or suspected Mau Mau were also widespread.[11]

Insurgents also committed many brutalities. Mau Mau forces massacred loyalist Kenyans at Lari in March 1953, for example. In Cyprus, EOKA assassinated informers and intimidated Greek Cypriots who were reluctant to support the insurgency.[12] Although this book analyzes government forces' abuses and attempts to hide those transgressions, it does not seek to excuse insurgents from blame for atrocities carried out in their name. Britain's post-1945 counterinsurgencies were terrible because combatants on all sides engaged in brutal behavior.

The terror and brutality of these wars stand in marked contrast to the professed values of the post-1945 international order. Supported by Western powers including the United States and United Kingdom, the postwar world was supposedly built on foundations of international law, justice, liberty, and equality. Ideas of "collective security," "self-determination," and "human rights" received significant attention in international politics immediately following the Second World War.[13] But this postwar vision emerged alongside growing Cold War tensions and violent contestations over colonial rule. For many in the West and the colonized world, the post-1945 international order was supposed to herald the coming of an "age of human rights," yet these rights appeared to have been absent during Britain's counterinsurgency wars.

This book explores the paradox of an international politics meant to advance rights and freedoms that existed alongside the simultaneous employment of systematic, brutal counterinsurgency methods.[14] British officials cloaked their repressive actions in the "legitimacy" of colonial laws—laws that those same officials had the power to change and manipulate as they saw fit. In this way, the British could keep their reputation as "protectors of rights" intact by claiming that their actions—whatever those actions were—supported the rule of law. In contrast, activists appealed to international law and human rights norms to define certain British actions as illegal or morally unjustifiable. British government officials and military commanders responded to activists' efforts by developing ways to hide human rights abuses. Activists sought to expose brutal British practices such as the torture of detainees during interrogation and the use of violence against civilians. This activism struck deeply at the British and shaped future counterinsurgency policies and practices, but not as the activists expected. Because they were most concerned with avoiding public scandal, British forces responded to human rights activists not by stopping their abuses but by developing new ways to hide their methods from scrutiny. British officials maintained a façade of restraint and respectability by attacking the credibility of their accusers, contesting the applicability of international legal agreements such as the Geneva Conventions and the European Convention on Human Rights, and developing dynamic responses to shield increasingly unpopular practices from public view.[15]

Rather than abandon brutal methods, senior British officials—including top-ranking colonial officers, army generals, and government ministers—devised dynamic responses to shield these increasingly unpopular practices from public view through what I call "cooperative manipulation." Cooperative manipulation means that when human rights activists succeeded in drawing public attention to British abuses, officials appeared to cooperate with them while simultaneously obscuring the continued use of those practices. Cooperative manipulation was a secondary reaction to human rights activism during counterinsurgency campaigns. Initially, British officials sought to deflect or deny activists' criticisms, often by undermining the credibility of those making the accusations.[16] But when they were unable to evade public scrutiny, government officials engaged in cooperative manipulation. This dynamic took several forms. For instance, officials gave the impression that they were cooperating with human rights activists' agendas by rescinding repressive emergency laws deemed nonessential to the counterinsurgency effort—particularly in the realm of intelligence collection. They also ordered official inquiries into possible abuses while simultaneously twisting the outcome of those inquiries in order to cast security forces' actions in a positive light. Often this manipulation involved limiting the scope of inquiries to keep knowledge of abuses out of public view. In addition, Britain was reluctant to allow international humanitarian and human rights organizations to develop a significant presence on the ground during counterinsurgency campaigns. When this proved impossible to prevent, however, British officials controlled those organizations' access to information and facilities in an attempt to shape the public narrative in Britain's favor.

Through cooperative manipulation, British forces employed effective countermeasures against activists. Sometimes these were implemented according to a preplanned strategy; at other times they were improvised solutions employed opportunistically in response to changing circumstances. Regardless, during Britain's post-1945 counterinsurgency campaigns, these efforts were responses to rights activists' criticisms and largely stymied those activists' attempts to stop what they saw as abusive practices. It was not until after the Northern Ireland "Troubles" began in 1969 that the government's use of cooperative manipulation began to elicit criticism rather than smothering it. Sustained public pressure over human rights issues became a central feature of the conflict and one that the British could no longer evade.

Despite the regular use of repressive measures during decolonization wars, Britain did not always encounter outraged human rights activists who sought to end these abuses. For instance, rights activists played little role in shaping counterinsurgency practices during the Malayan and Kenyan campaigns.[17] But even during conflicts such as the Mau Mau uprising in Kenya, colonial officials devised sophisticated efforts to conceal evidence of brutality and control public narratives of the war.[18] Why appeals to ideas of progress, modernization, or human rights emerged in different combinations during some conflicts but not others is a topic that deserves further research but is beyond the scope of this study. This book is concerned with British counterinsurgency wars in which human rights activism played a prominent role.

Toward this end, the book examines three post-1945 counterinsurgencies: Cyprus from 1955 to 1959, Aden from 1962 to 1967, and the Northern Ireland Troubles, with an emphasis on the period from 1969 to 1976. In each of these conflicts, rights issues emerged as a significant dimension of the war as a result of diverse forms of rights-based activism. Many, such as the Greek Cypriot legal elite and some Northern Irish civil society groups, were local partisan actors. Other groups, such as the ICRC, strove to alleviate the suffering of vulnerable populations through the provision of humanitarian aid or, like Amnesty International (AI) in Aden, helped civilians and worked to improve conditions for captured combatants.[19] Regardless of their motivations, rights activism lay at the heart of these organizations' agendas across all three conflicts.

The Cyprus, Aden, and Northern Ireland cases reveal the persistence of common trends in the relationship between rights activism and British counterinsurgency warfare across varied conditions. The Cyprus Emergency occurred from 1955 to 1959—a time when Britain was deeply engaged with additional wars in Malaya and Kenya. This period marked the height of the colonial counterinsurgency era, as British forces contended with three simultaneous, large-scale insurgencies. The 1950s were therefore a particularly intense period of colonial warfare.[20]

By the time of the 1963–67 Aden Emergency, however, most British wars of decolonization had ended. Prime Minister Harold Macmillan's 1960 "Wind of Change" speech in Cape Town, South Africa, signaled his desire to avoid anticolonial wars whenever possible by proceeding quickly with decolonization. During the mid-1960s, the British Empire rapidly contracted. Britain had lost many of its colonies to independence and was actively—and often chaotically—seeking to decolonize many of its remaining colonies. In addition to granting them independence as sovereign nation-states, Britain and other European powers at times attempted to group colonies into larger agglomerated "federations." The Aden conflict came to symbolize this chaotic end of the imperial era.[21]

The war in Northern Ireland was waged in different circumstances. In January 1968, after British troops had withdrawn from Aden, Prime Minister Harold Wilson announced a full-scale strategic withdrawal from areas "east of Suez." For many, this decision marked the end of Britain's position as a global imperial power.[22] But the influence of empire did not simply disappear during the late 1960s—it left lasting legacies within the United Kingdom in terms of race relations, social and economic influences, foreign policy, and national identity.[23] This book pushes beyond the traditional end of empire, into the era of the Northern Ireland Troubles, to analyze the impact of rights activism on a counterinsurgency campaign waged in a region that, although formally part of the United Kingdom, bore a distinctive colony-like legacy due to centuries of British domination and persistent religious discrimination. The story of activism and counterinsurgency during these three wars bears little resemblance to the myth of British exceptionalism.

The Myth of British Counterinsurgency

The myth of British counterinsurgency was born out of the multiple, simultaneous colonial wars waged during the 1950s and 1960s. Sir Robert Thompson's book *Defeating Communist Insurgency* (1966) has come to epitomize the mythologized understanding of British counterinsurgency. A former Royal Air Force officer and civilian defense official during the Malayan Emergency, Thompson wrote the book after he served as Britain's counterinsurgency adviser to the government of South Vietnam during the early 1960s. He advocated restricting violence to the minimum amount of force necessary and promoted political legitimacy by requiring colonial security forces to obey the rule of law. Political legitimacy, Thompson believed, was vital to convincing insurgents that they had a political future in the colony and would persuade many rebels to lay down their arms. Thompson's argument reflected an analysis of historical events from which he divined "best practices" for conducting counterinsurgency.[24] He did not write the book as a history of British counterinsurgency, but it contributed to the emergence of a historiography which presumed that the professed liberality and humanity of British doctrine corresponded with actual wartime practices.

The use of "minimum force" and rule of law to promote political legitimacy formed the cornerstone of the British counterinsurgency myth. Throughout campaigns in Malaya, Kenya, Cyprus, and elsewhere, colonial governments issued instructions designed to limit the circumstances under which soldiers could employ lethal force. During the Malayan Emergency, for instance, colonial laws permitted soldiers to use lethal violence only against armed insurgents who were actively resisting the security forces or "as a last resort" to prevent insurgents from escaping, to stop individuals who failed to halt when instructed, or in self-defense.[25] Officials intended such restrictions to reinforce Britain's political legitimacy as a colonial power interested in protecting its subjects. On paper at least, Britain seized the moral high ground.

The idea of minimum force was closely related to Thompson's call to uphold the rule of law. The rule of law—that is, the applicability of law to all imperial subjects regardless of status—was a key moral justification for imperial rule even though such equality before the law did not occur in practice.[26] Despite the inconsistencies with which colonial law was applied, Thompson believed that obeying the rule of law during counterinsurgency operations enhanced the government's legitimacy. He argued that acting outside the law not only was "morally wrong" but would also "create more practical difficulties for a government than it solves." Laws granting certain powers, such as arrest and detention, must be "clearly laid down within certain limits." Thompson was not averse to harsh measures, as long as they were *legal*: "There is nothing to prevent a government enacting very tough laws to cope with the situation, but the golden rule should be that each new law must be effective and must be fairly applied." Following the law, for Thompson, meant that officials were accountable for their actions—a key element of building and maintaining political legitimacy.[27]

In the 1980s and 1990s, as the British government began declassifying official documents from the decolonization era, many Anglo-American military historians embraced Thompson's ideas. Early studies supported the belief that British forces defeated insurgencies through minimum force, the rule of law, and political legitimacy rather than repression and coercion. This understanding contributed to the notion that the British waged "clean" campaigns, whereas the French, Portuguese, and Belgians fought "dirty wars" in Algeria, Indochina, Angola, and the Congo. Many studies from the 1980s and 1990s therefore reflected the Thompson narrative.[28]

Revisionist scholars have since convincingly overturned this myth by revealing that Britain actually waged extremely violent and repressive campaigns. These historians have recast the British counterinsurgency narrative to reveal the consistent and pervasive application of coercion, repression, torture, forced relocation, broad rules of engagement, and draconian laws. Although British security forces largely obeyed colonial governments' emergency regulations, these laws routinely permitted a wide range of repression, from population-control measures such as food rationing to open-ended rules of engagement in which British soldiers could shoot any curfew violator who failed to stop when hailed. As colonial officials claimed legitimacy from the rule of law, they simultaneously adopted wide-ranging executive powers on the basis that such powers were necessary to protect the colonial state.[29] Under these regulations, minimum force was often excessive, and the rule of law proved quite severe.[30]

Colonial officers also hid some of the most sensitive and embarrassing records concerning imperial rule, which contributed to the favorable studies initially written by scholars. In April 2011, the Foreign and Commonwealth Office (FCO) announced the "discovery" of a large collection of colonial-era documents: approximately 1.2 million files from thirty-seven colonies. Rather than depositing them in the National Archives at Kew, the FCO had retained the documents at its Hanslope Park facility. Most of these documents should have been declassified under Britain's Public Record Act, in which government documents are reviewed for public release thirty years after their creation. The files' existence also should have been declared after the passage of the UK Freedom of Information Act in 2000. Instead, the British government did not acknowledge the existence of the documents until forced to do so by court order in 2012 as part of a landmark lawsuit against it. Kenyans held prisoner during the Mau Mau war sued, alleging that colonial authorities had tortured them. Three historians of the conflict—David Anderson, Huw Bennett, and Caroline Elkins—testified as expert witnesses.[31] Their testimony contributed to the High Court's October 2012 decision to allow the case to go to trial. The plaintiffs won, and the government agreed to pay compensation to 5,228 Kenyans.[32] The "migrated archive," as it has been termed, was finally incorporated into the National Archives' holdings under the designation FCO 141.

Since the Mau Mau case, many scholars have criticized the government's failure to release official documents when legally required because such actions undermine the transparency with which democracies are supposed to operate.[33] The Hanslope Park archive's existence raised questions over the extent to which the British government had accounted for the "dark side" of decolonization and demonstrated the need for continued scholarly work in critically evaluating the legacies of empire and colonial counterinsurgency.

The FCO 141 files provide vital new evidence, but they also present an incomplete picture of the last days of empire. Sensitive material in the FCO 141 archive and any documents deemed unnecessary to keep were reviewed and potentially removed by colonial authorities. These newly discovered records provide new insights, but scholars cannot fixate upon them. This documentary record is a fragment, a glimpse of government records that colonial officials thought the public might one day be allowed to see. These documents present a pruned, manicured image of what colonial officials wanted to leave behind. It is therefore necessary to read the archive critically and incorporate sources beyond the official documents.[34] This book does so using personal papers, interviews, and records kept by nongovernmental organizations to place the government narrative in its proper context and reveal the mechanisms that went into constructing and protecting it from public scrutiny.[35]

The implications of scholars' work on British counterinsurgency extend beyond historical questions regarding the nature of the end of empire. Past counterinsurgency practices have shaped contemporary military debates while citizens of former colonies cope with the legacies of decolonization. Rights took on a renewed importance in international discourses after the Second World War, as the creation of the United Nations (UN) and the promulgation of the Universal Declaration of Human Rights (UDHR) seemed to usher in an era in which international relations would be regulated through principles of equality, justice, and rights. At the core of this vision was a desire to build a better future for humanity.[36]

Human Rights, International Law, and Counterinsurgency

The scholarly study of human rights history has centered on a search for the origins of contemporary human rights ideas and movements. But historians are divided as to when human rights truly started to matter. Some scholars view the establishment of the United Nations and the proclamation of the UDHR during the 1940s as the key moment in the emergence of global human rights norms and laws.[37] Others, following the pioneering work of Samuel Moyn, argue that the 1940s marked merely the appropriation of human rights rhetoric by great powers as a means of cloaking power politics in a moral guise. These historians assert that in fact the 1970s proved more important because broad-based social movements adopted human rights rhetoric in a manner that politicized moral sentiments.[38] Others push these developments farther back to the 1990s.[39] Yet these approaches tend to narrowly define human rights as applying only to notions of universal individual rights that transcend the nation-state—an idea that gained prominence beginning in the 1970s. From this perspective, categorizations of rights for groups of people, such as civil and political rights accorded to citizens of a state and legal protections for religious minorities, do not count as "human rights" in the contemporary sense.[40] Likewise, Moyn excludes anticolonial movements seeking national self-determination from his paradigm of human rights.[41]

This understanding may accurately describe the emergence of contemporary international human rights ideas in Europe and the United States, but various conceptions of rights have coexisted throughout the twentieth century. Humanitarianism is the moral sentiment to alleviate human suffering because of a shared sense of humanity. As such, it is not necessarily political, but Bruno Cabanes analyzes how actions motivated by moral sensibilities in the aftermath of the First World War contributed to political and social concepts of rights. Activists, he argues, asserted that various groups of sufferers—from starving children to disabled veterans—had the right to receive care and assistance because of their common humanity. This idea of a right to humanitarian assistance generated political consequences by shaping international laws pertaining to refugees and establishing new social policies to improve care for war veterans.[42] By exploring these notions of "humanitarian rights," Cabanes reveals the existence of a diverse range of social, economic, and political rights during the 1920s.

During the 1950s and 1960s, processes of decolonization and the actions of postcolonial states exerted a profound impact on the UN human rights agenda. As former colonies gained independence, they formed an increasingly numerous and influential voting bloc in the UN General Assembly. Newly independent states supported—and often led—UN initiatives that challenged colonial rule. In this context, UN debates over self-determination and human rights merged as Third World postcolonial states spearheaded an effort that resulted in recognition of national self-determination as the "first right" to which all peoples were entitled. In 1960, this understanding was enshrined in Article 1 of the UN Declaration on the Granting of Independence to Colonial Countries and Peoples. Throughout the 1960s, several postcolonial states therefore embraced and promoted human rights issues related to race and religion before Western societies "rediscovered" human rights during the 1970s.[43]

Activists in Cyprus, Aden, and Northern Ireland mobilized on the basis of a contested international politics of rights in which concepts of individual, group, humanitarian, and human rights overlapped. The most appropriate conceptualization of human rights for an analysis of these conflicts is the definition outlined in the 1948 UDHR. This definition would have been familiar to historical actors during the conflicts examined here. The UDHR classified human rights according to three general categories: the integrity of the human being, political and civil liberties, and social and economic rights.[44] Many activists and government officials referred to and based their interpretations of human rights on the principles articulated in the UDHR.[45] In the 1950s, Greek Cypriot lawyers and the Greek government invoked the European Convention on Human Rights to protect detainees' civil and political rights. In the 1960s, the ICRC, aided by Amnesty International, asserted humanitarian rights when it requested that the British government permit the provision of humanitarian relief to refugees in the Radfan region north of Aden. Amnesty International, which perceived itself as a human rights group, acted on behalf of prisoners in Aden to prevent colonial authorities from committing torture. In the 1970s and 1980s, a variety of civil society organizations, political parties, members of Parliament, and journalists vocally opposed brutal interrogation techniques in Northern Ireland as well. This book accepts how all these actors thought of human rights at the time, rather than imposing a current definition on them.

In addition to acting on their conceptions of human rights, national liberation movements often appealed to international legal traditions. Liberation movements justified anticolonial violence as a legitimate response to the denial of their right to national self-determination. In this way, they resuscitated older notions of just war theory at a time when the international law of war was state-centric. Modern understanding of international law as a means to regulate warfare is based on the legitimacy of the state as the sole entity that could rightfully wage war. This understanding laid the foundations for nineteenth- and early twentieth-century European attempts to constrain warfare through law. The 1864 signing of the first Geneva Convention reflected a desire among states to alleviate the suffering of war victims. International attempts to restrain the conduct of war by banning or restricting the use of certain weapons and military practices resulted in the 1899 and 1907 Hague Conventions. In contrast, anticolonial nationalists' assertions that the reason they fought mattered more than a belligerent's international legal status challenged the prevailing notion that only states could legitimately make war. Anticolonial nationalists argued instead that a struggle was legitimate if one's cause was just. According to this logic, anticolonial insurgent groups could claim that they were legally justified in fighting for the right to self-determination.[46]

But the relationship between international law and war was not limited to legitimizing a belligerent's cause or regulating the conduct of war—the law was also used as a tool for achieving military objectives. This concept, labeled "lawfare," is "the strategy of using—or misusing—law as a substitute for traditional military means to achieve an operational objective." Law, in this sense, is a weapon of war: "It is a means that can be used for good or bad purposes."[47] Lawfare has been applied in many contemporary contexts, including the Israeli-Palestinian conflict and the post-9/11 War on Terror, but it is not a twenty-first-century invention.[48] Despite the utility of the concept, there is a key limitation in how lawfare is often analyzed:

anticolonial nationalists often made legal claims that did not conform to the traditional definition of the term because those claims were not limited to formal legal agreements and institutions.

Anticolonial rhetoric appealed to broader, normative categories of rights. From the 1950s to the 1970s, soldiers, diplomats, and lawyers were only beginning to recognize the power of a language of rights that was not legally binding. But ideas of justice and rights encompassed more than merely the letter of the law or its customary application. Beliefs about which liberties the law should protect, how justice ought to operate, and what determined the legitimacy of the law held no formal power but were politically and emotionally powerful in the court of public opinion. Anticolonial nationalists used these normative beliefs by mobilizing the moral universalism of human rights to make political claims against their colonial adversaries.[49] Tanganyika's Julius Nyerere, for example, argued that colonial powers' refusal to grant self-determination prevented colonized peoples from achieving the degree of human dignity inherent in the UDHR.[50] Some liberation movements embraced the notion that they could reinforce their political legitimacy by following international law. In Kenya, for instance, the Mau Mau adopted "Rules of Conduct" on January 4, 1954, which prohibited killing children, raping women, and attacking hospitals or schools.[51] The idea of lawfare therefore is only one piece of a set of rights claims that derived from formal mechanisms of law in addition to the moral and ethical sensibilities upon which that legal corpus was based. For this reason, this book uses the broader term of "activism" rather than "lawfare" when discussing legal and moral claims.

Britain also used lawfare by categorizing anticolonial nationalists' struggles as internal rebellions and insisting that international law did not apply. Much of the argument centered on Common Article 3 of the 1949 Geneva Conventions, which stipulated that in "noninternational armed conflicts," noncombatants and prisoners must be treated humanely. But increased legal protections did not necessarily translate into stronger enforcement measures. Colonial powers simply claimed that this provision did not apply to colonial wars because those conflicts were internal security matters. Organizations such as the ICRC could not force states to comply with the Geneva Conventions but instead had to negotiate with belligerents for access to war victims and permission to provide humanitarian assistance. In practice, delegates from the ICRC prioritized gaining access to war-torn areas and providing humanitarian assistance over debating the interpretation of what constituted a noninternational armed conflict.[52]

Despite Britain's attempts to restrict the applicability of the Geneva Conventions, the postwar European regional human rights regime provided rights activists with another forum in which they could pursue their objectives. The European Convention for the Protection of Human Rights and Fundamental Freedoms—often shortened to the European Convention on

Human Rights (ECHR)—was the first binding agreement in European human rights law and became a focal point for anticolonial politics during the Cyprus Emergency.[53] The ECHR had its origins in a politically conservative Western European desire for Cold War unity—at least of a rhetorical kind—in the face of the communist challenge.[54] In Britain, influential statesmen such as the Labour foreign secretary Ernest Bevin supported the notion of a pan-European human rights project because of their interest in closer European security cooperation.[55] Conservative Party members sympathized with staunch anticommunists in the Labour government but wished to restrict the convention's purview to civil and political rights as a means of limiting Labour's ability to use it to transform domestic social and economic rights. Signed in 1951, the convention came into effect in 1953. The British government extended it to apply not only in the United Kingdom but also to forty-two dependencies, including Cyprus.[56] The legally binding nature of the ECHR and Britain's decision to extend the convention's protections to its colonies made Britain vulnerable to international criticism as the country's adversaries could use the ECHR to challenge its human rights abuses.

Although Britain and other Western European colonial powers embraced human rights and international law for themselves, they often treated colonies differently. Reprisals, punitive measures, and terror remained common methods for subduing these supposedly "uncivilized" peoples despite the rhetoric of minimum force.[57] Furthermore, colonized peoples were exposed to European ideas of law as part of the colonial "civilizing mission." From the nineteenth century to the decolonization era, imperial lawyers tried to replace native institutions with European-derived ones. Any notion of rights for colonized peoples was therefore tied to European forms of sovereignty and national identity.[58] The dynamics of colonial power structures provided an inherent advantage to the colonizer. Colonizers had established the legal framework within their colonies and could apply it as they saw fit. The idea that colonized peoples required instruction in the rule of law in order to become civilized also became part of the justification for colonial rule constructed upon racial hierarchies.[59]

Racial prejudice offers one explanation for British hypocrisy toward the rights of colonized peoples. British officials in Cyprus, Aden, and Northern Ireland often maintained a sense of racial superiority toward colonial subjects, and, in general, racism was central to the creation and maintenance of imperial systems of rule.[60] Nonetheless, British counterinsurgency techniques were remarkably similar even though the racial contexts of the conflicts in Aden, Cyprus, and Northern Ireland differed greatly from one another. Aden was a predominantly Arab Muslim colony with a large minority of South Asians. In Cyprus British forces fought white Europeans, but according to British Orientalist prejudices, "decadent" Ottoman rule had transformed Greek Cypriots into a "hybrid and mongrelized race" ruined by a "vague and spiritless lethargy."[61] Northern Irish, notwithstanding their political opinions or religious preferences, fell into the latter category. As one scholar described British attitudes, the Irish were "passionate, uncivilised, unreasonable." Even so, the Irish were seen as both white and Western European.[62] Regardless of racial attitudes toward the local population, British forces employed remarkably similar counterinsurgency techniques.[63] Racism can therefore explain why colonial administrators and soldiers viewed themselves as superior to their enemies, but it does not explain why colonial officials would be concerned with human rights rhetoric.

Human rights activism and international law mattered to officials because of concern with maintaining Britain's reputation. It was a widely held belief in Whitehall, particularly within the Colonial Office, that Britain was a paragon of virtue when it came to upholding and protecting rights, both domestically and internationally. The commitment to these ideals was so strong that many officials believed that the best way to lead colonies on the path toward self-government was through the enactment of constitutions and bills of rights that would supposedly help postcolonial states function according to the rule of law and with respect for citizens' rights. The result was what one scholar has called an "export trade in human rights."[64]

Belief in Britain's virtuous reputation meant that government officials were sensitive to moral criticisms. This sensitivity proved particularly true during colonial counterinsurgencies. In 1949, then colonial secretary Arthur Creech-Jones complained that documents such as the UDHR could easily become a "source of embarrassment" in the colonies because the perceived need to employ repressive policies would undermine Britain's reputation as a beacon of liberty and democracy.[65] Maintaining this reputation was an important priority for colonial governments. For example, in a 1957 meeting with a delegate from the ICRC, Cyprus's deputy governor Sinclair told his visitor that "the government of Cyprus is very conscious of preserving Britain's reputation as highly civilized."[66] Minimizing criticism of authoritarian colonial policies was of paramount concern.

Rights activists used the British concern with their reputation to put pressure on the government. For officials, embarrassment necessarily occurred only when mistakes, transgressions, or hypocritical actions were brought into the public view. Rather than exposing their actions to public scrutiny, government officials relied on secrecy. According to the historian David Vincent, this culture of secrecy was based on the notion that government figures saw themselves as holders of positions endowed with the moral authority to make decisions on the general public's behalf. For officials, this understanding meant that they had a duty to safeguard and control information by determining what could be released and what could not. They could rationalize decisions to withhold information from the public on the grounds that they bore the moral responsibility to protect the public's interest and therefore keep information secret on the public's behalf.[67] Activists, on the other hand, sought to strip this veil of secrecy away by attacking Britain in public forums with global audiences. The media-saturated environments of Cyprus's large newspaper-reading public, the predominance of radio in Aden, and the mass of newspapers, radio programs, and television stations covering the Northern Ireland conflict enhanced the effects of human rights activism.[68] Activists easily found platforms from which they could air their grievances against the British government, while British sensitivity to public embarrassment meant that the ensuing criticism stung particularly harshly.

The desire to avoid public embarrassment and maintain Britain's reputation as a guardian of human rights explains why British officials remained highly conscious of their public image. It also exposes the fundamental irony of the relationship between human rights and British counterinsurgency: Officials wanted to seem to be upholding the values central to Britain's reputation while using counterinsurgency practices that undermined those values. When confronted, they maintained this paradoxical stance by appearing to cooperate with their critics while actually manipulating the situation in order to continue their abusive practices with the least public embarrassment.

By investigating the relationship between human rights activism and British counterinsurgency practices, this book seeks to bring international histories of human rights into closer dialogue with military histories of insurgent movements and counterinsurgency warfare. Both military historians and historians of human rights have largely ignored the role of rights activists in shaping wartime policies and practices. These activists sought to influence diplomatic and strategic debates as well as counterinsurgency methods at the operational and tactical levels. Activism linked the metaphorical battlefield of law, diplomacy, propaganda, and public opinion with the physical battlefield of ambushes, house searches, arrests, and interrogations. Focusing the analytical lens on activists and the officials with whom they interacted places rights activists on the counterinsurgency "battlefield"—not as traditional arms-bearing combatants but as actors who nonetheless influenced counterinsurgency policies and practices.

A Lawyers' War

Emergency Legislation and the Cyprus Bar Council

On February 27, 1957, as the war in Cyprus raged, the Labour Party peer Lord Strabolgi rose during a heated debate in the House of Lords. Criticizing Britain's colonial government in Cyprus, Strabolgi demanded, "What sort of State is this? Is it a police State? Is it a State like that set up by Nazi Germany, or a State which is trying to copy the methods of Soviet Russia? I think that there is a very great need for the Government to investigate these allegations."[1] Put forward by a group of Greek Cypriot lawyers, the allegations in question criticized the use of emergency legislation to permit widespread press censorship, detention without trial, and abuse of prisoners in order to defeat the Greek Cypriot nationalist insurgency. These emergency regulations, which the Cyprus government adopted after the onset of violence in April 1955, were based heavily on those used to combat insurgencies in Malaya and Kenya. This draconian legislation was a common feature of postwar British counterinsurgency campaigns. Such laws facilitated counterinsurgency operations—particularly in the realm of intelligence collection through brutal interrogation measures.[2]

Scholars have viewed allegations of prisoner abuse in Cyprus from several perspectives. First, some commentators believe that the security forces usually did not abuse their powers but sometimes did so infrequently and only in exceptional circumstances.[3] Taking a different view, other scholars have argued that the allegations were credible.[4] Offering a variation on this interpretation, the historian David French argues that there is strong evidence of abuse, but EOKA propaganda (see below) exaggerated the extent of British brutality. French's interpretation is accurate but incomplete. EOKA certainly exaggerated British cruelty for propaganda purposes and British abuses clearly occurred, but torture was not primarily the result of increased frustration, nor was it limited to a small number of undisciplined "bad apples." Allegations of torture overwhelmingly concerned Special

Branch interrogations, suggesting that prisoner abuse was part of a calculated effort to obtain vital intelligence via coercive interrogation methods.[5] The Cyprus government's tough emergency legislation facilitated these intelligence collection efforts.

In response, Greek Cypriot lawyers' rights activism transformed the legal system into a battlefield in which both sides sought to manipulate the law to their advantage. These lawyers resisted the effects of the emergency regulations by defending detainees in court. But they soon realized that courtroom advocacy did not accomplish enough in the face of a judicial system stacked in Britain's favor. The lawyers then organized through their professional association, the Cyprus Bar Council, to protect detainees' rights. They lobbied colonial officials to establish and enforce the right of detainees to legal representation and the confidentiality of attorney-client relationships; publicized British cruelty when such standards were not met, including through complaints to members of Parliament in Britain; and documented cases of prisoner abuse for inclusion in international legal proceedings at the European Commission of Human Rights. These lawyers turned advocacy for detainee rights into a form of resistance to colonial authority that they framed as human rights activism.[6] Greek Cypriot lawyers' efforts convinced senior colonial officials—including the colonial secretary and Cyprus governor—to develop new ways of countering rights-based criticisms. This chapter examines the origins of the war in Cyprus and how the contest over emergency laws shaped counterinsurgency policies and practices up to the spring of 1957.

Enosis and the Cyprus Insurgency

The Cyprus insurgency began on April 1, 1955 over the Greek Cypriot desire for "enosis," or union, with Greece. Led by the National Organization of Cypriot Fighters, known by its Greek abbreviation EOKA, pro-enosis Greek Cypriots waged a nearly four-year war against their British colonizers. EOKA was commanded by a Cypriot-born retired Greek army colonel named George Grivas. Having fought in Greece's 1919–22 war with Turkey and in the Second World War, Grivas was an experienced officer who had been laying the groundwork for an insurgency in Cyprus since 1951. In contrast, when the war began, British forces were unprepared for a large-scale insurgency. After eight months of fighting, British officials had replaced an ineffective colonial governor with an experienced military commander who declared a state of emergency and enacted a harsh set of laws.

British forces had a difficult time subduing the insurgency in part because the overwhelming majority of Greek Cypriots supported enosis.[7] As over three-fourths of the five hundred thousand people living on Cyprus were Greek Cypriot, British forces faced a difficult task in subduing the insurgency. By 1957, violence between Greek Cypriot and Turkish Cypriot communities had erupted as Turkish Cypriots, who comprised approximately 18 percent of the island's population, asserted their desire for partition of the island rather than union with Greece. As the conflict descended into civil war, Greece and Turkey grew increasingly assertive in seeking to protect the interests of the Greek Cypriot and Turkish Cypriot communities, respectively.[8]

The involvement of Greece and Turkey ensured that an international settlement would be required to end the conflict. The war drew to a close after Greece, Turkey, and Britain, as well as the Greek and Turkish Cypriot communities, agreed to the establishment of an independent republic of Cyprus in which political power would be shared among Greek and Turkish Cypriots. In February 1959, these parties to the conflict signed the London and Zurich Agreements. The London Agreement ended the conflict between Britain, Greek Cypriots, and Turkish Cypriots. Britain, Greece, and Turkey signed the Zurich Agreement, which stipulated that neither union nor partition could occur without Greek and Turkish concurrence.[9]

Enosis supporters did not achieve their goal of unity with Greece, but they waged an effective insurgency that killed 371 British soldiers. Organized as semi-independent cells, EOKA units conducted assassinations, bombings, and ambushes and ran a complex propaganda operation to maintain support for the war among Greek Cypriot civilians. Although British forces developed a sophisticated understanding of EOKA's organizational structure, when the war began, British troops had a difficult time countering the insurgency. In November 1955, with violence mounting, the Cyprus government declared a state of emergency.[10]

The insurgency gathered momentum throughout the summer of 1955. EOKA attacked Greek Cypriot police officers, whom Grivas deemed antinationalist "traitors." Special Branch also emerged as a key EOKA target because of its intelligence collection mission. Without good intelligence, government forces would not be able to counter EOKA attacks. The Cyprus government, headed by Governor Sir Richard Armitage, had not expected a coordinated insurgent campaign. With the outbreak of violence, the British army arranged for Sir Gerald Templer, the officer who had served as high commissioner and military commander during the successful counterinsurgency campaign in Malaya, to visit Cyprus and assess the situation. Templer felt that Armitage's government was not taking the situation seriously enough and criticized them for carrying on with business as usual. He decided that Armitage was incapable of handling the situation. Templer also discovered that Special Branch, the organization responsible for intelligence collection, was woefully undermanned and unprepared. Prime Minister Sir Anthony Eden shared Templer's frustrations. Foreign

Secretary Harold Macmillan likewise argued that "we cannot afford to give any impression that we are on the run in Cyprus" because of the island's importance in British Middle East policy. Without the island as a base, Britain's ability to project power in the Middle East—a vital region because of its oil reserves—would be severely compromised.[11]

After Templer's visit, Colonial Secretary Alan Lennox-Boyd decided to replace Sir Richard Armitage with someone deemed more capable of combating the insurgency. The sense in Whitehall was that the situation demanded a "military man" to coordinate political and military activities as Templer had in Malaya. Field Marshal Sir John Harding was the logical choice. At the time of his October 1955 appointment as governor of Cyprus, Harding was the chief of the Imperial General Staff—the highest position in the British military. He was one of the most senior officers in the armed forces and an experienced commander. In a previous assignment as commander-in-chief, Far East Land Forces, he had worked with Templer during the Malayan Emergency. According to one scholar, the idea that terrorists and insurgents should be dealt with harshly "was not just an assumption of Harding's, it was one of his deepest feelings."[12] Harding approached his work in Cyprus with a hard-nosed determination to eradicate the insurgency through whatever means necessary.

While Harding understood that military action alone would not solve the conflict, he believed that a political solution could be reached only if British forces first destroyed EOKA. His objective was to obtain a settlement in which Greek and Turkish Cypriots agreed on a new constitutional framework of local self-government under British colonial rule.[13] This conviction was based on two assumptions: Harding thought that only a minority of the Greek Cypriot community actively supported EOKA and that the group maintained its influence by intimidating the rest of the more moderate population. To eliminate EOKA's hold, Harding planned to capture or kill EOKA fighters while coercing the population into submission. To do so, Harding determined that "it will be essential to employ the sternest and most drastic forms of deterrent open to us." He concluded that "one of the results of the various measures such as collective fines, curfews and other restrictions that have recently been increased is the restoration of respect" for British authority.[14] If EOKA could intimidate the Greek Cypriot population into submission, so could the British.

When Harding decided to declare a state of emergency in November 1955, Colonial Secretary Lennox-Boyd agreed but also sounded a cautionary note. Lennox-Boyd encouraged Harding, writing that "important though it is to seize any chance of a political solution [to the conflict], you must not let this hope interfere with firm action." Lennox-Boyd concurred with Harding's wish to eliminate EOKA but worried that tough measures could cause public controversy that he was keen to avoid. Even so, Lennox-Boyd had known Harding for many years and trusted his judgment. He authorized Harding to use collective punishments and order judicial whipping of juvenile offenders but urged him to be careful about using these powers. Lennox-Boyd did not want the Cyprus conflict to cause public controversy. He told Harding that "as you know, some forms of collective punishment have an ugly ring here." Collective fines and punitive seizures of civilians' property would "present real political difficulties" for the Colonial Office. Harding reassured Lennox-Boyd that he would "proceed as discreetly as the situation permits," and he declared a state of emergency in Cyprus on November 26. Harding knew that he had Lennox-Boyd's support in taking tough measures, but he also knew that there were limits as to what politicians in Britain would allow.[15]

The Emergency Regulations

Under the state of emergency, Harding's powers were nearly absolute. These powers were based on the First World War–era Defence of the Realm Acts (DORA), which permitted the executive to enact regulations concerning public safety without necessitating Parliament's approval. The 1921 Restoration of Order in Ireland Act applied similar provisions to Ireland after the First World War. Beyond this legislation, the government could amend legislation through the orders-in-council procedure. Akin to an executive order, an order-in-council could establish regulations that held the force of law without being submitted to the legislature for approval. Together, DORA, the Restoration of Order in Ireland Act, and orders-in-council formed the legal basis of Harding's emergency powers. By the time he faced the insurgency in Cyprus, emergency regulations regimes had become a common feature of colonial rule, having been employed in Ireland, Palestine, India, Malaya, and Kenya.[16]

Harding enacted seventy-six new laws that permitted security forces—a term that British officials used in reference to both police and military units—to wield significant coercive powers. Security personnel were authorized to arrest without warrant any person who was believed to have "acted or was about to act, in a manner prejudicial to public safety or public order, or who had committed or was about to commit an offence."[17] Any officer in the rank of major or higher could approve the detention of an arrested person for up to twenty-eight days without charges. Harding had the authority to sign a detention order extending any individual's imprisonment indefinitely and to deport anyone from the colony. Based on a similar measure passed during the Malayan Emergency, the Cyprus legislation also designated certain "protected areas" off-limits to all Cypriots except those with special government passes. Anyone in a protected area who fled from security forces could be shot.[18] Harding intended to use the emergency legislation regime as a tool for facilitating the collection of intelligence and for separating the Cypriot population from the insurgents by disrupting communication and supply between insurgents and civilian supporters.[19]

These regulations severely hampered civilians' freedom of movement and allowed the government to censor information available to the populace. Cypriots had to register with the government and obtain an identity card. Soldiers and police could demand to see this card at any time—failure to produce it when ordered could result in a fine or imprisonment. District commissioners could ban civilians from congregating in public spaces, close shops, and requisition property. Censorship regulations permitted government censors to regulate mail sent to or from any person in the colony and to control the content of radio broadcasts and newspaper reports. Propaganda—such as signs, slogans, graffiti, banners, and flags bearing political messages—was prohibited.[20] The Limassol district commissioner also outlawed the use of bicycles without a permit because EOKA fighters often used bicycles as "get-away vehicles." Other district commissioners followed suit.[21] Bicycle bans targeted teenagers and young adults—the primary demographic involved in EOKA attacks.[22]

Harding authorized the use of curfews and collective punishment as means of coercing local populations into submission. Curfews restricted movement in towns and could last for several hours or several weeks. An army report completed at the end of the conflict concluded that "by varying the forms and timings of the curfews, it was possible to keep EOKA leaders guessing and to disrupt their plans." But the report also asserted that punitive curfews "paid little dividend and tended to inhibit the police in their follow up action."[23] Even so, security forces often employed curfews as a form of collective punishment. Other collective punishments included fines levied on entire towns and collected in the form of a tax paid by each family or the closure of businesses and markets for a period of time determined by colonial administrators.[24]

In a move that shocked many Greek Cypriots, Harding approved the use of judicial whipping for youths up to age eighteen as a form of punishment for minors involved in "terrorist activities" such as the dissemination of propaganda or participation in civil disturbances. This measure meant that judges could sentence minors to a certain number of strokes with a cane rather than imprisonment. Police Force Order No. 86 governed the application of whipping, instructing officers that "a light rod or cane should be used and the blows should be delivered on the bare buttocks. The whipping should be carried out in the presence of a second police officer."[25] No more than twelve strokes could be applied.[26] Harding believed that judicial whipping would offer a more humane punishment for juveniles than imprisonment and saw no problem with implementing it, as it was a common punishment in British public schools when he was a child. Greek Cypriots, however, viewed the practice as repugnant. A group of lawyers later complained that although whipping was employed in Britain, "in no circumstances can this practice be tolerated in countries of Graeco-Latin culture."[27] Although Harding sought to implement tough measures, he would soon realize that whipping was counterproductive.

Harding also used the emergency regulations as a tool for improving the ability of British forces to conduct the vital but difficult task of collecting intelligence on EOKA. Finding and neutralizing EOKA fighters proved a less-than-straightforward task for the security forces. The authority to impose curfews and bicycle bans limited insurgents' freedom of movement. The designation of protected areas permitted British troops to use lethal violence with few restraints in mountainous areas where insurgents often sought sanctuary. Furthermore, frequent patrolling, house searches, and checkpoints for searching vehicle traffic would limit EOKA's ability to move around the island and hopefully lead to arrests, but security forces required actionable intelligence to identify, track down, capture, and interrogate or ultimately kill EOKA fighters.[28]

Although it was vital to military success, the security forces were initially unprepared for intelligence collection and analysis. Conflicts arose between representatives from Special Branch, the primary intelligence organization in Cyprus, and army liaisons, both of whom were assigned at the district level to ensure proper synchronization of intelligence work and military operations. Disagreements over decision-making authority were exacerbated by disparities in rank—the army often assigned officers to these positions, whereas most divisional Special Branch representatives were sergeants. Moreover, Special Branch had been reinforced at the outbreak of the emergency with officers from abroad who had little knowledge of local affairs. They lacked the local informant networks necessary for effective intelligence collection. EOKA quickly recognized the importance of experienced Special Branch officers and targeted them for assassination. Special Branch informants from within the Greek Cypriot population also became targets for assassination or intimidation.[29]

Because of the lack of informant networks, interrogation emerged as the most important source of intelligence. Information gathered from questioning suspects could lead to further arrests, seizure of supply caches, or the prevention of attacks. Suspects who confessed under interrogation to having committed crimes could face trial and punishment, but they would also sometimes turn against their fellow insurgents, perhaps in exchange for a reduced sentence or a pardon. British forces created plainclothes "Q-Patrols" in which these former insurgents patrolled with British police and soldiers to identify and capture EOKA suspects. These units worked in close cooperation with Special Branch and army intelligence.[30]

Despite the abundance of emergency laws that regulated in minute detail who could legally ride a bicycle and outlined specific procedures for how youths were to be whipped and how many strokes could be applied, the Cyprus government never produced specific guidance concerning which techniques were permissible during interrogation. In April 1956, Harding considered issuing specific instructions. He suggested that "we should consider sending out a confidential instruction to those directly concerned on what is and is not permissible in the interrogation of suspects."[31] But the commissioner of police, director of intelligence, and the heads of Special Branch and the Cyprus Police Criminal Investigation Division (CID) unanimously opposed the idea of issuing written instructions to interrogators. These officials believed that coercive interrogation was the most effective method of intelligence collection and did not want to inhibit the flow of valuable information by cracking down on abusive interrogators. The failure to articulate such restrictions ensured that the limits of the law remained ambiguous. This ambiguity permitted interrogators to use whatever methods they deemed necessary as long as they did not leave physical evidence that they had harmed a detainee.[32]

Senior officials knew of these brutal methods but maintained the public pretense that such treatment was forbidden and therefore did not occur. Colonial Secretary Alan Lennox-Boyd admitted that he knew some interrogations were conducted with "questioning of unusual rigour," but he suggested keeping the information from emerging in the public spotlight.[33] With Lennox-Boyd concerned that evidence of torture would embarrass British officials, Harding insisted that Cyprus Police "methods of interrogation follow the normal UK pattern. All forms of physical violence are forbidden by the Criminal Law and Police Force orders."[34] Although Lennox-Boyd, Harding, and other senior Cyprus security officers knew that interrogators were using physical violence against detainees, they chose to quietly tolerate such brutality rather than face the embarrassment of a public scandal.

Because of the operational advantages of ambiguous interrogation instructions and restrictions on Cypriots' freedom of movement, the emergency laws gave the security forces room to maneuver. The wide-ranging powers of arrest and detention authorized by the emergency regulations helped to offset the challenges of intelligence collection by allowing security forces to apprehend suspects and hold them for questioning with few legal constraints. Soldiers and police could more easily track insurgent groups in protected areas where few civilians were permitted. Restrictions on civilian movement through curfews, bicycle bans, and the requirement that all Cypriots obtain an identity card enabled security forces to disrupt EOKA communications and interdict supply lines. The emergency regulations were therefore more than simply a tool of repression—they facilitated counterinsurgency operations by manipulating the law to the colonial government's advantage.

In addition to using coercive measures, British officials recruited a variety of informers. Some of these were individuals who chose to collaborate in exchange for reduced charges or a reprieve from the death sentence, but a small number of Cypriots—perhaps several hundred—voluntarily elected to provide intelligence to the British. Colonial authorities paid for information, which satisfied those informers who desired financial rewards. Other informers often chose to testify in court against EOKA suspects out of anger at EOKA's intimidation tactics or out of personal revenge. One witness, for example, testified in court and denounced EOKA assassins both in the press and on the radio because EOKA had killed her fiancé. The most valuable informants, however, were former EOKA members who had turned against the organization. To EOKA, these "traitors" posed a significant threat because they could identify EOKA members and lead security forces to EOKA hideouts and weapons caches. EOKA targeted many of these collaborators for assassination. The exact figures are in doubt, but EOKA likely killed between 180 and 220 Greek Cypriots who, for a variety of reasons, chose to cooperate with the British. If EOKA discovered an informant's identity, colonial officials often offered the informant sanctuary in Britain. The number of Greek Cypriots who cooperated with colonial intelligence officers was small, but along with coercive legislation and abusive interrogations, their efforts supported British counterinsurgency operations.[35]

By 1956, the military campaign had begun to turn in Britain's favor. In June, the army nearly captured EOKA leader George Grivas. Operation Pepperpot resulted in the capture of several weapons caches and the annihilation of two EOKA operational cells, and it inflicted heavy casualties on a third. In December, British forces captured fifty-two guerrillas, including one of Grivas's couriers and his second in command. Interrogations after each arrest operation generated new intelligence, which was then used to arrest more insurgents.[36] The war was going well for Harding.

Although the emergency regulations provided British forces with wide-ranging coercive powers, the rule of law technically remained in place, even if the law had been distorted to suit the demands of the counterinsurgency campaign. Officials revoked basic legal rights such as due process, the right to move freely, and the right to freedom of speech. Other traditional tenets of the justice system were ignored or reversed, such as the change to criminal proceedings on capital offenses that shifted the burden of proof from the prosecution to the defense. All these changes had occurred legally—that is, at the governor's discretion and with the colonial secretary's approval. But throughout all of this, emergency laws never officially allowed the use of violence against a prisoner during interrogation. Unofficially, senior officials including Colonial Secretary Lennox-Boyd and Governor Harding knew that such brutality often took place. Despite the permissiveness of the emergency legal regime, security forces still had to obey its dictates. If members of the security forces were caught violating the law, they could face punishment. Any such violations would also embarrass the colonial government. Pro-EOKA lawyers sought to exploit this situation by using the colonial legal system to challenge the emergency regulations regime.

EOKA's Lawyers

Historians understand colonial legal systems as pluralistic spaces in which law often applies to different groups in different ways. Various actors—including imperial agents, cultural intermediaries, and colonized subjects—could use this system to assert agency and contest the colonial order through legal processes. Colonial legal regimes therefore operated with a degree of flexibility and room for negotiation between colonizer and colonized. In these systems, the application of law was always contested and based on mixtures of metropolitan and local ideas.[37] Colonial powers relied on "imperial intermediaries" to navigate these legal spaces. Angered by Britain's refusal to grant self-determination to Greek Cypriots and the subsequent enactment of Harding's harsh emergency regulations regime, many Greek Cypriot lawyers chose to resist colonial rule. But the lawyers' initial forays into the courtroom battlefield exposed the extent to which emergency laws had tilted the legal system in the colonial government's favor. As a result, a group of Greek Cypriot lawyers mobilized their professional association, the Cyprus Bar Council, to disrupt brutal interrogation practices, protect prisoners' rights, and publicize security force abuses.

Before the insurgency, these lawyers often played key roles in the administration of law and order on the island. In fact, the colonial government would have been hard-pressed to function without them. Colonial authorities used intermediaries' local connections and social status to reinforce imperial administrative structures. Cypriot lawyers filled positions as government attorneys and acted as civic leaders. Many served as town mayors. A select few were appointed to positions on the colony's Legislative or Executive Councils, in which select colonial elites advised the governor on local affairs. In exchange for their cooperation with colonial rulers, local intermediaries generally benefited from imperial connections to increase their economic status or social prestige.[38]

John Clerides, his son Glafkos, and Stelios Pavlides exemplified this class of imperial elites and became three of the most influential lawyers during the emergency. All three studied law in London and were admitted to the bar as members of the Gray's Inn society of barristers. From 1946 to 1949 John Clerides served as mayor of Nicosia. In 1952 the governor appointed him to the executive council. Clerides was also one of a handful of Cypriots to be named a Queen's Counsel and awarded the title of Commander of the Order of the British Empire.[39] Glafkos served in the Royal Air Force during World War II before returning to Cyprus in 1951 after completing his studies at Gray's Inn.[40] Pavlides joined the Cyprus government in 1916 as a civil servant and rapidly rose through the ranks, eventually receiving an appointment to the Legislative Council. From 1944 to 1952, he served as attorney general of Cyprus. He was the first and only Cypriot to hold the post under British rule. Pavlides was also a Queen's Counsel and a Companion of the Order of St. Michael and St. George.[41] These lawyers and others like them had much to gain from Cyprus's imperial connection with Britain, but British actions had alienated them from their imperial masters.

To many Greek Cypriot lawyers, the draconian nature of emergency laws violated basic notions of justice that formed a core component of the "civilized" British self-image. "British justice is fair in England, but not abroad," recalled Renos Lyssiotis, a lawyer who returned to Cyprus in 1955 after being called to the Bar at Gray's Inn. To Lyssiotis, the emergency regulations perverted hallowed principles of British justice—innocence until proven guilty, the liberty of speaking and associating freely, and respect for the rights of the individual citizen. In its place was erected a system of repression that undermined the most fundamental elements of human dignity and permitted the government to wield nearly totalitarian powers. After the insurgency began, Lyssiotis started defending EOKA fighters as an assistant to John and Glafkos Clerides. But he also supported EOKA by running a youth propaganda group of about two hundred students who painted pro-EOKA slogans on buildings and walls and distributed leaflets.[42] Another lawyer to return from Gray's Inn, Lellos Demetriades, also joined EOKA and defended insurgents in court. Many lawyers who defended EOKA fighters were formally inducted into the organization but kept this affiliation secret to avoid arrest. These and other Greek Cypriot barristers turned against British rule because of the contradictions that they saw between British ideals and British practice. They had learned British justice in the United Kingdom before returning home, only to find political frustration. At a time when other British colonies such as India, Burma, and Ceylon had gained independence, many Greek Cypriots expected that their turn to assert their right to national self-determination would come next. But Britain's insistence on maintaining colonial rule in Cyprus and the repressive legislation that followed EOKA violence appeared to these lawyers hypocritical.[43] Ironically, in the minds of many Greek Cypriot lawyers, British officials' repressive reassertion of colonial rule damaged the very credibility that those officials hoped to maintain.

Although the judicial system functioned throughout the Cyprus conflict, security imperatives often trumped legal procedure. Emergency legislation created a system of Special Courts to hear insurgency-related cases. British expatriate judges administered the courts. Single judges would rule in juryless trials, but death sentences were heard by three-judge panels at the Supreme Court in sessions chaired by the island's chief justice. The trappings of court procedure remained the same during the emergency as in peacetime: defendants could be represented by a barrister, evidence was submitted, prosecutors and defense counsels argued the merits of the case, and the judge came to a decision. But Harding had the power to order the immediate arrest and indefinite detention of anyone found not guilty in the courtroom. As the *Manchester Guardian* reported in July 1957, such arbitrary power fomented "public resentment" toward the government that was "stirred up by an apparent injustice." Often, those found not guilty only to be immediately rearrested and imprisoned under a detention order were EOKA operatives who were not convicted either because of a legal technicality or lack of sufficient evidence to warrant a conviction.[44] Greek Cypriot barristers were at a profound disadvantage when defending EOKA fighters in court.

The EOKA lawyers' highest-profile initial forays into the Special Court system ended in failure. The cases of Michelakis Karaolis and Andreas Demetriou seized the attention of many Greek Cypriots because they were the first capital punishment cases related to the emergency. Demetriou's case was straightforward. He was caught after shooting and wounding a British civilian businessman. In normal circumstances Demetriou would have faced charges of attempted murder that did not carry the death penalty, but under the emergency regulations he was subject to the death penalty.[45] He was convicted and hanged. The Karaolis case, however, was a different matter. The prosecution alleged that Karaolis had killed a police sergeant in October 1955. Defense attorneys Stelios Pavlides and Glafkos Clerides argued that it was a case of mistaken identity and submitted evidence that Karaolis had an alibi—he claimed that he was at his uncle's house when the murder occurred.[46] Karaolis was found guilty, but his lawyers appealed to the Cyprus Supreme Court and then to the Privy Council. The Privy Council dismissed the appeal. Harding, who had the power to issue a reprieve, decided "that the law shall take its course." Karaolis was executed in April 1956.[47] Harding was committed to keeping Karaolis in custody. He wrote to Lennox-Boyd that if the conviction were overturned, he would have Karaolis rearrested and detained indefinitely, as was Harding's prerogative under emergency laws. Even if Pavlides and Clerides had won the case, their client would not have gone free. The lawyers were battling against a system that inherently favored the British side.[48]

Occasionally, Greek Cypriot lawyers obtained favorable verdicts through innovative legal arguments. The case of Michael Rossides illustrates the impact that the lawyers could have. Two soldiers had been killed in retribution for the Karaolis and Demetriou executions, and British forces arrested Rossides for the death of one of the soldiers. Rossides confessed to the killing and was sentenced to death. His lawyers—Michael Triantafyllides, Stelios Pavlides, and Glafkos Clerides— turned to a common-law precedent. They argued that Rossides had killed the British soldier only because other EOKA members threatened to kill him if he failed to follow their orders. In a clemency submission to the governor, Clerides and Triantafyllides cited two sources of common-law precedents that acknowledged that "if a man were placed in the agonising situation of having to choose between his own life and somebody else's and preferred his own no capital sentence would be carried out." The argument succeeded—Harding commuted Rossides's sentence from death to life in prison. Despite Cyprus's repressive emergency legislation, Harding backed down when faced with a legal argument based on English common law.[49] Greek Cypriot lawyers used the rule of law to their advantage. But even in this situation, a defendant's fate ultimately rested in Harding's hands.

Greek Cypriot barristers realized that the legal system was stacked against them, but their engagement in the courtroom helped them identify British vulnerabilities that they could exploit. Colonial officials were averse to public criticism, and judges proved willing to enforce the law regarding the use of coercion during interrogation—that is, coercion was illegal and any confession obtained through intimidation or violence was inadmissible in court. Executions of EOKA fighters inflamed Greek Cypriot public opinion and sympathetic foreign audiences in countries such as Greece and Egypt. In the month following the Karaolis and Demetriou executions, the Foreign Office received nine petitions from organizations in Greece and one from Argentina denouncing the death sentences as well as several statements of support for the Greek Cypriot struggle from civic organizations in Egypt.[50] The outrage that the Karaolis and Demetriou executions incited across the island and overseas demonstrated that every execution would cause intense public outcry.[51] Harding's decision to execute Karaolis and Demetriou also invited criticism from home. In March 1956—one month before Karaolis's execution—the House of Commons voted to suspend the death penalty within the United Kingdom. The resolution stated that "this House believes that the death penalty for murder no longer accords with the needs or the true interests of a civilised society, and calls upon Her Majesty's Government to introduce forthwith legislation for its abolition or for its suspension."[52] The Commons' decision put the Cyprus government on the defensive. Concerned that journalists or politicians in Britain might criticize Harding's use of the death penalty, public relations officers in Cyprus designed talking points for the press which emphasized that "there is no inconsistency between the execution of Karaolis and the recent resolution in the House of Commons on the abolition of the death penalty." The rationale was that "even when enacted into law, [the resolution] will have no validity outside the United Kingdom." Harding had the authority to "take into account local circumstances in deciding how far he should go" in restricting capital punishment.[53] The combination of Greek Cypriot outrage at the Karaolis and Demetriou executions and the Cyprus government's response to the House of Commons vote on capital punishment in the United Kingdom revealed a key British vulnerability—public criticism.

Although emergency laws permitted security forces to exercise wide-ranging powers, these laws did not permit the use of violence during interrogation, a fact that led EOKA lawyers to attack the admissibility of prisoner confessions as evidence during trials. According to one expatriate British judge in Cyprus, Justice Bernard Shaw, if a defense attorney alleged that a prisoner had confessed as a result of any form of coercion, the law required

Crown prosecutors to prove that the confession was "free and voluntary." The burden of proof therefore lay with the Crown, whereas the defense needed only to establish "reasonable doubt" that the confession might have been obtained through coercion.[54] In one such case, the EOKA fighter Nicos Sampson was arrested in September 1956 for the murder of a police sergeant. After arresting him, police officers told Sampson to remove his shoes and socks—ostensibly to prevent an escape attempt—and forced him to lie in an open truck bed as a cold, steady rain poured down on him. Sampson confessed to the crime only after enduring this treatment. According to the head of the Cyprus police criminal investigation division, "the Special Branch man had taken [Sampson's] original confession down in a way that would not stand up in court." Sampson's lawyers successfully argued that Special Branch had beaten Sampson's confession out of him.[55] The judge, Justice Shaw, concluded that Sampson might have admitted to his crime out of fear that he might receive further poor treatment. These circumstances were enough to establish reasonable doubt.[56] Greek Cypriot lawyers frequently succeeded in having confessions ruled inadmissible on these grounds.[57]

After the declaration of a state of emergency, British security forces operated in an environment in which the Cyprus government could arbitrarily confer additional powers upon them with few legal restrictions. Greek Cypriot lawyers saw the emergency legislation as a sham, and they were not alone in that sentiment. In a protest letter, a group of Greek Cypriot mayors criticized the laws for being "enacted with utter disregard to the basic principles of Justice and human rights." They went on to deride the colonial government for granting "a deceptive cloak of legality to the virtually criminal excesses of the Security Forces."[58] But EOKA lawyers also sensed an opportunity to defend prisoners from punishment and undermine the impunity with which the Cyprus government could operate under emergency laws. In doing so, Greek Cypriot barristers turned the courts into part of the counterinsurgency battlefield. But they also realized that the courtroom was not the only place in which they should fight on behalf of prisoners. These lawyers found that they could pressure British officials by targeting the government's aversion to public scrutiny. Toward this end, they transformed their professional association, the Cyprus Bar Council, into an activist organization dedicated to protecting prisoners' rights to legal representation and publicly criticizing the excesses of the emergency regulations—including coercive interrogations.

The Bar Council Goes to War

Greek Cypriot lawyers used their professional association, the Cyprus Bar Council, as a vehicle for organizing resistance to the emergency regulations. The Bar Council existed to regulate professional standards and conduct. According to the 1955 Advocates Law, which was enacted before the emergency, all practicing barristers were required to join the Bar Council. It oversaw five local bar associations, each representing one of Cyprus's five districts. Despite its formal independence from the government as a professional society, the Bar Council maintained a close association with the colonial administration. The solicitor general had a seat on the council and the attorney general served as the council's titular head. The council was led by a committee elected by the council members. The committee consisted of fifteen barristers, including two members each from Nicosia, Paphos, Limassol, Famagusta, Kyrenia, and Larnaca, as well as three at-large members.[59] But the majority of Bar Council members—and particularly its leadership committee—were Greek Cypriots with pro-EOKA sympathies. The Bar Council's close association with the Cyprus government meant that the council's Greek Cypriot leaders were well placed to lobby British officials.[60] Through the auspices of the Bar Council, Greek Cypriot lawyers negotiated a memorandum of agreement with the government and lobbied colonial officials to ensure that security forces followed the terms of the memorandum.

Although the Cyprus Bar Council also included Turkish Cypriot members, they did not take part in the organization's activism because they objected to Greek Cypriot political aspirations. After the war began, the Turkish Cypriot leader Fazıl Küçük told the governor that "any direct or indirect means of bringing about Enosis will meet, as hitherto, with the bitter and determined opposition of the Cypriot Turks."[61] In general, Turkish Cypriots supported the Cyprus government against EOKA—a trend that continued in the courtroom. Turkish Cypriot barristers often worked on behalf of the colonial government as prosecutors and civil servants. Rauf Denktaş, for instance, studied in London at Lincoln's Inn before joining the colonial administration as a Crown Counsel. During the insurgency, he prosecuted EOKA fighters and, in 1958, founded a Turkish Cypriot resistance group that fought against EOKA.[62] In late 1956, as Greek Cypriot barristers began to transform the Bar Council into a platform for activism, Turkish Cypriot members withdrew from council proceedings altogether.[63] The council's Greek Cypriot leadership claimed that the organization was a professional association without political affiliation, but the absence of Turkish Cypriot involvement indicated the extent to which the council had become an activist organization supporting the enosis struggle.[64]

The Bar Council sprang into action not only to protect detainees' rights to legal representation but also to gain advantages for EOKA. As British forces began to strike back at EOKA throughout 1956, the number of detainees rose steadily from 169 in March to 447 in August and 623 by November. At the end of the year, there were 735 detainees in British custody.[65] As the number of arrests increased, lawyers demanded to know who had been detained, where they were held, and how they had been treated. As soon as barristers could obtain this information, they could take the necessary legal steps to best protect their clients from an emergency legal system that was stacked in Britain's favor. But there were other, military advantages to be accrued from ensuring that prisoners could hold confidential discussions with their legal representatives. EOKA commanders wanted to know who had been captured or killed in order to reorganize and reconstitute their forces. Lawyers could gather this information in their confidential meetings with captured insurgents and pass it on to EOKA leaders. For these lawyers, protecting detainees' rights went hand in hand with aiding EOKA.

To many attorneys the best way to protect detainees' rights and support EOKA was to ensure that the government respected prisoners' right to legal representation. But British forces grew suspicious of the lawyers' motivations and often prevented or delayed attorneys from speaking with detainees. Denying a prisoner the right to see an attorney was illegal under ordinary Cyprus law—emergency regulations had not changed this fact. As a result, Stelios Pavlides and George Chryssafinis, the Bar Council leadership committee's Nicosia representatives, complained to the attorney general's office in February 1956. Deputy Attorney General Nedjati Munir responded by reaffirming the right of detainees to consult an attorney. To prevent security forces from obstructing this right in the future, Munir informed the chief of staff that "I think this principle [of detainees' right to legal representation] and the statutory provisions in our law, should be drawn to the attention of Area and Unit Commanders."[66] On February 18, Brigadier J. S. Aldridge, the chief of staff, circulated a memorandum to his subordinate commanders conveying Munir's instruction that arrested persons had the right to see an attorney if they wished. Aldridge also ordered that when an interview between an attorney and a detainee occurred, guards were to locate themselves within eyesight of the meeting but not within range of hearing. This procedure was intended to satisfy the right of confidentiality in attorney-client discussions. The memorandum further proclaimed that powers of arrest and detention without warrant "do NOT override the ordinary law of the colony in one important respect, namely that any arrested person must be given reasonable facilities for obtaining legal advice." Soldiers and police who inhibited this right were therefore acting "contrary to the spirit of the law."[67]

Munir's response to the Bar Council complaint underscores British officials' complex and somewhat contradictory conceptualization of the rule of law during the insurgency. On the one hand, Munir asserted the primacy of law by reminding security force units that detainees had a right to legal representation. He wrote that "it is a fundamental principle of British justice, almost dating back to the Magna Carta, that a person in custody must be given reasonable facilities for obtaining legal advice and for arranging his defence." Munir insisted that the denial of an arrested person's right to meet with a lawyer was illegal and could result in charges against the government. But on the other hand, he acknowledged that the EOKA insurgency permitted deviations from "normal" principles of justice. He admitted that "it is in the public interest to stretch, and in some cases to modify, some of the basic principles which we all like to see operating in normal peaceful conditions."[68] Like many officials, Munir wanted to uphold the law but was willing to compromise on legal principles in order to end the insurgency. The survival of the state mattered more than justice for the state's subjects.[69] The subsequent August 17, 1956, memorandum on detainee legal representation reflected these competing priorities.

This memorandum amounted to a government guarantee that detainees could exercise their rights to legal representation, but it also included a compromise that permitted Special Branch officers to interrogate detainees before the detainee met with a lawyer. Chryssafinis, Pavlides, the assistant commissioner of police, a representative from the chief of staff's office, and Munir confirmed the details of their February discussion. In addition, the assistant commissioner of police agreed to provide a liaison officer at a central office available to answer all calls and inquiries from lawyers regarding a detainee's whereabouts and legal representation. From the perspective of the Greek Cypriot lawyers, this memorandum clarified and codified some important detainee rights but did not go far enough. To collect vital, time-sensitive intelligence, security force commanders believed it necessary to interrogate detainees during the first forty-eight hours following capture. They insisted that lawyers should be allowed to meet with detainees only after interrogation was complete. The memorandum also included an ambiguous caveat: "There may be cases where it will not be practicable" to allow advocates to interview detainee clients. Security forces could still prevent an attorney-client interview if the officer in charge of a police division believed that an interview "would be likely to hinder urgent enquiries or to prevent further arrests."[70] Although the August agreement curbed some government powers for arrest and detention, officials retained the power to limit lawyers' access to clients on the basis of suspicion rather than evidence.

The compromise inherent in the August 17 memorandum represented an attempt by British officials to balance their concerns with upholding the rule of law and maintaining security, but it undermined both. By granting interrogators forty-eight hours in which to question detainees, officials expected the detainees to provide information before receiving legal counsel and potentially incriminate themselves. This measure undermined the perception of fairness that was a hallmark of how British and Cypriot lawyers perceived the judicial system. The forty-eight-hour rule suggested that the preservation of standard legal proceedings was of secondary importance to security considerations—the rule of law mattered only insofar as it supported counterinsurgency operations. On the other hand, permitting detainees to have legal representation at all allowed their lawyers to use the legal system against the security forces. Lawyers' accusations that interrogators had abused detainees during questioning hampered the security effort by making convictions more difficult to obtain. Despite the memorandum's contradictions, Greek Cypriot attorneys used the terms of the document to their advantage.

Bar Council barristers successfully attacked the government for holding detainees longer than permitted under the August 17 agreement and often insinuated that interrogators abused prisoners to obtain confessions. When they met with detainees, lawyers sometimes passed messages from EOKA and could determine what information the detainee provided to the British during interrogation. The fact that the lawyers often claimed that their detainee clients had been abused in custody succeeded in reducing the number of cases that went to trial. The attorney general's office would not press charges if a detainee was held in Special Branch custody for too long because of the likelihood that defense attorneys would claim that interrogators had coerced the detainee into confessing. The government could have countered these allegations by ordering interrogators to appear in court as witnesses. Instead, the head of CID noted, British officials "dared not make a case" in court because of the potential risk of exposing interrogators. Security officials were concerned that interrogators would be in danger of assassination if EOKA discovered personal information or travel schedules, such as the dates and times when interrogators would make court appearances.[71] One additional rationale did not appear in the official record: instructing interrogators to testify in court would have put them in the awkward position of answering defense attorneys' probing questions over whether detainees were tortured.

Regardless of their reasons, some security officials resisted the rules outlined in the August 17 memorandum. One approach was simply to ignore the memorandum. When this occurred, Bar Council lawyers lobbied Attorney General Sir James Henry. Throughout the conflict, Henry regularly received complaints from Greek Cypriot lawyers when British forces failed to follow the memorandum's guidelines. In October 1956, British paratroopers captured thirty-one insurgents, including the leaders of two EOKA cells and members of four additional groups.[72] Following the operation, security forces prevented the lawyers Demetrios Demetriades, Stelios Pavlides, and Michael Triantafyllides from meeting with the captured insurgents. The Cyprus police also refused to identify who had been captured and where they were held. Under the terms of August 17 memorandum, the lawyers were entitled to know all this information.[73] Demetriades asked for Henry's immediate intervention. Henry's priority as attorney general was to uphold the law, which included the procedures outlined in the memorandum. Within twenty-four hours, Henry provided the Bar Council with a list of ninety detainees and their place of detention.[74] He consistently instructed police and prison staff "not to hold up [attorney] visits longer than is absolutely necessary in the cases of persons detained for interrogation" and reminded the security forces that "persons should be enabled to see advocates as soon as possible."[75] Greek Cypriot lawyers' appeals to the attorney general helped enforce the terms of the August 17 agreement.

Bar Council activism resulted in the August 17 memorandum, which the lawyers used to chip away at the edifice of the colonial state's emergency powers by defending the right of detainees to legal representation. Bar Council lawyers could also rely on Attorney General Henry's willingness to uphold the agreement even though some security officials ignored it. The lawyers had made some progress toward protecting prisoners' rights, but they faced a new challenge when Harding decided to issue a new set of emergency laws in November 1956.

Courting Controversy: The Expanded Emergency Regulations

During the second half of 1956, Harding had to balance two parallel military crises. Within Cyprus, he faced the EOKA insurgency. The second crisis, however, involved the British government's plan to attack Egyptian forces occupying the Suez Canal. In July 1956, Egyptian president Gamal Abdel Nasser nationalized the Suez Canal, which had been under French and British control. British prime minister Anthony Eden viewed Nasser's act as a threat to the use of the canal as a vital conduit for Middle Eastern oil. Eden coordinated with France and Israel to seize the canal. Cyprus became a key staging ground for the assault. Although Harding was not involved in the attack, he received orders to divert two brigades from counterinsurgency operations in Cyprus to prepare for the Suez invasion. Throughout the autumn, Harding was shorthanded. But in November, after the Suez intervention ended, he heard good news—his two brigades returned to Cyprus and he received 8,500 additional reinforcements, bringing his total troop strength to 31,000.[76] Without the Suez intervention siphoning his resources, Harding could redouble his efforts against EOKA. He chose to enact additional emergency laws that would facilitate an intensification of military operations by further protecting interrogators from scrutiny and improving their leverage over captured EOKA fighters during interrogation. EOKA lawyers responded to Harding's actions by expanding their activism to target Opposition politicians in Britain.

On November 22 and 23, 1956, Harding launched a legal offensive. He expanded the emergency regulations by passing a series of laws designed to stifle dissent, protect interrogators and other intelligence officers, and induce prisoners to provide information. An earlier measure already included a broad prohibition against the publication of any statements "likely to cause alarm or despondence." The new regulation allowed Harding to ban publications deemed threatening to the security forces' counterinsurgency efforts. Furthermore, the new law prohibited the publication of anything that fell under the vague description of a "disturbing report." Finally, possession of prohibited publications "without a lawful excuse" could result in six months' imprisonment.[77] Harding had the power to prohibit virtually any publication that he did not like.

Another new law, the public officers' protection regulation, was intended to shield Special Branch interrogators from charges brought by EOKA lawyers. The regulation dictated that private citizens could not file civil or criminal proceedings against any government official unless the attorney general consented to the charges. Detainees might have been able to identify their interrogators, but under this law their lawyers could not take interrogators to court unless they could first persuade the attorney general to allow the case to proceed. This law empowered the colonial government to act as a filter for charges against members of the security forces, preventing cases of abuse during interrogation from going to court. As one EOKA leaflet complained, the public officers' protection meant that "if you have been unjustly treated or ill-treated, if you are the victim of a theft or of the English justice [sic], you have no right to take the persons responsible to court."[78] The public officers' protection regulation limited Cypriot subjects' right to seek redress through the courts and protected interrogators from prosecution.

The expanded firearms law was perhaps the most notorious emergency regulation enacted during the conflict. The original law prohibited the use of firearms, bombs, or any other form of explosive "with intent to cause death or injury." Anyone violating this law could face the death penalty. The law also stipulated that anyone in possession of a firearm, bomb, grenade, or other explosive could face imprisonment for life. The expanded regulations of November 1956, however, took these punishments further. The new law prescribed a mandatory death sentence for anyone caught using or possessing firearms or explosives, as well as a mandatory death sentence for anyone "consorting" with persons possessing or using firearms or explosives. Anyone carrying an "incendiary article" other than a bomb, grenade, or ammunition was liable to a life sentence. In addition, the law reversed the burden of proof from the prosecution to the defendant. Now any individual charged with possession or use of a firearm would have to prove his or her innocence beyond a reasonable doubt.[79] These harsh sentences were intended to convince captured EOKA fighters to trade information for their lives. Unburdened by the need to prove that a suspect had actually used firearms or explosives, interrogators could offer a reprieve from the mandatory death sentence—granted by the governor on the security forces' recommendation—if a suspect provided useful intelligence. The mandatory death sentence became a tool in the intelligence collection effort.[80]

This manipulation of the law to facilitate counterinsurgency operations incensed Greek Cypriot lawyers, who used the Cyprus Bar Council as a means of registering their complaints with government officials. Stelios Pavlides and John Clerides called for a meeting of the Bar Council's general membership on December 8, 1956. As the president and vice president of the council, Sir James Henry and Ned Munir were also invited. During the meeting, Pavlides introduced a resolution stating that the members of the bar "strongly deprecate[d] and condemn[ed]" the mandatory death sentence for firearms offenses, the new censorship regulations, and the public officers' protection legislation. The lawyers argued that the mandatory death penalty removed the "discretionary power of trial judges of the Special Court to impose a sentence of imprisonment in the case of certain offences (which ordinarily would not carry a capital sentence)," instead "leaving no alternative to the judges than to pass a sentence of death upon every person convicted for any such offence." The members of the bar also objected to the structure of the Special Courts, where a single judge determined the verdict. The lawyers insisted that "no court should have power to pass a death sentence unless composed of three judges as in the case of Assize Courts," which before the emergency had presided over the most serious cases in the colony and consisted of a panel of judges. The lawyers' ire also extended to censorship, in which the Bar Council members asserted that "Emergency or no Emergency, there can be no excuse or justification for the promulgation of provisions which strike at the very root of matters connected with the administration of justice and the freedom of the press." Finally, the lawyers wrote that the public officers' protection regulation would "prevent free access to the Courts of the Colony by persons having a grievance against public officers for offences committed against them and ill-treatment applied to them." The new regulations were therefore "contrary to well established principles and policy of law."[81] Bar Council members voted overwhelmingly to pass the resolution. Only Henry and Munir, in their capacities as colonial officials, voted against it because it criticized government policy.[82] Through the December 8 resolution, Greek Cypriot lawyers asserted that the expanded emergency regulations violated Cypriots' civil rights. But they did not limit their activism to lobbying local officials.

Beyond Cyprus, Bar Council attorneys found a receptive audience among anticolonial left-wing British politicians. A key connection was made when a British lawyer named Peter Benenson arrived in Cyprus. Although he would later gain renown as a cofounder of Amnesty International, in 1956 Benenson was a member of the Society of Labour Lawyers—a group of attorneys who belonged to the Labour Party—and chaired its foreign relations subcommittee.[83] He first visited Cyprus in 1956 as a war correspondent for the *Spectator*. Benenson was supposed to cover the Suez Crisis, so he was flown to Cyprus while British troops staged for the assault on Egypt.

Being a barrister, he wandered into the Nicosia law courts and began speaking with Greek Cypriot lawyers. In December, Benenson joined the legal team retained by Charles Foley, who owned the *Times of Cyprus*, a newspaper that was highly critical of Harding's repressive policies. Benenson worked alongside John and Glafkos Clerides to defend the newspaper against libel charges filed by the Cyprus government. Foley described Benenson as "red-haired, rabidly energetic, and had a warm heart for lost causes."[84] At some point between October and December 1956, Benenson met John and Glafkos Clerides, who told him of their problems with emergency legislation and allegations of prisoner "ill-treatment"—the colonial government's preferred euphemism for torture.[85] Benenson decided to help by raising awareness of these problems in Britain.

In December 1956, Britain's Conservative Party government was under siege from Opposition MPs over the Suez Crisis, but the Opposition quickly expanded its critique to include Cyprus policy. On December 4, spearheaded by the Labour MP Lena Jeger and the Liberal Party leader Jo Grimond, a group of twenty-seven Labour and Liberal MPs tabled a motion in the House of Commons condemning the "ruthless severity" of Harding's expanded emergency laws, particularly the extension of the death penalty and the governor's power to censor the press.[86] Grimond argued that the curtailment of free speech in Cyprus amounted to a "sad day for this great liberal country." In the House of Lords, Lord Listowel criticized the new press restrictions. He found the public officers' protection regulation particularly repulsive, calling it "contrary to our ideas of justice that a citizen should be unable to go to law without the consent of the Attorney-General, himself a member of the Government." Lord Jowitt lamented that "I do not think I have ever seen a more draconian set of rules than these regulations."[87] Lord Jowitt's point was clear—harsh laws fed resentment and created new enemies, which only made Britain's colonial problems worse.

The debate continued throughout the month as Harding's expanded emergency laws faced further criticism. On December 21, several Labour backbench MPs criticized the new regulations as overly repressive. The Labour MP Kenneth Robinson condemned the "repressive government and draconian legislation" as an "almost total denial of civil liberties." He rebuked Harding over press restrictions, telling the Commons that the Cyprus regulations amounted to "a fantastic interference with the rights of free speech and freedom of expression." Robinson also decried the public officers' protections, saying that under the law "the Government become judge and jury in their own case." Lena Jeger linked repression in Cyprus to the dynamics of other colonial rebellions: "We have had enough experience in Cyprus and in other parts of the Colonial Empire to know that repression of this kind is simply a sowing of dragon's teeth and that, in fact, violence in Cyprus has increased in direct relationship to the severity of the Regulations."[88] Harding's decision to expand the emergency regulations incited

Opposition politicians' ire at the very moment when Benenson began corresponding with Greek Cypriot lawyers. This combination would soon put Harding under intense political pressure.

Cyprus Bar Council lawyers sent Benenson evidence that security forces regularly used torture during interrogation—information that Benenson passed along to Labour MPs such as James Callaghan.[89] On December 17, 1956, John Clerides penned a letter to Benenson containing a spate of complaints that he had recently filed with the Cyprus government. On November 1, Clerides filed six allegations of ill treatment. The administrative secretary pledged that investigations would occur, but Clerides had not yet received news of the investigation results. By the end of November, Clerides claimed that he had filed an additional thirty complaints, which colonial officials had failed to answer. "I have been submitting complaints," he wrote to Benenson, "for the purposes of remedying a situation which discredits the prestige of British Administration."[90] In a direct reference to Stelios Pavlides and John Clerides, James Callaghan told the House of Commons of his concern over "examples—I think I am not putting it too highly—of torture": "Investigations were made by persons of the highest repute in Cyprus, namely, a former Attorney-General, who I believe is well esteemed by the Administration, and another former member of the Governor's Executive Council. They have sent the Administration 30 documented cases of *prima facie* brutality by Security Forces." The colonial government in Cyprus, however, had thus far failed to investigate the complaints. "There is a responsibility upon the Administration," Callaghan asserted, "to ensure that every complaint of this nature is investigated." Until then, "we are under a cloud of suspicion."[91] As a result of Cyprus Bar Council activism, British MPs called for a formal inquiry into torture allegations.

At Callaghan's behest, Benenson returned to Cyprus on December 28 with a series of informal proposals to reform detention and interrogation procedures. He suggested that CID interrogate suspects—a measure that revealed his personal understanding of the purpose of police questioning. To Benenson, interrogation was designed to gather evidence that would determine whether a case should go to trial, not to collect intelligence in support of military operations. Because CID was the police organization best equipped to prepare case evidence for trial, it made sense to have CID conduct the interrogation. Benenson also disagreed with the stipulation that interrogators could prevent detainees from meeting with their lawyers during the first forty-eight hours after capture. Instead, an accused person should be allowed to communicate with an attorney "as soon as he is handed over for interrogation" but certainly "no later than 48 hours after his arrest." A lawyer, Benenson continued, "should be allowed to see his client at any time after notification of the arrest of his client," although he conceded that this measure did not mean that an attorney must be present during interrogation or that interrogation should be delayed until the lawyer arrived.[92] Benenson saw interrogation as part of the trial process—a mind-set that explains his preference that CID conduct interrogations and his desire to allow suspects to meet with an attorney immediately after arrest.

At the time, however, interrogations were conducted by Special Branch rather than CID. Special Branch officers perceived interrogation differently than Benenson did. For them, interrogation provided intelligence that would enable security forces to disrupt EOKA operations by interdicting supplies and capturing or killing insurgents. Special Branch's priority was to collect vital, actionable intelligence rather than meticulously documenting evidence for eventual use in a court of law to convict captured EOKA members. Because of their emphasis on intelligence collection, Special Branch officers avoided testifying in court, whereas CID officers routinely provided testimony during criminal trials.[93] Special Branch officers viewed interrogation as a security operation against the enemy, not part of a process for the administration of justice.

Attorney General Henry's perspective on interrogation procedures aligned with Benenson's. Henry supported Benenson's suggestion to assign CID officers to interrogation duty "both as a safeguard and because he will be at hand if any information useful in the investigation of the particular offence is obtained." CID's involvement would help gain convictions as well: "Difficulties are frequently occurring over cases in which alleged confessions have been made to C.I.D. officers at the end of a period of 14 days detention during which the accused had been in the custody of the Special Branch. The onus is on the prosecution to prove that the confessions are voluntary, and it will not be possible to do this unless the Special Branch officers in whose custody the accused was held are called to give evidence. The Judges insist on this." Henry continued, writing that when a confession is introduced during a trial, "it is invariable that allegations of beating and ill-treatment are made in respect of the period during which the accused has been held by Special Branch." Special Branch officers' aversion to appearing in court "nullified any chance of securing a conviction on a capital charge" in one recent case "and there are several other similar cases now pending."[94] This internal interrogation debate resulted from Cyprus Bar Council activism, which led several Opposition MPs to scrutinize Harding's harsh security policies such as the expanded emergency legislation.

Harding did not want Benenson's interference—or anyone else's, for that matter—to disrupt the successes achieved as a result of the new laws. When he learned of Benenson's return to Cyprus in December 1956, an angry Harding ordered Deputy Governor George Sinclair to "keep Benenson on the rails."[95] As Sinclair tried to control whom Benenson could talk to and where he went, Harding cabled Colonial Secretary Lennox-Boyd to explain the value of the new regulations:

> For your private information . . . you may wish to know that the new Regulations extending the death penalty are believed to be responsible in great measure for recent successes in the liquidation of terrorists at Limassol. One youth, who was plainly aware that he was liable to the death penalty declared his intention of implicating others as well and proceeded to make a 26 page statement admitting his complicity in earlier murders and giving material which has led to the arrest of many terrorists in the area and the break-up of a number of killer groups. The same occurred also, to a lesser degree, in Famagusta and was also attributable to the knowledge of the death penalty. For these reasons I consider that the new measure has justified itself although of course it will be kept constantly under review.

According to Harding, the application of mandatory death sentences for firearms possession had led to an intelligence boon. Interrogators could use the threat of the death penalty as leverage to obtain a confession in exchange for a reduced sentence.

Expanding the death penalty also proved strategically useful because it enabled the government to convict more insurgents. Security forces often lacked evidence to try EOKA fighters for serious crimes such as murder, yet they had obtained sufficient intelligence to know that an insurgent was probably guilty. Such circumstantial evidence would not produce a murder conviction in court, but regulations such as the firearms law allowed the government to severely punish insurgents for lesser offenses. Harding described an example in which members of an EOKA cell that "had probably been responsible for several murders" faced charges for the possession of firearms rather than murder because the prosecution lacked sufficient evidence to win a murder case. Before the extension of capital punishment to firearms possession cases, the members of this cell could not have been sentenced to death. After broadening the application of the death penalty, Harding noted, such cases required judges "to impose the punishment such conduct deserves."[96] These laws permitted the government to implement serious punishments without the need to assemble enough evidence to prove that the suspects had committed serious crimes with the firearms in their possession.

Harding's decision to expand the emergency regulations encountered resistance not only within Cyprus but also at home. By December 1956, the Cyprus Bar Council's overtures to British politicians had brought detention and interrogation issues into public view. Faced with pressure from Parliament, Harding was primarily concerned with avoiding the establishment of formal limitations on interrogation practices. His opposition to Benenson's presence on the island reflected this priority. Harding would remain committed to this course of action as criticism mounted throughout 1957.

Harding under Pressure: III Treatment and Interrogation

The winter of 1956–57 was a difficult time for Britain's Conservative government. Sir Anthony Eden resigned as prime minister in the aftermath of the Suez Crisis and was replaced in January 1957 by Harold Macmillan.[97] In Cyprus, a series of factors had put Sir John Harding's administration under pressure. Parliamentary criticism, stimulated by the Cyprus Bar Council's efforts, continued into 1957. In the wake of the Suez Crisis, Prime Minister Macmillan committed the government to a political settlement in Cyprus. Finally, the government of Greece had sponsored a complaint—or "application," in legal language—at the European Commission of Human Rights. From December 1956 to the spring of 1957, Harding remained steadfast in his desire to preserve emergency laws that facilitated intelligence collection.

During the first months of 1957, Harding continued to face censure from Opposition politicians in Britain over the expanded emergency regulations. On February 19, MP Lena Jeger criticized the Cyprus government's press restrictions by questioning the case against Charles Foley's *Times of Cyprus*. "I have been reading all the cuttings from the *Times of Cyprus* very carefully, including those articles which have brought down such wrath on Mr. Foley's head," Jeger told the Commons. "If one reads his articles and then reads the Government's reproof of him," she continued, "one is surprised and dismayed. One is left with the conclusion that the Government do not want newspapers at all."[98] A February 20 article in the *Manchester Guardian* reported James Callaghan's condemnation of Cyprus policy as "lost in a blind alley."[99] On March 8, Jeger asked Colonial Secretary Alan Lennox-Boyd if the government would set up an independent inquiry into "irregularities in the administration of justice in Cyprus."[100] Finally, the Cyprus Bar Council leadership also wrote to Lennox-Boyd asking for the appointment of a parliamentary committee to investigate allegations of prisoner ill treatment. He demurred.[101] The Bar Council's connection with British politicians ensured that the Opposition was well informed of the state of the emergency regulations in Cyprus.

Harding also faced new geopolitical concerns as the Macmillan government adopted a different political course in Cyprus. The Suez Crisis had severely damaged Britain's relationship with its primary ally, the United States. When Macmillan met with President Dwight Eisenhower in March 1957, Eisenhower suggested that Macmillan release Archbishop Makarios from exile in the Seychelles. Macmillan agreed, hoping that Makarios's release would pave the way for a political settlement to the conflict. The Macmillan government also presented a new plan for self-government in Cyprus and invited Greece and Turkey to a three-power conference with Britain to negotiate a solution. Peace in Cyprus was especially important given the April 1957 release of the Defence White Paper, which signaled the end of conscription and the consequent reduction of the army to half its size over the next five years. Cyprus's airfields were still considered vital to British security, but the new Minister of Defence, Duncan Sandys, was not convinced that retaining sovereignty over the entire island was either necessary or practical.[102] Meanwhile, the United Nations General Assembly debated the island's fate, with a weakly worded resolution calling on the parties involved to resume negotiations toward a solution.[103] Diplomatic momentum had turned toward a negotiated settlement.

Although Harding could anticipate the change in British policy, neither he nor the Macmillan government foresaw Greece's decision to submit an application to the European Commission of Human Rights on behalf of Greek Cypriots alleging that Britain had violated the European Convention on Human Rights through its conduct of the war in Cyprus. The European Commission of Human Rights, based in Strasbourg, France, oversaw the implementation of the convention. The convention contained eighteen articles protecting civil liberties such as the right to life, privacy, marriage, and a fair trial; and the freedom of expression, thought, assembly, and religion. Of particular relevance to the Cyprus Emergency, Article 3 prohibited torture and "inhuman or degrading treatment," while Article 15 permitted states to derogate from the convention if three conditions were met: there must be a public emergency threatening the life of the nation, the measures taken in response to an emergency must be "strictly required by the exigencies of the situation," and those measures must be consistent with the state's other obligations under international law.[104] The convention also allowed, but did not require, its signatories to accept individual or group petitions. Britain rejected the right of individual petition but accepted the right of a fellow state party to the convention to petition the European Commission. The implication for Cyprus was that only states could formally complain about British actions, not the Cypriots themselves.[105] But the government of Greece, sympathetic to Greek Cypriot nationalist aspirations, proved a willing international patron.

The Greek application of May 1956 was a reaction to allegations of abuse during interrogation and the executions of Karaolis and Demetriou, which contributed to a sense among many mainland Greeks and Greek Cypriots that British forces operated with impunity. By filing the application, the Greek government entered uncharted territory—this case marked the first interstate complaint under the auspices of the European Convention on Human Rights. At a June 1956 hearing in Strasbourg, British legal officers, the commission members, and the Greek delegation settled on the scope of the application. The Greek representatives agreed to limit the proceedings to a general inquiry into whether the state of emergency and its associated legislation constituted a breach of the European convention. The commission, however, permitted the Greek government to submit a second application addressing individual cases of abuse at a later date if it so desired. With the terms set, the European Commission appointed a subcommission to oversee the proceedings of the case.[106] Although the convention was an international agreement, it generated highly localized consequences for the colonial administration in Cyprus.

To support the Greek application, the Cyprus Bar Council established a local "human rights committee" in Nicosia in October 1956. Its objective was to document evidence of torture and other forms of abuse for use in local legal proceedings and inclusion in a potential second Greek application under the European convention. John Clerides and Stelios Pavlides led the effort, receiving support from approximately a dozen other barristers, many of whom were also involved in defending captured EOKA fighters. The Bar Council's island-wide activist network facilitated the creation of human rights committees in other cities and towns.[107]

Human rights committee lawyers found that most complaints concerned mental and physical abuse during interrogation. In the case of Ioannis Christoforou, the lawyers called on the attorney general to investigate what their private inquiry had disclosed as "an overwhelming prima facie case of grievous bodily harm" committed against Christoforou. Maria Lambrou, who was pregnant when taken into custody, claimed to have been beaten at the Kyrenia police station and alleged that her interrogator told her to confess or else he would beat her so hard that she would miscarry.[108] Another prisoner, Takis Kakoullis, held at Omorphita Police Station, reported that guards threw salt on the floor and forced him to lick it. They subsequently placed a tin can on his head and beat it for fifteen minutes. George Koursoumbas alleged that police officers ordered him to raise his arms, then punched him in the armpits. They then ordered him to lie down, placed his feet on a chair, and beat the soles of his feet with a leather bandolier. In Nicosia, Konstantinos Ionannou endured a mock execution. Ionannou alleged that an interrogator pointed a revolver at his head and said, "I will count to seven. If you do not confess you will die." The interrogator counted to seven and pulled the trigger. The pistol clicked—the chamber was empty.[109]

Suspicious deaths in custody also attracted scrutiny. The *Times of Cyprus* routinely published reports on inquests and criminal procedures. In one, an inquest into the death of Nicos Georghiou, the newspaper reported that the coroner had determined Georghiou's cause of death to have been "intercranial haemorrhage and purulent bronchitis 'occasioned by some unknown external agency of which there is no direct evidence.'" Georghiou died at Akrotiri hospital in January 1957 after four days in British custody. Dr. Clearkin, a government pathologist who testified at the court hearing, reported that Georghiou's death "was unnatural." The lack of direct evidence meant that the mysterious circumstances of Georghiou's death were not pursued further. No one was convicted for causing his death.[110]

The Cyprus government did not officially sanction physical cruelty—in fact officials cited the conviction of a police officer in Limassol on ill-treatment charges as well as the March 1956 court-martial of two army intelligence officers on assault charges as "proof of the resolution with which Government and the military authorities deal with such cases."[111] As of March 1957, the Cyprus government had punished four additional members of the security forces for ill-treating Cypriot civilians. Three police constables were charged with assault, fined from £10 to £25, and forced to resign. One police auxiliary was found guilty of inflicting grievous bodily harm on a civilian and was sentenced to three years' imprisonment.[112] In June 1957, a UK police sergeant Gash assaulted a Greek Cypriot civilian over a private quarrel unrelated to detention or interrogation. The Nicosia Special Court convicted Gash on July 5, 1957. He was reprimanded and fined £5.[113] The colonial administration proved willing to punish security forces if the evidence against them was overwhelming or if the crimes were relatively petty, but the punishments were far from severe.

As the Strasbourg inquiry progressed, British officials in Cyprus and Whitehall realized that they required a coordinated response to the Greek application. Britain could not simply ignore or dismiss the application because, as one official noted, it "falls too clearly within the ambit of the Convention, which we have signed, to be brushed aside."[114] The Foreign Office legal adviser, Sir Francis Vallat, articulated a strategy to slowly give ground on issues that the Cyprus human rights committees and the Greek government found objectionable while continuing to contest the application before the subcommission. Vallat described this approach as a "policy of gentle co-operation and the gradual whittling away of the sting of the Greek application by one means or another."[115] Harding applied this strategy to good effect in Cyprus while simultaneously preserving laws that he deemed vital to the counterinsurgency effort.

As a result of parliamentary criticism and the Greek human rights applications and out of a desire to win Greek Cypriot support for a new colonial constitution, Harding revoked collective punishment and juvenile whipping regulations in December 1956.[116] These laws had proved more burdensome than useful.[117] They had little impact in practice on the security forces' efforts to kill or capture EOKA fighters but proved particularly controversial and infuriating to many Greek Cypriots. Harding needed to preserve laws that allowed the security forces to gather intelligence, like those on interrogation practices, deemed vital to the counterinsurgency effort. Appearing to give ground on the collective punishment and juvenile whipping regulations would assuage angry Greek Cypriots and Opposition critics at home without sacrificing legal powers that were actually useful for countering EOKA.[118]

Among the regulations that Harding designated as essential to the success of counterinsurgency operations, however, were the public officers' protection regulation and the firearms law. He left these laws in effect. When explaining this decision to the colonial secretary, Harding wrote that he preferred for the regulation to "remain in force at least until it has been possible to garner the results from the interrogation of persons arrested in the course of recent operations. There is no doubt that far more information is coming in than ever before, and this has assisted towards recent successes." Harding argued that the public officers' protection regulation "had an extremely limited object, to protect Government servants whose anonymity was necessary for their personal safety while performing their duties during the present emergency." This "limited object," however, had broad ramifications—it shielded interrogators from scrutiny, ensuring that they could continue without concern for the actions of EOKA lawyers.[119]

Militarily, by the spring of 1957, the Cyprus campaign was going well for the British thanks to operations conducted under a legal framework designed to facilitate intelligence collection and security operations. Captured documents and prisoner interrogations had reduced EOKA's mountain gangs and town-based assassination squads to a shell of their previous strength. Intelligence estimates indicated that only 40 percent of EOKA's most experienced and dedicated fighters remained at large. The rest had been killed or captured. Logistically, EOKA had also suffered losses as British forces seized several major arms caches and disrupted the organization's Limassol-based smuggling network. EOKA's leader, George Grivas, was on the run and had almost been captured.[120] He ordered a unilateral ceasefire so that EOKA could regroup.

On April 4, 1957, with the desire for a political settlement driving policy in Whitehall, Harding further relaxed the emergency regulations. He decreed that the death penalty would apply only in cases in which the defendant was charged with discharging or carrying firearms and bombs with the intent to cause bodily harm. Furthermore, Harding removed all restrictions on the use of taxis and bicycles and canceled the 1956 orders controlling the sale and circulation of publications. He portrayed these actions as generous steps toward peace and hoped to placate the subcommission in Strasbourg.[121] Harding had preserved the laws that were most useful to the intelligence effort, but activism from the Cyprus Bar Council and the resultant parliamentary criticism pressured him into revoking some repressive regulations.

When first enacted, the emergency regulations regime tilted the balance in the colonial government's favor. This legislation granted security forces wide-ranging powers of arrest, detention, and interrogation. British officials sought to wield the law as a weapon that could restrain their enemies' freedom of action while enabling the security forces to operate with fewer restrictions. Through courtroom advocacy, Greek Cypriot barristers undermined the emergency regulations by turning the judicial system into a battlefield in its own right, but they also shaped the war beyond the courtroom.

By transforming the Cyprus Bar Council from a professional society to an activist organization, Greek Cypriot lawyers protected detainees' rights to legal representation, appealed to sympathetic British politicians, and documented torture allegations in support of the Greek government's application before the European Commission of Human Rights. Although the firearms law and public officers' protection regulation remained in place, the Bar Council lawyers forced Harding to eliminate some of the most repressive laws such as those concerning collective punishments, juvenile whipping, and press censorship.

When in December 1956 and April 1957 Harding decided to rescind some repressive regulations—a selection of the most offensive yet least useful emergency laws—he actually hoped to protect the interrogation system that he deemed to be so valuable to the war effort. Ultimately, for both Greek Cypriots and the British, human rights activism and the law proved useful as instruments of war—instruments that would continue to be applied as the conflict dragged into the second half of 1957.

The Shadow of Strasbourg

International Advocacy and Britain's Response

International diplomacy played an important role in the Cyprus conflict, both as a site of confrontation between the protagonists and, eventually, as the forum in which Britain, Turkey, and Greece—the three states most heavily invested in the outcome of the war—arrived at a satisfactory agreement that ended the insurgency. Diplomatic wrangling at the United Nations, squabbling among NATO allies, and ministerial-level negotiations between Britain, Turkey, and Greece defined much of the political and diplomatic history of the Cyprus Emergency. But the Greek government's actions on behalf of Greek Cypriots at the European Commission of Human Rights shaped the conduct of the war in new ways. Greece's May 1956 application to the commission amounted to a general inquiry into the justifiability of a state of emergency in Cyprus, but on July 17, 1957 the Greek government followed this complaint with a second application concerning specific allegations of torture. Although Britain won the case regarding the first (1956) application, the European Commission compelled British officials to permit an international human rights investigation. Greece's second (1957) application accused Britain of torturing prisoners in forty-nine individual cases. The evidence used in this application was based largely on documentation collected by Greek Cypriot lawyers associated with local human rights committees.[1]

Combined with the Cyprus Bar Council's lobbying efforts, these two applications and an EOKA propaganda offensive—which colonial officials labeled the "atrocity campaign"—convinced the Cyprus government of the need to devise a coherent, effective response to human rights activism. At first, colonial administrators tried to prevent an international human rights investigation in Cyprus. When those efforts failed, the deputy governor, administrative secretary, and senior security force commanders within the Cyprus government sought to control public discussion of abuse allegations. The Special Investigation Group (SIG) became a key component of this effort. SIG was a counterpropaganda unit that existed to preserve Britain's reputation by whitewashing abuse allegations and providing British officials with plausible deniability or an alternative narrative to undermine EOKA propaganda efforts.

In addition to the creation of SIG, colonial officials covered up evidence of security force culpability in two 1958 incidents: the deaths of eleven unarmed Greek Cypriots killed by Turkish Cypriots after soldiers released them from custody near the Turkish Cypriot village of Geunyeli, and the army's unsanctioned reprisals after the murder of Catherine Cutliffe in Famagusta. After the Geunyeli incident, several senior military and civilian officials whitewashed the results of a judicial inquiry. Following the Famagusta incident, Director of Operations Sir Kenneth Darling asked the governor to eliminate pretrial inquests in cases involving security operations—an initiative that would have further shielded soldiers and police from public scrutiny concerning the circumstances in which soldiers used lethal force. These local consequences—the creation of SIG, the Geunyeli and Famagusta incidents, and the inquest debate—resulted from rights activism in the international arena.

The International Arena

Before calling upon the European Convention on Human Rights, Greek Cypriots pursued many different avenues to mobilize international support for enosis, but Britain effectively kept these attempts in check. Greek Cypriots obtained Greek support at the United Nations, condemned British violations of the Geneva Conventions, and appealed to the International Committee of the Red Cross. But many of these overtures proved ineffective. The European Convention on Human Rights, however, offered a viable option for Greek Cypriots and their Greek sponsors to force Britain into relaxing its repressive policies. Greece's decision to submit two applications before the European Commission should therefore be seen as one part of a multifaceted strategy to pressure Britain in the international arena.

In the early 1950s, under the leadership of Archbishop Makarios III, Greek Cypriots sought to "internationalize" the enosis question by establishing a global network of support. As head of the Cyprus Greek Orthodox Church and the primary religious and political leader of the Greek Cypriot community, Makarios regularly traveled abroad to establish religious links with other Greek Orthodox communities. He simultaneously used these trips to build support for enosis among anticolonial politicians and journalists in Egypt, Lebanon, and Syria. Makarios could also call on an extensive network of Christian groups in the United States, cultivated during his studies in Boston and later involvement with the ecumenical World Council of Churches. When Makarios visited New York in 1952, he pursued UN delegates' support for enosis and publicized the cause through speeches and radio interviews in the American media.[2] In 1954, the right-wing Greek government under former field marshal Alexandros Papagos committed to backing Makarios's diplomatic efforts at the United Nations.[3]

The United Nations became the site of an annual diplomatic battle between Britain and Greece over whether the "Cyprus Question" qualified as an international issue. Britain argued that since Cyprus was a colony, its affairs were a domestic issue; the island's international status should not be a topic for discussion. British diplomats tried to undermine support for the Greek position among other UN member states. But many states, particularly former colonies of the emerging Third World such as India and Indonesia, advocated a broader UN mandate that included self-determination for colonies. Britain attempted to gain American support on the Cyprus issue with the argument that Cyprus was strategically valuable and therefore essential to Cold War defense. Furthermore, British diplomats argued that self-determination for Greek Cypriots would alienate Turkish Cypriots and inflame relations between Greece and Turkey, both of which were vital NATO allies.[4] Within Cyprus, EOKA was highly conscious of the international arena's importance.[5]

One way in which Greek Cypriots sought international support was by invoking international agreements that prevented torture. In 1956, the Cyprus Bar Council complained to Governor Harding that physical and mental ill treatment during interrogation constituted a breach of the 1949 Geneva Conventions. Bar Council lawyers insisted that the security forces' use of torture was a blatant violation of the conventions. The 1949 conventions required all signatory governments to "pledge themselves to leave unaltered and unrestricted the existing processes for the vindication of civil rights." Emergency regulations, the lawyers argued, violated this stipulation by overriding normal legal processes.[6] British officials disagreed.

Although Britain had signed the convention in 1949, the government had deliberately avoided ratifying the treaty out of concern that the convention would restrict British forces' ability to deal with insurgents as law-breaking rebels rather than as internationally recognized combatants. Even after the British government finally ratified the convention in 1957, government lawyers identified and exploited legal loopholes to ensure that it did not restrict British freedom of action.[7] For example, Britain insisted that Common Article 3, which stipulated that the Geneva Conventions applied to "noninternational armed conflict" as well as interstate conflict, did not apply in Cyprus. British officials based their argument on a technicality. No clear definition of what constituted a noninternational armed conflict existed, so the British government insisted that rebellions and insurgencies did not constitute full-scale war and did not qualify as noninternational armed conflicts. Therefore, they argued, the laws of war did not apply.[8]

The International Committee of the Red Cross, which worked to improve conditions for prisoners, also proved ineffective at recognizing and stopping British abuses. Throughout the conflict, the ICRC conducted visits to British detention camps. In one March 1957 visit to the Nicosia Central prison, the ICRC representative David de Traz was allowed to interview many detainees without oversight from camp officials. A British report on de Traz's visit noted that he heard "numerous complaints concerning harsh treatment suffered during questioning by the police. In many cases the delegate saw actual traces of such treatment." All the detainees claimed that they had sustained their injuries during interrogation, not at the detention camp. De Traz raised the issue with Deputy Governor George Sinclair, reminding him of Britain's obligation "for the detainees to be treated with humanity in all circumstances." De Traz asked to be allowed to visit the police interrogation centers on his next visit to Cyprus.[9] He believed that brutality had probably occurred but was limited: "My personal opinion is that at no time did the top British officials order or tolerate deliberate ill-treatment of prisoners. However, I think it quite possible that in moments of exasperation, lower-ranking police officers will get carried away to excess."[10] When he visited Omorphita interrogation center in August 1957, de Traz spoke with only one detainee and used a British interpreter. Since the dialogue occurred in the presence of a British official, the detainee unsurprisingly stated that he had no complaints about his treatment. De Traz concluded that "nothing untoward is happening there."[11] He reported that he did not see any suspicious marks or signs of abuse on detainees' bodies. As the war continued, de Traz regularly visited detention camps—visits that resulted in marked improvements in living conditions. But Greek Cypriot detainees insisted that it was the interrogation centers rather than the detention camps that were the source of abuse and encouraged the ICRC to investigate those sites. De Traz, however, did not push British administrators to let him visit the interrogation centers on a regular basis. Although he believed that at least some abuse had occurred, he was also suspicious of the often-exaggerated EOKA propaganda alleging that British forces tortured prisoners. De Traz acted cautiously so as not to appear a pawn in EOKA's propaganda game. His caution backfired. By November 1958, many Greek Cypriots had grown to believe that the Red Cross was biased in favor of the British.[12]

Despite Britain's resistance at the UN and rejection of the Geneva Conventions' applicability, Greece's applications to the European Commission of Human Rights accomplished what other international appeals so far had not—the applications struck at key aspects of counterinsurgency operations in Cyprus. Greece's May 1956 application amounted to a general inquiry into the justifiability of a state of emergency in Cyprus. This application targeted the emergency regulations regime. If the European Commission determined that the state of emergency was unjustified, Britain would face tremendous international pressure to revoke emergency laws in Cyprus. The second application's emphasis on individual torture cases aimed at the interrogation system. Most accusations included in the second application involved Special Branch police interrogators using brute violence to extract information. Techniques included beatings with fists and canes, whips, or belts; a form of water torture meant to simulate drowning; and the twisting of male genitals.[13] In two cases, prisoners died. One died when attempting to escape. According to colonial officials, the man died when he hit his head on a rock after being tackled by a British soldier. The other man died from intercranial hemorrhage. There was no evidence indicating that he had been mistreated in custody, but there was also no evidence to suggest how he had developed a head injury. The fact that a seemingly healthy man died in custody without evidence to indicate how he had received a fatal injury was in itself suspicious.[14] Upon reviewing Greece's second application, the European Commission of Human Rights appointed another subcommission to investigate. The two Greek applications meant that by the summer of 1957, the Cyprus government faced international human rights challenges to the emergency regulations regime and the interrogation system, both of which were seen as vital to the counterinsurgency effort.

The Atrocity Campaign

In addition to scrutiny from the European Commission of Human Rights, Britain had to contend with an EOKA propaganda offensive that publicized allegations of British abuses in Cyprus. Officials often viewed these accusations as nothing more than false propaganda and labeled EOKA's efforts the atrocity campaign. In response to EOKA's propaganda effort, Colonial Secretary Lennox-Boyd and Governor Harding attempted to undermine their accusers' credibility and defended British policies through propaganda of their own, but they shied away from ordering a public inquiry into the allegations because they believed that British forces had in fact committed abuses.

EOKA waged a sophisticated propaganda campaign to discredit the security forces. EOKA's propaganda wing, Politiki Epitropi Kypriakou Agona (PEKA), distributed leaflets, painted slogans on buildings, organized demonstrations, and coordinated other propaganda activities. EOKA leader George Grivas ordered his subordinates to collect reports of vandalism committed by the security forces, physical brutality toward civilians, torture of prisoners, and any other abuses that could possibly be considered ill treatment. Ill-treatment allegations became so prominent in the press that journalists from Cyprus, Greece, Britain, and the United States reported sordid tales of abuse. Publications could be found in prominent British, American, and Cypriot papers such as the *Tribune*, the *Manchester Guardian*,

Newsweek, the *New Statesman*, the *Spectator*, and the *Times of Cyprus*. In Athens, the Panhellenic Committee for Cyprus Self-Determination printed millions of booklets, pamphlets, and leaflets for worldwide distribution.[15]

In its eagerness to discredit the security forces, EOKA publicized British misdeeds even when some of those "misdeeds" were false or exaggerated. Given the prominence of torture accusations in the press, PEKA eagerly compared British counterinsurgency practices to "the Nazi methods of Hitler."[16] The group's often hyperbolic rhetoric raised doubts as to the veracity of its claims. British forces documented several instances in which pro-EOKA villagers purposefully destroyed property after cordon-and-search operations and claimed injuries by bandaging nonexistent wounds. Greek-language newspapers often published inaccurate or exaggerated stories. In May 1958, *Ethnos* published the allegation that several young Greek Cypriot girls were "offensively searched" by a soldier disguised "as a Turkish woman." But British soldiers were not involved in this incident, and the searcher was in fact a Turkish woman.[17] Captured EOKA fighters also had reasons to fabricate abuse allegations. Prisoners who were released after interrogation—rather than being detained—were regarded suspiciously by EOKA. Released prisoners could claim that they had been tortured to avoid suspicion that they had informed on their comrades as a condition of their release.[18] But not all of EOKA's claims were false or embellished.

Fabricated claims did not appear to have been included in the forty-nine cases submitted to the European Commission of Human Rights. In his exhaustive study, the legal scholar A. W. B. Simpson found that the allegations included in the second application were "not in the main implausible; what is alleged is the sort of thing which might well have occurred, given the situation in Cyprus and the importance of intelligence." Simpson believes that the Greek Cypriot lawyers who handled the documentation for these cases must have realized the importance of selecting cases in which the evidence was strong enough to potentially sway a body of expert international lawyers such as the members of the European Commission of Human Rights. Unsubstantiated allegations therefore would not have been included.[19] The lawyers wanted to win their case.

Many British officials, however, perceived the Cyprus Bar Council lawyers as nothing more than propagandists. When the barrister John Clerides filed thirty-six ill-treatment complaints in December 1956, Colonial Secretary Alan Lennox-Boyd insinuated that Clerides and his colleagues simply wanted to obstruct the government's functionality. Clerides bristled at this suggestion: "It is a grave mistake of Lennox-Boyd even to think that a person of my standing would be putting up allegations of ill-treatment for the purpose of consuming the Administration's time and energies."[20] But Clerides, was not as naive as his response suggested. Lawyers who defended EOKA clients in court, participated in Cyprus Bar Council activism, or joined the human rights committees often coordinated with EOKA to ensure that they prioritized key fighters or avoided defending anyone with communist sympathies.[21] These lawyers and their local human rights committees were partisan actors in the conflict who fought for enosis through human rights activism.

Because human rights committee members were not impartial, scholars and commentators have typically embraced the British view that they were little more than propagandists. The British journalist Nancy Crawshaw, who worked in Cyprus during the war, believed that the lawyers were "motivated by political aims rather than a desire to establish the truth and to ensure humane treatment for their clients."[22] Crawshaw attended many trials and knew several of the lawyers personally, but she remained biased in favor of the Turkish Cypriot desire to prevent enosis. Writing in 2015, the historian David French agreed with Crawshaw's assessment that the human rights committees "were not impartial bodies of lawyers intent only on the pursuit of the truth."[23] It is certainly accurate to note that the lawyers were partisan actors and the human rights committees were concerned about the human rights of only Greek Cypriot nationalists. But these insights do not mean that the lawyers were not principled rights advocates.

The human rights committees' partisanship should not automatically cast them into the realm of propagandists who promoted lies and misinformation. The critical flaw in both Crawshaw's and French's assessments of the human rights committee lawyers lies in their assumption that justice is always impartial. Their assessments assume that the pursuit of justice and political activity are mutually exclusive motivations. But this assumption does not account for how colonial officials and Greek Cypriot lawyers perceived the idea of justice in different ways. For the Bar Council lawyers, their principles and politics aligned. By ending detainee mistreatment and undermining draconian emergency laws, Greek Cypriot attorneys could both support the war effort and assuage their concerns over an unfair justice system. For them, the choice was simple: because they opposed what they saw as the unjust emergency regulations regime and supported EOKA, their rights activism served the interests of both justice and the enosis movement. British officials, too, were far from impartial in their quest for justice. The Cyprus government believed that they were working on behalf of justice by enacting laws designed to facilitate counterinsurgency operations and intelligence collection. From the perspective of colonial officials, it could be said that subduing the insurgency legally, regardless of how harsh those laws were, served the interests of justice by reestablishing order. In their pursuit of different visions of justice, both Greek Cypriot lawyers and colonial officials sought to manipulate the law to their advantage. Impartiality was impossible.

To counter the Cyprus Bar Council's local human rights committees, Governor Harding ordered the compilation and publication of an official government white paper entitled "Allegations of Brutality in Cyprus." Intended to serve as a weapon against atrocity allegations and designed for widespread dissemination, copies of the white paper were dispatched to UK delegations in Athens, Ankara, Washington, and New York.[24] Harding wrote in the foreword that "I do not think any unbiassed [sic] person who has lived through the past two years in Cyprus could be in any doubt that the Security Forces here have been subjected to a darefully [sic] organised campaign of denigration." Harding presented "evidence that this campaign has been a deliberate and organised conspiracy."[25] The white paper attacked the Cyprus Bar Council's human rights committees as politically motivated EOKA supporters who abused their profession to serve the cause of enosis rather than the interests of justice. Bar Council attorneys issued a twofold response. First, they charged that Harding's white paper constituted an assault on the lawyers' professional integrity and that they were merely defending their clients as any barrister would. This claim was partially disingenuous—pro-EOKA lawyers used the courts for the promotion of both justice and enosis. Second, they asserted that the white paper did not adequately answer the ill-treatment allegations they had previously documented. The Bar Council called for an independent public inquiry.[26]

In defense of the security forces' conduct, Harding insisted that "it would be unrealistic, when men are fighting terrorism, to exclude the possibility of occasional rough-handling of terrorists in the heat of the moment when their capture is being effected." Even so, Harding argued, "I have made it clear that I will not tolerate misconduct by members of the Security Forces." He cited evidence that the courts had "found fault with the Police for the way in which evidence of terrorist offences was obtained" in "very few" cases. Harding wrote that, when it was substantiated, his administration punished security force brutality, such as in the Linzee and O'Driscoll cases. Finally, Harding described an incident in which soldiers from the Gordon Highlanders were playing football in Lefkoniko when a bomb exploded and a soldier was wounded. The troops immediately searched the vicinity for suspects. After the search, "wild allegations of ill-treatment and malicious damage were made" against the soldiers. But a "very thorough" inquiry determined that the soldiers did not abuse villagers or cause serious damage to property. "The people of Lefkoniko," Harding insisted, "have reason to be thankful that it was British troops with whom they had to deal on that day."[27]

But rough handling at the point of capture was not the source of most ill-treatment allegations. Upon his July 19, 1957, return to Athens from detention in the Seychelles, Archbishop Makarios attacked the white paper during a press conference. Repeating allegations often made against interrogators, Makarios described sexual abuse—claiming that torturers would twist the genitals of male detainees, force women to strip naked before plucking their pubic hair, and threaten women with rape—as well as more "mundane" harassment such as the placement of a metal rubbish bin on a detainee's head, which security forces would beat with a stick; the metal amplified the noise and vibrated as it was hit, which created a disorienting effect.[28]

Colonial Secretary Lennox-Boyd publicly labeled the allegations "wild charges" that were clearly part of a pro-EOKA denigration campaign, but he privately considered ordering an inquiry.[29] In the Colonial Office, officials debated the idea and weighed various arguments for and against an inquiry, including the potential that a special inquiry could forestall an international one related to Greece's applications under the European Convention on Human Rights. One colonial officer in Whitehall, D. J. Kirkness, believed that "it must be admitted that there is a great deal of quite responsible opinion in this country which is seriously concerned about the allegations, largely from a feeling that there is no smoke without fire." He referred to articles that had appeared in the *Manchester Guardian*, the *New Statesman*, the *Spectator*, and the *Economist*. Kirkness concluded that "we have to weigh the possible desirability of meeting the increasing concern in responsible circles about the allegations now current against the likely feeling of the Governor that, the administration and even his personal honour, would be called into question by any investigation."[30] To Kirkness, the damage wrought by an investigation would severely damage both Britain's reputation and that of Sir John Harding.

Ironically, Lennox-Boyd chose not to order an inquiry because of the likelihood that at least some of the allegations were true. Kirkness identified the crucial factor in Lennox-Boyd's decision:

> It seems increasingly probable that an investigation would unearth certain instances of brutality, probably by the Special Branch or by interrogators, which cannot be contained in the category of violence in the course of arrest of desperate men. I am not suggesting that we should refuse to consider investigation because we are afraid of what it might bring out; but we shall have to consider what we would do if it did bring out even one or two more discreditable incidents, after the Governor has stated repeatedly that all allegations are investigated and those found to be guilty of any misconduct punished.[31]

On June 26, 1957, Kirkness informed Harding that "a special enquiry is unnecessary and would do positive harm." Instead, Lennox-Boyd entered the counterpropaganda battle by resolving to "publish a White Paper with detailed answers to all specific allegations recently made."[32]

Lennox-Boyd's decision to avoid an inquiry reflected the attitude that exposing security force misconduct would undermine rather than reinforce the Cyprus government's legitimacy. According to Lennox-Boyd's thinking, an inquiry that uncovered valid instances of ill treatment would damage the counterinsurgency effort and Britain's reputation as a protector of human rights. It was better to deny allegations than face the possibility of their validity. Within six months, however, Whitehall's resistance to an inquiry had eroded.

"Embarrassing Nonsense": The Subcommission Investigation

Having rejected the possibility of a government inquiry into the substance of the second Greek application, British officials bristled at a proposal from the Strasbourg subcommission that was investigating the May 1956 Greek ECHR application. Because of the ongoing investigation into the Greek application, the subcommission requested that colonial authorities temporarily suspend the emergency laws that Greece had challenged. The final straw came when the Greek press published leaked reports of the subcommission's supposedly confidential proceedings. Britain refused the subcommission's request, claiming instead that "the continuance of the emergency threatening the life of the nation in Cyprus requires the application or maintenance in force of a substantial part of the emergency measures."[33] In response, the subcommission resolved to visit Cyprus and conduct an on-ground investigation into whether British emergency regulations were justified.[34] Lennox-Boyd acquiesced to the investigation only after it became clear to him that Britain could not legally refuse. The investigation brought an unprecedented degree of international scrutiny onto the Cyprus government and contributed to the emergence of a siege mentality among many colonial officers on the island.

Many officials in Whitehall and Cyprus vehemently opposed the idea of an on-the-ground inquiry. At the Colonial Office, A. S. Aldridge recommended rejecting the proposal. He recognized the implications of an investigation under the auspices of the European Convention on Human Rights: "Thought has not yet ranged beyond Cyprus to the question whether the whole Convention is not an embarrassing nonsense if we can be put to trial over any of our colonial territories."[35] In Cyprus, Harding was also frustrated. Already in February 1957, he had expressed dissatisfaction with the way the Foreign Office had handled the first Greek application. He was dismayed that "the Commission is allowing the Greeks constantly to extend and multiply their malicious accusations and to obtrude on supposedly judicial proceedings all manner of extraneous political matter." Harding insisted that Britain's lawyers act more aggressively. They should launch a legal counterattack—an action that would be "bad law but good tactics."[36] Administrative Secretary John Reddaway agreed with Harding and condemned the subcommission's planned investigation as unwarranted interference in what he saw as an internal matter. "I trust," Harding wrote, "that Her Majesty's Government will be adamant in refusing to countenance such an invasion of our authority here."[37] He was wrong.

Harding, however, had already decided to resign from his position regardless of whether an investigation occurred or not. He sensed that an intense military effort against the insurgency could no longer be sustained. Makarios's release from exile and international pressure for a political solution—coming from the United Nations and the human rights sub-commission—indicated a shift in the political winds. At the 1957 Labour Party conference, MP Barbara Castle announced that if Labour won the next election, the new government would radically alter Britain's Cyprus policy in favor of self-determination. Harding had grown disillusioned at the lack of a political consensus at home, the explosion of communal violence between Greek and Turkish Cypriots, and the likelihood of troop reductions in the Cyprus garrison. He did not believe that, faced with these difficulties, a Labour government in London would fully support the tough military measures he believed were necessary to defeat EOKA.[38]

Despite objections from within Whitehall, Foreign Office legal advisers determined that there were no legal grounds for rejecting the subcommission's request. At the Colonial Office, Lennox-Boyd and Minister of State Lord Perth concluded that Britain would stand in violation of the European Convention if it refused to permit the investigation. On November 6, the cabinet agreed to permit an on-ground investigation.[39] At this point, a refusal to allow the investigation to proceed would make it appear that Britain had flouted international law. For Lennox-Boyd, letting the investigation happen would do less damage to Britain's reputation than repeated objections to an investigation that Britain had no right to stop. Faced with a choice between protecting the Cyprus government from scrutiny and safeguarding Britain's vaunted reputation as a leader in the human rights field, Lennox-Boyd chose to uphold Britain's reputation. Deputy Governor George Sinclair expressed the sentiments of many within the Cyprus government when he wrote despondently that "London has failed us."[40] The investigators arrived in January 1958.[41]

On September 26, 1958, the European Commission determined, on the basis of the subcommission's report, that Britain had not exceeded its powers by implementing emergency regulations. The commission's report established several legally nonbinding rulings. The first two rulings concerned the commission's jurisdiction. The commission asserted that it had the authority to pronounce judgment on emergency laws that had since been revoked as well as the "competence," in legal language, to decide whether Britain's declaration of a state of emergency was justified. Having established that it had the authority to decide the case, the commission then ruled that an emergency that "threatened the life of the nation" existed in Cyprus and that British officials' use of emergency regulations—curfews, detention without trial, arrest without warrant, and deportation—still in effect on the island were also justified.[42]

It appeared as though the British government had avoided a disastrous ruling. If Britain were held to be in violation of the convention, according to the legal scholar A. W. B. Simpson, "there would have to be a complete reappraisal of the mechanisms of repression which had been developed over the years, and which had never previously had to be justified in international proceedings." Simpson notes that this decision reinforced the government's power over its citizens: "It can hardly be said that the outcome was a triumph for the international protection of human rights."[43] Simpson is correct from a legal perspective, but despite the favorable result, the victory was not as clear-cut as it first seemed for the British.

The outcome of the application had broader implications for the conduct of the war in Cyprus. The Greek application and subsequent investigation marked the first time that a group composed almost entirely of foreigners—there was one British member of the subcommission—had formally investigated and judged whether a British colonial government had violated the human rights of its subjects. Greek actions at Strasbourg therefore forced British officials to publicly defend repression in Cyprus to an international audience before an internationally recognized human rights organization. A precedent had been established that allowed for international oversight, intervention, and investigation into alleged human rights violations under the terms of the European Convention. This precedent limited the sovereignty of states that had signed the convention in a way that did not previously exist in international law.[44]

Combined with Greek Cypriot lawyers' efforts to document abuses, file complaints, and defend clients in court, the Greek applications contributed to the emergence of an operational environment in which the legality of British actions faced constant scrutiny. As one report on interrogation procedures noted, "The shadow of the Committee of Human Rights, which sits in Strasbourg, looms large over Omorphita and over Police Headquarters."[45] Despite winning the case, British officials believed that they would face further scrutiny over abuse allegations. The "shadow of Strasbourg" had created a siege mentality within the Cyprus administration. When officials' attention turned to the second Greek human rights application, the Cyprus government improved its ability to deflect future allegations rather than taking concrete steps to prevent abuse from occurring in the first place.

Responding to the Shadow of Strasbourg

Greece's May 1956 application galvanized British resistance to a possible investigation into the second application and contributed to the Cyprus government's siege mentality regarding human rights abuses. Although officials were relieved at the European Commission's decision on the first Greek application, many were concerned with the precedent that the investigation had established. At the Colonial Office, Aldridge worried that a subsequent investigation into the second Greek application's torture charges would "hamstring the security forces." In Cyprus, Deputy Governor George Sinclair deemed "the thought of a local enquiry" into the second application "intolerable."[46]

The prospect of another international investigation and the fact that Whitehall had seemingly caved to international pressure in permitting the investigation to occur unsettled members of the security forces to such an extent that they did not wish to cooperate with representatives from Whitehall who were supposed to help prepare the government's defense against ill-treatment charges. In January 1958, the Foreign Office dispatched Hilary Gosling, a retired prosecutor, to Cyprus in order to gather evidence to support the government's side of the case. But several security officials refused Gosling's request to interview them. According to Sinclair, inquiries from the Colonial Office for details on the forty-nine torture cases "have inevitably caused deep misgivings in army, police and other Government circles." Special Branch officers were especially disconcerted with "the fear that they may individually be brought before an international tribunal, either here, or in Strasbourg, on ludicrous but personally damaging charges."[47] Gosling managed to convince these reticent officials to participate only after promising that they could refuse to answer particular questions if they wished.[48]

Officials remained concerned about the potential negative consequences of an investigation because of the likelihood that physical abuse had indeed occurred. Foreign and Colonial Office lawyers realized that "the political disadvantages of a breach of the Convention would be serious. It would receive widespread publicity and might seriously damage our reputation as one of the principal guardians of Human Rights. Many of our friends would be puzzled and dismayed, and our opponents elated." Because protecting Britain's reputation was so important, officials sought to avoid international criticism. British diplomats expected to suffer most from such negative ramifications at the United Nations, where they depended on NATO and Commonwealth countries to support their position on the Cyprus issue. Government legal officers determined that a negative verdict from the European Commission of Human Rights or a British refusal to cooperate with the commission "might even contribute to the adoption of a resolution hostile to us; it would also encourage the Greeks to call for a United Nations Commission of enquiry in Cyprus."[49]

As Foreign Office lawyers prepared Britain's defense against the second Greek application during the spring of 1958, a second wave of ill-treatment accusations marked the beginning of another EOKA atrocity campaign, Sir Hugh Foot replaced Harding as governor, and the Special Investigation Group was created. Greek Cypriot human rights committees resumed their advocacy efforts against British ill treatment in April 1958. Numerous allegations of British brutality emerged in the aftermath of a detention camp riot. Then, on May 5, John Clerides held a press conference to chastise British troops for mistreating Greek Cypriot civilians in the aftermath of an EOKA attack on two military police officers.[50] EOKA had initiated a second atrocity campaign.[51]

In the midst of this controversy over human rights investigations and torture allegations, Sir Hugh Foot arrived as Cyprus's new governor. Foot hailed from a well-known left-wing political family. His father, Isaac, was a prominent Liberal MP and former president of the Liberal Party. Sir Hugh's older brother, Sir Dingle Foot, was a lawyer and Liberal MP who switched parties to Labour in 1957. He later became solicitor general for England and Wales. Michael Foot, the youngest brother and a journalist, was a Labour MP from 1945 to 1955. After leaving Parliament, Michael Foot became editor of the *Tribune*, a position from which he launched several sharp attacks on the Conservative Party and its Cyprus policy.[52]

Sir Hugh Foot's political orientation toward Cyprus differed tremendously from Harding's. For instance, Foot was reluctant to carry out death sentences.[53] Those convicted of capital crimes such as murder or possession of firearms still faced mandatory death sentences, and Foot ordered his solicitor general to provide a fortnightly list of all pending capital cases. During 1958, the list usually included between eleven and twenty-seven pending cases. Throughout the second half of 1958 there were twenty to twenty-five capital cases pending at any given time. But Foot regularly granted reprieves for these cases—no Greek Cypriots were executed for emergency-related offenses during Foot's governorship.[54] The new governor was also less likely to ignore abusive interrogation practices and excessive violence from security forces. In his September 29, 1958, message to the troops, Foot insisted that "there must be no bullying or brutality."[55] This approach, however, contributed to strained relations between Foot and his senior security officials.

Tension between the new governor and his senior advisers soon emerged over security policy. Director of Operations Major General Douglas Kendrew, Administrative Secretary A. J. Reddaway, and Deputy Governor George Sinclair hoped to continue tough military measures against EOKA, whereas Foot intended to reach a negotiated settlement with Greek Cypriots. Many within the army and police had given up hope that peace could be negotiated and believed that they had lost Greek Cypriot loyalties for good. Foot's peace orientation meant that political decisions—such as the release of detainees—often trumped military considerations. These differences contributed to a growing rift between the security forces and the new governor.[56]

Foot's concern with ill-treatment rumors also did not ingratiate him with the security forces. Bothered by the persistence of abuse allegations, Foot asked Reddaway for advice on what to do. Reddaway said to make a short-notice visit during the next military operation to see for himself how the troops conducted interrogation. Foot did and did not see any untoward behavior, but the "point was the deterrent effect of the Governor going out on the spot to see for himself." Reddaway admitted that these visits were "much criticized in Army and Police circles at the time," but he believed that they were beneficial.[57] Foot's on-the-spot visits during ongoing operations may have convinced him that ill-treatment rumors were exaggerated, but if so, he was looking in the wrong place. Allegations most often resulted from interrogation at Omorphita Police Station, not the point of capture. Although Foot was genuinely interested in stopping abuses, his more immediate concerns were the potential of a second Strasbourg inquiry and the renewal of EOKA's atrocity campaign. With public allegations in the spotlight, Foot turned to Reddaway and Sinclair for help in preventing future accusations of brutality.

The Special Investigation Group

Reddaway and Sinclair collaborated with Major-General Kendrew and Attorney General Sir James Henry to establish the Special Investigation Group. The European Commission of Human Rights investigation into Greece's first (1956) application demonstrated that the Cyprus government might not be able to stop an inquiry into the second (1957) application concerning torture. Recognizing this situation, administrators shifted tactics from trying to prevent investigations into torture allegations to trying to control the tenor of public discussions on those allegations. To do so, the Cyprus government created SIG. SIG recorded the worst examples of exaggerated, ill-founded Greek Cypriot torture and abuse claims while documenting an "official" British narrative of each incident so that the Cyprus government could protect soldiers and police from local or international scrutiny. By emphasizing the outlandishness of some Greek Cypriot allegations, these officials hoped to undermine all such allegations. SIG therefore formed a shield against both EOKA propaganda and the encroaching shadow of Strasbourg.

According to Sinclair, SIG's purpose was "to enquire into allegations against the Security Forces with a view to establishing the facts and disproving malicious misrepresentations." Sinclair highlighted SIG's importance to the administration's counterinsurgency effort: "Experience with the Human Rights Committee locally and in Strasbourg and in dealing with the smear campaign in the press abroad has shown us that we cannot afford to let the allegations pass uninvestigated and unchallenged. We therefore must make this investigating team an important unit in our campaign to defeat EOKA."[58] The group comprised military and police CID members able to "operate quickly and effectively" in response to allegations of Security Force abuses.[59] The three permanent members of SIG were

Chief Superintendent R. A. P. H. Dutton of the Cyprus Police CID, Detective G. E. Whitcomb, also of CID, and army Major M. F. Drake. They received temporary assistance from CID officers, the army's Special Investigation Branch, and the Royal Air Force Police.[60] Later, an additional eight police, army, and civil service officers were assigned as regional SIG liaisons to the Famagusta, Larnaca, Limassol, Paphos, and Kyrenia districts.[61]

Sinclair and Reddaway viewed SIG as an important element of the British counterpropaganda campaign rather than an independent and objective investigatory arm. Sinclair informed Reddaway of his desire to "keep to the principle and practice, which we have followed for the last 2½ years, namely that if a properly supported complaint is made against the Security Forces it will be carefully investigated and those concerned will either be cleared or have the matter brought home to them."[62]

Yet SIG's importance as a counterpropaganda tool was emphasized during a May 8, 1958, meeting at Government House between Sinclair, Henry, Reddaway, and Chief of Staff Brigadier Gleadell. They noted that "in countering the smear campaign Government should select the ground for its counter attack and make an all-out effort where the detractors of the Security Forces had obviously put themselves in a false position."[63] SIG's purpose, therefore, was to exploit embellished or falsified allegations, not to prevent members of the security forces from committing abuses in the future. Gleadell made this clear in a June 12 memorandum to all area commanders. SIG's duties were

> to investigate immediately, and record, the facts in major cases of allegations against the conduct of the Security Forces, with a view to:
>
> (a) issuing a prompt, positive and accurate denial of any false allegations.
> (b) Preparing the ground in cases where legal action could be taken against the offenders [meaning those individuals or organizations making false allegations], with minimum delay.
> (c) Maintaining a record for use, if required, before the Human Rights Committee.
> (d) Forestalling subsequent faked or exaggerated allegations.[64]

Chief Superintendent Dutton also clearly understood his role: "The immediate tactical aim of SIG is to wrest the initiative from EOKA in the propaganda field relating to allegations. The over-riding and ultimate aim encompasses the prevention of any allegations arising from Security Forces' action." SIG existed to find false allegations and thereby discredit all of EOKA's claims. It was not created to punish those who committed real abuses.

SIG investigations helped the Cyprus government defend security force actions against its critics among the Greek Cypriot community and alleviate Governor Foot's apprehension over abuse allegations. In September 1958 the mayor of Kyrenia complained that British troops had ransacked a nearby village. Foot acknowledged that "damage was done and personal injuries were caused" but stated, "I am satisfied from the report of the special investigation team that, although they were extensive, the damage and injuries were minor."[65] Personally averse to the cruel treatment of civilians, Foot was reassured by the SIG report. SIG investigations could also exonerate Special Branch interrogators from ill-treatment allegations. A September 1958 investigation cleared interrogators accused of beating Georghios Panayi while he was in custody at Omorphita. These findings, too, assuaged Foot's concerns. "Thank you," he wrote, "I have been worried by some of the accounts given of interrogation methods at Omorphita—and I am therefore glad to see this report."[66]

Over the course of its existence, from June 1958 to February 1959, SIG investigated a total of 191 incidents.[67] Rapid investigation of the most serious allegations enabled SIG to compile a report and present it to public relations officials who would then release a press statement. Chief Superintendent Dutton bragged that "the resulting statement, often published within 24 hours of the incident occurring, has forestalled major and protracted allegations." But the speed with which SIG completed its investigations and public affairs officers released press statements calls into question SIG's thoroughness. To investigate allegations of British misconduct by collecting the facts, analyzing that information, and providing it to public relations personnel within twenty-four hours suggests that SIG's real purpose was not to discover the truth but to document the pro-British narrative before accusations could be made. By September 1958, Dutton confidently assessed that SIG efforts were having "a telling effect on EOKA propaganda."[68]

SIG's close relationship with public relations officers improved the government's ability to respond to atrocity allegations. Before SIG's creation, British officials were on the defensive. News reports would often appear in the local press two or three days after an incident had occurred. But SIG's immediate on-the-spot investigations meant that the first reports about an event were British reports. SIG-derived press releases "became news items and, at the same time, forestalled gross exaggerations and false allegations." In August 1958, during Operation Swanlake, the investigations provided the material for four press statements. During operations around Paphos in September, SIG contributed to four additional press statements. "It is true to say that a denial lacks the news-catching appeal of a sensational rumour or first report. It is a dull negative statement. Hence SIG have persistently avoided use of 'flat denials' and clichés such as 'a tissue of lies.' " Instead SIG reports proactively circulated positive accounts from the very first. SIG officers proved adept at learning how to conduct what Dutton described as the "battle of words" in Cyprus.[69]

British forces quickly integrated SIG into operations. By October 1958, British forces in Kyrenia had developed "a set drill" for using SIG during house searches. Troops would cordon an area, impose a curfew for the duration of the operation, and search the area. Once the search was complete, SIG would move in before the curfew was removed and investigate any major complaints. They would have a statement ready for release to the press soon after the operation concluded. "The resulting statements to the press," Dutton wrote, "have, almost invariably, scotched the wild and exaggerated allegations that, hitherto, always used to appear in the local press after such operations."[70] By being proactive, SIG ensured that British officials could quickly answer EOKA allegations with facts gathered in the aftermath of an operation.

SIG seized on any aspect of a complaint that could possibly invalidate it. On August 7, 1958, troops searched the village of Pano Panayia. After the search, twelve villagers alleged that they had been forced to stand for three hours facing a wall with bayonets pointed at their chests. But SIG revealed contradictions in the villagers' stories. The villagers, Dutton reported, "failed to explain how the bayonets were pointed at their chests when they were facing a wall." None of the villagers were able to "show any marks of ill-treatment whatsoever." Regarding damage to property, SIG noted that "in two cases where damage to radio sets was alleged, both sets were actually found to be in working order." SIG documented the allegations, investigated, and determined that "in practically all cases, the allegations of damage to property and furniture could not in any way be substantiated by the complainants." SIG needed only to raise enough doubt to make a plausible case that allegations might have been falsified. Establishing reasonable doubt would discourage a potential future European Commission of Human Rights investigation from confirming Greek Cypriot claims.[71]

SIG counterpropaganda tactics included the use of photography to prevent civilians from making false or embellished claims. In the aftermath of one cordon-and-search operation, SIG officers surmised that "villagers have been taught to exaggerate damage" and "apply for heavy compensation from Government." Subsequent Greek Cypriot claims of damages exceeded those documented by SIG, and SIG reported that one villager was "caught in the very act of disarranging the furniture of a house" which "proved beyond any doubt the purposeful 'rigging' of certain premises after the Security Forces had withdrawn." To forestall such problems in the future, SIG determined "to take photographs of all premises likely to be used as a basis for allegations of serious damage."[72] SIG's use of photography spread to other units, which, Dutton reported, "were issued with cameras and encouraged to carry out this practice as a matter of normal routine after a thorough search of any premises." Dutton extolled the tactic of photographing damaged property as "a psychological factor in that complaints of damage were not exaggerated when the owner/occupier was present to see his premises being photographed."[73] Photography could therefore serve as a deterrent for preventing false or exaggerated claims.

Some allegations, however, contained at least a kernel of truth. As EOKA began using pressure mines against British patrols and convoys, some troops started taking Greek Cypriot civilians as "hostages" and would force them to ride on British vehicles with the soldiers. The idea was to deter EOKA from planting mines or attacking patrols when Greek Cypriot civilians were in danger. When Greek Cypriots complained about the practice, SIG quickly investigated. According to Dutton, "investigation into a few cases revealed a measure of indiscretion in three instances," but he found that in general the troops "were well aware of the rules" prohibiting the practice.[74]

Instead of investigating the use of "hostageship" more thoroughly, SIG sought to deflect attention by documenting the most egregious examples of false claims. One example is the case of the teenager Demos Xenophontos. On November 27, 1958, Xenophontos told his relatives and neighbors that British troops had arrested him during the night and kept him as a hostage in a British patrol car. The Greek-language newspaper *Harvaghi* quickly published his account. But when SIG contacted Xenophontos to investigate his claims, Xenophontos admitted to having concocted the entire story "to cover his amours and thus allay the cajolings of his co-villagers." At SIG's request, colonial public relations officials met with *Harvaghi*'s editor and demanded that he print a retraction, which was published on December 19.[75] SIG cast such false or exaggerated allegations not as the extreme of Greek Cypriot behavior but as the norm.

Most SIG investigations resulted from army searches of civilian communities rather than the abuse of prisoners during interrogation. On the occasions when SIG addressed ill treatment during interrogation, the group reported what had become a standard line: "In cases of ill-treatment alleged to have occurred whilst in detention—particularly in Omorphita cells, Nicosia—complainants talk of the 'water treatment'; genitals being twisted or given electric shocks; receptacles being placed on the head and beaten endlessly; being made to stand up all night; and being deprived of food and water." Under the emergency regulations, however, the burden of proof lay with the accuser. Chief Superintendent Dutton observed that in interrogation cases complainants were "unable to show any injury received as a result of these 'tortures.'" But some of these abuses—water treatment, deprivation of food, and standing all night, for instance—would not have left visible injuries. Rather than scrutinize Special Branch, SIG chose not to pursue these cases further.[76]

In 1956 and 1957, Greek Cypriot lawyers had raised credible allegations that British forces tortured detainees during interrogation, but by 1958 EOKA and its sympathizers publicized many false or overstated accusations of British brutality. SIG discovered several occasions in which Greek Cypriots faked or exaggerated allegations against the security forces. SIG's existence ensured that many of these accusations were identified and discredited. EOKA's atrocity campaign was based on tangible evidence and reasonable suspicions of abusive British practices, but the campaign also involved instances of fabricated or exaggerated accusations.

EOKA's actions, however, did not exonerate British forces from having to answer for their worst excesses. British authorities established SIG to prevent *allegations* of ill treatment, not to prevent ill treatment itself. They created SIG to turn EOKA's propaganda campaign against itself. By using evidence of falsified EOKA allegations to cast the atrocity campaign in a negative light, SIG was able to attack EOKA in a previously unrealized way. By challenging the credibility of ill-treatment allegations, SIG protected the security forces from embarrassing disclosures of abuse. This desire to avoid embarrassment led to subsequent attempts to whitewash criticism of the security forces after two incidents in Geunyeli and Famagusta.

The Geunyeli Incident

On June 12, 1958, outside Geunyeli village, eight Greek Cypriots died at the hands of Turkish Cypriot attackers in what the Greek Cypriot press labeled the "Geunyeli massacre." To assuage Greek Cypriot anger, Governor Foot ordered the island's chief justice, Sir Paget Bourke, to conduct an inquiry into the incident and announced that the findings would be made available to the public. Chief Justice Bourke produced a straightforward and honest draft report in which he mildly criticized British troops' actions at Geunyeli. But the fact that the report was intended for public release meant that Bourke's critique triggered a concerted effort to shield the security forces from criticism. In an attempt to protect the security forces' reputation, senior military and civilian officials in Cyprus and Whitehall took exception to Bourke's opinion and intervened to remove the offending language from his final report.

The Geunyeli incident occurred against a backdrop of escalating tensions and communal violence between Greek and Turkish Cypriots. Violence broke out in response to international developments concerning the island's future political status. With Greece and Turkey each supporting one of the two Cypriot communities, British policymakers realized that any settlement to the conflict would require a negotiated settlement to which Greek Cypriots, Turkish Cypriots, and the governments of Greece and Turkey agreed. In May 1958, Foot convinced Prime Minister Macmillan to advance a solution for the Cyprus conflict on the basis of partnership between Greek and Turkish Cypriot communities. This proposal proved unsatisfactory to both sides. It offered Turkish Cypriots wide powers of autonomy but not the preferred Turkish Cypriot solution, which was the partition of the island. Under the British plan, Cyprus would remain a single political entity, but Greek Cypriots still objected to sharing power with Turkish

Cypriots. The plan also allowed for Turkey and Greece to each appoint a representative to the Cyprus government. Extremists from both Cypriot communities reacted with a wave of killings and rioting. On the night of June 6, Turkish Cypriots looted and burned Greek Cypriot houses. The security forces reacted slowly, failing to place a curfew on Turkish Cypriot neighborhoods until two days later. Suspicious Greek Cypriots believed that the British had colluded with Turkish Cypriots by allowing them to harm Greek Cypriot neighborhoods. The communal divide grew so sharp that British officials compared the situation to Arab-Jewish violence that had preceded British evacuation from Palestine in 1947.[77]

On June 12, a police patrol encountered thirty-five Greek Cypriots congregated around two buses in a dry riverbed near Skylloura village. The men were armed with sticks, shovels, stones, and pitchforks. The policeman on scene, Sergeant Gill, believed that the men were planning to attack Skylloura's Turkish Cypriot community. Gill arrested the men and loaded them into the nearby buses. Escorted by two army armored cars, the buses drove toward the nearest police station to process the prisoners. But a radio message instructed the troops not to bring the prisoners to the police station. According to the official inquiry report, the armored car escorts received new orders "to send the prisoners out of town into the country and make them walk home." The armored car squadron leader, Major Roy Redgrave, decided to drop the prisoners off north of Geunyeli village. From there they could walk the ten miles to Skylloura and the additional three and a half miles to Kondemnos, where many of the prisoners lived. The convoy drove through Geunyeli and stopped four hundred yards north of the village. The patrol released the prisoners and told them to walk home. Several soldiers stood behind the prisoners with bayonets fixed—a not-so-subtle threat that the prisoners should begin their walk. The soldiers remained on the road and watched as the walkers crested a ridgeline and were out of sight. During the walk, a group of fifty to a hundred Turkish Cypriots armed with sticks, axes, knives, and a few firearms attacked the Greek Cypriots. They "cut and bludgeoned" several Greek Cypriots. The British armored car patrol responded to the attack within five minutes. By the time the troops intervened, a large crowd of Turkish Cypriots had gathered outside Geunyeli, and four Greek Cypriots lay dead. Four more later died of their wounds. Five others were severely wounded.[78]

The deaths generated outrage across the Greek Cypriot community, which led Foot to order a special inquiry under Chief Justice Bourke.[79] Many Greek Cypriots believed that British troops had purposely deposited the unarmed victims in an area where they were sure to face a Turkish Cypriot attack. For this reason Foot instructed Bourke to determine whether British forces were culpable for the Greek Cypriot deaths. Foot also announced that he would release Bourke's findings to the public.[80] On June 20 Bourke began taking evidence from witnesses. Attorneys representing four concerned parties attended the hearings—Sir James Henry represented the government; George Chryssafinis, John Clerides, and Stelios Pavlides led a team of five other lawyers representing the Greek Cypriot survivors of the incident and relatives of the deceased; Colonel J. C. Hamilton represented the British military; and Turkish Cypriot attorney Rauf Denktaş appeared on behalf of four Turkish Cypriot police and auxiliary police officers. Over the next eight days, attorneys called thirty-seven witnesses.[81]

Bourke concluded that British troops had not intended to cause a massacre, but he criticized the practice of driving recalcitrant civilians to isolated areas and forcing them to "take a walk" home.[82] He noted that it was an "accepted practice" among the army for arrested persons "to be brought off some distance and caused to walk back to their homes." According to Bourke, this tactic was an unofficial practice that security forces used "to give troublesome persons 'a little exercise' so that they should behave themselves and have 'time to meditate upon their doings.' It was a way of teaching people a 'lesson.'" The armored car squadron commander Major Redgrave said that "it was quite a normal thing."[83]

Senior police officers found the practice repugnant. Assistant Chief Constable Rice, the top police officer in Nicosia District, and Assistant Superintendent Trusler, responsible for the region that included Geunyeli, said that they had never heard of the practice before the June 12 incident. Trusler tartly observed that he was not aware of the technique because "I think irregularities of that nature would not be brought to our attention, that is the reason." Although soldiers used the practice regularly, all the army witnesses who testified at the Geunyeli hearing concurred with Redgrave's commanding officer: "To be perfectly honest," the commander said, "it is an unlawful practice."[84]

Bourke decided that he could not in good conscience exonerate the security forces. He noted that "I have been invited by Colonel Hamilton [the lawyer representing the army] to find not only that everyone acted in good faith, which I have had no difficulty in doing, but also that the order given and action taken upon it were reasonable. I am unable to do so."[85] Bourke concluded that although the army did not intend to cause harm, the commander's decision to release the Greek Cypriots between two Turkish Cypriot villages and force them to walk out of sight of the security forces was both a poor decision and illegal. Bourke asserted that given the recent spate of communal violence, the commanding officer should have realized the potential dangers facing his former prisoners.

Some influential military officers and civilian officials rejected Bourke's findings and tried to change his report to avoid any acknowledgment of security force culpability in the Greek Cypriot deaths. General Sir Roger Bower, commander in chief of Middle East Land Forces, declared Bourke's assessment of the security forces' conduct to be "a non sequitur quite unsupported by the facts." Bower believed that Bourke's criticism would "cause some comment if the Report is published as it stands. I hope that it will not be."[86] Bower's main objection was Bourke's condemnation of the soldiers' decision to release the prisoners in the vicinity of a Turkish Cypriot village during a time of communal violence. Specifically, Bower wanted Bourke to delete two sentences and the record of questions that Bourke had asked Major Redgrave. Bourke had written, "The only conclusion I can reach is that the course adopted was unimaginative and ill-considered." He followed that sentence with "It was also, in my opinion, unlawful."[87] Major General Kendrew agreed with Bower. Kendrew wrote that "although this particular action [the walking home practice] has been technically ruled unlawful, under the circumstances it was justified." Kendrew insisted that the practice "had been most effective" in averting civil war between Greek and Turkish Cypriots. The section of the report containing Bourke's criticisms—paragraph 38—was, to Kendrew, "unacceptable in its present form." Chief of the Imperial General Staff Sir Gerald Templer concurred with Bower's and Kendrew's assessments.[88]

Senior civilian officials in Whitehall also objected to Bourke's findings because of concerns over the potential legal and political consequences for the security forces. Colonial Secretary Alan Lennox-Boyd insisted that publication of the report could "further exacerbate inter-communal feeling and I fear that particularly the statement in paragraph 38 that the course adopted was 'unlawful' would produce worst possible reaction amongst Security Forces themselves." Lennox-Boyd and Secretary of State for War Christopher Soames lodged their "strongest objection to publication." They declared that "publication of report in present form might well lead to civil action against individuals and even pressure for prosecution." Soames preferred that Bourke's report never be published, but Lennox-Boyd thought that it might be possible to convince Bourke "that he should draft a shorter statement of conclusions which could be published with less embarrassment."[89] Driven by a concern for guarding Britain's reputation, Lennox-Boyd and Soames wanted to avoid the possibility of legal action.

In Cyprus, George Sinclair concurred with his superiors in London, recognizing that Bourke's criticism of the walking home practice could carry significant consequences with the European Commission of Human Rights: "The local 'Human Rights' organisation no doubt intend to use this incident as part of their campaign of vituperation of the Security Forces at Strasbourg and possibly the U.N."[90] Bourke's criticisms opened the possibility not only of encouraging further Greek Cypriot protest and communal violence between Greek and Turkish Cypriots but also of international censure.

In the midst of debate over the report's publication and content, Foot maintained his position that publishing the report was necessary to counter Greek Cypriot allegations of British collusion in the killings. He believed that Bourke's report fulfilled the purpose of the inquiry, which was to investigate the "terrible accusation" levied in the Greek-language press that security forces "acted in collusion with Turks to destroy the Greek villagers." Foot concluded that "the Chief Justice's report provides a very able and clear and fair account of what took place." "I myself," he continued, "consider that the practice of putting down arrested people a long way from their villages and making them walk home at a time of inflamed intercommunal feeling was wrong. I cannot disagree with the Chief Justice when he said that the course adopted was 'unimaginative and ill-considered.'"[91] Foot ordered the army to stop using the practice and insisted on publicly releasing the report.[92]

Officials in Whitehall continued to resist Foot and Bourke on the issue of publication. Conveying the colonial secretary's sentiments, assistant secretary J. D. Higham and assistant legal adviser J. A. Peck suggested that Bourke prepare a short statement for publication that did not include a reference to unlawful conduct on the security forces' part.[93] In early September, Bourke met with Peck and Higham in Whitehall. Peck explained his apprehension: "Publication of the full report might, however, create certain difficulties and embarrassment, in particular the opinion given in paragraph 38 that the action of the Security Forces was unlawful." Peck also believed that as a result of the Cyprus Bar Council lawyers' success in turning the judicial system into a battleground, Bourke's report "might make it difficult for Greek Cypriots not to take criminal or civil proceedings against the members of the Security Forces concerned." Higham added that "it had been officially stated on a number of occasions, in a 'human rights' context, that misconduct by members of the Security Forces would not be tolerated and that offenders would be punished." He worried that "if the Chief Justice's opinion was made public, there might be a good deal of pressure on the Cyprus Government itself to prosecute those concerned."[94] Peck and Higham preferred to expunge the offending parts of the report rather than allow the critique to stand and potentially expose the security forces to embarrassing legal actions.

Peck and Higham attempted to convince Bourke to remove his statement that the walking home practice was unlawful on the grounds that Bourke's comments represented a legal opinion, not an official finding. Peck pointed out that Bourke's inquiry had been established to ascertain the events that occurred on June 12, 1958, in Geunyeli and whether British forces bore any responsibility for the deaths of eight Greek Cypriots. The inquiry was not designed to pronounce judgment on the walking home practice. Bourke agreed that he would omit the sentences in which he deemed walking home unlawful. He also agreed to remove Major Redgrave's evidence in paragraph 32 because it was "merely an extract of evidence, and not a finding." But Bourke refused to eliminate all of paragraph 38 from the record. Legally, Bourke insisted, "it was doubtful whether a Commissioner, having heard his inquiry and submitted his report, had the power to alter or amend it."[95] Echoing Peck's rationale, Solicitor General Ned Munir argued that Bourke's assertion about the unlawfulness of the security forces' decision to make their prisoners "walk home" was not a "fact" in "the strict sense of the term"—it was merely the chief justice's legal interpretation. As such, Munir argued, Bourke's opinion could "properly be omitted from the findings to be published."[96]

In November, Foot mediated a compromise.[97] Foot convinced the generals that "much more harm will be done if we refuse to publish than if we do. Refusals to publish the findings may well be taken as indicating that there is some foundation for the terrible accusation that British Security Forces acted in collusion with Turks to bring about the murder of the Greek villagers." Foot also believed that he could not delay the report's publication much longer—over four months had already elapsed since the Geunyeli incident. Foot fully expected "that the matter will be raised again before long—possibly in the U.N. debate or at Strasbourg."[98] But Bower remained insistent on publishing the report only after deleting the entire paragraph in which Bourke criticized the walking home practice. Bourke still refused to remove the paragraph. Foot supported Bourke: "There surely could be no justification for publishing the findings with the omission of one of the findings because we disliked it."[99] In the end, Bourke agreed to delete the sentences to which army commanders had originally objected, while Bower and the new director of operations, Major General Sir Kenneth Darling, acquiesced in principle to the publication of Bourke's report.

Even with this agreement, the upcoming UN General Assembly session further delayed publication of the report. On November 22, Lennox-Boyd authorized Foot to publish Bourke's report "with omission of 2 sentences of para. 38 agreed by Chief Justice" and the exclusion of "[Major] Redgrave's evidence in para. 32."[100] But he quickly changed his mind after learning that the UN intended to discuss plans for a political settlement in Cyprus. One week later, Lennox-Boyd recommended that Foot defer publication of the report until after the UN session.[101] Lennox-Boyd wanted to delay publication so that the report could not be used at the UN to criticize Britain. Bourke's report was finally published on December 9—almost six months after the incident and five months after he completed the inquiry.[102]

Senior leaders such as Lennox-Boyd, Soames, Bower, and Darling shielded the security forces from criticism over the Geunyeli incident in two ways. First, they pressured Foot and Bourke to change the content of the judicial inquiry. Second, they delayed the release of the report to avoid having to confront international criticism at the UN. With the shadow of Strasbourg hanging over them, these officials worried that a negative report from the island's chief justice could lead to international legal actions or force the government to press charges against the soldiers involved. But the report that was eventually submitted, with Bourke's criticisms removed, meant that the security forces had little to fear.

The Cutliffe Murder

Officials also whitewashed criticism of the security forces' brutal response to the murder of Catherine Cutliffe. On October 3, 1958, two sergeants' wives from the Royal Artillery's Twenty-Ninth Field Regiment—Catherine Cutliffe and Elfriede Robinson—along with Cutliffe's eighteen-year-old daughter, Margaret, visited the picturesque Famagusta suburb of Varosha for a shopping trip. As they left a dress shop, two EOKA gunmen confronted them. The women tried to run away but were shot as they fled. Catherine Cutliffe died instantly, while Robinson fell wounded. The gunmen shot Robinson two more times as she lay on the ground, but she survived. Margaret Cutliffe escaped unharmed. A Greek Cypriot shopkeeper phoned the police to report the murder.

Upon hearing that the victims of the attack were the servicemen's wives, British soldiers reacted furiously. Royal Military Police units were the first to arrive on scene and ordered the arrests of everyone in the immediate vicinity of the murder and all males between the ages of fifteen and twenty-seven in the neighborhoods around Varosha. Soldiers and police rounded up the town's inhabitants with little regard for niceties.[103] Civilian property damage compensation payments later totaled £14,223. One shop was looted, with the owner later receiving £91 in compensation. Several storefront windows and car windows were also smashed. The troops made 1,423 arrests in the vicinity of the murder.[104] The detainees were kept in three holding centers—the local police station, Karaolos Camp, and the government hospital. Soldiers moved with such fury that 258 people suffered injuries of varying severity, from bruises and scratches to fractures. It took the rest of the day and much of the night before the army had screened all detainees. The last detainees to be released were sent home at 3:00 a.m. on October 4.[105]

As they were brought to holding centers, many prisoners suffered further abuse. By evening, Karaolos Camp—headquarters of the Twenty-Ninth Field Regiment—held 396 of the 1,423 detainees. Troops transported prisoners by truck to a drop-off point seventy yards from the entrance to a detainee holding center nicknamed the "snake pit." SIG chief Dutton later recorded that the arrival of Greek Cypriot detainees "was soon common knowledge among soldiers not on duty in the camp, as, indeed, was the knowledge of the atrocious shooting of the wives." Dutton concluded that "it cannot be denied that cold fury took a tangible form in goading the Greek Cypriots on their way as they doubled [ran] the 70 yards."[106] One Twenty-Ninth Regiment veteran described the events more candidly: "All the other units in Famagusta were ordered out to arrest all males in Varosha . . . and transport them to Karaolos Camp. We lined the roads from the Royal Ulster Rifles Gate. They were de-bussed and had to run the gauntlet to the Snake pit."[107] Bill Packham, a regiment veteran, said that at the snake pit he "saw bodies laid out in rows, with the Medical Officer and medics attending to the injured Greek Cypriots."[108] They had been beaten by soldiers from the Twenty-Ninth Regiment or the Royal Ulster Rifles. According to a technician at the British military hospital, Nicosia, the Royal Ulster Rifles "had the reputation of being one of the roughest regiments on the Island."[109] Sixty-one of the Karaolos Camp detainees suffered injuries either during their arrest or after being imprisoned in the snake pit.[110]

For Foot, the security forces' anger at the murder of a family member was understandable, but their retaliation was counterproductive. When Governor Foot visited the detainee holding sites, he found that "about fifty [detainees] were being given first aid for head wounds and other injuries and the nurses told me that another fifty had already been sent to hospital." Foot admitted that "as I feared when the report of the shooting came in it was impossible to prevent the troops from dealing very roughly with many of those they arrested" because "some troops and some Police too are inclined to deal very hardly with Greek Cypriots when they get the chance." Yet he sternly insisted that "the very rough treatment of last night is quite inexcusable" and informed Whitehall that "I shall do my utmost to prevent it in future." He understood that brutality could generate negative consequences at the United Nations, in Strasbourg, or in Britain. Foot ordered SIG to investigate.[111]

Foot had not witnessed the troops' worst excesses. When word went out that the governor was on his way to Famagusta, soldiers began cleaning up the mess they had made. Lance Corporal Chas Baily of the 227th Provost Company later recalled that "we rounded up as many squaddies as possible and told them to pass the word and got everybody cleaning up the main roads. We knew from past experience that no one would look down the side roads." The side roads, however, "were a right mess. Blood, bits of clothing, odd shoes, shopping. . . . Ambulances were everywhere, the hospitals were full, and surgeries the same." Regardless, "by the time HE [His Excellency, Governor Foot] arrived there was not much out of place."[112]

On the morning of October 4, after the cleanup, SIG began its investigation. For four days, it collected forty-four statements, including twenty-four from Greek Cypriots alleging ill treatment. In addition, SIG met with senior civilian officials—including the district medical officer and staff at the Famagusta hospital—and military officers "to gain as clear a picture as possible on the general discipline and conduct of all units involved on the operation."[113] Dutton realized that SIG's findings would prove vital in the event of another Greek human rights application "as a record to refer to should the matter ever be raised at the Strasbourg Council." In his report, Dutton stated his usual intention "to present the facts, as revealed by a quick on-the-spot investigation, with which to counter false allegations or subsequent faked or exaggerated allegations."[114] The facts, however, were damning. Trying his best to minimize the severity of the situation, Dutton wrote that soldiers had used "some force" to make arrests, "as a result of which a large number of persons sustained injuries varying in degree."[115] In fact, of the 258 Greek Cypriots injured, 3 died, 2 were wounded when soldiers fired on them, 5 suffered bone fractures, and 21 were hospitalized for further treatment.[116]

Faced with significant evidence that soldiers had committed brutal violence toward Greek Cypriot civilians, Dutton could not reconcile his instructions to both shield the security forces from scrutiny and report the facts. On October 14, as he finalized his report on the Famagusta events, Dutton visited Foot. He told Foot that he was "somewhat uneasy about attempting to record a conclusion." Dutton explained that he could not in good conscience report that British forces had acted properly—because they had not—but SIG's approach of documenting the "facts of the case" was supposed to protect the security forces from ill-treatment allegations. Foot provided the answer: "I told him that in my view it was not possible to say that the Security Forces carried out their duties with commendable restraint and I told him that to include this final sentence would, it seemed to me, detract from the value of the factual report which he had submitted." In this case, Dutton was to record the facts but to neither defend nor accuse the security forces.[117] He could file a factual report but did not have to write anything that could undermine the security forces. Even in a situation where British forces had obviously behaved brutally, officials could not bring themselves to formally criticize the troops.

The Inquest Debate

British attempts to cover up the actions of the security forces continued in the aftermath of the Famagusta arrest operations as part of a broader approach to suppressing public criticism. Several senior officials in the Cyprus government sought to avoid conducting inquests into the deaths of the three Greek Cypriot civilians who had died under mysterious circumstances in British custody following their arrests. Major General Sir Kenneth Darling was foremost among them.

Darling took over as the Cyprus director of operations in October 1958. He quickly realized the importance of countering EOKA propaganda by mitigating public criticism. Shortly after arriving in Cyprus, Darling informed General Sir Hugh Stockwell, military secretary at the War Office, that "I am deliberately cultivating the Press and using them as a vehicle (although they do not know this) for increasing my initiative and deflating EOKA." Darling happily noted that "this tactic is working better than I expected."[118] "The trick is," he proclaimed several years after the war, "to disguise what is propaganda so that it appears to be perfectly ordinary news."[119] One way in which Darling attempted to disguise his manipulation of the public narrative was through changing the law to prevent public questioning of the security forces' conduct in instances where soldiers or police killed Greek Cypriots.

Cyprus law required that a coroner conduct an inquest in the event of an "unnatural" death. During the emergency, inquests continued to be held on those who died as a result of security operations. Coroners therefore were required to hold inquests into the deaths of each of the three Greek Cypriots who perished during the October 3 arrest operations. Inquests were judicial proceedings in which the court could compel soldiers and police to testify. An inquest served four primary purposes: to determine who died, when the death occurred, the place of death, and the circumstances of death. Inquests were not meant to determine who was responsible for an unnatural death, but because they established the cause of death in a particular case, inquests into deaths resulting from security operations could have important consequences for the security forces. Family members of the deceased were permitted to attend the proceedings and entitled to legal representation. Family lawyers could also question witnesses testifying before the court.[120] In Cyprus, the involvement of local human rights committee lawyers ensured that members of the security forces faced intense questioning during inquest proceedings. Darling recognized that in this environment, inquest verdicts suggesting that the security forces bore responsibility for a civilian's death would lead to public outrage among Greek Cypriots—outrage that would fuel support for EOKA and invite additional international scrutiny as the second Greek human rights application proceedings continued in Strasbourg.

Darling therefore sought to shield the security forces from legal action and mitigate the potential for public outcry by eliminating inquests. On October 16, while inquests into the Famagusta deaths were under way, he approached Attorney General Henry and Solicitor General Munir with a suggestion: amend Cyprus law to eliminate inquests in certain circumstances.[121] Darling argued that inquests simply slowed the judicial system. Holding inquests "takes up a great deal of time," and many inquests were never completed because the law required them to stop if criminal proceedings began. In these situations, the trial fulfilled the functions of an inquest by determining the facts of the case. But Darling's most strenuous objection to inquests was what he saw as the needless involvement of soldiers in court proceedings. In a reference to the Cyprus Bar Council's human rights committees and EOKA's atrocity campaign, Darling argued that soldiers "are very apprehensive of being brought up before the coroner and asked a great many questions about their actions by persons whose object was to make dishonest political capital and not just to safeguard the interests of deceased persons and their families."[122] During an inquest, soldiers became targets for Greek Cypriot lawyers who would probe troops' testimony for inconsistencies. Testifying at inquests exposed the security forces to scrutiny that Darling wanted to avoid.

Chief Justice Bourke supported Darling's view. Bourke, who had previously served as a justice during the conflicts in Malaya and Kenya, believed that "this whole inquest business is a nightmare. It was not allowed to worry us in the Kenya Emergency."[123] Although Bourke had criticized the security forces during the Geunyeli investigation, he had no problem with taking a hard line against insurgents. He informed Henry that "personally I would welcome the adoption of the Kenya and Malaya legislation substituting a procedure that would bring terrorists more speedily to trial."[124]

Security force commanders had previously raised the issue of dispensing with inquests. In 1956 Munir prepared a draft law based on regulations previously enacted during the 1946–47 Palestine conflict as well as the Malayan Emergency. Munir's draft stated that "where the Coroner responsible for holding an inquest upon the body of any person is satisfied that such person has been killed as a result of operations by Her Majesty's Forces or by the Police Force for the purpose of suppressing disturbances or for maintaining public order, the Coroner may dispense with the holding of an inquest on the body of such person."[125] If Munir's draft had been enacted, it would have allowed the Cyprus government to avoid conducting inquests into the circumstances in which three Cypriots died during the British reprisals on October 3. The coroner would simply have had to declare that the deaths occurred in the process of maintaining public order.

Henry agreed with Darling and Bourke to an extent, but he noted that in some circumstances an inquest might prove beneficial to the government. Henry believed that dispensing with inquests "might be the very strong factor in re-inforcing morale" by removing the possibility that soldiers' conduct might be publicly questioned by Greek Cypriot lawyers during an inquest.[126] Retaining inquests could also help to dispel "otherwise unfounded and malicious allegations" against the security forces. In Avgorou, for instance, British forces opened fire on rioters and killed one bystander. Greek Cypriot newspapers criticized the soldiers' actions, but the inquest determined that villagers had thrown rocks, sticks, and bottles at the troops, inflicting several injuries on British forces in the process. The soldiers fired one machine gun burst of fifteen rounds. The bystander died from a ricochet. Instead of eliminating inquests altogether, Henry recommended a measure that would have allowed "the Coroner or some other authority such as myself" to conduct an inquest only "if it was thought advisable in the public interest."[127] But it was left in the hands of colonial officials to determine what constituted the public interest.

Foot ultimately decided to retain the existing inquest procedures.[128] He informed the Colonial Office that "I very well understand how the Army feel about this and I should greatly like to help in shielding them from the public ordeal to which they are sometimes subjected at the inquests." But Foot determined that inquests were necessary because "the fact that an inquest is to be held restrains Press comment and tends to prevent wild accusations." The elimination of inquests would result in allegations "of attempting to cover up evidence of ill-treatment or worse by Security Forces and such criticism would obviously be particularly damaging at this time following the inquests at Famagusta."[129] Foot recognized the anger that emergency legislation fostered and did not wish to contribute to it further. Revoking standard legal practices such as inquests would have damaged, rather than enhanced, Britain's reputation.

Army commanders need not have worried. Finalized between November 24 and December 3, the Famagusta inquest reports exonerated British troops through masterful equivocation. The first detainee to die in custody was Panayiotis Chrisostomou, who collapsed as he was unloaded from an army truck. The coroner concluded that he died from heart failure brought on by breathing difficulties "caused by seven broken ribs." The coroner determined that Chrisostomou's ribs "were not broken before his arrest, and, consequently, they must have been broken whilst he was on the truck." Although he found that Chrisostomou sustained his injuries in army custody on an army vehicle, the coroner refused to hold British forces responsible.[130] The inquest succeeded in determining the cause of death but did not identify a culprit. Chrisostomou was in British custody, but the coroner skirted the issue of whether British troops were culpable for his death. Since the coroner had not identified a specific incident or person responsible for Chrisostomou's injuries, law officers did not have to pursue the matter further.

Despite evidence to the contrary, the coroner also downplayed the security forces' role in the death of Andreas Loukas, who was the second person to die in British custody. According to SIG's description of the coroner's report, Loukas was killed "by a blow from a blunt instrument which fractured the skull." Furthermore, the coroner stated that he "had not sufficient evidence to enable him to say when or by whom such a blow was struck." SIG's assessment of the coroner's report was equally cautious and carefully ambiguous: "It was obvious from this inquest that during the arrests or thereafter, there was used on some of those arrested a degree of force that would appear to be entirely unjustified."[131] Additional evidence suggested that an officer might have injured Loukas. At one point during the aftermath of Catherine Cutliffe's murder, Captain Blakesley of the Royal Military Police had struck Loukas on the head. But, as Foot reported to Whitehall, the coroner conveniently concluded that "he could not with any confidence say that it was Capt. Blakesley's blow which fractured the deceased's skull and that such being the case he did not propose to examine in detail the question of criminal liability or exoneration in so far as it affected Capt. Blakesley." Grasping for a possible explanation for Loukas's death, the coroner added that he could have sustained the fatal injury "during his journey in the vehicle or when he alighted and was placed in the cage to which the arrested persons were taken."[132] As with the Chrisostomou case, the coroner determined that Loukas had sustained his injuries while in British custody but refused to find that British forces were at fault for his death.

The coroner's report on Ioanna Zacharidou—the third individual who died during the October 3 roundup—proved inconclusive. Zacharidou's death became a point of contention between British authorities and Greek Cypriots. Colonial administrators insisted that since security forces had not apprehended her, her death therefore had nothing to do with the military response to the Cutliffe murder.[133] After conducting an inquest, the coroner reported that Zacharidou "died of shock accelerated by status lymphaticus brought on by fear but there was insufficient reliable evidence to deduce what brought on the state of fear."[134] "Status lymphaticus" was a diagnosis that doctors began using routinely during the nineteenth century as a cause of death in children. Medical professionals believed that it was a fatal disease in which the primary symptom was an enlarged thymus identified during autopsy. Later, doctors began to doubt whether the condition existed at all. By the 1950s, advancements in medical research convinced many doctors in Britain that status lymphaticus was a misdiagnosis—a false understanding of childhood deaths brought on by other circumstances.[135] The coroner's diagnosis of Zacharidou's death does not, therefore, provide a convincing explanation of her death. The inquest findings, however, prevented further investigation by denying all connection with the actions of the security forces.

The coroner's findings demonstrated that Foot's decision to reject Darling's request to eliminate inquests was not a departure from the government's desire to prevent further scrutiny into counterinsurgency practices. Foot's decision simply buried the source. The elimination of standard judicial procedures such as inquests would appear too obvious as a form of manipulation. But by retaining inquests, Foot shifted the site of manipulation from the act of the inquest itself onto the coroners who conducted inquests. When investigating the deaths that resulted from the Cutliffe murder roundup, the coroner interpreted the available evidence in ways that exonerated members of the security forces from blame. On the surface, the situation appeared unchanged—inquests remained in force, as they always had. But in practice, they became tools for protecting soldiers and police from scrutiny rather than serving as impartial instruments of justice.

Beyond their attempts to cover up the details of what had happened, senior officials understood the damage done by the Cutliffe reprisals. "I must say," Foot wrote, "that we should prevent any such actions ever taking place again." George Sinclair concurred that "much harm was done to our reputation at Famagusta on that day."[136] Foot and Sinclair knew that the implications of events like the Famagusta reprisals could reverberate beyond Cyprus. The second Greek application under the European Convention on Human Rights was under way. From November 12 to 18, 1958, oral hearings were held in Strasbourg. The subcommission eventually accepted thirteen of forty-nine individual torture cases for further investigation. The Foreign Office legal adviser, Sir Francis Vallat, concluded that "we are now faced with the prospect of being called upon to fight the thirteen cases and to produce witnesses."[137] Further public admission of mistreatment and misconduct would not help Britain's case.

Ultimately, officials deflected allegations against the security forces long enough that the possibility of a second Greek human rights application was overcome by events. As the communal conflict between Greek and Turkish Cypriots continued into the winter of 1958, British, Turkish, and Greek diplomats negotiated a political settlement above the heads of Cypriot leaders. In February 1959, discussions between the Turkish and Greek governments in Zurich and between the Turkish, Greek, and British governments in London produced an agreement between all three state parties. Greece and Turkey then strong-armed their Cypriot compatriots to adopt the agreement. Rather than achieving enosis or partition, Cyprus gained independence and remained a single political entity. As part of the settlement, the Greek and British governments jointly terminated proceedings on Greece's second European Commission of Human Rights application.[138] The shadow of Strasbourg had receded.

Greek Cypriot lawyers' efforts, the Greek government's two applications under the European Convention on Human Rights, and EOKA's atrocity campaign created new challenges for the Cyprus government. Colonial officials responded to these challenges in three ways: they publicized false or embellished accusations, they whitewashed British actions, and they managed the information that was publicly available during the Geunyeli incident and the Cutliffe reprisals in Famagusta. Through these measures, Cyprus officials largely succeeded in resisting rights activism on the part of the lawyers and their connections in Greece by defending their actions through an effective counterpropaganda campaign. After Deputy Governor Sinclair and Administrative Secretary Reddaway ordered its creation in June 1958, the Special Investigation Group stood at the forefront of this effort. In addition, Governor Foot's decision to order a judicial inquiry into the Geunyeli incident was an acknowledgment of the need to placate a severely disgruntled Greek Cypriot population, but the subsequent manipulation of the chief justice's report ensured that British soldiers would go unpunished. Likewise, after the Cutliffe murder in Famagusta, the continued use of inquests masked other forms of manipulation, such as the coroner's report into the deaths of two Greek Cypriots, which produced vague findings that obscured British soldiers' possible culpability in the deaths.

Although colonial officers and military commanders managed to deflect human rights activists' efforts, they were often indignant about activists' involvement in the conflict. Brigadier Geoffrey Baker, the former chief of staff to the director of operations in Cyprus, authored an after-action report on the Cyprus Emergency in which he concluded that dealing with human rights complaints "was a bitter and distasteful experience."[139] Deputy Governor Sinclair later passed a copy of Baker's report to the governor of Aden, where activists and security officials clashed again.

"Hunger War"

Humanitarian Rights and the Radfan Campaign

When Brigadier Baker's report on the Cyprus Emergency arrived in Aden, it generated such interest that the Aden government decided to send a four-person liaison team to visit Cyprus in an effort to learn more about countering insurgencies.[1] The Aden government would soon put this new knowledge to work. By 1960, it was clear to British policymakers that the empire was crumbling. In February, Prime Minister Harold Macmillan gave his famous "wind of change" speech in South Africa, in which he described the emergence of African anticolonial nationalism as "a political fact." British withdrawal from many of its remaining African colonies was increasingly becoming a policy priority. Withdrawal from Africa, however, went hand in hand with the desire to maintain British influence east of the Suez Canal, meaning that Britain sought to maintain access to Persian Gulf oil. Three years after Macmillan's speech, an anticolonial insurgency erupted in the colony of Aden—one of the three territories comprising the South Arabian Federation and a valuable base for securing the sea lanes between the Suez Canal and Persian Gulf. Within a decade, British forces had completely withdrawn from Aden in what many contemporaries viewed as the symbolic end of the British Empire.[2]

British officials used many of the same coercive tactics in Aden as their colleagues had in Cyprus, such as curfews, collective punishments, and abusive interrogations. Officials also tried to control the public narrative concerning brutal actions in order to protect Britain's reputation as a guarantor of human rights and justice. In one campaign, British troops launched a massive operation in the Radfan, a mountainous region approximately sixty miles north of Aden city.[3] British forces intended to wage a scorched-earth campaign in the Radfan that was consistent with how they had handled tribal revolts in the past. Such tactics harmed combatants and noncombatants alike while also creating a refugee crisis.

This humanitarian crisis, combined with the detention of many anticolonial nationalists in Aden, elicited scrutiny from the International Committee of the Red Cross and a newly established activist group called Amnesty International. The ICRC's interest in providing humanitarian assistance to refugees fleeing a British offensive in the Radfan region and to prisoners detained in South Arabian Federation jails was consistent with its support for what the historian Bruno Cabanes has called "humanitarian rights," in which the ICRC asserted the right of all people to receive humanitarian aid.[4] It was also similar to ICRC efforts during Britain's colonial wars in Kenya and Cyprus.[5] Amnesty International, however, added a new dimension to the Aden Emergency that was not present in Cyprus. Whereas most human rights activism during the Cyprus war came from partisan Greek Cypriot lawyers and their Greek government patrons, AI was a British-based group dedicated to protecting the rights of individuals across the world.

When the Radfan operation began in April 1964, colonial officers resisted calls by the ICRC to uphold humanitarian rights by preventing the ICRC from entering the South Arabian Federation. In February 1965, after the campaign had ended, the ICRC delegate forced his way into the federation on an "unofficial" visit. The ICRC's actions, supported in Britain by Amnesty International, forced colonial officials to make a difficult choice. They could either permit an ICRC visit that was likely to lead to private censure through the ICRC's confidential reporting system, or they could refuse the ICRC's request to enter the South Arabian Federation—a choice that British administrators expected would lead to public accusations that the government had something to hide. Officials at the Aden High Commission solved this dilemma through cooperative manipulation. But unlike in Cyprus, where colonial officials consciously manipulated the results of inquiries and created the Special Investigation Group to systematically counter abuse allegations, the Aden High Commission's response was an opportunistic reaction to ICRC involvement in the Radfan.

Middle East Politics and the Threat to Aden

The Aden insurgency was embedded in a regional balance of power in which Egypt challenged British influence in the Middle East. By the early 1960s, this struggle had expanded into a proxy war in Yemen that threatened the stability of the South Arabian Federation. For an important clique of Conservative Party policymakers, the maintenance of Britain's great-power status and geopolitical role in the Middle East depended on control of Aden.[6] After losing control over the Suez Canal in 1956, Aden became the linchpin of British security in the Middle East.

Aden was a key air and naval base for securing oil supply routes from the Persian Gulf to Britain. Persian Gulf oil was shipped from the gulf to the

Red Sea, through the Suez Canal, to Mediterranean and European markets. At the time, two-thirds of European oil traveled through the canal. To ensure that the British economy had access to the Gulf States' vital oil resources, Britain established a series of defense treaties with states such as Kuwait and Oman. These defense arrangements influenced British policy in Aden. As one diplomat wrote, "If we were forced out of Aden our prestige in the Gulf would suffer severely."[7] Maintaining a strong position in Aden would bolster Arab monarchies' confidence in their British ally.

Aden also played a valuable role in British Cold War strategy. It acted as a regional hub for deterring Soviet incursions into the Middle East and as a base for a potential deployment of Britain's strategic reserve of ground forces. In 1963, the British signaled their continued interest in bolstering their position in the Middle East when they merged the Crown Colony of Aden city with the Western and Eastern Aden Protectorates—rural territories governed by local Arab sheikhs, sultans, and emirs under British "protection"— into the South Arabian Federation.[8] Britain had essentially constructed a state of its own to counter the possible emergence of a pro-Nasser Yemen to the north.

Under the 1963 merger, the South Arabian Federation became a hybrid polity that combined elements of direct colonial rule with limited local sovereignty. Local rulers retained sovereignty in the federation territories of the Western and Eastern Aden Protectorates, but their rule was circumscribed by a series of "advisory treaties" with Britain. The original nineteenth-century treaty system consisted of a series of agreements between Britain and local tribal chiefs in which the chiefs received British protection in exchange for British political officers who would advise them on political and military matters. The treaty terms, however, mandated that local rulers obey this advice. In the 1930s and 1940s, new treaties extended this mandatory advice to welfare and development policies as a reaction to what the British perceived as Arab "misrule." According to colonial officers, local sheikhs had done little to improve the lives of their followers. The new treaty terms gave British advisers control over internal governance, making indirect rule far more direct. After the Aden Crown Colony merged with the two protectorates in 1963, Britain retained advisory powers related to defense, foreign affairs, and internal security throughout the federation.[9] British officials could therefore make all key security-related decisions.

Middle East politics, however, were more complex than the Cold War struggle between superpowers as regional actors pursued independent agendas. The greatest threat to British primacy in the Middle East came from Egyptian president Gamal Abdel Nasser. Nasser opposed colonialism and advocated Egyptian nationalism, stating that "to be an Egyptian patriot was to struggle to cleanse Egypt of the British presence and to safeguard Egypt's territorial integrity."[10] In addition to his calls to rid Egypt of

British influence, Nasser encouraged similar programs for all Arab territories. Under Nasser, Egypt adopted an assertive foreign policy advocating pan-Arab solidarity, liberation from colonialism, and freedom from the interference of Cold War superpowers. In truth, Nasser's relationship with each superpower was complicated. He cultivated close relations with the Soviet Union but did not embrace communism. In the United States, the Eisenhower administration alternated between containing Nasser and trying to win his support.[11] Britain, however, was Nasser's implacable enemy.

Throughout the 1950s, Nasser challenged Britain's Middle Eastern supremacy. In 1955 he took a leading role at the Bandung Conference in Indonesia, where he joined with delegates from newly independent states such as India, Sri Lanka, Burma, Pakistan, and China in denouncing colonialism. The following year he nationalized the Suez Canal, which resulted in Britain's failed Suez Canal intervention. In the aftermath of the Suez Crisis, Britain seemed to have reached a nadir in terms of its influence in the Middle East as Nasser saw his popularity surge throughout the region.[12]

Nasser's challenge to British primacy in the Middle East led to a series of confrontations between republican governments supported by Egypt and the Soviet Union against conservative Arab monarchies supported by the United Kingdom and United States. In September 1962 a coup d'état in Yemen installed a pro-Nasser republic in the country neighboring Britain's Aden base. Republican conspirators failed to assassinate the ruling imam of Yemen, Mohammad al-Badr, who fled to the northeast seeking refuge with supporters. The Yemen revolution quickly descended into civil war.[13]

In response to the confrontation with Egypt and the 1962 Yemen revolution, defeating Nasser became an obsession for British political leaders, including Colonial Secretary Duncan Sandys, Minister of Aviation Julian Amery, MP Neil McLean, and Defence Secretary Peter Thorneycroft. Dubbed the Aden Group, these policymakers intended to strengthen British forces in the Middle East in order to curb Egyptian influence in the region.[14] Prime Minister Macmillan supported the Aden Group and described the Egyptian threat in the gravest terms. Upon receiving a telegram urging reconciliation with Nasser, Macmillan furiously scribbled in the margins "for Nasser put Hitler and it all rings familiar." Macmillan and the Aden Group were committed to resisting Nasser and refused any suggestion of "appeasement."[15]

Obsession over the Egyptian threat drove the British government's decision to intervene in the Yemen civil war. Although anticolonial resistance to British influence preceded Nasser's rise to power, British policymakers were convinced that Nasser was the driving force behind unrest in Yemen and Aden.[16] Prime Minister Sir Alec Douglas-Home, having replaced Macmillan, maintained an official policy of nonintervention in the civil war but authorized covert military assistance to support Mohammad al-Badr's royalist side. Britain waged a secret war, code-named Operation Rancour, against the Egyptian-backed Yemeni republicans by supplying weaponry and financial aid and building a mercenary organization in cooperation with French intelligence. British and French intelligence organizations also collaborated with Saudi Arabian intelligence officials to hire private aircraft, purchase weapons and ammunition, and recruit experienced ex-soldiers. Many of the organization's recruits were former British Special Air Service commandos or French veterans of the Algerian and Indochina wars. The South Arabian Federation played an important part in the effort—the mercenary force used Aden as a logistics hub and established a field communications center in Bayhan, along the border with Yemen.[17]

In Aden, High Commissioner Sir Kennedy Trevaskis worried that the Yemen civil war could lead to Nasser's gaining influence in Aden. "It became apparent," Trevaskis wrote in his memoirs, "that the Yemen was not far short of being an Egyptian satellite." He worried that Yemen would become a base from which Egyptian forces could subvert the South Arabian Federation. Trevaskis arrived as high commissioner to Aden in 1963. By the time of his appointment to this post, he had served for more than a decade in the territories that had become the South Arabian Federation. Trevaskis knew the region, its customs, and its rulers, and, perhaps most important for the leaders of Britain's Conservative Party government, he shared their views on Aden's strategic importance. To Trevaskis, Nasser "in effect declared a cold war on Britain, with the object of removing her from the Middle East." Yemen's increasingly intimate relationship with Egypt therefore "had sinister implications."[18] The Aden Group member Julian Amery agreed, labeling the Aden situation "potentially our most explosive Colonial problem."[19]

Trevaskis feared links between Aden's well-organized labor movement and Nasser's influence in Yemen. Connections between the Aden Trades Union Congress (ATUC) and Yemeni labor organizations strengthened throughout the 1950s. Primarily composed of Yemeni migrant workers, ATUC sponsored strike actions to protest arbitrary arrests, low wages, and discriminatory employment practices. ATUC members largely embraced Nasser's message of pan-Arab unity, which spread rapidly in the South Arabian Federation through radio services such as *Voice of the Arabs*, a program broadcast from Cairo. In August 1962, ATUC established a political wing, the People's Socialist Party (PSP). This move allowed the PSP to mobilize ATUC's collective action networks toward political ends without violating colonial laws stipulating that labor unions could not strike for political purposes.[20] The combination of Arab nationalist sentiment and labor militancy worried colonial administrators, who justified breaking strikes and imprisoning labor activists on the basis of political connections with Arab nationalism. Trevaskis saw the PSP and ATUC as pawns in Nasser's quest for Middle Eastern supremacy—a perception that was reinforced by escalating violence between socialist activists and British security forces.

After the September 1962 Yemen revolution, Trevaskis's concerns multiplied as he fretted over the possibility that a pro-Nasser government in Yemen would exacerbate Aden's labor problems: "The ATUC/PSP could expect to receive ready and active support from the new regime in the Yemen."[21]

To limit PSP and ATUC political influence, Trevaskis limited the voting franchise to eight thousand people—mostly members of propertied, established Aden families likely to vote for pro-British candidates—banned labor strikes, shut down the ATUC weekly newsletter, and deported hundreds of trade union activists.[22] Violence escalated throughout 1963, culminating in a December 10 grenade attack at the Aden airport in which Trevaskis was wounded and two others died. The next day, Trevaskis and the Federal Supreme Council declared a state of emergency.[23]

Unrest in the Radfan

In addition to PSP agitation in the city of Aden, Trevaskis had to contend with an uprising in the South Arabian Federation's hinterland. As Britain's covert war in Yemen continued, Egyptian and Yemeni republican forces increasingly sought to expand the anticolonial conflict into the federation. They established a guerrilla force called the National Liberation Front (NLF), smuggled arms across the border, and trained sympathetic villagers. In 1962, Yemeni and Egyptian forces began to develop close relations with the rulers of the Radfan, a region with a population of about twenty-seven thousand people, most of whom were Arabs of the Qutaybi people. Yemeni troops began supplying automatic weapons, grenades, land mines, and military advisers to the Radfan. As the British had feared, civil war seeped beyond Yemen's borders, finding a receptive audience among the Qutaybi.[24]

In 1963, a dispute between the Qutaybi and federation forces led to open revolt. In October, an exchange of gunfire between a Federal Regular Army (FRA) patrol acting on behalf of the local federation authority, the emir of Dali, and Qutaybi residents resulted in the death of a Qutaybi sheikh.[25] The Qutaybi complained that the emir had been hoarding the state's finances for himself, had changed the system of customary law, and favored some clans at the expense of others. Trevaskis dismissed the Qutaybis' appeals, instead seeing the nefarious influence of Nasser, Yemeni republicans, and the NLF as the true source of Radfan discontent.[26] The NLF had, in fact, taught guerrilla warfare techniques to several Radfan family groups like the Qutaybi. Trevaskis also knew that Radfan peoples had also traveled to Yemen and returned with arms supplied by the NLF. By 1963, residents of the Aden hinterlands had spent a decade listening to broadcasts that spread Nasser's vision of "Islamic World Power" and glorified anticolonial struggles in Cyprus, Algeria, and Kenya. Radio had a tremendous impact on isolated Arab populations. After the Second World War, the proliferation of portable wireless receivers enabled villagers to listen to broadcasts from Cairo Radio and the Egyptian-backed Sana'a Radio. During the 1950s, Cairo Radio's *Voice of the Arabs* became the most popular radio program in the Middle East.[27] Both stations' anticolonial rhetoric proved popular in the South Arabian Federation. News traveled quickly and easily by radio, making it almost impossible for the British to control the flow of information in Aden. As one Sana'a Radio broadcast recognized, "Could the iron screen which the British imperialists put around the Arab South prevent the spread of news about our struggling people?"[28] The answer was a resounding no.

Anticolonial propaganda, however, was not the sole reason for the Radfan revolt. Local politics also influenced tribal leaders' competition with each other and their decisions to ally with Britain or its enemies. Radfan peoples' grievances derived as much from local conflicts such as that between the Qutaybi and the emir of Dali as from the influence of Nasser's pan-Arab nationalist vision. The NLF, however, perceived local tensions in the Radfan as an opportunity to organize sympathetic populations outside Aden city to harass British and federation forces with raids and ambushes. On December 22, 1963, the FRA reported that convoys along the Aden-Dali' Road, which ran through the Radfan, had come under attack. For Trevaskis, the situation was "now getting seriously out of hand."[29] As one scholar described, British officials often pejoratively labeled local unrest as "the result of 'subversion' cross-cut with 'tribalism.' "[30]

With the Qutaybis challenging British rule through open revolt, Trevaskis decided to launch a punitive operation to reassert British and federal authority. In January 1964, the FRA, supported by a small British contingent, attacked the Radfan. In a campaign dubbed Operation Nutcracker, three FRA infantry battalions and an armored car squadron assembled at the nearby village of Thumair. British support consisted of a tank troop, artillery battery, several helicopters, and RAF bomber support. Over the next three weeks, federation and British troops drove deep into Radfan, using helicopters and air support to move from ridge to ridge. Each forward movement was followed with the construction of a gravel road to facilitate resupply. The NLF-trained Qutaybis, nicknamed the "Red Wolves of the Radfan," harassed the attackers with long-range sniper fire, raids, and small-scale ambushes, but as federation forces drew near, Qutaybi forces would withdraw. By the end of January, as a result far more of the rebels' hit-and-run strategy than of the FRA's skill, the Radfan was largely under federation control, and most rebel groups had negotiated peace. Still, NLF attacks against FRA forces continued sporadically into February. The campaign succeeded in driving the rebels out of the Radfan, but as soon as the federation withdrew its forces, the rebels returned.[31]

Qutaybi attacks resumed in March and April, but when Trevaskis outlined his plans for a harsh counteroffensive, Whitehall encouraged him to be mindful of the potential for international censure.[32] In response to the resumption of hostilities, federation authorities requested that British forces lead a new offensive in the Radfan. Trevaskis sent his recommended courses of action to Colonial Secretary Sandys, who briefed Prime Minister Douglas-Home. Sandys proposed that Douglas-Home should authorize "whatever methods are necessary to ensure the success of the operation while endeavouring, as far as possible, to minimise adverse international criticism." Trevaskis also asked for £200,000 to "strengthen the loyalty of the tribes"—that is, bribe them into submission—which "might well save expensive and embarrassing military operations later on." In terms of propaganda, Trevaskis wanted £39,000 to support pro-British politicians in Aden as well as £44,000 to fund pro-British radio broadcasts and news services. Sandys called the initiative "well worth this expenditure."[33] Acutely aware of how brutal counterinsurgency methods negatively affected Britain's public image, Sandys prioritized the need to avoid criticism.

Militarily, Trevaskis intended to strike hard through a scorched-earth campaign. The political directive issued to British forces outlined his expectations: "The effectiveness of punitive action" depends "on the firmness with which it is conducted." British troops, therefore, "must take punitive measures that hurt the rebels, thus leaving behind . . . memories that will not quickly fade." The idea was "to make life so unpleasant for the tribes that their morale is broken and they submit."[34] In line with Trevaskis's directive, British troops employed "ground proscription" tactics in which they designated certain areas as off limits, or "proscribed." All inhabitants, regardless of their status as civilians or combatants, were required to leave, which turned virtually the entire population of a proscribed area into refugees. Trevaskis's strategy was to wage war against the entire Radfan population.

In preparation for the campaign, British military officers and colonial officials did articulate rules of engagement to regulate the use of violence, but the scope of actions allowed under these rules was immense. Regulations authorized the use of force against both noncombatants and combatants. Rules of engagement stipulated that in proscribed areas "all movement of any kind in the open (i.e. human or animal) should be treated as hostile and engaged," although with the tepid caveat that "deliberate casualties to women and children" should simply be "avoided." And yet, British soldiers were ordered to destroy standing crops, "confiscate property, burn fodder, destroy grain, grain stores, and livestock." Livestock and crops were sources of wealth and sustenance for Radfan peoples. Attacks against these targets amounted to economic warfare waged with little distinction between civilian and combatant. By devastating villagers' food stores, British troops ensured that women and children would suffer from malnutrition and starvation. In any areas where the villagers refused to surrender, British rules of engagement allowed commanders to use aerial and artillery bombardment "to the maximum extent necessary." In such circumstances, the directive bluntly stated, "casualties to women and children must be accepted."[35]

Still, Trevaskis thought that a successful campaign would require even harsher methods than ground proscription tactics. As British forces continued planning the offensive, Trevaskis wrote to Lieutenant General Sir Charles Harington, the commander in chief of Middle East Command, that "ground forces cannot deal effectively with rebels." Trevaskis based this assessment on his experiences as a colonial political officer in the Middle East. Believing that he was far more of an expert on the "Arab mind" than Harington, Trevaskis insisted that actions such as "the taking of hostages, banning tribesmen from markets, dismissing members of rebel tribes from the security forces" were useful methods against rebels but were not enough to end the rebellion entirely. Victory required "interfering with their livelihood and . . . doing and threatening to do damage to their property." Trevaskis argued that damaging a population's livelihood required persistent punitive action—it took time to generate an effect. Since it was often too difficult to sustain ground troops on long-term deployments to remote areas, Trevaskis insisted that "the only means which has proved effective has been air proscription with our other weapons employed in an auxiliary role."[36] He repeated this message to Colonial Secretary Sandys, describing punishment by air as "the only form of action" that had been successful against past Arab revolts.[37] The general commanding the Radfan operation, Brigadier Cecil Blacker, agreed with Trevaskis's assessment. Blacker later told the Associated Press that "this is largely a political war and undoubtedly an economic squeeze is the most effective weapon against the dissidents."[38]

Trevaskis's proposed air proscription was a resuscitation of a popular colonial policing technique called "air control." Developed by the Royal Air Force (RAF) during the 1920s and employed throughout Britain's Middle Eastern dependencies since then, the concept of air control rested on the notion that the act of bombing would inspire fear and terror among rebel groups. Physical destruction was not the objective but the means to achieving a psychological effect. RAF air control advocates argued that policing the colonies by air was cheaper than maintaining large ground forces. Aircraft could also easily traverse mountain ranges and deserts, identify rebel troop movements from afar, concentrate quickly to attack rebel troops or villages, and deliver significant damage through bombs and machine guns. A racist dynamic also fed the air control myth, as RAF and colonial officials felt it was best suited for use against "primitive" peoples and "certain stubborn races" in underdeveloped areas.[39] The assumption was that such "semicivilized" peoples would be so awed by Britain's ability to strike any target by air that they would quickly submit to British authority.

In a 1937 lecture at the Royal United Services Institution, an RAF senior officer described how air control functioned in practice. When so-called primitive peoples—such as seminomadic Arabs in the Aden protectorates—upset the balance of British rule, a political officer would visit the community in question and deliver an ultimatum that usually instructed the sheikh to pay a fine or hand over the individual "miscreants" responsible for causing trouble. During the period before the ultimatum expired, the RAF would conduct aerial reconnaissance to identify key targets. If the sheikh failed to fulfill the terms of the ultimatum, "aircraft appeared all over the country and dropped a few small bombs in the principal villages." The local population, who knew that the bombing raids were coming, would usually have evacuated their villages and relocated to the mountains. RAF aircraft would then patrol above the abandoned villages, bombing anyone who had remained behind as well as destroying crops and cattle until the sheikhs agreed to make peace. No matter how defiant, the officer concluded, eventually the sheikhs would realize "that if they did not start ploughing soon they would lose their crop."[40]

Perversely, airpower advocates argued that air control was not only cheaper and more effective than maintaining large ground forces but also more humane. They suggested that air control methods protected political officers, allowing them to travel into frontier zones without fear. Guarded by the shield of airpower, political agents could safely immerse themselves in Arab society, gaining the familiarity and expertise necessary to understand and manipulate the local populace, thus minimizing further conflicts. Air control created a benevolent regime that promoted cooperation and understanding despite being built on coercive foundations.[41] In this sense, air control served as the military equivalent of indirect imperial rule, offering control without occupation, much like the maintenance of British political authority through informal collaboration with emirs, sultans, and other local elites.[42] Although air control doctrine gained an almost mythical reputation for effectiveness, in reality its effects were largely temporary, and its appeal to policymakers was due more to fiscal than to military logic.[43]

After the Second World War, aerial bombardment persisted as a common British response to local rebellions in the territories that eventually became the short-lived South Arabian Federation. Groups displaying "insolence" or "disobedience" toward colonial rule faced overwhelming force. In 1947, the RAF bombed the Mansuris of Lower Awlaqi. Over the course of three days in November 1947, the RAF pummeled Qutaybis with sixty-six tons of bombs and fifteen thousand pounds of rockets. Another community was bombed for failing to deliver its salt taxes.[44] In 1957, the commander of British forces in Kenya, Lieutenant General Sir Gerald Lathbury, expressed his support for similar tactics.[45]

As a colonial officer with a long history of service in the Middle East, Trevaskis enthusiastically promoted air proscription, but officials in London balked because of the consequences from a March 1964 attack on Harib,

Yemen. The fort at Harib served as a distribution center for arms smuggling and the movement of recruits and advisers into the South Arabian Federation. On March 28, less than two months after the first Qutaybi uprising in the Radfan, with approval from the Cabinet Defence Committee, eight RAF bombers dropped leaflets on the fort as a warning for civilians to evacuate. A mere fifteen minutes later, however, the RAF attacked with rockets and bombs. When Yemeni forces claimed that the attack had killed twenty-five civilians, Nasser and all Arab League governments condemned it.[46] The bombing generated a wave of international condemnation at the United Nations. The UK permanent representative reported to Whitehall that sentiment at the UN was overwhelmingly negative, with many claiming that the bombing represented "methods of the last century" that engendered "no public support" from the international community.[47] Trevaskis originally planned to initiate the Radfan offensive on April 6, but Sandys asked him to postpone the operation. A renewed offensive, in Sandys's words, "could scarcely happen at a worse moment in relation to our United Nations position."[48] To launch a massive aerial bombardment so soon after the Harib incident would be a public relations nightmare for Britain.

Concerned with international criticism following the Harib attack, British officials at the United Nations and Whitehall opposed Trevaskis's appeals for air proscription. From the UN, the UK permanent representative wrote of his surprise at the extent of hostility toward Britain after the Harib bombing and warned that by continuing air attacks "we shall constantly be playing into the hands of our enemies," who made good propaganda use of the Harib strike.[49] In London, Sandys instructed Trevaskis not to proceed with the Radfan operation or air proscription until gaining his approval.[50] Likewise, after consulting with Sandys, the chief of the Defence staff notified Harington, who had overall responsibility for Aden military operations, that "air strikes against the Radfan were politically unacceptable at present."[51] But Trevaskis resisted, listing a litany of problems:

> The resolutions of the United Nations Security Council and the Committee of 24, the hostility of the Arab League and most Arab Governments, the virulent propaganda from Cairo and Sana [sic] Radios, the universally hostile and to some extent menacing tone of the Aden press . . . the critical tone of important sections of the British press on the Harib incident . . . our failure to deal with the rebellion in Radfan and the knowledge that [anticolonial forces] are planning to provoke rebellions and disorders throughout the Federation.

These British setbacks had "made a serious impact on the morale" of federation rulers, Trevaskis argued. "They know only too well of our fear of criticism in the United Nations and the United Kingdom."[52] His protestations failed to entirely overcome Whitehall's reluctance to employ proscription bombing, but Trevaskis's superiors did authorize the use of air attacks in a close air support role to assist ground troops. Final instructions to Trevaskis specified that close air support "will be kept to the minimum necessary" and "will not repeat not include the use of bombs."[53]

Trevaskis yielded to the Colonial Office's instructions, and the campaign began without using air proscription. To carry out the attack, the military established a temporary organization—the Radfan Force, or Radforce—consisting of Royal Marines from Forty-Five Commando, a company each from Third Battalion, the Parachute Regiment and First Battalion, the East Anglian Regiment, two FRA battalions, and a Special Air Service (SAS) squadron, as well as armored car and artillery support. Assessing the Qutaybis' capabilities and available British forces, military planners expected the campaign to last three weeks.

British troops began the operation on April 30 with several night assaults to occupy key terrain features, allowing Radforce to isolate the Radfan from access to Yemen. The greatest danger to British troops came from sniper fire. Radfan fighters who knew the terrain would occupy well-protected positions on high ground near villages or above mountain passes. As British patrols moved into these areas, rebel snipers would fire on them at long range and quickly withdraw before the patrol or British air support could engage them. British troops grew frustrated with their enemy's ability to initiate contact and quickly melt away, but the British also faced challenges unrelated to the enemy. The harsh terrain proved difficult for British logistics: front-line troops consumed ammunition, food, and water as fast as the supplies could be brought forward. Helicopters and animal transport by pack mule or camel ameliorated the supply situation, but frustration with logistics and the enemy only grew as the campaign ground on. After only three days, British commanders realized that they were embroiled in what had rapidly become a protracted operation.[54]

Impatient with the campaign's slow progress, Trevaskis again requested authorization for air proscription. In a lengthy personal memorandum to Sandys, Trevaskis condemned "half-measures" and "half-hearted action," reiterating his conviction that success demanded "stern repressive measures undertaken thoroughly and with determination."[55] In a reflection of his growing sense of desperation, Trevaskis cabled colonial officials in London on May 2, calling the situation "every bit as menacing as I have believed." He implored Sandys to reconsider the ban on air proscription and ominously warned that "failure to deal effectively with Radfan will, of course, enhance the possibility of serious trouble elsewhere."[56] Lieutenant General Harington cabled the Ministry of Defence also requesting authority to begin proscription bombing.[57] Still concerned with air proscription's negative public image, Sandys resisted withdrawing the embargo.[58] For Sandys, public criticism remained a greater problem than the Radfan offensive's slow progress. Trevaskis soon persuaded Sandys to change his mind.

Airpower Unleashed

Facing multiple, simultaneous security crises over Britain's covert involvement in the Yemeni civil war, labor unrest in Aden, and now a revolt in the Radfan, Trevaskis grew increasingly desperate to begin proscription air attacks. Throughout the first week of May, he continued pressuring officials in London. Ground proscription, he argued, had been "slow and restricted" while also imposing "a terrible strain on our troops." Trevaskis lamented that "quite frankly we cannot afford to go on like this much longer" because "if we are to forego the use of the most powerful weapon in our armoury, we shall have to pay for it with further loss of life and limb . . . without even a reasonable prospect of success." Only "proscription . . . and punitive action against the rebel villages" could win the campaign. Trevaskis insisted that failure to quickly subdue the Radfan would lead to "three more Radfans" in the federation territories of Dhala, Haushari, and Subeihi that could easily overwhelm Britain's limited military capabilities.[59] Besides, Trevaskis argued, British forces were already employing aircraft in a close air support role to assist ground forces pinned down by enemy fire. To him, using aircraft in any capacity would inevitably generate "all kinds of vicious criticism." Air proscription tactics therefore would not "make a halfpenny worth's difference internationally."[60] Trevaskis described the use of air proscription as absolutely necessary for the success of the operation. His lobbying worked.

Concerned with Trevaskis's gloomy assessment that the offensive might fail and that violence might spread if the campaign was not successful, ministers in London approved air proscription on May 8. Sandys, however, remained anxious over a possible international backlash and decided to visit Aden immediately to discuss the implementation of air proscription with Trevaskis in person.[61] Sandys arrived on May 11 and met with Trevaskis right away. At this meeting Trevaskis convinced Sandys that proscription bombing was necessary. After the meeting Sandys cabled the prime minister and defence secretary that "air proscription is absolutely unavoidable" and "the sooner we start it, the better."[62] Concerned as usual with the potential for international criticism, Sandys reassured himself and his London-based colleagues that airstrikes could be justified publicly by stretching the circumstances. He wrote that since "tribesmen have been regularly firing at our aircraft and have hit several of them, we might be able to claim that our aircraft were shooting back."[63] As Sandys approved the use of methods that he knew would garner criticism, he began coming up with cover stories with which to deflect the potential controversies.

As with ground proscription, approval of air proscription came with certain restraints. During Sandys's visit to Aden, he and Trevaskis decided that before an attack began, British forces should warn villagers to evacuate. The idea was to air-drop warning leaflets on villages at least twenty-four hours prior to bombing them. A written warning would be printed on each leaflet stating "the crimes of violence committed by the Radfan tribes, followed by a demand that they should . . . send a representative delegation to make submission to the Federal Government."[64] But the typical leaflet message, according to the War Office's official after-action review, did not actually specify the consequences facing villagers who refused to leave. Instead it stated vaguely, "Let it be known to you that for the maintenance of law and order the Federal Government has declared the district in which you live to be an area of military movement. For your own safety you should therefore leave the district by dawn tomorrow, taking your women and children with you."[65] By dropping leaflets prior to an attack, British officials could claim that those villagers who failed to evacuate had made a conscious decision to stay despite knowing the consequences. Yet by not including an actual threat of the consequences for remaining in a proscribed village, British forces could avoid condemnation in Arab media and at the United Nations. As Sandys reported, "For international reasons it seemed to me desirable to avoid including in the leaflets any threat about the consequence of non-compliance." He did not want to provide written evidence of British threats to destroy villages, kill livestock, or attack potentially unarmed villagers. A leaflet threatening military action against civilians could become a propaganda tool in the hands of Arab nationalists. Instead of written warnings, Sandys and Trevaskis proposed sending FRA soldiers of Radfan origin into the villages to "put the fear of death" into the population. By word of mouth, "the message would quickly spread from village to village and would no doubt improve with the telling."[66] As the Sandys-Trevaskis proposal suggests, intimidation was the real benefit of forewarning the population.

With the approval of air proscription, the Radfan population felt the full force of colonial coercion as the RAF bombed villages, slaughtered livestock, and destroyed crops. For the RAF, the approval of air proscription meant that "villages may be attacked with cannon and grenades," and it allowed pilots to shoot cattle, goats, crops, and people loitering in proscribed areas.[67] It was a scorched-earth campaign waged from the air. In one attack, a single Shackleton bomber expended 600 20 mm cannon rounds and dropped sixty aerial grenades—lightweight twenty-pound bombs. The pilot reported firing his cannon at a herd of goats, while dropping six aerial grenades on another goat herd, eleven on cattle, eight on people—without specifying civilian or combatant—four on "people in Wadi," six more on "people and four camels," and an additional fourteen on "people under trees." In another instance, a flight of two Hunter Mk 9 fighter-bombers fired 370 rounds of 30 mm cannon, reporting "cows attacked."[68] Later, two Hunter Mk 9s fired 1,040 cannon shells while strafing "houses and crops."[69] Such battle damage reports were commonplace. In early May, the RAF usually reported between three and five ground attack sorties per day, but this rate increased to between eight and fifteen sorties beginning on May 26 as

British reinforcements entered the fight and the campaign's intensity escalated. The Aden High Commission ordered the RAF to maintain "continuous harassment of the area by day and by night by: (a) attacking all signs of movement; (b) shooting up inhabited areas and agricultural areas; and (c) generally causing damage to property."[70] By the end of the campaign, the RAF had flown more than 600 sorties, launched 2,500 rockets, and fired 200,000 cannon rounds.[71]

Although senior leaders deemed harsh punitive measures necessary, British troops were often unenthusiastic about enforcing them. One East Anglian Regiment lance corporal called the destruction "a bloody shame."[72] Soldiers' hesitancy to destroy homes and burn crops was enough of a problem that the War Office's official after-action report specifically addressed the issue: "Soldiers were reluctant to embark on punitive operations, which although mild in nature, seemed to them to be directed against comparatively innocent people." Such operations "inevitably involve hardship for some, and the need was not always apparent to the troops and junior officers involved."[73]

This resistance incensed political and military leaders like Ian Baillie, the British agent in the Western Aden Protectorate. On May 8, Baillie received a radio message indicating that "very little was happening in the villages other than a thorough search of houses." On May 11, he went to the front to see for himself: "When I flew up to the forward areas and talked to our troops in a village . . . with my own eyes I saw many stacks of fodder and a grain store with grain in it (both these items are specifically mentioned in the political directive), but the forward commanders had specific orders to the effect that the relevant paragraphs of the political directive were in abeyance."[74] To his horror, Baillie discovered that the political directive had been ignored on orders from Middle East Command—the military headquarters overseeing the Radfan operation. Furious, he told the commanding general, Lieutenant General Harington, that "Paragraphs B(iii) and B(vi) of the political directive attached to the Radfan Operation Order dated 29th April 1964 deal with the punitive activities of troops in abandoned villages and fields" and warned that "if they are not complied with, military domination of the area can have little or no lasting effect."[75] Harington assured Baillie that he would reinstate the political directive in full. Political and military leaders overcame soldiers' reluctance by cajoling them—as Baillie had—and providing information briefings intended to create an appreciation among the troops for the "political requirement" of punishment.[76]

Many troops may have been reluctant to destroy civilian livelihoods, but by the end of July, Radforce had captured all its territorial objectives and had pushed the rebels out of the Radfan. British troops occupied the Radfan and continued enforcing proscription through air and ground patrolling. These measures effectively sealed access to the Radfan, preventing combatants and civilians alike from returning to their homes until after they agreed to peace terms with British and federal authorities. With the planting season coming to an end, colonial officials knew that denying access to the region would pressure rebels to make peace so that they could return "to their land before it is too late to grow a crop this year." Unable to tend their herds or crops, Radfan fighters faced the agonizing choice of surrender or starvation.[77]

The British were prepared to wait as long as necessary. On June 21, Trevaskis's deputy, Timothy Oates, triumphantly reported that "ground and air operations in Radfan have been successful insofar as they have, up to the present moment, prevented the revolt from spreading and have effectively put a stop to attacks on the road." Although he noted lamely that proscription "inflicted some casualties and much damage and inconvenience," Oates cautiously observed that "the tribes of Radfan have already been taught a sharp lesson, but it cannot yet be said that we have reasserted our authority. . . . Any slackening of our pressure on the tribes may lead to renewed attacks."[78]

The Refugee Crisis and Britain's Response

Proscription tactics had targeted both combatants and noncombatants in order to break Radfan resistance, but these methods caused a refugee crisis that elicited the very criticism that Colonial Secretary Sandys had hoped to avoid. In what Britain's *Sunday Telegraph* labeled a "hunger war," British actions caused thousands of civilian refugees to flee the Radfan.[79] One British expatriate living in Aden recorded that the Radfan peoples had been "punished as never before" with "their homes destroyed and families scattered; crops and livestock lost" as well as "many dead and the remainder suffering from hunger and privation."[80] The Arab League claimed that there were an astounding thirty thousand people—a figure larger than British estimates for the entire Radfan population—fleeing "British aggression."[81] On May 25, the *New York Times* reported that only "about 1,000 refugees from the Radfan area, mostly women and children, have left rebel territory."[82]

Publicly, however, colonial officers downplayed the refugee crisis. In June, the *Guardian* reported information fed to its reporters by colonial public relations officers: "Earlier accounts of a thousand refugees arriving at Jaar, in the Yafai region south of Radfan, are now described here as greatly exaggerated." The *Los Angeles Times* also noted that British officials "counted no more than 500 refugees."[83] Private calculations, however, contradicted public pronouncements. In reality, the numbers were far higher. Hugh Hickling, Trevaskis's legal adviser, visited the Radfan and recorded the relatively conservative number of eight thousand refugees.[84] According to Don McCarthy, the Foreign Office's liaison to Middle East Command

(Aden), "when situation was at its worst in April and May perhaps ten thousand people had moved to Yafa, Abyan and elsewhere."[85] By November, most rebel groups had decided to agree to peace terms before their people starved.

Punitive tactics had indeed proved their effectiveness, but the refugee crisis elicited sharp criticism internationally as many Middle East and Third World leaders demanded that the refugees receive humanitarian aid. In June, the PSP leader Abdullah al-Asnag traveled to Cairo, where he delivered a press conference decrying the ICRC's failure to intervene on behalf of the people of South Arabia, who faced British "genocide" in the Radfan. Al-Asnag blamed the British, accusing the British government of opposing the entrance of ICRC representatives into the "occupied South."[86] In November, ten leaders of a group affiliated with al-Asnag's PSP wrote to the colonial secretary decrying the Radfan campaign for "exposing the lives of the population to death and rendering them homeless after destroying their property."[87] Meanwhile, broadcasts on Cairo Radio and Sana'a Radio condemned the RAF for having "carried out brutal raids on peaceful citizens in Radfan." Cairo's *Voice of the Arabs* also reported on the International Red Crescent Society's efforts to aid the refugees with an initial installment of £1.25 million.[88] Sana'a Radio, meanwhile, informed its listeners that "Britain left the rebels to die of hunger because they demand their rights in life in accordance with international laws and human rights issued by the United Nations."[89] Reactions in former British colonies were also negative. Indian newspapers criticized the damage done to cultivated land and the effects of the campaign on the civilian population.[90] The British High Commission in Delhi reported that Indian newspapers "were generally unsympathetic" to the British campaign.[91] In the UN Committee of 24, Indian prime minister Jawaharlal Nehru and Tanganyikan president Julius Nyerere cosponsored a resolution condemning British operations in the Radfan.[92]

Faced with this controversy, Colonial Secretary Sandys sought to publicly justify British operations. As they had done during the Cyprus Emergency, British officials prepared a public relations campaign of their own. On May 10, Sandys met with Commonwealth Relations Office (CRO) officials to complain that "not enough is being done to put across our case" in defense of the Radfan operation.[93] The strength of Radfan resistance meant that "the relatively simple security operation in Radfan, to which we wished to give minimum publicity, is assuming proportions which compel us to take stronger action locally." On May 12, the CRO sent a telegram to high commissions in all Commonwealth states to notify British diplomats that "our objectives and motives are being misrepresented by undue publicity and unjustified criticism." The intent of this initiative was to bolster Commonwealth states' support for Britain at the United Nations. The telegram included a series of approved talking points and instructions to "make positive use in publicity and other media."[94] Diplomats in some embassies, such as Cairo, were placed in the unenviable situation of having to explain British actions to a decidedly hostile public. The Foreign Office informed the Cairo embassy that diplomats "should take the line" that "although every precaution is taken to keep hardship to a minimum it is inevitable that in such operations the civilian population should suffer some disturbance." The Foreign Office instructions followed this apparent admission of civilian suffering with the denial of British culpability: "The responsibility for this [civilian hardship] lies with those who initiated and have sustained the revolt"—that is, with those who "compelled" the British to escalate their response.[95] Seeking to manipulate the public debate over operations in the Radfan, British officials prepared to defend proscription tactics by denying that they had done anything wrong.

Commanders recognized that, in addition to the public relations campaign, rebuilding the Radfan would help to combat international disapproval of British actions. In June, Lieutenant General Harington and High Commissioner Trevaskis agreed that "it is desirable to demonstrate that our military presence can be constructive as well as repressive." Although he believed that "the time is not yet ripe," Harington proposed to "provide direct assistance in the areas adjoining Radfan and in the Radfan itself." But the purpose of economic assistance was not necessarily to win the Radfan population's hearts and minds. Harington worried that focusing economic development efforts on the Radfan would send the wrong message—that is, rebellion results in economic assistance. Instead, Harington believed that economic aid should also go to neighboring rulers who had remained loyal "to demonstrate that it is not only the tribes that have misbehaved that we are prepared to reward" with assistance.[96] Unenthused, Ian Baillie reluctantly agreed: "We should probably find ourselves with little alternative but to make some contribution to the rehabilitation of Radfan. The only type of rehabilitation I was contemplating at the moment was the provision of wells and minor irrigation works, but the time was not yet ripe for such work in Radfan itself."[97] Baillie's reluctance to help the Radfan population reflected the cynicism with which British forces approached economic development in the Radfan. Colonial officers planned to terrorize the Radfan population into submission by destroying their economic livelihoods while simultaneously planning to demonstrate British "goodwill" by rebuilding the very livelihoods that British forces had destroyed.

Cynicism was rife in Britain's response to the refugee crisis and subsequent international censure. British forces used the refugee crisis as leverage to compel Radfan leaders to negotiate peace settlements. Officials then crafted a public relations strategy which denied British culpability for civilian suffering and blamed the Radfan people for bringing this suffering upon themselves by rebelling in the first place. British methods in the Radfan amounted to a wholesale rejection of the population's rights to receive care and relief from suffering. Civilian suffering, however, invited attention from the International Committee of the Red Cross and a recently established activist group called Amnesty International.

Humanitarian Rights: The ICRC and Amnesty International

Helping victims of war lay at the heart of the ICRC's organizational identity. This assistance extended to such vulnerable populations as the wounded and sick, prisoners, and vulnerable civilians. The ICRC also embraced a rule of silence in which the organization pledged not to publicize states' violations of international humanitarian law. This provision was meant to encourage governments to permit the ICRC to provide humanitarian assistance in even the most devastating conflicts without fear of being criticized by the group. Amnesty International, however, was founded as a human rights group that embraced public activism. By 1963, Amnesty International and the ICRC developed what AI cofounder Peter Benenson termed "a tacit agreement" in which AI lobbied governments on the ICRC's behalf to obtain invitations for the ICRC to visit prisoners and report on their treatment.[98] The ICRC and AI worked to protect two vulnerable populations during the Aden Emergency—civilians and prisoners.

A Swiss businessman, Henri Dunant, had founded the Red Cross after seeing the horrors endured by wounded French and Austrian soldiers during the 1859 Battle of Solferino. Dunant's subsequent memoir, *A Memory of Solferino*, amounted to a clarion call for the alleviation of human suffering during war. In 1863, the Genevan Society of Public Utility formed a committee of leading citizens that led to a conference of states and the 1864 Geneva Conventions as well as the establishment of the International Committee of the Red Cross. All state parties to the Geneva Conventions agreed to recognize the ICRC's mandate to protect victims of war and to permit the ICRC to carry out this mandate in wartime. National Red Cross branches emerged across Europe as volunteers embraced the ICRC's mission.[99] From its inception, the ICRC focused on alleviating the suffering of those populations deemed most vulnerable to violence, such as prisoners, civilians, the wounded, and the sick.[100] These efforts formed the basis of international humanitarian law.

The ICRC's commitment to protecting victims of war amounted to an assertion of what the historian Bruno Cabanes called humanitarian rights. International organizations embraced humanitarian rights in the aftermath of the First World War. Its proponents claimed that all people had the right to receive humanitarian assistance and aid in ameliorating human suffering. These rights were usually applied to groups—such as refugees, veterans, or civilians—and claimed during or after a war.[101] The ICRC was one of the most influential and long-standing of these organizations. For the

ICRC, the interwar period marked a time in which the organization grew in confidence and asserted a general right to take "humanitarian initiative" in international wars and internal unrest.[102] The ICRC's humanitarian rights claims persisted after the Second World War as it advocated increased rights for combatants and protections for civilian victims of war through international humanitarian law.[103]

Although international humanitarian law and human rights law emerged independently from each other, the concepts underlying these two strands of legal thought overlapped in some important respects. For example, both forms of law sought to protect human dignity, whether in war or peace. In the post-1945 international system, human rights law rested on the foundation of UN documents such as the Universal Declaration of Human Rights as well as regional human rights agreements such as the European Convention on Human Rights. International humanitarian law, in contrast, was grounded in the 1949 Geneva Conventions. This conceptual overlap formed the basis of a slow convergence in which the UN and regional bodies such as the ECHR asserted the importance of human rights law during armed conflict.[104] It was in this context of two overlapping legal regimes that the ICRC and Amnesty International sought to protect vulnerable refugees and ensure that prisoners received humane treatment.

The ICRC did not engage in political activism, even as it sought to provide humanitarian aid to victims of war and violence. As a rule, it did not condemn governments for wartime decisions that caused suffering. It shared its reports and findings with the government concerned but kept those reports confidential. Each government, however, was allowed to publicly release ICRC reports if it desired. ICRC leaders believed that criticism would simply cause governments to prohibit further ICRC assistance. Such censure would result in continued human suffering; lives would not be saved if the ICRC could not provide aid. It was heavily criticized for this stance, particularly after the Second World War. For the organization's detractors, the fact that the ICRC did not speak out about the treatment of Jews and other persecuted minorities in ghettos and concentration camps during the Holocaust marked a serious moral failing.[105] During the Aden Emergency and in other colonial wars, the ICRC remained committed to this principle of confidentiality.

Yet the group's leaders insisted that the organization was not blind to government abuses. ICRC president Léopold Boissier later defended the organization's position, writing that delegates' impartiality "does not mean that these witnesses remain silent." Instead, when delegates "observe a breach of the Geneva Conventions or acts contrary to morality or law they protest to the authorities and demand that such acts be stopped." But, Boissier stressed, "these facts are not publicized" precisely because of the danger that any "indiscretion" would result in the loss of ICRC access to the war zone.[106] The ability to immediately provide aid to those in need mattered more to the ICRC than legal accountability for violations of the Geneva Conventions.

The ICRC's reluctance to speak publicly about inhumane conditions continued during post–World War II colonial conflicts. The problem was that the ICRC espoused the idea that victims of war had the right to receive humanitarian aid, and under the Geneva Conventions, it was the ICRC's responsibility to provide such aid. Despite their refusal to apply these conventions to the Aden conflict, British officials had allowed ICRC delegates to provide humanitarian assistance during past colonial wars. During the Cyprus Emergency, for instance, the Red Cross periodically visited detention camps. But in Kenya during the 1955–60 Mau Mau conflict, British officials opposed ICRC attempts to visit prison facilities, detention camps, and resettled populations. Britain eventually acquiesced in 1957, when military operations began winding down and colonial officers had already decided to release most detainees.[107] Relying on the precedents of Cyprus and Kenya, as well as the ICRC's commitment to confidential reporting, ICRC leaders expected Britain to permit them to work in the South Arabian Federation as well.

Unlike the ICRC, Amnesty International did not embrace confidentiality and was committed to publicly chastising governments that failed to act humanely. Founded in London in 1961 by the British Labour Party lawyer Peter Benenson as well as several colleagues such as the Quaker peace activist Eric Baker, Irish international lawyer and politician Seán MacBride, and British lawyer Leon Blom-Cooper, AI embraced activism on behalf of the dignity of the individual. Although the group is often categorized as a human rights organization, AI's activism overlapped with other concepts such as the humanitarian rights espoused by organizations such as the ICRC. For example, the protection of prisoners' rights was central to the ICRC's humanitarian mission, but it also formed a core component of AI's agenda.

Benenson's experience working with the Cyprus Bar Council lawyers on detainee abuse allegations during the 1955–59 Cyprus conflict contributed to his desire to work on behalf of prisoners.[108] In 1960, he authored the foreword to the anonymously written book *Gangrene*.[109] *Gangrene* was about torture committed by French and British forces in Algeria and Kenya, but Benenson's foreword largely concerned similar allegations of abuse during the Cyprus Emergency. He described, for example, torture allegations against British troops, the use of repressive legislation, and the obstacles that police and prison authorities placed in the way of lawyers seeking to defend their clients. The *Gangrene* foreword suggests that Benenson's experiences in Cyprus profoundly affected his opinions on the ubiquity of government repression on both sides of the Iron Curtain as well as how best to promote human rights in the future.[110]

These ideas found expression in Benenson's 1961 "Appeal for Amnesty"— the document that marked the birth of Amnesty International. Published in the *Observer* on May 28, 1961, Benenson's article called on governments to grant an amnesty "for all political prisoners everywhere." The *Observer* article was republished across the world.[111] Within the first six months of the organization's existence, about twenty such groups had formed in Britain. Other branches formed in several European countries. In particular, AI focused on "prisoners of conscience," whom Benenson described as persons imprisoned for expressing an opinion that he or she "honestly holds and which does not advocate or condone personal violence."[112] AI worked for the release of prisoners of conscience, supported the notion of a fair and public trial for all prisoners—even those who had committed violence—and advocated for their humane treatment while in jail. Benenson wanted to shift the debate over political prisoners away from the beliefs that those prisoners espoused, instead focusing on the fact that they had been imprisoned *for a belief*.[113]

To Benenson, public scrutiny was the solution to prevent governments from wielding power arbitrarily and secretly. In his "Appeal for Amnesty," he identified a "growing tendency all over the world" in which governments consistently concealed "the real grounds upon which 'non-conformists' are imprisoned." Such "cover-up charges," Benenson wrote, suggested "that governments are by no means insensitive to the pressure of outside opinion." The greatest implication of a government's susceptibility to public pressures was that "when world opinion is concentrated on one weak spot, it can sometimes succeed in making a government relent."[114] Benenson believed that "human freedom depends on public opinion. So long as public opinion is prepared to accept arrests of people who have committed no crime beyond holding a certain belief, Governments can and will continue to make inroads into personal freedom." The "re-awakening of conscience," he wrote, was the pathway to stimulate public interest and activism.[115] He continued, "There are few, if any states, totally immune from the influence of collective world opinion."[116] Amnesty International would therefore place a premium on public activism to engage civic and social groups, individuals, and governments in the interest of unveiling injustice and ill treatment. Given the declaration of emergency in Aden and subsequent large-scale detentions, it was no surprise that Benenson's fledgling group of activists would soon find itself embroiled in Britain's next colonial conflict on behalf of the ICRC.

The 1963–64 Aden Detention Controversy

Although the Radfan refugee crisis elicited the ICRC's interest in protecting refugees, it was not the first occasion in which the ICRC had sought to fulfill its humanitarian mission during the Aden Emergency. Both the ICRC and Amnesty International first became involved in the conflict in the immediate aftermath of High Commissioner Trevaskis's December 1963 declaration of a state of emergency—over a year before the Radfan campaign began. Trevaskis's subsequent crackdown resulted in numerous arrests and drew the attention of the ICRC and AI.

After his 1963 declaration of emergency, Trevaskis targeted socialist anti-colonial activists. Within a week, he had ordered the arrest of fifty-five people associated with the People's Socialist Party and deported three hundred socialist activists, many of whom were Yemeni migrant workers residing in Aden.[117] Trevaskis did not have proof of the PSP leaders' complicity in the December 10 attack, but in a controversial move he held them without charges in federation territories outside Aden city. The World Federation of Trade Unions (WFTU), which British officials perceived as a communist front organization, complained that many of those arrested were imprisoned "in bad conditions." The head of the WFTU wrote to the director general of the International Labour Organization to report that "there has been no attempt to provide any evidence that these arrested leaders had anything to do with the grenade incident" and called the arrests "a pretext to repress the anti-colonial movement" in Aden.[118] Colonial officers responded that "under the Emergency Decree, a group of five or more people constitutes an illegal gathering," and this measure therefore did not discriminate against ATUC because it applied to all organizations and individuals.[119] This excuse conveniently ignored the fact that PSP and ATUC tactics relied heavily on rallies and strikes. Trevaskis had clearly targeted both groups with these decrees.

Trevaskis's actions incited criticism in Britain. In Parliament, Labour MP Albert Oram raised concerns over whether the detainees' civil liberties had been violated. Colonial Secretary Duncan Sandys insisted that no such abuse had occurred. Sandys said that a British doctor visited the detention site three times. "I have the report from the British medical officer with me," Sandys continued. "He examined all the detainees and, apart from minor ailments of a normal character, found no signs of ill-treatment of any kind whatever."[120] Peter Benenson, on behalf of Amnesty International, added his voice to the criticism by writing to Sandys with a request that the government "permit a delegate of the International Committee of the Red Cross to inspect the prisons."[121] Trevaskis's crackdown on the PSP and ATUC raised concerns within the ICRC and Amnesty International. Both groups sought to ensure that detainees in Aden received humane treatment.

Trevaskis, however, rejected calls for an ICRC inspection of prisoners' conditions. On December 20, in response to a complaint from ATUC, the British Red Cross Society requested that Trevaskis allow an ICRC delegate to visit the prisoners.[122] But when colonial officers in Whitehall cabled Trevaskis to suggest that the federation government might "wish to consider advantage to be gained by inviting impartial investigation of this kind, which could be expected to provide unimpeachable proof that A.T.U.C. allegations are false," they received a curt reply.[123] Trevaskis insisted that "I would prefer not to press Federal Government to agree to a Red Cross inquiry" in another telegram. Instead, he chose to conduct an inquiry that he could control—he ordered a local investigation to be carried out by the colony's chief justice. The subsequent report, Trevaskis conceded, would be released to the ICRC. Unsurprisingly, the chief justice found no evidence of ill treatment.[124]

Trevaskis's reluctance to allow ICRC inspections struck Benenson as suspicious. He made his concern quite clear: "Great Britain has regularly allowed such inspection in Kenya, Cyprus and Singapore; so has the Government of Southern Rhodesia. It would be gratifying to learn that the Colonial Secretary was prepared for a visit of the International Red Cross delegate." While the chief justice's inquiry was welcome news, Benenson was not satisfied. He pressured colonial officers further, writing that the local government inquiry "does not wholly deal with the point raised in my letter." Regardless of whether the detainees had been mistreated in the past, Benenson insisted that "the important principle is that wherever there are political prisoners held without judicial process, the International Red Cross should be invited to inspect their conditions."[125]

Peter Benenson sought to establish a mechanism for independently reviewing the treatment of prisoners. An ICRC mission to monitor prison conditions and the treatment of detainees would provide the independent, impartial oversight mechanism that he desired. Toward this end, Benenson wrote to the Colonial Office again, this time asking for a private meeting to speak off the record. Benenson conveyed the news that "the International Red Cross are not 'quite satisfied with the arrangements made by the High Commissioner' and we ourselves feel that the role of the International Red Cross in Aden has not, perhaps, been considered as fully as it deserves."[126] On March 19, 1964, Benenson met with Minister of State for the Colonies Nigel Fisher and explained his views. Fisher agreed to pass the information to Trevaskis, requesting that he "consider the matter."[127] With the looming unrest in the Radfan, however, Trevaskis had other concerns.

ICRC efforts to gain access to the South Arabian Federation received renewed impetus shortly after the Radfan campaign began. Brutal British tactics provoked international censure. On May 19, 1964, with the Radfan operation in full swing, the Arab League decided to act by formally requesting that an ICRC delegation visit the "occupied Yemeni South" to investigate the humanitarian effects of British military operations in the Radfan. The ICRC was willing to help. British officials, however, were less enthused. They knew that a request from the ICRC to provide humanitarian aid in the federation would invite further scrutiny.

Britain Obstructs the ICRC

Trevaskis's large-scale detentions in the aftermath of the December 1963 declaration of emergency piqued the ICRC's interest and stimulated Amnesty International's lobbying on the ICRC's behalf, but the Radfan campaign changed the ICRC's priorities from inspecting prison conditions to caring for refugees. The ICRC was already providing humanitarian assistance in Yemen, having established a field hospital near the Yemen-South Arabian Federation border. Most Radfan refugees fled toward Yemen, and no doubt some of them encountered Red Cross workers on that side of the border.[128] For the ICRC, the conduct of the Radfan campaign reinforced the organization's interest in gaining access to the South Arabian Federation. British officials, however, chose to obstruct the ICRC's efforts in order to avoid criticism over the Radfan campaign's brutality.

On May 24, 1964, André Rochat, head of the ICRC delegation in the Arabian Peninsula, approached Britain for permission to visit the South Arabian Federation, ostensibly for a fund-raising trip.[129] British officials delayed the ICRC's request through June on the basis that "it was not possible to raise with Minister of External Affairs the question of visit to Federation of International Red Cross delegate on fund-raising mission" because all federation ministers had traveled to London for a conference on the federation's future constitution.[130] ICRC representatives accepted the explanation, but further delays soon tested their patience.

By July, the ICRC still had not received a response to its visitation request. On July 14, ICRC president Léopold Boissier wrote to British foreign secretary R. A. Butler. Boissier tactfully conveyed his exasperation, indicating that although the ICRC had been in contact with the British government since May, Britain had not yet responded to its request to send a delegate to the federation. The mission, Boissier reiterated, was "to visit the prisoners and wounded in the hands of the authorities concerned" and "to enquire on the needs, if any, of the civilian population." He also expressed his desire to "avoid any undesirable publicity." Finally, Boissier reminded Butler that the ICRC's request to act "as a neutral intermediary between two parties to an internal conflict" was "in conformity with the stipulations of the Geneva Conventions. Article 3, common to all four Conventions, authorizes the Committee to offer its humanitarian services on behalf of the victims of such conflicts."[131]

Neither British nor federation officials objected to the idea of an ICRC fund-raising trip, but they still did not want ICRC delegates to investigate prison conditions. Mohammad Farid, the federation's minister of external affairs, told Colonial Secretary Duncan Sandys that he saw no reason to object to an ICRC fund-raising trip. He also agreed to allow a Red Cross representative to assess whether the ICRC could help "to alleviate any hardship suffered by the civilian population as a result of operations in Radfan." On the issue of ICRC prison visits, Farid echoed British sentiments in saying that such an investigation "would be regarded as unwarranted interference."[132] To officials in Whitehall, the matter seemed straightforward and routine: allow the Red Cross to raise funds and assess the humanitarian situation in the Radfan, but deny ICRC access to prison facilities. Duncan Sandys, however, urged Trevaskis and Federation leaders to allow the Red Cross fund-raising visit. He worried that blocking the visit of a reputable humanitarian organization such as the ICRC would suggest that British officials had something to hide.[133] They did.

Colonial officers at the Aden High Commission stridently opposed allowing the ICRC to visit South Arabia in any capacity because of the devastation that military operations had wreaked in the Radfan. On August 20, Timothy Oates, Trevaskis's deputy in Aden, cabled Assistant Undersecretary of State W. B. L. Monson at the Colonial Office's Central African and Aden Department. Oates revealingly argued that "the Radfan operations were undertaken under British direction, and largely with British troops." As a result, "the operations themselves and their repercussions on the civil population are therefore a British responsibility." The repercussions were severe:

> H.M.G. has been obliged to take stern measures in Radfan. They have inevitably caused widespread distress and suffering and H.M.G. has come in for bitter criticism. Now that the situation is mending, I believe it would be directly contrary to H.M.G.'s interest to permit a factual exposé of the unfortunate side-effects of the Radfan campaign. Criticism of H.M.G. would be redoubled and our actions in Radfan would be used to belabor us in the councils of the world for months to come.

Oates concluded by informing Monson that Mohammad Farid and other federal ministers—who in July had not opposed the idea of an ICRC visit—had, after returning to the federation, changed their minds. Oates proposed to help Farid "draft a reply to the letter from President of the I.C.R.C. politely declining to permit the visit."[134]

Oates's opposition was not well received in Whitehall. Monson informed Oates that he was "frankly puzzled at your criticism of our position" and wrote that the "Red Cross have always been helpful to us in the past, their visits being conducted in a non-controversial manner." Because the ICRC shared its reports only with the government concerned—in this case Britain—negative findings would remain private. "On the other hand," Monson explained, "a refusal to permit a visit would be treated as evidence that allegations of brutality are true." Monson suggested that ICRC attention could be directed toward improving living conditions in refugee camps if the High Commission did not want Red Cross delegates to spend time in the Radfan itself. Monson concluded that "unless there are overwhelming reasons against such visits, we are not in general opposed to I.C.R.C. missions." But he also included a caveat: "We would not wish to strain relations with Federal Ministers if they should be firmly opposed to a visit."[135]

On August 29, Oates further explained the High Commission's position by elaborating on the damage done in the Radfan. He wrote that "operations in Radfan, by their very nature, have involved the entire population." Refugees made their way out of Radfan to neighboring territories within the federation. Federation authorities, however, decided not to establish formal refugee camps, leaving the refugees to their own devices. Oates added a positive spin to the humanitarian crisis, insisting that refugees "have been able to enjoy health and other services not available to them in Radfan. In the context of Arabian tribal life" the refugees' situation "does not present the same degree of difficulty or hardship that it would in more sophisticated urban societies." He cautioned, however, that "to anyone not versed in the grinding poverty of Radfan in times of peace, the apparent side effects of our military operations might well seem distressing" and warned that "if Rochat visited Radfan there would be the very real risk that he would find himself unable to report in favourable terms."[136]

Oates also exploited Monson's aversion to straining relations with the federation. "I confirm," Oates reported, "that Federal Ministers are firmly opposed to an ICRC visit" and "they do not wish to create the impression internationally that their social services are unable to cope with the situation" in Radfan. But Farid, although "generally agreeing with his colleagues in not wishing to allow the visit," was now reluctant to inform the ICRC of the federation's decision to refuse the Red Cross delegation.[137] Farid wanted British reassurances that if he refused the ICRC's request now, High Commission officials would not overrule his decision at a later date. On September 10, the High Commission received authorization from Whitehall to provide Farid with the assurance he desired.[138]

The federal rulers' change of heart and Farid's subsequent reluctance to notify the ICRC reflect the extent to which British High Commission officials controlled the federation's policy decisions. When approached by Foreign and Colonial Office representatives in London, federation leaders did not object to a Red Cross presence in the federation as long as the ICRC mandate did not include detention facilities. Their sudden change of heart upon returning to Aden could only have been the result of Trevaskis's and Oates's influence. Farid's hesitation to write to the ICRC and the subsequent "help" provided by High Commission officials in drafting a formal refusal—colonial officers heavily edited the content of the letter, if they did not write the entire document themselves—suggests that in practice, the High Commission held power in Aden by operating behind a federal façade.[139] The federation ministers' change of heart concerning an ICRC visit can therefore be seen as the product of British colonial administrators' influence. It was the High Commission that delayed the ICRC's visit, not the federation.

ICRC representatives were losing patience as the Radfan campaign wound down during the autumn of 1964. Farid, for instance, waited until mid-October before formally notifying the ICRC of his refusal to permit a visit.[140] By November 1964, when Radfan peoples finished negotiating peace settlements and returned to their homes, the ICRC's primary interest in the federation shifted from aiding refugees to protecting detainees. On December 29, Sir Patrick Renison, vice chairman of the British Red Cross Society, informed the Colonial Office that a group of Aden political prisoners had complained to the ICRC of torture and poor conditions.[141] British officials promptly denied the allegations—and denied that the detainees were political prisoners—but Renison persisted.

The ICRC reassured British officials that they were less concerned with the detainees' legal status than with ensuring the prisoners received humane treatment. Renison acknowledged that "on no occasion has H.M.G. admitted that the Geneva Conventions were applicable in territories under its control" and explained to colonial officers that "the I.C.R.C. have no interest in the legal status of the detainees." Furthermore, Renison argued that there was "everything to gain" by allowing an ICRC delegation to visit and "nothing to lose" because "if no visit is made it is all too likely that allegations of inhumane treatment will continue."[142] ICRC officials believed that such practical arguments might resonate with governments stretched by wartime crises better than overtures to uphold the spirit of international law. Even so, after the Colonial Office forwarded Renison's letter to Aden, Red Cross representatives waited a further two weeks without receiving a reply. Meanwhile, André Rochat decided to act on his own.

Forcing the Issue: The Red Cross Enters Aden

In February 1965, as Renison attempted to break down government obfuscation in the United Kingdom, Rochat made an unexpected private visit to Aden—over eight months after the ICRC first asked to provide humanitarian assistance in the Radfan.[143] By conducting a private visit, Rochat was not coming on a formal trip as an ICRC delegate. As a private citizen of Switzerland, he was entitled to fly to Aden on his own. He stayed for two weeks. Rochat met with Sir Richard Turnbull—who had replaced Kennedy Trevaskis as High Commissioner—Mohammad Farid, and Sultan Saleh; visited hospital facilities; and received a helicopter tour of the Radfan areas affected by the previous year's fighting.[144] In the aftermath of this visit, British officials realized that they could turn the ICRC presence into an advantage. By allowing the ICRC to provide aid and inspect prison conditions, colonial administrators could cultivate the public image that Britain was adhering to international standards of humane treatment.

Initially, though, Rochat's sudden appearance took colonial officials off guard. Don McCarthy, a diplomat since 1946, had lived and worked in the Middle East for much of his career. Having previously served in Saudi Arabia and Kuwait, he was familiar with the region. McCarthy was an insightful commentator, provided honest and outspoken assessments, and at times he criticized British policy in Aden. By 1964, McCarthy had been named political adviser to Middle East Command. He recognized the trouble that Rochat's arrival in Aden could cause: "On the main point we are in a jam. M. Rochat has forced the issue. I do not see how we could let him return without contact with the Federal Government if we are not to create a deplorable impression in Geneva and, very probably, in London." Rochat had established personal relationships with several federation ministers, which created the social expectation that he would be able to meet them again on subsequent visits. McCarthy recognized that if Rochat were permitted to visit the federation again, he would be able to meet with federation officials and potentially influence federal policy.

Although Rochat's visit seemed to cause a problem for the British, McCarthy also sensed an opportunity. "My feeling," he reported, "is that with Radfan just about over we have less to be timorous about than we had last summer." McCarthy recommended that the High Commission should instruct Farid to host Rochat, but "we should advise Farid against access to detainees at present because of the conditions in Aden prison and the tendentious and harmful political use which would be made of M. Rochat's access." Later, McCarthy suggested, "When the new detention centre is ready and, perhaps, [constitutional] conference problems are less acute, it might suit us to facilitate access." The Red Cross request therefore should be "turned aside rather than turned down."[145] By 1965, High Commission officials had begun to see the ICRC's presence as potentially advantageous but not until the potential for a negative ICRC report had abated. The end of the Radfan campaign, return of the refugees, and the opening of a new prison with modern facilities meant that the ICRC was unlikely to find violations of humanitarian rights. If ICRC delegates did find and report abuses, the public would never know because of the organization's confidentiality policy. Besides the ICRC, only members of the British and Federal governments would have access to the reports.[146] As a result, British officials allowed Rochat to file a formal trip report with ICRC headquarters and granted permission for him to make official visits to South Arabia in the future.[147]

As Rochat built a fledgling ICRC presence in the federation, Amnesty International continued its lobbying efforts on the ICRC's behalf. The October 1964 UK general election brought the Labour Party to power, led by Prime Minister Harold Wilson. As a well-connected barrister and member of the Labour Party, Peter Benenson used his connections to contact the new colonial secretary, Anthony Greenwood. Greenwood had been an MP since 1946, but this was his first cabinet post. As a member of the Movement for Colonial Freedom, however, he supported moves to grant greater sovereignty to the South Arabian Federation and other colonies.[148] In October 1965, several months after Rochat's private visit to the federation, Benenson asked Greenwood "for an invitation to the Red Cross to visit detainees in Aden." He reminded Greenwood that "there was some difficulty about an International Red Cross delegate going to Aden at all" and that once the delegate finally arrived, "he was not able to visit any of the prisons." Permitting such access would, Benenson argued, assist the ICRC and serve as "a useful political move for Britain."[149] Greenwood agreed. He believed that ICRC inspections would help Britain counter "the constant flow of false allegations about both the number of detainees and the conditions of their detention." Fully expecting Red Cross visits to confirm the benevolence of British detention procedures, Greenwood wrote effusively to Turnbull that "I very much hope that you will agree that an invitation may now be extended." From Greenwood's perspective, Britain had "nothing to hide."[150] Benenson had won over the new colonial secretary.

By the time Benenson met with Greenwood, the danger of an adverse ICRC report had already subsided with the November 1964 completion of the state-of-the-art Mansoura detention center. Deputy High Commissioner Timothy Oates noted that poor prison conditions in Aden were no longer a problem: "This source of embarrassment, with the use of Al Mansura for detainees, has been removed. So in that respect we have nothing to fear from a I.C.R.C. visit." In many federation territories beyond Aden city, however, the High Commission's concerns over prison conditions persisted. Oates suggested that "it might be politic to ask Ian Baillie to ensure that detainee conditions in the States would stand up just as Al Mansura would stand up to I.C.R.C. scrutiny."[151] But in terms of Britain's reputation, ICRC inspections of federation-administered prisons mattered little. Colonial officers wanted to avoid criticism of detention facilities managed by Britain, not the federation. If anything, Greenwood noted, critical ICRC reports might provide enough "embarrassment" to persuade federation ministers to improve substandard facilities.[152] Greenwood expected the supposedly less civilized tribal federation rulers to fall short of ICRC standards, but he was convinced that Britain treated its prisoners humanely.

With the ICRC now officially working in the federation, officials used its presence to buttress British credibility. The Foreign Office wanted to use Red Cross visits to counter anti-British propaganda from Egypt, the PSP, and the NLF. They hoped that making Rochat's visit public would help British and South Arabian authorities to "discourage those concerned from pursuing their original intention of making propaganda out of alleged inhuman conditions in the South Arabian territories"[153] After Rochat's

February visit, the South Arabian Federation press service hailed the arrival of "the delegate of the International Committee of the Red Cross" as if Rochat's visit were officially sanctioned. Federal authorities published a press release that highlighted Rochat's Radfan tour, meetings with government ministers, and time spent reviewing "the organisation of medical services in the Federal territory."[154] Rochat was even allowed to make a second trip in May 1965. British officials seemed satisfied with the scope and substance of Red Cross reports on the South Arabian Federation because Rochat had not reported any negative findings. In August, the prevailing perception at the Aden High Commission was that Rochat has "established friendly relations" and indicated that "he was given everything he wanted in the way of reception and touring."[155] But High Commissioner Turnbull was skeptical. Formerly the chief secretary in Kenya, Turnbull had been intimately involved in countering the Mau Mau uprising. After his service in Kenya, he took a position as governor of Tanganyika before it became independent. He was experienced in dealing with anticolonial nationalists and believed that winning hearts and minds was "a vain hope." Instead, for Turnbull, "wearing down" rebels and their supporters was the best way to defeat colonial insurgencies. Such methods involved treating the civilian population harshly.[156] Relying on this conviction, he explained that "I am rather doubtful whether we should stimulate the I.C.R.C.'s renewed interest gratuitously."[157]

Ultimately, the propaganda potential of ICRC visits to the new detention facility outweighed Turnbull's reluctance. On November 25, Greenwood instructed Turnbull to "secure [the] Federal Government's agreement to an invitation being formally conveyed to Rochat through normal Foreign Office channels."[158] The Whitehall official J. V. Mullin expressed the colonial secretary's sentiments succinctly: a Red Cross inquiry "would help us to counter the constant allegations of brutality and torture in detention camps, the gross exaggerations of the numbers under detention, the damaging effect of hostile propaganda over our alleged refusal to permit the International Red Cross to visit the detainees." He boasted that "we have nothing to hide: the detainees have now been transferred to the new prison at Al Mansura where the conditions are excellent."[159] Officials in the Foreign Office believed that a formal request would be more beneficial than Rochat's earlier informal visits, in which the lack of a formal report meant that colonial authorities "were unable to take any propaganda advantage of the very favourable impressions he [Rochat] formed of conditions in South Arabia."[160] British opinions had shifted from preventing ICRC visits to promoting formally documented prison inspections. Colonial administrators needed a way to counter torture allegations with credible evidence—ICRC prison inspections would provide that credibility.

Rochat visited detention facilities on two occasions in 1965, but colonial officers did not allow him to interview detainees—he could only visit the facilities and speak with British officials.[161] Despite this setback, prison inspections had finally begun. It had taken the ICRC over nine months since the beginning of the Radfan campaign and about six months since the rebels negotiated their return home. Over a year had elapsed since December 1963, when the first reports of detainee abuse surfaced and Benenson began his overtures on the ICRC's behalf. This delay had allowed colonial officials to clean up the damage they had caused in the Radfan. By November 1964, most Radfan refugees had returned home and British forces had opened a new prison with facilities capable of satisfying ICRC humanitarian standards. Turnbull had preferred to refuse ICRC access to Aden prisons but reluctantly came to understand the potential propaganda value of allowing the inspections. This approach appeared to pay off, as the ICRC's initial visits produced positive assessments that British officials could use to defend themselves against allegations of abuse. By permitting ICRC inspections, Britain cultivated a public image in which it appeared to be playing by the rules.

The Radfan campaign and subsequent refugee crisis heightened the involvement of the International Committee of the Red Cross in South Arabia. British officials knew that military operations in Radfan had intentionally created the need for humanitarian assistance. Homelessness and the threat of starvation, however, were clearly articulated and acceptable means for ending the conflict. The War Office's official report on the campaign recognized as much by noting that "the policy of 'big stick and no carrot'" had proved "to be the right one in South Arabia."[162] Officials also willingly perpetuated the humanitarian crisis by blocking ICRC access to the region. Going further, colonial officers also obstructed the ICRC's attempts to visit detainees. British authorities in Aden did not want the ICRC involved because they did not want their actions scrutinized.

When it proved impossible to prevent ICRC access to the federation, colonial administrators leveraged the organization's presence to their advantage. By early 1965, British officials had embraced High Commissioner Turnbull's dictum that it was "better to avoid than win a public controversy."[163] Colonial authorities dropped their objections to the ICRC's presence in the federation because they spied an opportunity to manipulate that presence to shield Britain from criticism. With the refugees having returned to their homes after the fighting and with the construction of a new, modern prison facility to house detainees in humane conditions, colonial officers realized that the ICRC was unlikely to find negative information to report. Officials could therefore benefit from the public image of allowing the ICRC to visit but without the danger that this scrutiny would lead to public criticism. By controlling the ICRC's physical access to these sensitive sites, British officials sought to neutralize rights activists' potentially reputation-damaging findings by restricting public knowledge of the Radfan campaign's brutality. As in the Cyprus Emergency, these efforts were reactive—they were responses to appeals by Amnesty International and the ICRC on behalf of civilians caught in the war zone. But in contrast to the reaction in Cyprus, where the creation of the Special Investigation Group epitomized the colonial government's conscious approach to undermining abuse allegations, the colonial government's response after the Radfan campaign was improvised.

Despite their ad hoc character, these efforts were largely successful. Colonial administrators in Aden were far more proactive in shielding Radfan operations from scrutiny than their counterparts in Cyprus, where Greek Cypriots' aggressive publicity efforts often caught British officials off guard. During the Radfan campaign, colonial officers succeeded in waging a brutal campaign while avoiding public controversies on the scale of the European Commission of Human Rights investigation in Cyprus, although the Radfan's relative isolation would certainly have helped reduce the campaign's public exposure. By the time the ICRC was permitted to visit prisons in late 1965, British priorities had shifted away from the Radfan toward the insurgency in Aden city. But the decision to authorize ICRC prison inspections soon raised awkward questions as ICRC delegates—and suspicious colonial officers—uncovered evidence of torture.

"This Unhappy Affair"

Investigating Torture in Aden

At two in the afternoon on July 28, 1966 Selahaddin Rastgeldi—a medical doctor and Swedish citizen born in Turkey of Kurdish parents—landed at Aden International Airport.[1] He traveled on behalf of Amnesty International's Swedish section to investigate persistent allegations that British interrogators had tortured detainees. As in Cyprus, British forces in Aden employed violent and degrading interrogation techniques to obtain vital intelligence because they lacked other means of collection and continued to believe that coercive measures were effective. The Aden High Commission's legal adviser, Hugh Hickling, had discovered evidence of these abuses as early as October 1965. But rather than stopping the practices, High Commissioner Sir Richard Turnbull, his deputy Timothy Oates, land forces commander Major General John Willoughby, and senior intelligence officials adopted the same approach taken by their colleagues in Cyprus: they sought to preserve the effectiveness of their intelligence apparatus by covering up the evidence.

Where Hickling's inquiries stalled, Amnesty International's investigation proved marginally more successful. Unlike the ICRC, which imposed a rule of silence in which delegates' reports were shared only with the British government and South Arabian Federation, AI intervened in the Aden conflict using a mixture of public activism and behind-the-scenes politicking. British officials worried that AI's inquiry would embarrass Britain by publicly exposing evidence of torture in Aden. Amnesty International's involvement in Aden pressured officials to such an extent that the Cyprus-era tactics of denial and obstruction were no longer enough to counter human rights activism.

In October 1966, Foreign Secretary George Brown responded to AI's pressure by ordering an official investigation that resulted in a series of reforms to the detention and interrogation regime in Aden.[2] Once it proved impossible to prevent a public inquiry, Aden High Commission officials appeared to co-operate with rights activists' agendas by implementing the reforms while simultaneously manipulating oversight mechanisms created by the reforms to ensure that the interrogation system remained shielded from scrutiny. Protected by the High Commission, interrogators resumed the use of torture.

"An Uncoordinated Mess": Intelligence in Aden

As in Cyprus, the British believed that intelligence was vital to countering the Aden insurgency. Obtaining intelligence on local political allegiances and insurgent activities, however, proved extremely difficult. To gather the intelligence that the counterinsurgency effort depended upon, British forces used a method considered reliable and effective in previous campaigns: interrogation. As the counterinsurgency campaign grew more desperate, the security forces clung to this last option with everything they could, even in the face of mounting criticism.

Local circumstances undermined intelligence officers' attempts to recruit spies and conduct surveillance strategies. Because of widespread hostility within the local population, intelligence officers had a difficult time recruiting spies and developing knowledge of insurgent capabilities. Furthermore, insurgents assassinated police informants, which deprived colonial forces of access to informant networks and deterred others from cooperating with the police. Wiretapping telephones proved ineffective because the insurgents did not often use telephones to communicate operational details. Surveillance operations were also unproductive—Aden's dense urban landscape made it difficult for British troops to travel unseen or remain in hideouts without being noticed by the inhabitants. The only remaining option for collecting intelligence was the interrogation of captured suspects.[3] As the former chief of staff for Middle East Land Forces recorded, "Pretty well all our information comes from interrogation."[4]

By the summer of 1965, the insurgency was gaining momentum. Insurgents frequently assassinated police informants. Special Branch officers were also vulnerable to attack because the Aden Intelligence Centre was located in the Crater neighborhood, a hotbed of anti-British sentiment. In July, insurgents killed the only two Arab officers in Special Branch.[5] On August 29, gunmen assassinated Harry Barrie, whom Major General John Willoughby, commander in chief of Middle East Land Forces, called "the mainstay in Police Special Branch & the only one left who really knew the town." By killing Special Branch's most experienced officers, the insurgents were crippling British intelligence capabilities. Willoughby lamented that Barrie's death "puts us back 6 months" in the intelligence collection effort.[6] On September 14 the NLF killed another Special Branch sergeant: "Tied up, 25 bullets, message pinned to the body," Willoughby recorded.[7] By the end of the year, Special Branch had lost half of its officers. British forces had also endured attacks on bars frequented by servicemen and the bombing of Middle East Command's officers' mess. The NLF was gaining strength while its attacks on Special Branch reduced British forces' ability to identify and capture NLF insurgents.[8] It was no surprise that the intelligence effort was, as one Special Branch officer later noted, "an uncoordinated mess."[9]

Aden Special Branch adopted an approach toward intelligence similar to that of their predecessors in Cyprus—they justified the targeted application of physical and psychological violence on detainees as a necessary and effective measure for gathering intelligence on the insurgency.[10] With the assassinations of many experienced Special Branch officers, however, interrogation in Aden was often conducted by military interrogators who were legally required to abide by the Joint Directive on Military Interrogation in Internal Security Operations Overseas. This directive had not existed during the Cyprus Emergency. Designed by Whitehall's Joint Intelligence Committee in February 1965, the directive ordered military interrogators to obey the Geneva Conventions and the laws of the territory in which they were operating. It banned "torture" but did not define what that meant in practice.[11] Furthermore, the laws of the territory in which they were operating included all emergency legislation in effect during the insurgency.[12] In addition to the Joint Directive, a local High Commission regulation entitled "Instructions on Detainees" outlined the proper treatment of prisoners during interrogation and detention. Issued on September 30, the instructions stipulated that despite the declaration of a state of emergency, Section 5 of the Aden Constitution remained in force. As a result, the document directed that "no person shall be subjected to torture or to inhuman or degrading punishment or treatment" during interrogation and detention.[13] These legal restrictions appeared to restrain interrogators from using violence against detainees, but the failure to define the practices that constituted torture meant that British forces could claim that they did not torture prisoners.

The primary venue for monitoring detainee affairs was the Review Tribunal, which adjudicated detention orders and oversaw prisoners' welfare. The tribunal did not have the power to order release, but it could recommend to the high commissioner whether to release or continue holding a detainee. Under the 1965 emergency regulations, detainees were not supposed to be held longer than six months unless the tribunal had reviewed the case and recommended continued detention. Six months' imprisonment without trial and without review of a detainee's case file made a mockery out of due process, but according to Hugh Hickling, "the detainee always had a right to appear in person before the Tribunal" to contest his detention or make complaints. In Hickling's opinion, the Review Tribunal adopted "a liberal and humane approach."[14] It was the only appeal process available.

Hickling tried to enforce the ban on torture. As High Commissioner Turnbull's personal adviser on matters concerning the drafting and application of law in Aden and the South Arabian Federation, Hickling paid special attention to monitoring detainee treatment. The son of a police inspector, Hickling had earned a law degree at Nottingham University and served in the Royal Navy during the Second World War. After the war, he worked in Malaya, where he drafted much of the legislation used during the Malayan Emergency. Later in life, he spoke of his concern that the postcolonial Malaysian government continued to use legislation that he had drafted to arbitrarily detain political opponents and rights activists.[15] He was intelligent and humane and had a strong sense of justice. He would find these qualities sorely tested in Aden. Hickling's desire to ensure that detainees were treated in accordance with the law quickly brought him into conflict with military commanders and civilian officials who were far less concerned with abiding by the legal requirements regulating detainee treatment than with collecting intelligence through the only effective means available.

Hickling's Detainee Abuse Inquiries

In October 1965, Hickling learned of several reports that detainees had been abused while in British custody.[16] But after he recommended an inquiry, Turnbull and Willoughby tried to minimize knowledge of the abuses, in public as well as within government circles. Over the next nine months, Turnbull and Willoughby successfully deflected additional pressure from Hickling, a visiting member of Parliament, and the ICRC. Willoughby sought evidence from medical professionals to prove that detainees had not been tortured. Turnbull delayed ordering a local police inquiry into torture allegations until Hickling presented compelling evidence to the High Commission's senior staff members that such abuse had occurred. When Turnbull finally initiated an investigation, he limited its scope to avoid the conclusion that torture had taken place. These efforts succeeded in containing scrutiny from Parliament and Whitehall and within the Aden High Commission.

Hickling first inquired into abuse allegations after the head of the Review Tribunal reported several instances of suspicious injuries. When he visited the Mansoura detention center in October, an army medical officer notified him "that there was some evidence of physical maltreatment of detainees arriving at the centre."[17] Hickling raised his concerns with his superiors. In an October 19 memorandum to Deputy High Commissioner Oates, Hickling noted that "evidence of the physical maltreatment of detainees" required a judicial inquiry. But no such inquiry materialized. Two weeks later, Hickling again wrote to Oates, saying that he was "very disturbed" by allegations of cruelty and torture during interrogation and expressing his conviction that every allegation of abuse demanded "a full inquiry." Three weeks later, Hickling reiterated his assessment that "a case exists for an enquiry by a judicial officer," still with no results. Hickling was not the only voice calling for an investigation. On November 14, the army's director of health services wrote to Oates that "the injuries sustained by the detainees . . . indicate that their interrogation was assisted by physical violence." Oates did not want to see the High Commission embarrassed by this assessment, nor was he interested in inviting scrutiny into the interrogation program at a time when intelligence on enemy activities was scarce. Oates again chose to evade Hickling's overtures by failing to order an inquiry.[18]

The High Commission also managed to avoid criticism from most of the Aden legal community. One reason why many Aden lawyers did not advocate on behalf of detainees, as Greek Cypriot barristers had in Cyprus, was that they often did not share Arab nationalist aspirations. South Asian migrants had settled throughout the Indian Ocean basin during the height of British imperial expansion, and Aden was no exception. As a result, most lawyers in Aden were of South Asian descent. They had little incentive to support the avowedly pan-Arab aspirations of the PSP and ATUC. A similar dynamic occurred during the Kenya Emergency, when few African lawyers existed to defend Kikuyu prisoners.[19]

When the few Arab lawyers practicing in Aden challenged British interrogation practices, colonial officials contained the attorneys' influence. Several cases concerning detainee treatment went before the Aden courts, but British officials found creative ways to evade contentious legal proceedings. In one instance, colonial officials bribed the detainees into dropping their complaints. In 1966, the chairman of the Aden Bar Council, Saeed Hassan Sohbi, agreed to defend several detainees who alleged that British forces had tortured them. But on the day of the High Court hearing, Sohbi arrived at the courthouse to discover that his clients had dropped their complaints after the High Commission offered them scholarships to study in London. The detainees were released, stayed in London for three months, and then settled in Cairo.[20]

At the international level, local lawyers in Aden could not rely on the support of a state belonging to the European Convention on Human Rights, as Greek Cypriots did during the Cyprus Emergency. Instead, the Aden Bar Council, PSP, and ATUC advocated for trades union rights protected under the umbrella of the International Labour Organization (ILO). Since the Second World War, the ILO had sponsored several international initiatives to reduce forced labor, restrain penal labor, and protect workers' freedom of association. For the ILO and Aden's anticolonial nationalists, workers' rights formed an important element of the emerging international human rights regime. British lawyers, however, convinced the ILO not to take formal legal action.[21]

Although Arab lawyers had not effectively challenged Britain through legal action, the visit of Lord Beswick, parliamentary undersecretary of state for Commonwealth relations and the colonies, brought unwanted scrutiny of the detainee situation.[22] The visit lasted from November fifth to twenty-third, and much of the agenda involved meetings with federal ministers. Discussion topics revolved around constitutional affairs and movement toward South Arabia's eventual independence, but Lord Beswick also made a point to inspect the Mansoura detention center on three separate occasions.[23] His detainee visits bothered Willoughby, who complained that "Lord Beswick who has come out here for 3 weeks to become an 'expert'" has "given the terrorists a shot in the arm. He has enforced the release of 6 Trades Union Leaders who were 'inside' for dubious activities."[24] According to Willoughby, "almost the first action of Lord Beswick during his stay here was to visit the Detention Centre, which is exclusively for members of the National Liberation Front and included at that time amongst some 90 inmates." Willoughby later fumed that Lord Beswick's visits to Mansoura were "a marvellous satisfaction to the NLF, whose morale had been severely lowered by our successes in Aden State." Lord Beswick declared the living conditions at the new Mansoura Detention Centre "eminently satisfactory," but after hearing detainees complain about their treatment, he cautioned that "there is a strong case for an enquiry by a suitably qualified lawyer."[25] Hickling agreed.

After Lord Beswick's visit, Hickling resumed his search for evidence of torture. He quickly found it. Hickling visited Mansoura on November 24, 1965. Accompanied by an Arabic-speaking colleague, he heard detailed complaints in which prisoners described specific acts of violence and degrading treatment. Hickling recorded that prisoners were allegedly "compelled to stand in the sun for hours with arms raised," had "pig's fat smeared on the body," and "a wooden stick inserted in the anus." He further reported that he had seen "evidence of violence having been applied to the bodies of some detainees, who anxiously presented scars, bruises and weals as additional testimony." Despite his own biases—Hickling described the "native histrionic ability of the Arabs" and their "tendency to dramatise and exaggerate"—he found "a substantial body of evidence" pointing toward the systematic abuse of prisoners during interrogation.[26] He then examined detainees' medical records. The documentation he found led him to conclude that "there was prima facie evidence to the effect that the handling of detainees" at the Fort Morbut interrogation center "had been accompanied by physical violence."[27] On November 27, Hickling described his findings to the High Commission's senior staff members, including Turnbull and Oates. They did not take kindly to Hickling's interest in detainee treatment. Concerned about the embarrassment that these findings could cause, Willoughby confided in his diary, "Thank God Lord Beswick isn't here any more."[28] Exasperated, Willoughby called Hickling "a great ferret" who had been "scouring around the Detention Centre" looking for evidence.[29] Hickling had uncovered evidence that senior High Commission officials and military commanders wanted to keep hidden.

Turnbull and Willoughby now faced uncomfortable scrutiny both within the High Commission and from London. On December 2, Colonial Secretary Anthony Greenwood informed Turnbull that the allegations of physical violence during interrogation required "immediate attention" and "cannot be ignored." Greenwood believed that "if the allegation of physical violence designed to extort confession were true the servicemen concerned would be guilty of a criminal offence triable by court martial." Cautiously—and perhaps hoping that he could change Hickling's mind—Turnbull asked him to review the evidence and advise the High Commission on what to do next.[30] Turnbull was under pressure. So was Willoughby. Because the abuse allegations implicated soldiers, the Ministry of Defence (MOD) got involved. Defence Secretary Denis Healey notified Greenwood that "whatever the character of the further investigations which are being made, I am sure the Commander-in-Chief should associate himself with them."[31] Willoughby faced the prospect of investigating his own troops.

Willoughby was an experienced commander in conventional warfare and counterinsurgency operations. He was a veteran of the Dunkirk evacuation during the Second World War and led an infantry company during the Korean War. He later commanded a battalion during the Cyprus Emergency. In addition to patrolling urban areas, hunting for insurgents, and dispersing riots, Willoughby's battalion was responsible for administering the Pyla Detention Camp. In his Cyprus diaries, Willoughby frequently complained of bad intelligence, inept prison officers, and poor communication with his civilian district commissioner counterpart. He understood the challenges of counterinsurgency warfare and placed a premium on the importance of good intelligence. He was also steadfastly loyal to his soldiers, even when they made mistakes—a quality that he demonstrated in abundance during his Aden assignment.[32]

Willoughby hoped to present medical evidence that would exonerate his interrogators. He ordered RAF Air Commodore William Thorburn, the senior medical officer in Aden, to examine the medical records belonging to detainees who had complained of physical abuse. Thorburn investigated the claims of twenty-one detainees. In five detainees' records, Thorburn found no evidence of injury. He identified seven detainees who were injured in transit from the Crater jail to Mansoura during an isolated incident that Hickling uncovered in October. Finally, Thorburn found that the records of nine detainees confirmed that they had been injured. He found "medical evidence that these nine men sustained injuries at Fort Morbut, or Al Mansoura or in transit between these places." Between October 12 and November 1, four of the nine detainees reported suffering ruptured eardrums, which Thorburn described as "consistent with being struck or pushed." But on December 11, when Thorburn had a specialist from the RAF hospital examine the four men with perforated eardrums, the specialist "reported that the ears of each were healthy and showed no signs of perforation or scarring." Six to eight weeks after reporting their injuries, the detainees had recovered. Using circular logic to dismiss the severity of their injuries, Thorburn concluded that "none of the injuries was gross since none persists." This statement offers a window into Thorburn's twisted logic. He assumed that torture could have occurred only if physical violence had resulted in "gross" injuries, but injuries that healed after several weeks could not qualify as gross. Furthermore, since his investigation had occurred well after the injuries were first reported, Thorburn claimed that it was not "profitable to speculate how the injuries came about." Yet he conclusively declared that there was "no consistent pattern to suggest brutal interrogation," and therefore "the evidence does not support systematic ill treatment of detainees."[33]

When Hickling examined the detainees' medical records, he arrived at an entirely different conclusion. Hickling believed that the similarity of injuries among four of nine detainees and the type of injury—perforated eardrums were known to result from blows to the head—suggested a consistent pattern worthy of a formal inquiry.[34] Thorburn's conclusion is evidence of a careful attempt to deflect Hickling's call for an inquiry and clear the security forces of any potential wrongdoing. Thorburn did not want to speculate as to how four out of nine detainees received the same traumatic injury because the likely explanation was that the perforated eardrums had occurred during interrogation. But he did speculate in concluding that systematic ill treatment had not occurred. He may have felt that he could reasonably claim that indications of abuse were not systematic if injuries had not occurred in a majority of prisoners. The word "systematic" is critical to Thorburn's assessment because it removed the possibility that violent interrogation methods were a concerted British strategy. After Lord Beswick's visit and Hickling's unrelenting calls for an inquiry, Turnbull was under pressure to order an official investigation. Thorburn's assessment led Turnbull to believe that if he ordered a limited inquiry into detainee abuse, investigators would not find sufficient evidence to conclude that torture had occurred. They would be in the clear.

Air Commodore Thorburn's medical report may have convinced Turnbull that an inquiry would not find evidence of torture, but to Turnbull's chagrin, the investigating officer confirmed Hickling's suspicions of torture rather than Thorburn's benign findings. Hickling suggested a judicial inquiry—a formal investigation by an officer of the court—but according to Hickling, "no such inquiry was held."[35] Instead, on December 26, Turnbull ordered a police investigation. A British police officer was assigned to take statements from all detainees who had complained of abuse. The officer was instructed only to record detainees' statements, not to offer analysis or conclusions. Hickling viewed the inquiry's limited parameters as evasive and deceptive: "No investigation, in any real sense of the word, had been ordered." But the investigating officer stepped beyond his mandate and provided a conclusion based on his findings. In his final report the officer suggested that detainee complaints were "more or less localized to two rooms at the Interrogation Centre and circulate round three men."[36] When the investigating officer filed his report with Hickling on March 6, 1966, Hickling cross-checked the report with existing evidence and concluded that the detainees' new statements, previous testimony, and documentation from medical records indicated "at least degrading and humiliating treatment, at worst vicious brutality." The evidence reaffirmed Hickling's opinion that the common pattern of abuse at Fort Morbut established a prima facie case against several military interrogators. Hickling recalled sardonically that "after a lapse of several months, we appeared to have established the accuracy of evidence that had already been known."[37]

As Hickling challenged his superiors over detainee abuse allegations, the military and political situation in Aden deteriorated further. Attacks against British troops escalated from 23 in 1964 to 286 incidents in 1965. The following year would be worse, as British forces faced 480 attacks. Casualties also increased from 2 killed and 26 wounded during 1964 to 6 killed and 78 wounded. In 1966, 5 soldiers died, but 216 were injured.[38] Politically, the sheikhs and sultans who dominated the South Arabian Federation ruled territories in the countryside beyond Aden city but held little sway within Aden itself. British political efforts emphasized winning support from federation leaders for a slow, evolutionary process toward South Arabian independence. In contrast, the NLF and an umbrella group encompassing various anticolonial factions, the Front for the Liberation of South Yemen (FLOSY), demanded nothing less than immediate British withdrawal. Despite a lack of political progress, the British government remained committed to transferring sovereignty to the South Arabian Federation. A February 1966 Defence White Paper outlined Britain's desire to remove its forces in Aden by January 1968, at which time the federation would achieve full independence.[39]

Meanwhile, although British forces' abusive interrogation methods had resulted in an influx of useful intelligence and the identification of approximately one hundred suspected insurgents, attacks against British forces and pro-British Arab collaborators persisted throughout 1965. Insurgents threw grenades into coffee shops and bars that British servicemen and their families frequented, while British homes and bases also often came under attack. Arms caches were hidden throughout the city, which provided anticolonial fighters with easy access to weapons. When intelligence from detainee interrogations helped to identify the locations of arms caches or known insurgents, joint army and Special Branch patrols cordoned the area and thoroughly searched the buildings. Such raids, however, often angered Adeni civilians. Riots and street demonstrations also occurred frequently.

Faced with a hostile population and an enemy that blended in with the population, British forces continued to rely on intelligence gleaned from detainee interrogations.[40]

It was in this atmosphere of periodic street fighting that the ICRC delegate André Rochat also uncovered evidence that Fort Morbut interrogators had tortured detainees. In March 1966, Rochat visited Mansoura with Don McCarthy (the Foreign Office political adviser to Middle East Command), Major General Willoughby, and a delegation of camp officials including the camp commandant, medical officer, and an interpreter. Rochat asked the detainees to speak with him if they had been abused. Approximately fifteen complained that interrogators had beaten them. For two hours, Rochat asked detailed questions to probe the validity of detainees' accounts. Ultimately he determined that about half of the complaints were invalid, but the other half appeared credible and accurate. In each case of the credible cases, detainees complained of brutal treatment during interrogation at Fort Morbut.[41] Willoughby recalled that "one detainee showed a thin 4"–5" scar behind one of his knees which he said had been made some months previously by a British soldier with a bayonet." The detainee's medical records corroborated his story, indicating that a "sharp instrument" had caused the wound. Another detainee reported being "stripped, beaten, kicked and burned with cigarettes and matches" while held at Fort Morbut. Willoughby noted, perhaps reluctantly, that "there were certainly marks on the man." Rochat interviewed five additional detainees and concluded that British interrogators had physically abused some of these prisoners as well.[42]

In his March 1966 report to ICRC headquarters, Rochat unequivocally declared that detainees had been abused. He classified the abuse according to two categories. In the first category, Rochat indicated that approximately 25 percent of detainees appeared to have been "slapped around" during interrogation in a relatively "minor" manner. But 5 percent of them had been subjected to what Rochat considered "physical torture"—a category that included practices such as forcing the prisoner to strip naked, punching and kicking his body, and beating genitals with sticks. Interrogators did not mindlessly apply wanton brutality motivated by frustration or anger. A cold, calculated logic lay behind their decisions about which detainees should face torture. Rochat found that a detainee's alleged crime did not determine whether interrogators tortured him. Many detainees had clearly been involved in bombings, murders, and other forms of violence, but they were not necessarily the ones tortured. Instead, Rochat wrote, "The use of torture is applied to those who are likely to know a lot." Rochat's findings suggested that physical abuse occurred regularly to specifically selected prisoners.[43] As in Cyprus, interrogators in Aden used torture to gather intelligence rather than as punishment or retaliation for terrorist acts—and they had grown proficient at evading responsibility for these actions.

Interrogators abused prisoners in such a way that they could maintain plausible deniability when questioned about detainees' injuries. After a May 1966 visit to Fort Morbut, Rochat concluded that among the interrogators, "many precautions are taken so that detainees cannot in any way prove that they have been maltreated." When injuries were more obvious, prison officials simply claimed that they were self-inflicted—detainees wanted to convince the ICRC that they had been tortured when such allegations were clearly false. British officers also tried to insist that detainees had sustained injuries through such mundane activities as recreational football matches or when running up the stairs. In one instance, prison officials attempted to explain how two detainees had developed similar bruises and sores on the soles of their feet. The detainees had apparently worn ill-fitting sandals during their exercise periods, when detainees were allowed a daily walk. Rochat found the officials' explanations unconvincing. "Is it not a little strange," he wondered, that on the same day, these two men developed "the same kind of injury on the soles of their feet?" He concluded "this problem [of ill treatment] is serious," and he wanted British officials to improve the situation.[44]

Willoughby and McCarthy immediately challenged the allegations. Willoughby declared that "it was not accepted that ill-treatment had taken place." He tried to undermine the credibility of detainees' testimony, reminding everybody that these were individuals detained for "complicity in violent acts of terrorism." Willoughby also suggested that detainees could have received bruises and scars as a result of "involvement in riots before arrest" or while resisting arrest.[45] To shift the burden of proof onto the detainees, McCarthy asserted that "proving a negative is always difficult." In a final passive-aggressive dismissal of the matter, McCarthy and Willoughby explained the high commissioner's willingness "to have Rochat visit Morbut at any time he liked."[46]

In keeping with the Red Cross's desire to alleviate suffering and improve prisoners' conditions, Rochat's goal was not to punish security forces for allowing abuse to occur but to prevent abuse from continuing. Rather than taking on Willoughby and McCarthy, Rochat proposed to delay visiting Fort Morbut so that British officials could stop abusive interrogations and therefore avoid receiving a negative ICRC report. He suggested to Willoughby and McCarthy that he was willing to keep the evidence quiet as long as they worked to prevent future abuse. Rochat knew of the police investigation of Fort Morbut that had finished on March 6, but he declared that he would file a positive report on Mansoura and would not directly implicate Fort Morbut before visiting it. He hinted hopefully to Willoughby and McCarthy that if he investigated at a later date, he would "find nothing to worry him."[47]

McCarthy believed that Rochat was providing a tactful "hint against recurrence," but he saw no incentive for stopping the abuses. Rochat's and

Hickling's claims increased McCarthy's suspicions that the allegations might have been true: "I must say, nevertheless, that the allegations of ill-treatment under interrogation carry some degree of conviction and I think that they should be looked at again. The Legal Adviser [Hickling], who has not recorded other comment, has remarked that he is perturbed by the frequency with which allegations of being stripped naked for interrogation are made by detainees."[48] But McCarthy was less concerned with the validity of the detainees' accusations than with the confidentiality of them. He reminded Turnbull that Red Cross reports were shared only with the government concerned. Colonial officers would, at worst, only have to explain a negative ICRC report to the British government. As McCarthy explained to Turnbull, "What Rochat is doing is to give us time to create conditions in which he could then say that there was nothing currently wrong." But in the end the confidentiality of Red Cross reporting assured that Britain would not face the specter of public humiliation. McCarthy therefore concluded that "we have nothing really to fear from the International Committee."[49] For McCarthy and Turnbull, the problem with torture allegations was not how detainees were actually treated but whether such treatment would cause a public scandal.

Turnbull knew that Rochat's reports would not reach the public, but he still had to deal with the police investigation and Hickling's constant calls for a judicial inquiry. Civilian authorities did not have jurisdiction over military personnel, so the decision to prosecute the "three men" belonged with the army commander, Major General Willoughby, and his superiors. On March 28, Turnbull instructed Hickling to send evidence of abuse—detainee statements, medical records, and the police investigator's report—to the director of Army Legal Services. Writing on July 12, the directorate informed Hickling's deputy legal adviser that, in their opinion, the evidence "did not in the main appear to substantiate the allegations." Army lawyers, however, were willing to question the three men if the director of intelligence in Aden, Brigadier Cowper, consented. But by June 1966 each of the men had been conveniently reassigned outside Aden.[50] Cowper, too, was on his way out. He had received orders reassigning him to Malaysia. July 19 was Cowper's last day as director of intelligence in Aden. To judge from the surviving records, he apparently never consented to the Army Legal Services request and neither Turnbull nor Oates pursued the issue further.[51]

Cowper's replacement, John Prendergast, was the most experienced Special Branch officer in the empire, and after his September 1966 arrival in Aden, he revitalized British intelligence operations. Prendergast had begun his police career in 1946 during the insurgency in Palestine before being promoted to head of Special Branch during the Mau Mau war in Kenya. In November 1958, after his Kenya service, he took over the intelligence effort in Cyprus. When the Cyprus Emergency ended in 1960, he served as a deputy police commissioner in Hong Kong before retiring. In both Kenya and

Cyprus, Prendergast earned a reputation as a no-nonsense, effective intelligence chief, but he also left a legacy of torture and abuse in his wake. These abuses, however, were covered up at the time.[52] With the increasingly desperate need for better intelligence in Aden, Prendergast was called out of retirement to replace Brigadier Cowper. Upon taking over in Aden, he reorganized interrogation operations by creating B Group, which was responsible for both interrogating detainees and using intelligence gained from interrogation to capture additional suspects.[53]

With Special Branch reorganized, Prendergast was not willing to allow the ICRC to interfere in interrogations and proved adept at smothering torture allegations. In September 1966, Rochat interviewed Prendergast but found him impenetrable. When Rochat asked Prendergast about prisoners' humanitarian concerns, Prendergast replied, "I do not think we have problems of this kind" and denied that interrogators obtained confessions through violence. Judging by Prendergast's answers, Rochat concluded, Prendergast was either "absolutely not aware of any detail concerning F. M. [Fort Morbut]," or he "could not answer us" truthfully. Rochat was convinced that "'reasons of state' barred us from the way to the truth."[54] Prendergast's expert obstructionism protected the interrogation apparatus from in-depth ICRC scrutiny.

Ultimately, Turnbull dealt with detainee abuse allegations by taking the minimum action possible. He chose to not fully investigate the allegations and not punish the culprits. On April 24, 1966, Turnbull wrote to the Colonial Office claiming, "I cannot put my hand on my heart and say that at no stage in the past was anyone under interrogation clouted or otherwise maltreated. It is simply not possible to check things many months old." But he reassured them that "there has never been 'torture' and I am satisfied that . . . no maltreatment takes place" at Fort Morbut.[55] Prendergast's arrival also helped reinforce the charade that torture had not occurred. By the fall of 1966, Turnbull and other senior officials such as Oates, Willoughby, and Prendergast had successfully sidestepped scrutiny of the interrogation system by Lord Beswick, Hickling, and the ICRC. Turnbull may have been satisfied, but Amnesty International's leaders were not.

Amnesty International's Intervention

As British officials in Aden tried to avoid torture controversies, Amnesty International launched a parallel process designed to pressure the government into investigating the allegations. In March 1966, as Turnbull dismissed the detainee abuse allegations and Rochat agreed to delay his visit to Fort Morbut, an Amnesty International delegation visited the new colonial secretary, Lord Longford, to demand greater government transparency over prisoner treatment in Aden. AI representatives asked that he either publish Red Cross reports on the treatment of prisoners or permit an independent investigation. However, Longford delayed. When confronted with the British government's obfuscation, AI leaders launched an investigation of their own and threatened to make the findings public if Britain did not take action to formally investigate the Aden torture allegations.

It is unclear whether Longford's delay was due to his own reticence to discuss the matter or was the result of bureaucratic tangles. Administrative responsibility over Aden was in the process of transferring from the Colonial Office to the Foreign Office, which could have contributed to officials' slow to response to AI's subsequent queries. Regardless, Eric Baker, the chairman of AI's British section, criticized the government's "dilatoriness" and later complained that "it took seven weeks to get an answer to a simple question despite repeated letters and telephone calls."[56]

The AI delegation had reason to expect a faster response because of the organization's close ties with the British government. The relationship had begun in 1962 under the Macmillan government when Amnesty leaders met with Peter Thomas, Conservative MP and undersecretary of state in the Foreign Office, to discuss the right of individual appeal under the European Convention on Human Rights. AI made the anticommunist argument that supporting individual petition and the European Court would "deprive our enemies [by which he meant the Soviet Bloc] of a possible propaganda point." This perspective left Thomas convinced that Amnesty International shared many of the government's interests. In 1963 the Foreign Office notified its overseas posts that Amnesty International was to receive the government's "discreet support."[57] Many of Amnesty's senior leaders had close ties with Harold Wilson's Labour government. Benenson was a long-standing member of the party, as were several other founding members including Peter Archer, an MP, and Elwyn Jones, MP and attorney general for the Wilson government. Lord Gardiner, named the lord chancellor in the new government, was a Labour peer, vigorous campaigner for legal reforms, and a vocal Amnesty supporter. Robert Swann, Amnesty's general secretary, was a former diplomat who understood the Foreign Office's inner workings.[58] The Labour Party's 1964 electoral victory offered an opportunity for Amnesty to broaden its relationship with the government even further.

AI used its relationship with the government to advocate on behalf of detainee rights in Aden. Throughout June and July 1966, Robert Swann exchanged a series of letters with Minister of State for Foreign Affairs Walter Padley. Swann explained that AI's mission included the protection of political prisoners detained for expressing political beliefs contrary to colonial policies, even if those prisoners participated in violence.[59] Eric Baker later clarified this position when he stated that Amnesty worked to prevent torture and support the right to trial of all prisoners—even violent ones—but would advocate for the *release* only of "prisoners of conscience" who did not advocate violence.[60] He requested that the British government take one of two actions: the government should publish the Red Cross reports on Aden or support an independent Amnesty International mission "to investigate the conditions under which persons are at present detained there under the emergency regulations."[61] Although the ICRC kept its reports confidential, it did not oppose the public release of its reports if it was the British government that published them. So far the government had refused to do so. In arguing for an independent investigation, Swann noted that Britain already faced accusations at the United Nations that colonial authorities were holding political prisoners. It would therefore be "in the best interests of Her Majesty's Government that these allegations should be investigated by an impartial and experienced organisation like ourselves."[62]

Padley denied Swann's request for an AI investigator to interview detainees, although he expressed "considerable sympathy" for Amnesty's work. First, he argued that an investigation into the reasons why authorities decided to detain particular individuals would "inevitably acquire the character of a judicial enquiry." Padley claimed that it would be unacceptable for Britain to submit itself to such scrutiny by a nongovernmental body. Second, he perceived Amnesty International as "being concerned only with the interests of political detainees." Padley denied that any such prisoners existed. Instead, he insisted that prisoners in Aden were terrorists jailed for acts of violence and "none of the persons at present detained in Aden is held because of his political opinions." AI therefore had no business interfering.[63] The government would not facilitate an AI visit to Aden. In the end, although Padley refused to allow an Amnesty delegate to meet with detainees, he did assure Swann that High Commission officials would at least meet with the Amnesty International representative, discuss detainee treatment, and answer his questions.[64]

Padley also rejected Swann's request that the government publish the Red Cross reports. He reiterated the High Commission's argument that the ICRC's presence was enough to ensure prisoners' well-being. Padley asserted that the Red Cross had already sent a delegate to Aden on multiple occasions. The delegate had investigated prison facilities and detainee conditions but had found nothing untoward. This was not entirely true, but Padley insisted that investigations into prison conditions by an esteemed international organization such as the ICRC ought to provide "sufficient assurance to the world at large" that the government's treatment of prisoners "is in fact as humane as possible." He insisted that the government was not hiding anything by refusing to publish the ICRC reports. Instead, he argued that the reports contained positive assessments of prison conditions. In a final evasive stroke, Padley informed Swann that despite the potential advantages of publishing these positive reports, British policy held that they were confidential and therefore could not be made public.[65]

Rather than backing down, AI leaders pressured the government into re-forming the treatment of prisoners in Aden. First, Amnesty committed to launching an independent investigation. The organization's Swedish section selected a delegate—Selahaddin Rastgeldi, the Swedish doctor—and the British section pledged to fund half the cost of Rastgeldi's trip. Rastgeldi planned to travel first to London and Cairo before departing for Aden. He arrived in London on July 18.[66] Publicly, Amnesty-affiliated Labour MPs pressured their party leadership in Parliament. Privately, however, Robert Swann offered a compromise.

On the day of Rastgeldi's arrival in London, Peter Archer pressured Padley during Parliament's question time. Reiterating much of the substance of the Swann-Padley private correspondence in the public domain of Parliament, Archer asked Padley "on what grounds he informed Amnesty International that he did not think it appropriate for them to send an observer to Aden; whether he will reconsider this and provide every facility for the Swedish observer who is going; and whether he will publish the recent International Red Cross reports on Aden." Benjamin Whitaker, a first-term Labour MP, supported Archer. Whitaker suggested that Padley should "place a copy of the Red Cross report in the Library" so that other MPs could examine it. Facing dissent within the ranks of his own party, Walter Padley responded with the same explanation he had offered to Swann. He argued that the detainees were being held as a result of "their implication in terrorist activities" and that none of the detainees were political prisoners, "which is the kind of detention with which Amnesty International is usually concerned." A visit by Amnesty International would therefore serve "no useful purpose." Padley also claimed that the Red Cross reports were confidential and "Her Majesty's Government are not at liberty to publish them." He said that "no report by a Red Cross representative on a visit to a detention camp or similar establishment in a British dependent territory has been published by the British Government." Archer pressed his point further, asking, "If there is nothing to conceal, would not my honorable Friend agree that the sooner the fact is confirmed by an independent observer the better?" Padley insisted that "the International Red Cross is the appropriate body" for monitoring the treatment of detainees. The answer to Archer's question, apparently, was no.[67]

Swann knew that Padley and others in government would prefer to avoid public embarrassment along the lines of Archer's tirade in Parliament, so he wrote privately to Padley with the intention of using the threat of additional adverse publicity as leverage to change government policy. "Should the High Commissioner not be able to alter the decision conveyed in your letter of 18th July," Swann wrote, "we feel it would be useful to set out our point of view in writing so that it can be published together with your reply as an appendix to Dr. Rastgeldi's report." Having established

Amnesty's willingness to publish, Swann created an escape for the government. He proposed an arrangement similar to what Rochat had offered to McCarthy and Willoughby: "If Dr. Rastgeldi is given the facilities necessary to carry out a complete and impartial investigation of the conditions of detainees, we, on our part, are prepared to delay the publication of his report for a period to be agreed, so that, if there should appear from his visit to be any matters capable of improvement these can be attended to prior to publication." In an appeal to policymakers' concern with avoiding embarrassment, Swann wrote that until the government offered evidence that British forces had not tortured prisoners, "public opinion both in Britain and at the United Nations will continue to accept prima facie the allegations of ill-treatment made on behalf of the detainees." More menacingly, however, Swann wrote that if Rastgeldi did not receive permission to visit detainees, "then the inference must be that there is something there which the authorities wish to conceal"—something embarrassing that Rastgeldi's visit could uncover.[68]

The Rastgeldi Mission

Rastgeldi's visit to Aden removed the shroud that the High Commission had used to hide abuses committed during interrogation. Through the course of his investigation, Rastgeldi found evidence that British interrogators had tortured prisoners. Recognizing the British government's concern with embarrassment, Amnesty International used the threat of publicly releasing Rastgeldi's findings to compel Whitehall into ordering an official inquiry. AI effectively employed a combination of public criticism and private lobbying to convince Foreign Secretary George Brown that it was in the government's best interest to order an inquiry.

In Aden, Rastgeldi's meetings with two civic groups and several former prisoners convinced him that an investigation was warranted. Representatives from the Graduates' Congress, an association of Adeni university graduates, described the case of Adel Mahfood Khalifa, a law graduate of Hull University and member of a prominent Aden family who worked for the South Arabian Federation government as undersecretary to the Aden chief minister.[69] One morning British soldiers broke into Khalifa's house, upended the furniture as they searched the premises, and threw him into the back of a truck. The truck drove to a camp where soldiers forced Khalifa "to stand up for seven hours" before transporting him to the Fort Morbut interrogation facility, where he was physically and psychologically abused. He was beaten until he vomited blood and held in a room with the air conditioner set at its coldest temperature, as a result of which he contracted influenza.[70] Khalifa complained that "I have never been charged with any offence. The treatment at Ras Morbut is like that of Nazis against the Jews and the French against the Algerians." Representatives of the Civil Service Association of South Arabia (CSASA), a group of Adeni government workers, also gave Rastgeldi the sworn testimony of Abdul Majid Mockbel Sabri, who "was made to undress completely and was kept in a room with the air-condition and ceiling fan switched on at maximum capacity." Sabri also reported that "a wooden stick was inserted forceably in my anus causing bleeding." Several other detained civil servants reported similar experiences of guards forcing them to stand naked in rooms with the air-conditioning at its coldest settings, beating them, and spitting on them. None of them were charged with a crime.[71] In addition to testimony from the Graduates' Congress and CSASA, Rastgeldi met with former detainees. He found some allegations unconvincing, but, like the legal adviser Hugh Hickling after his earlier inquiries, Rastgeldi found enough evidence to conclude that British officials should order an independent inquiry.[72]

For AI, the purpose of an investigation into torture allegations was not simply to determine whether detainees had been abused but to improve the administration of justice and treatment of detainees in Aden. Toward this end, Robert Swann called on Walter Padley with four proposals for improving the administration of justice and treatment of detainees in Aden. The proposals echoed many of the same issues that Peter Benenson had encountered during his trips to Cyprus in the 1950s. First, Swann suggested that every detainee should receive access to a lawyer within forty-eight hours of arrest. He recommended that the families of those arrested should be notified quickly because authorities' refusal to do so "gives rise to rumours and lends credence to stories of ill-treatment." Swann also endorsed the idea that British civilian police should replace military interrogators. Finally, he insisted that the government initiate an independent, external inquiry into the abuse allegations.[73]

High Commissioner Turnbull bristled at Amnesty's suggestions and argued that existing interrogation and detention processes were absolutely necessary to the security effort. He rejected each of Amnesty's recommendations in turn, declaring that "there can be no question of lawyer's access before interrogation has been completed." Turnbull claimed that keeping a suspect's family and colleagues in a state of uncertainty allowed security forces to collect intelligence from the detainee and act on it before his close associates could warn insurgents. Turnbull likewise lambasted Swann's idea of replacing military with civilian interrogators. He labeled "slanderous" the implication that "military interrogators are brutal and civilians not" and quipped that if the Foreign Office "could find us a body of civilian policemen from the United Kingdom trained in techniques of interrogation and fluent in Arabic we should be delighted."[74] But Turnbull's most passionate rebuttal concerned AI's recommendation for an independent investigation. Such an inquiry, Turnbull believed, would fuel NLF and FLOSY efforts "to destroy our interrogation system." Interrogators, he argued, carried out "an exacting, unpleasant and difficult task" worsened by the abuse allegations they had faced in the past. Turnbull warned that if the British government allowed inspections from Amnesty International or supported a judicial inquiry, the interrogators' morale "would be utterly destroyed." The consequences, Turnbull insisted, would be severe: "Interrogation would either have to cease entirely or become a purely token procedure yielding nothing." Without effective interrogation, security forces would have "virtually no forewarning against terrorism or information on its development." British forces would lose "the only intelligence weapon we have."[75] For Turnbull, preserving the interrogation regime was crucial to winning the war.

Military commanders agreed with Turnbull's dire assessment. Admiral Michael Le Fanu, the commander in chief of Middle East Command and Willoughby's direct supervisor, stressed that "unhindered operation of the interrogation centre in Aden is critical to all our operations." Le Fanu insisted that "interference" with the center "would result in a very sharp deterioration of the security situation" that would lead to "a more sophisticated and determined form of terrorism" if interrogation operations were disrupted. Echoing Turnbull's language, Le Fanu despaired that if the security forces lost access to "virtually our only avenue of intelligence," the consequences would be "incalculably damaging" to British interests in both South Arabia and the Persian Gulf.[76] The Foreign Office agreed, informing the MOD of their opinion that "Amnesty International requests in any form should be refused."[77] For Le Fanu, Turnbull, and Foreign Office officials, the success of the military campaign depended on good intelligence. To them, Amnesty International's scrutiny therefore undermined the counter-insurgency effort.

Despite resistance within the British government, refusing AI's dogged insistence on an investigation was not so simple. In 1965, Ian Smith, leader of Rhodesia's white minority government, unilaterally declared independence from Britain in an attempt to prevent black majority rule. Rhodesia soon became an international pariah state. In 1966, Smith ordered the arrest of four British expatriate university lecturers. In response, the British High Commission to Rhodesia formally protested against the Smith regime's actions and requested the detainees' release. Smith rejected the request.[78] By September, he had authorized police to detain for up to thirty days anyone believed to have committed—or who might commit—an act "prejudicial to the public safety."[79] Smith promptly jailed many black political leaders. Opposed to what they perceived as an illegal regime illegally detaining people for political purposes, the British government worked with Amnesty to provide financial and legal aid to the Rhodesian detainees' families.[80] Rejecting AI's request would have made Britain vulnerable to accusations of hypocrisy and could have jeopardized the government's work with AI in Rhodesia. For these reasons, Foreign Secretary George Brown believed that the government could not "return a completely negative reply" to AI's suggestions in Aden.[81]

Brown did not wish to interfere with measures that senior military leaders believed to be necessary for the war effort, but he also could not afford to court embarrassment by ignoring AI. Brown asked for Turnbull's opinion on which of AI's demands the government could accept that would inflict the "least harm" to military operations. Following the Foreign Secretary's lead, John Marnham, the Foreign Office assistant undersecretary responsible for Aden and southern Africa, conceived of two options. The government could either allow an Amnesty representative to visit Fort Morbut or "agree to an independent investigation" led by "someone of judicial standing"—a British judge or lawyer. Marnham also suggested that "an investigation of specific complaints would be better than an investigation of general allegations of ill-treatment."[82] On September 29 Brown met with Swann and Benenson. The Amnesty representatives suggested that Brown choose an external investigator suitable to Amnesty and government ministers. Brown did not commit but indicated that he would make a decision over the next week.[83]

Predictably, Turnbull found the notion of Amnesty International's involvement in an investigation to be "highly objectionable." He did, however, note that an inquiry headed by a "personal representative" of the Foreign Secretary "would of course be welcome."[84] Turnbull did not want to invite scrutiny, but he knew that he had little choice in the matter. If Brown chose a personal representative, Turnbull would have to comply with the representative's instructions. As a civil servant, he could not openly defy a cabinet secretary. However, the foreign secretary's personal representative was likely to be better disposed toward Turnbull's position than an investigator who was unconnected with the British government.[85] As a result of AI's persistence, the decision to order an inquiry was no longer in Turnbull's hands.

By October 10, Brown had made up his mind to order an inquiry by a personal representative, but who that representative might be and the scope of the investigation remained vague. George Thomson, as minister of state in the Foreign Office, met with Defence Secretary Denis Healey to obtain Healey's opinion on the matter. Thomson told Healey that the inquiry would examine only "the procedures for the arrest and detention of suspects." Healey expressed his "high regard for Mr. Benenson personally" and agreed with Brown's decision. But he also voiced two reservations. His first priority was to ensure that "efficient interrogation" continued. He did not want the investigation to undermine intelligence collection efforts. Healey was also concerned about the publication of the investigator's report. He suggested that Brown should not state in advance that he would publicly release the report. Publication would be dealt with later.[86]

Swann and Benenson grew increasingly frustrated that their private appeals had generated at most the nebulous acknowledgment of a future government inquiry. On October 11, Swann and Benenson were informed that Brown had agreed to appoint a representative to visit Aden but had not decided who the representative would be, when the investigator would travel to Aden, the scope of the inquiry, and whether the report would be released to the public.[87] In the opinion of Amnesty's leadership, Brown's offer was "a poor 'concession.'"[88] They resolved to drive the government into action. On the night of the eleventh, Swann and Benenson conferred with the head of Amnesty's Swedish section and decided to make Rastgeldi's findings public. On October 12 an official from the Foreign Office called Swann to ask if Amnesty intended to publish Rastgeldi's report. Swann said yes.[89] The following day the Foreign Office issued a new press release stating, "The Foreign Secretary has decided to appoint a personal representative to examine the procedures for arrest, interrogation and detention of suspected terrorists in Aden."[90] But for AI, it was not enough. The organization increased its campaign to pressure the government into action.

Beginning in mid-October 1966, Swann took a series of steps that caused serious public embarrassment to the British government. On October 17, Amnesty International's London-based headquarters issued a press release that announced the existence of Rastgeldi's independent inquiry into torture allegations in Aden and deplored the British government's refusal "to allow proper investigation" or improve existing detention procedures.[91] Rastgeldi appeared in a television interview on the BBC to discuss the allegations.[92] The following day, Hans Göran Franck, chairman of AI's Swedish section, wrote to Prime Minister Harold Wilson to formally condemn the "unlawful, inhuman practices of the British military personnel in Aden." Franck argued that incarcerating individuals without trial amounted to "a violation of the United Nations Declaration of Human Rights." Likewise, the use of physical brutality and torture was "unworthy of a civilized nation." He insisted that Amnesty would continue to monitor the treatment of political prisoners in Aden "until the day when they are released."[93] In an October 20 press conference, AI blamed the government for its "procrastination and vacillation" in response to AI's private overtures. Public controversy could have been avoided, Amnesty representatives declared, if the government had simply "shown 'a little bit of good will and intelligence.'"[94] The *New York Times* reported that "Britain has been embarrassed by the actions of a Swedish doctor."[95] It was embarrassment that British officials would not take lightly.

Once publicity became inevitable, British officials tried to shape the narrative that emerged in the media. The Foreign Office would not concede that their announcement of Brown's decision to send a personal representative to Aden resulted from Amnesty's advocacy on behalf of detainee rights. In its first story on the inquiry, the *Times* noted that "the decision to appoint a special representative was taken before it was known that Amnesty International was to publish Dr. Rastgeldi's report."[96] The *Times* story, however, simply reproduced off-the-record comments that Foreign Office public relations personnel purposely conveyed to *Times* reporters.[97] In private, there was no doubt about the link. A note from the MOD to Le Fanu and Willoughby expressed regret that "the Swedes have forced the issue." Officials at the ministry were "sorry we have not been able to prevent this."[98] Government officials admitted that AI's intention to publish details of Rastgeldi's visit forced the inquiry. By announcing the inquiry, however, Foreign Secretary Brown had managed to delay the publication of Rastgeldi's report. Rather than releasing the report to the public, AI's Swedish section passed it to the British Embassy in Stockholm with a note addressed to Prime Minister Wilson asking him to conduct a serious investigation of the allegations.[99] Ultimately, Amnesty's efforts compelled British officials into a course of action they had hoped to avoid.

When it became clear that they could not prevent negative publicity, British officials undermined Rastgeldi's credibility. The Foreign Office insisted that "none of the allegations made by Dr. Rastgeldi appears to be corroborated."[100] The Labour MP and Amnesty International member Christopher Mayhew, who had previously served as Minister of Defence, telephoned Peter Benenson to express his displeasure that AI had publicized the allegations. Some sections of the British press accused Rastgeldi of bias on the basis of his Kurdish-Turkish background. The MOD's British Forces Broadcasting Station accused Rastgeldi of supporting Nasser and al Asnag because of his Cairo meetings. Newspapers such as the *Daily Express* carried the story as well.[101] Government officials gave journalists nonattributable briefings in which they suggested that Rastgeldi was anti-British and "naturally" preferred the Arab cause because of his Kurdish origins.[102] This public smearing went so far that Peter Benenson felt obliged to comment publicly that Rastgeldi was "not an Arab" and that his Kurdish origins were not a source of pro-Arab bias because "the Kurds have been conducting a bitter war against the Arabs."[103] Rastgeldi also faced criticism in newspaper editorial columns. Lady Listowel, a former journalist and the wife of Labour peer Lord Listowel, found "the conditions under which Dr. Salahadin Rastgeldi carried out his investigation and reached his conclusions far less credible" than the allegations themselves. She claimed that Rastgeldi said he had investigated three hundred torture cases during his seven-day visit and asked incredulously, "How has he done this single-handed in seven days?" Rastgeldi never stated that he had investigated three hundred cases—this was a misprint in an earlier issue of the *Times*—but Lady Listowel's letter to the editor contributed to the emerging aura of disbelief that Defence and Foreign Office officials sought to create.[104]

Officials in Aden responded to the negative publicity with utter indignation. Turnbull criticized Rastgeldi's "Middle Eastern background" and called him an "unscrupulous little Levantine."[105] Willoughby perceived the shadowy hand of Cold War communism operating behind Amnesty's façade. "As we suspected," he confided in his diary after the Rastgeldi smear attempts began, "the Swedish Branch of Amnesty International which has started all this up is Communist controlled and hand in glove with Egypt."[106] Don McCarthy reiterated Willoughby's perspective. In a telegram to the Foreign Office, he wrote that "as seen from here, Amnesty International have succeeded in carrying the UAR's objective of destroying our only major source of operational intelligence nearer to achievement than ever before."[107]

As Aden officials lamented the coming inquiry, Foreign Secretary Brown selected Sir Roderic Bowen to conduct the inquiry. Bowen was a deeply religious Presbyterian, barrister, lifelong bachelor, and former Liberal Party Member of Parliament for Cardiganshire, on Wales's west coast. Upon leaving Parliament Bowen became the national insurance commissioner for Wales, where he worked until Brown selected him to conduct the Aden inquiry.[108] On October 24, two days before he left for Aden, the foreign secretary hastily brought Bowen to Whitehall to brief him on his terms of reference. Brown outlined a narrow purpose—Bowen was to examine and suggest improvements to existing detention and interrogation procedures. Brown did not authorize Bowen to investigate or offer judgment on specific allegations. The inquiry was restricted in scope to avoid the potential for embarrassing disclosures that could result in legal action against colonial officials or security forces.[109]

Rastgeldi's independent fact-finding mission and AI's threat to publish his critical report had compelled Foreign Secretary Brown to conduct a formal inquiry. British officials also shaped the narrative surrounding Brown's announcement of an inquiry by coordinating a public assault on Rastgeldi's reputation and motives. The official response to AI pressure was therefore simultaneously cooperative and manipulative. The Foreign Office cooperated with AI by ordering an inquiry into the allegations but manipulated the situation by publicly undermining AI's credibility and quietly limiting the scope of the inquiry to prevent possible future legal action against British officials.

The Bowen Inquiry

From October 27 to November 8, 1966, Bowen conducted a thorough inquiry into torture allegations in Aden. Despite his narrow terms of reference, he produced a critical report that resulted in some, albeit limited, reforms to interrogation procedures and oversight. Brown, Turnbull, and Oates appeared to act in an accommodating, transparent manner by publicly releasing Bowen's findings over the objections of senior military commanders, implementing Bowen's suggested reforms, and permitting the

ICRC to visit the Fort Morbut interrogation center. But the High Commission also manipulated the Bowen reforms by ensuring that Turnbull retained authority over interrogation oversight procedures, closely supervising ICRC visits, refusing to punish those implicated in torture allegations, and resuming the use of torture during interrogation several months after implementation of the reforms.

During the inquiry, Bowen's thoroughness worried Major General Willoughby. Willoughby complained that Bowen was "tapping the walls" of the interrogation center "to discover hidden torture chambers." Bowen toured detention and interrogation facilities, reviewed interrogation and detention files, examined medical records, and interviewed military and civilian personnel. Willoughby recalled that Bowen even insisted "on the drawer of a table that was stuck being forced open."[110] Bowen also received an unexpected piece of evidence from the editor of the *Sunday Times*. The newspaper had found a member of the British army who provided information to support Amnesty's findings. Corporal Glen Lennox served as a guard for a unit billeted near the interrogation center. One of his duties, patrolling the perimeter fence, brought him in close proximity to the interrogation center, where he could occasionally hear "pathetic screaming and howling." Upon inquiring into what had happened, soldiers assigned to the interrogation center told him "in boastful fashion, of the beatings and tortures which they had had a hand in." Lennox reported that on one occasion, he witnessed three interrogators drag a detainee into the exercise yard and beat him into unconsciousness. The interrogators revived him with a fire hose and resumed the beating.[111]

Bowen's final report balanced praise with criticism. He commended the concept of oversight that lay behind the Review Tribunal and Committee of Inspection, but he also found ways to improve their work. He determined that members of the Review Tribunal did not always receive enough information about detainees to make a well-informed judgment on whether prisoners should remain in detention. The High Commissioner's office also regularly failed to inform the tribunal whether the high commissioner agreed with the tribunal's recommendations. Ultimately, the decision to release or continue to detain a prisoner rested with High Commissioner Turnbull. But Turnbull frequently did not approve the tribunal's recommendations for the release of detainees, a practice with which Bowen was "disappointed." Bowen also criticized the practice of allowing detainees to remain incarcerated for long periods without the tribunal's review. After a detainee's initial appearance before the tribunal, Bowen concluded, he might not appear before it again even though he could remain in detention "six, twelve, or even eighteen months" after his first appearance. The detainee bore the burden of ensuring that the tribunal heard his case. Bowen considered the six-month detainee-initiated review process an unsatisfactory protection of detainees' rights. He suggested that "the Tribunal should be required to examine each case every three months irrespective of the wishes of the detainee himself."[112]

The Committee of Inspection also appeared to Bowen a useful entity for protecting detainees' rights. Consisting of two civilian Arab officials, the committee was responsible for monitoring detainee conditions and treatment at Mansoura. Bowen found that the committee was efficient and that prison authorities took its recommendations seriously. But the committee lacked authority to monitor interrogations at Fort Morbut. Bowen believed that extending the committee's mandate to include Fort Morbut was necessary for enabling it to "take note and report on allegations of cruelty and torture." In short, Bowen suggested the creation of a civilian oversight committee to monitor the treatment of detainees at Fort Morbut.[113]

Although Bowen found positive aspects of the Review Tribunal and Committee of Inspection, he criticized the length of time that detainees were held without charges. The High Commission's failure to prosecute detainees in court gave Bowen "considerable concern." After interrogation and after the High Commissioner approved a detention order, detainees simply sat behind bars to await the end of the conflict. Authorities in Aden cited several mitigating circumstances for why trials were not held. They argued that witnesses were "either too frightened or too hostile" to provide evidence required to convict suspects. Bowen recognized the "considerable strength" of arguments against trying detainees in court, but he insisted that authorities should prosecute insurgents whenever possible. He also censured the practice whereby interrogators continued to question detainees at the interrogation center after the High Commissioner had granted a detention order. A detention order was supposed to result in transfer from Fort Morbut to Mansoura. Sometimes, however, detainees remained at the fort for further interrogation. On other occasions, security forces transferred prisoners confined at Mansoura under a detention order to Fort Morbut for additional interrogation. Bowen labeled both practices "highly undesirable."[114]

Bowen saved his gravest condemnation for the way in which Turnbull and Deputy High Commissioner Timothy Oates had handled the earlier allegations of prisoner abuse that had surfaced between October and December 1965. During his investigation, Bowen received forty written complaints from detainees and several petitions from detainees' family members and civic associations. He also interviewed colonial officials and received unrestricted access to interrogation records, medical records, and other official files. Like Hickling and the police investigator before him, Bowen concluded that the interrogation center was the main site of complaint. His review led him to believe that "there was a most regrettable failure to deal expeditiously and adequately with the allegations of cruelty." Failure to take action occurred even though "the existence of serious allegations came to light" and "it was recognized that they should be investigated without delay." Bowen surmised that early investigations of detainee complaints would have either disproved the allegations or identified problems that required corrective actions.[115]

Bowen concluded his report with seven suggested improvements to existing detainee procedures designed to "enable the investigation of allegations to take place with greater promptitude and thoroughness." He proposed relocating the interrogation center to a special annex at the detention facility; recruiting civilian interrogators; caring for prisoners using civilian rather than military medical personnel; assigning a civilian High Commission official to the detention center with the responsibility of recording and investigating all abuse allegations; conducting a daily medical examination of all detainees held at Fort Morbut to prevent physical abuse; instructing the Review Tribunal chairman and director of Health Services to report all detainee complaints "without delay"; and having the High Commission prepare a monthly report on all complaints made, investigations carried out, and actions taken in response to the allegations.[116]

Brown's decision to publish the Bowen report led to a weeks-long bureaucratic battle with the army and MOD. Although Brown acknowledged that the report contained "a number of criticisms," he decided to publish the document "in its entirety" because of the Foreign Office consensus that the government would face strong public pressure to do so, particularly in the aftermath of AI's criticism.[117] Although they eventually agreed to publication of the full report, several senior officers expressed their "grave misgivings" at any hint of criticism directed at the security forces.[118] Willoughby called Bowen "the Foreign Secretary's inquisitor." The inquiry itself struck Willoughby as "a disgraceful act of Political dishonesty."[119] He confided in his diary that "I no longer trust our government to support us."[120] But what most irked Willoughby was the foreign secretary's decision to adopt some of Bowen's recommendations and publicly release the report without waiting for High Commissioner Turnbull's input—that decision was "inexcusable and unforgivable."[121] At Middle East Command headquarters, Admiral Le Fanu also chafed at Bowen's report and its potential publication, claiming that "the hands of our interrogators are clean. They need support not suspicion." Le Fanu believed that an admission of torture or physical cruelty would provide Britain's adversaries with a significant propaganda victory.[122] Within the MOD, officials worried that the report faulted "a number of authorities in Aden, including, for example, the Director of Intelligence," Brigadier Tony Cowper.[123] A few officials objected that some of Bowen's comments were "not within his Terms of Reference" and hoped to restrict publication of the report to only the part within those terms. Such restrictions would have ensured that the army's failure to act on known, credible abuse allegations remained private.[124] In the end, however, Brown determined that publicly releasing the entire report would "do less harm than the continuing cloud of allegation and suspicion."[125] Brown realized that releasing Bowen's findings in full would assuage critics such as Amnesty International—a beneficial result considering the trouble that AI had put the British government through.

Despite hostility from Middle East Command and some offices in Whitehall, the Bowen inquiry changed interrogation and detention procedures. First, it resulted in the assignment of a civilian High Commission official to the Mansoura detention center for the purpose of documenting and acting upon detainee complaints. Before he left Aden, Bowen discussed the idea with Turnbull, who implemented it immediately. Each time security forces transferred a detainee from Fort Morbut to Mansoura, the High Commission representative would ask him if anyone had tortured or beaten him or otherwise treated him cruelly. The High Commission official would then document the detainee's complaints and follow up with an investigation. He was to report the results and make recommendations for further action to the legal adviser and deputy high commissioner. The rationale for handing responsibility for detainee complaints to a single individual and collecting those complaints immediately upon transfer was that past allegations often did not surface until several weeks or months after abuse occurred. Some detainees were afraid to accuse their captors while incarcerated, whereas others complained only when their cases arrived before the Review Tribunal during the mandatory review scheduled six months after detention. On other occasions, detainees first raised allegations of abuse to third parties such as the Red Cross, sometimes well after the abuse had occurred. Bowen believed that the creation of a systematic approach to collecting, categorizing, and acting on detainee complaints would permit faster investigations of abuse allegations. Soldiers could be questioned before the end of their deployments to Aden, and medical records could be reviewed while the detainee still bore the physical marks of maltreatment.[126] In Bowen's opinion, assigning an official to record detainee allegations would help to screen out false or exaggerated complaints and would ensure that interrogators knew that someone was watching their activities.

On November 21, Turnbull implemented another Bowen-recommended reform by establishing a system for reporting detainee complaints to the Foreign Office on a monthly basis. The monthly reporting requirement meant that officials in Whitehall could ensure that all detainee abuse allegations were being addressed. Each report included an individual "case sheet" for every detainee. Case sheets indicated personal details such as the detainee's name, place of origin, and date of arrest, as well as the details of the complaint, investigation conducted, and actions to be taken by the High Commission.[127] The first report documented fifteen complaints, ten of which had first been raised to Rochat during his visits in September and November 1966. The remaining five complaints were reported to High Commission officials during November and December. Systematic documentation and review along the lines that Bowen had suggested ensured that all allegations were investigated, but these investigations almost always determined that detainee complaints could not be substantiated.[128] The inability to prove abuse, however, did not mean that abuse had stopped.[129]

The problem with these reforms was that the same officials whom Bowen criticized in his report for failing to take action to investigate past torture allegations—Turnbull and Oates—retained authority over most oversight mechanisms. The reforms did not create *external* oversight in Aden. On the basis of Bowen's recommendations, Oates oversaw the day-to-day management of the High Commission official charged with documenting detainee complaints. Turnbull oversaw the process for determining whether detainee complaints required formal investigation. Turnbull also instructed the Aden Police Criminal Investigation Division (CID) to conduct the resulting inquiries. CID's role as the investigating arm ensured that an organization independent from the interrogation and detention apparatus held responsibility for investigating abuse allegations.[130] The result was a system in which civilian High Commission staff members monitored the actions of military interrogators and prison guards at Fort Morbut and Mansoura. A November 21 directive reinforced this system by requiring the director of intelligence to investigate his own staff members in detainee abuse cases.[131] These reforms left Turnbull with wide decision-making authority over the conduct of investigations and how to respond to investigatory findings. The Bowen reforms required Turnbull to report allegations to the Foreign Office, investigate those allegations, and report the results of the investigations. But Turnbull controlled the information sent to the Foreign Office because all the government bodies charged with conducting investigations—CID, the director of intelligence, the legal adviser, and the civilian High Commission official—reported to him. The Bowen reforms established an ostensible sense of accountability in which colonial officers were expected to follow the procedures and guidelines established for them. But this accountability was largely self-imposed—officials monitored themselves, and the practice of interrogation remained an internal affair.

The only organization responsible for monitoring interrogation and detention that remained beyond Turnbull's complete control was the ICRC. As a result of the Bowen reforms, the High Commission adopted a more cooperative approach to its dealings with that organization. Turnbull established formal protocols for handling Red Cross inspections. He also allowed Rochat access to previously off-limits facilities. Beginning with his January 1967 visit, Rochat was taken to Fort Morbut and allowed to examine the premises and observe the detainees. Security forces also provided him with unprecedented access to the Mansoura detention facility. He received a list of all detainees held at the facility and was permitted to interview each detainee individually. Furthermore, Turnbull instructed the head of the detention center "to give M. Rochat any help he may require in recording allegations or complaints." Turnbull insisted that Rochat submit all future reports "in the form of a written document" and that if detainees complained to him, "a separate document should be submitted in respect of each case." All allegations were to be submitted to a designated High Commission official, the colonial civil servant A. C. W. Lee. The Lee and the assistant legal adviser maintained individual case files containing evidence on each detainee's allegations. Lee then circulated the files to the director of intelligence and director of health services for their assessment prior to final review by Oates. Oates would consult civilian attorneys from the legal adviser's office and military lawyers from Army Legal Services on actions to be taken in response to the allegations. Once Oates made a decision, Lee would inform Rochat of the outcome.[132]

But Turnbull's newly cooperative attitude toward the ICRC masked his subtle manipulation of ICRC visits. At first glance, the creation of a systematic process for handling detainee complaints would appear to have streamlined the High Commission's ability to investigate abuse allegations. But this system also meant that British officials were embedded in every step of the process and so could keep a close eye on ICRC activities. By collaborating on detainee complaints, British officials could quickly document *their* account of what had happened to a detainee in custody. Turnbull allowed Rochat to visit Fort Morbut on a regular basis, but this was done according to a schedule set by High Commission officials and only with a British official escorting him during the entire visit.[133] By contrast with the terms of his visits to Mansoura, Rochat was also prohibited from speaking to detainees held at Fort Morbut.[134] ICRC reports on these investigations, meanwhile, remained private under the ICRC's rule of silence.[135] If Rochat found evidence of torture or cruelty, colonial officials could rest assured that the Red Cross would not publicly release his discoveries. Turnbull's cooperation with the ICRC was a tactic for appearing transparent while simultaneously ensuring that he could exercise as much control over ICRC activities as possible and that the High Commission would stay as informed as possible on the allegations made against British interrogators.

Besides the ICRC's expanded access to interrogation and detention facilities, new oversight mechanisms such as the establishment of a centralized complaints system relied on the High Commission to scrutinize itself. High Commission officials, however, quickly reached the limits of their self-scrutiny. By embracing reform and opening prison facilities to the ICRC, Turnbull and Oates could avoid further public embarrassment by claiming to have implemented the required changes. But under the surface, they turned the reforms to their advantage. They managed local oversight procedures and defined the terms of the ICRC's access to Aden prisons. The significance of the Bowen inquiry therefore lies not solely in the reforms themselves but also in British officials' resilience in shielding the interrogation program: Amnesty International forced the foreign secretary to order a public inquiry after months of resistance, and the inquiry report forced the

High Commission to implement reforms, yet officials still managed to manipulate the circumstances to their advantage in order to preserve the interrogation regime.

A Hollow Victory

During the months following the Bowen inquiry, Turnbull proved willing to conform to the postinquiry reforms as long as those reforms did not obstruct the counterinsurgency effort. He restricted some activities but, with one exception, refused to punish those implicated in torture. In addition, Turnbull allowed interrogators to continue torturing detainees despite the regular ICRC visits to Fort Morbut. Amnesty International, meanwhile, faced an internal crisis that prevented the organization from continuing its watchdog role. The enforcement of compliance with the Bowen reforms was left in the High Commission's hands.

After implementing the Bowen reforms, Turnbull restricted some detainee treatment practices but only when those practices did not interfere with interrogation. For instance, in January 1967 several detainees complained that during transfer from Morbut to the detention facility, soldiers blindfolded them and beat them with rifle butts. In line with the new detainee investigation protocols, an inquiry began immediately. The army commander issued new orders to his soldiers designed to prevent such conduct in the future, but he also determined that "formal disciplinary action was not justified."[136] In February 1967, a detainee complained that guards had placed a hood over his head and pushed him against a wall. Guards commonly hooded detainees prior to moving them within the facility. A doctor examined the detainee and found that the right side of his forehead was swollen. The guard involved in the incident claimed that "the injury was caused by the detainee walking away when told to wait, and striking his head on a pillar." Although Turnbull did not challenge the guard's version of events, he instructed the guard force to stop hooding detainees except under "exceptional circumstances."[137] He proved willing to restrain some procedures such as hooding, but he and other officials refused to punish soldiers for interrogation-related transgressions.

British officials involved in the interrogation controversies described in the Bowen report escaped punishment. The three men identified during the January–March 1966 police investigation and referenced again in the Bowen report were investigated but not prosecuted. The men—named as Lieutenant Edmund Briffa de St. Vincent, Warrant Officer Second Class Joly, and Sergeant Knibbs—faced inquiries from the Royal Military Police Special Investigations Branch (SIB). SIB investigators interviewed over two hundred members of the battalion that provided guards for the interrogation center, ten doctors, seven detention center staff members, eight interrogators, and the three men themselves. Of the two hundred guards interviewed, sixteen claimed to have witnessed the use of force against detainees. The decision of whether or not to prosecute the three men put MOD officials in a bind. Gerald Reynolds, minister of defence for the army, lamented that he would face criticism regardless of his course of action. In a telling note, Reynolds wrote that if the army did not prosecute the three men, the government "shall no doubt be accused of trying to 'whitewash' the people involved." But if he proceeded with a court-martial, "there will inevitably be a lot of dirty linen washed in public."[138] Attorneys from the Army Legal Services directorate decided that the available evidence was insufficient to bring any of the three men to trial on torture charges. But army lawyers also determined that "there is *prima facie* evidence of common assault." Despite this evidence, Army Legal Services insisted "that a court martial would be unlikely to convict any of the three men" because the sixteen guard force witnesses "would be testifying to events 18 months old," and all members of the interrogation center staff "firmly denied" that detainee abuse had occurred. In a letter to the minister of defence for the army, the army's adjutant general, Major General Reginald Hewetson, concluded, "I do not propose to take disciplinary action of any kind against any of the 'three men.'"[139] Sir Richard Turnbull, Timothy Oates, and Tony Cowper—the three officials whom Bowen criticized for their failure to quickly investigate abuse allegations—also escaped formal censure.[140] The MOD and Foreign Office were willing to reform interrogation and detention practices, but legal sanctions against individual soldiers and civil servants proved unacceptable to Whitehall functionaries.

Only one colonial official faced prosecution for the abuse of detainees in Aden during the emergency. On March 29, 1967, a Fort Morbut doctor, following the Bowen-recommended procedure of medically examining detainees on a daily basis, discovered that a detainee had two black eyes. The detainee identified P. J. Hurr as the assailant. Hurr, an Arabic-speaking member of the diplomatic service assigned to Fort Morbut, was the sole civilian interrogator. He was therefore the only interrogator subject to civil law rather than military jurisdiction. Hurr admitted to slapping the detainee one time, but claimed that he slapped the man because the detainee became hysterical during the interrogation. Hurr denied that he beat the detainee and rejected the notion that his one slap could have caused the detainee's injuries. Hickling reviewed the available evidence and determined that the evidence was sufficient to file charges. On April 24, the Aden attorney general decided to prosecute Hurr.[141] Don McCarthy noted the irony that "criticisms of interrogation have included the fact that the executive investigates itself and that interrogators are military," but in this instance "post-Bowen procedure has now worked admirably at the expense of the only civilian interrogator."[142] Hurr did go to trial, but in the end the court delivered a "not guilty" verdict.[143]

Several senior officials in Aden and London saw the case as an unpleasant but useful way to prove their commitment to the Bowen reforms, but the trial amounted to no more than a token attempt to demonstrate that the interrogation oversight procedures were working. Turnbull thought it "distasteful" to prosecute Hurr for "a momentary loss of temper" but insisted that "the public interest in this case demands first and foremost that the carefully devised procedures we have ourselves elaborated to deal with these cases should be scrupulously and manifestly followed out."[144] McCarthy concurred. In a letter to Turnbull he declared that "after all your sufferings from Amnesty International, the Bowen report and so on it ill behooves anyone in London to complain about Hurr going to court."[145] Officials in London also saw the case as a vindication of the Bowen reforms. Lord Shackleton, minister for the RAF, believed that "there is clearly advantage for the Government to be seen to be following the procedure it has established for dealing with complaints by detainees."[146] In a letter to Robert Swann at Amnesty International, Minister of State for Foreign Affairs George Thomson applauded the Bowen reforms for ensuring "that a case of this kind does not get smothered."[147] The High Commission was seen to have followed the proper procedures by taking the case to trial—a perception that appeared to demonstrate that British forces took the Bowen reforms seriously. The failure to prosecute other interrogators, however, suggested otherwise.

The new procedures under the Bowen reforms did not extend to "unofficial" questioning conducted beyond the formal interrogation system. Bowen's inquiry never touched issues beyond Fort Morbut and Mansoura, such as allegations that British forces operated secret, undisclosed detention sites in Ahwar, Perim, Kamaran, and the Kuria Maria islands.[148] One paratrooper recalled how his unit interrogated recalcitrant prisoners by having them "accidentally" fall down stairs.[149] In 1967, the Argyll and Sutherland Highlanders operated according to what has infamously been termed "Argyll Law." The battalion ran an independent, unofficial interrogation center in the basement of its headquarters building. Soldiers from the reconnaissance platoon conducted raids to capture suspected insurgents and delivered them to the battalion's interrogators, who often beat information out of their captives.[150] The Royal Northumberland Fusiliers also ran their own interrogation operations. According to one officer, Special Branch intelligence collection capabilities were so degraded by the beginning of 1967 that "we were over trying to invent our own Special Branch crew."[151] Many of these makeshift Special Branch sections included soldiers who had little or no intelligence training. The Lancashire Regiment relied on the battalion band, reporting that their temporary Special Branch squad "consisted of an officer, sergeant and 10 men from the Corps of Drums."[152] Colonial authorities were not monitoring these unofficial units, but neither was the only external oversight organization in Aden—the ICRC.

Throughout 1967, the ICRC continued to visit Fort Morbut and Mansoura. The Bowen reforms had generated a sense of optimism within the ICRC hierarchy. The organization determined that Bowen's recommendations aligned closely with Rochat's desire to improve detainees' conditions by providing better oversight for interrogation operations. Rochat saw Britain's acquiescence to periodic ICRC visits to both detention and interrogation facilities as an important positive step. When he visited Fort Morbut in February 1967, he noted that abuses seemed to have declined. He reported that "despite some negative aspects, Fort Morbut is no longer a state within a state, fully autonomous. On the contrary, we feel that the situation is normalizing little by little."[153] It seemed that British forces were committed to improving detainee treatment, but Rochat's rosy view soon proved illusory.

Insurgent violence intensified during the first months of 1967, which put colonial officials under pressure to gain control of the security situation. Between January and March, the security forces noted over three hundred "security incidents"—a significant increase in insurgent activity. Beyond Aden city, British camps routinely came under mortar and rocket fire as the NLF sought to seize control of rural areas. Special Branch officers remained key targets for NLF fighters, but insurgents also targeted Arab collaborators such as federation officials and Adenis who worked for the British. The chief minister of Aden, Abdul Mackawee, died along with his three sons during a February 27 bomb blast at his home. Another bomb went off during a High Commission cocktail party in which the wives of two intelligence officers were killed. Ten others were injured. From April to June 1967, the security forces recorded more than one thousand incidents of violence. Despite some operational successes in capturing suspects and seizing arms caches, British forces struggled to impose order.[154]

In May, as the Bowen inquiry faded from public view, Rochat discovered that torture had resumed at Fort Morbut. Rochat found that "incontestably, the scandalous practices of some interrogators are starting over again." He described three categories of abuse: "violence beyond what is acceptable" during interrogation, "using soldiers to increase detainee suffering outside of interrogation," and sheer cruelty. This third category included behaviors such as breaking a detainee's nose and then spitting in his mouth; forcing prisoners to stand naked; alternating between making detainees take cold showers and ordering them to stand in front of air conditioners; exposing them to the sun for long hours; forcing them to stand on hot sand, causing foot burns; prohibiting them from using the bathroom; and beating them in the genitals. Although he did not believe every aspect of the detainees' stories, Rochat was convinced that they had not entirely manufactured allegations either. Of thirty-seven Fort Morbut detainees who had complained of their treatment, Rochat assessed that thirty had indeed been tortured. Finally, he believed that British medical officers were complicit in the torture regime. He blamed the doctors for failing to effectively treat detainees' injuries. Medical personnel preferred to believe that detainees had simply faked their injuries. In one case, two doctors had disagreed over how to treat a detainee's injuries. When they finally operated on the prisoner, it was too late—the man remained disabled for life. Rochat concluded that Fort Morbut remained "the center of the problem."[155] He realized that the British promise of routine access to Fort Morbut did not mean that British forces had abandoned torture. The reforms that had at first appeared to herald a new period of cooperation between the ICRC and High Commission merely masked the revival of brutal interrogations.

As Rochat's reports grew increasingly dour, British officials tried to undermine his assessments by discrediting him personally. One official, E. F. G. Maynard, called Rochat "neither impartial nor intellectually honest" and opined that "there seems to me clear evidence of bias on Rochat's part in that each time he comes back to Aden he finds things a little worse." Maynard seems to have discounted the possibility that things had in fact gotten worse. He charged that Rochat was "quite unable to bring a logical mind to bear on the relative credibility of terrorist detainees and British officials with a tradition of regard for human rights." Officials like Maynard embraced the assumption that Britain valued human rights and therefore British interrogators would not stoop to torture. In Maynard's calculus, the detainees, by their very status as individuals linked with terrorist acts, were untrustworthy. He continued with this logic, writing that detainees "are briefed beforehand what to say to Rochat," which meant that "when he sees a continuing theme in the stories presented to him by detainees this becomes to him evidence of a continuing pattern in our maltreatment."[156] Humphrey Trevelyan, who succeeded Turnbull as high commissioner, was more direct than Maynard. He told the Foreign Office that "we should dearly like to get rid of M. Rochat and find it difficult to believe that anyone could be worse." Trevelyan asked if the Foreign Office could "insert a little poison into the ears" of Lady Limerick or Dame Ann Bryans—two senior figures in the British branch of the Red Cross society, which was separate from but affiliated with the ICRC—to convince the ICRC that Rochat was "bringing their organization into disrepute."[157] Despite officials' efforts, Rochat retained his position. By using these personal smears to challenge his credibility, officials such as Maynard and Trevelyan appeared to cooperate with the ICRC while also undermining its efforts.

With the ICRC neutralized, Amnesty International remained the only other organization that could have maintained public pressure on the British government. Initially, AI felt vindicated by the results of the Bowen report and encouraged by the subsequent changes to British interrogation and detention policies. In December 1966, Eric Baker wrote to the group's British members that "it is clear now that it was only Amnesty's consistent pressure that finally exposed these facts to the public." Having prodded the government into an investigation, however, Baker declared that "so long as action is in fact taken to change procedures, we have no wish to pursue the matter indefinitely."[158] An editorial in the *Guardian* applauded AI's efforts and the results of the Bowen report, claiming that "the detention and 'extremely grim' interrogation centres have been opened up for a time to public scrutiny, and nothing is so strong a deterrent of torture." Triumphantly, AI leaders proclaimed that "almost all the recommendations in the Bowen Report to change existing procedures have been accepted." According to AI, all their efforts had succeeded.[159]

AI's declaration of victory in the struggle for Aden prisoners' rights masked a severe internal crisis in the organization—a crisis that reinforced Eric Baker's December 1966 pronouncement that AI had no interest in monitoring the treatment of Aden detainees indefinitely.[160] The previous month, after reading Rastgeldi's report, Benenson felt compelled to visit Aden and see the situation for himself. He returned extremely distressed with what he saw and went on "sabbatical" to a Trappist monastery in France "to think things out."[161] He was shocked that a British Labour government could have allowed such abuses to occur. Furthermore, he worried that British intelligence services had tapped Amnesty's telephones.[162] News reports suggesting that the International Commission of Jurists, headed by the Amnesty board member Sean MacBride, had received funds from the American Central Intelligence Agency (CIA) further aroused Benenson's suspicions. He began to doubt MacBride's independence from government manipulation.[163] Benenson also became convinced that Robert Swann was somehow involved in a government conspiracy, labeling him "a secret British intelligence agent." To Benenson, Swann's past record of employment with the Foreign Office contributed to his "conflict of loyalty" that jeopardized "the whole of Amnesty's future."[164]

AI also faced financial problems. Göran Claesson, from AI's Swedish section, determined that the primary problem was a "lack of goals, standards, instructions and control measures" in addition to the shocking realization that AI's London headquarters operated "without a budget."[165] AI's international executive committee convened in March 1967 to solve the crisis. The meeting marked the end of Peter Benenson's service as AI's president. Committee members voted to create the new position of director general, which would supersede that of president. Eric Baker became the first director general and implemented several financial reforms.[166] Amnesty International emerged from the crisis intact, but the organization had been too preoccupied to follow up on its initiatives in Aden.

With AI distracted and the ICRC nullified, British forces in Aden could conduct brutal interrogations without fear of public scrutiny. Torture generated intelligence that led to further arrests, but the NLF's tactic of assassinating Special Branch officers and Arabs who collaborated with the British nullified any advantage gained through interrogation.[167] By spring 1967, Adenis who had previously supported the colonial regime realized that

British forces would soon depart. Britain's Labour government had committed to withdrawing from Aden before the Bowen inquiry, but the pace of withdrawal accelerated through the spring and summer of 1967. Meanwhile, a power struggle broke out between the two competing nationalist groups in Aden, the NLF and FLOSY. FLOSY had formed around a core group including Abdullah al-Asnag and his former PSP cadres. Committed to pan-Arabism, FLOSY wanted to incorporate the Marxist NLF into its ranks, but their opposing goals escalated into violence. Each group fought the other while also continuing to attack British forces. British troops responded with curfews, large-scale security sweeps, and arbitrary searches. These measures further alienated many Aden residents.[168]

In the aftermath of the June 1967 Arab-Israeli War, Britain's situation in Aden deteriorated rapidly. British forces withdrew from federation territories in the Western Aden Protectorate. The NLF filled the resultant power vacuum. On June 20, South Arabian Federation soldiers and police mutinied. They seized several neighborhoods across the city, including the densely populated and stanchly anticolonial Crater district, where the mutineers killed twenty-two British soldiers after ambushing a patrol. Now desperate to withdraw, the British government moved the date for South Arabian independence from January 1968 to November 1967. The federal government collapsed in the wake of the June mutiny, leaving the NLF and FLOSY to fight over who would control the soon-to-be independent South Arabian Federation. By November 1967, the NLF had defeated FLOSY. British troops evacuated Aden on November 29. On the following day, the NLF proclaimed independence for the newly christened People's Republic of South Yemen.[169]

"The truth of this unhappy affair," Hugh Hickling lamented in his unpublished memoirs, "was not, in spite of all our efforts, discovered." Although Hickling, Rastgeldi, Swann, Benenson, and Bowen sought to reform the interrogation apparatus to prevent torture, other officials at the High Commission and in Whitehall obstructed attempts to restrict interrogation operations. Senior officials such as Turnbull, Oates, and Willoughby proved willing and able to cover up evidence of torture when suspicions surfaced from within the colonial bureaucracy. It was only after AI used a combination of private lobbying and public reproach to convince the Foreign Secretary to order an investigation that the High Commission had to submit to an external inquiry.

Although the Aden High Commission implemented many of the Bowen reforms, Turnbull managed the reforms in a manner that was carefully calculated to avoid interfering with interrogation—the rationale driving prisoner abuse in the first place. Furthermore, military leaders chose not to prosecute or otherwise punish the three men specified in the Bowen report. The only person who faced prosecution was the seconded diplomat, P. J.

Hurr. Incidentally, he was the only interrogator under civilian jurisdiction. Neither of the senior civil servants whom Bowen criticized—Turnbull and Oates—faced sanction. Again, Hickling said it best: "neglect, delay, and an unwillingness to seem to act in a manner detrimental to those members of Her Majesty's forces" permitted regular and systematic detainee abuse.[170]

Amnesty International's efforts proved only partially effective. Even so, AI's intervention pressured colonial officials in new ways. The group's actions were not governed by legal procedures or formal agreements such as international treaties; it could therefore act as independently as it wished, deciding to launch an on-ground investigation of its own that the British government could do little to stop. Caught in the midst of internal upheaval, AI disengaged from Aden as officials began to implement the Bowen reforms.

Colonial officials appeared to follow the post-Bowen reforms while simultaneously minimizing the impact of those reforms. Turnbull and Oates preempted future public criticism by controlling the information about detainee abuse that could become public. The High Commission regulated all forms of oversight except ICRC visits, but the ICRC's rule of silence meant that its reports remained confidential, to be shared only with the British government. Turnbull had effectively covered his tracks. The only variable that he could not control was Amnesty International. AI's internal crisis, however, allowed Turnbull to manipulate the Bowen reforms without concern for external intervention beyond the already neutralized ICRC.

"A More Talkative Place"

Northern Ireland

As the Union Jack came down over Aden for the final time in November 1967, Britain's departure from the "last post" of empire seemed to mark an end to two decades of counterinsurgency warfare. The Colonial Office had disappeared as an organ of government when it was merged with the Foreign Office in 1968. The British army also seemed to have left colonial wars behind as it focused on other challenges such as Cold War commitments in West Germany. But by August 1969, the army was again operating against insurgents. This time, the conflict occurred within the United Kingdom—in Northern Ireland.[1] This chapter does not seek to offer a comprehensive assessment of all human rights activism during the Northern Ireland "Troubles"—a topic that would warrant a separate book in its own right—but rather to explore the dynamics of cooperative manipulation beyond the traditional colonial context.

British efforts to hide controversial practices and deflect allegations of brutality persisted into the Northern Ireland Troubles even though British policymakers viewed the conflict differently than they had past colonial wars. When the British army intervened in the conflict in August 1969, commanders did not simply copy colonial practices. But after communal violence and attacks on soldiers had escalated sharply throughout 1970 and into 1971, British forces resorted to harsher tactics such as internment without trial and "interrogation in depth." Such methods included the use of torture during interrogation. Allegations of torture soon surfaced and led to widespread condemnation from members of civil society and human rights groups both in the United Kingdom and abroad. Confronted with this criticism, British officials—including the prime minister, cabinet ministers, civil servants, and soldiers—engaged in practices reminiscent of the Cyprus and Aden conflicts by ordering limited government inquiries, the results of which cleared interrogators from accusations of having committed torture and absolved them from legal liability. But the public consequences of these actions in Northern Ireland differed from those of past colonial campaigns.

In Cyprus and Aden, British officials were largely able to contain the relatively limited efforts of small groups of activists. But during the Troubles, rights activism and legal proceedings that challenged British actions were pervasive and persistent as the war generated a host of government inquiries and investigations conducted by human rights organizations.[2] As one officer said of the intense public scrutiny surrounding the use of brutal interrogation methods, "The world has become a more talkative place than it was when we used these techniques in colonial situations."[3] The growing global human rights consciousness of the late 1960s and 1970s combined with Northern Ireland's constitutional position as a constituent member of the United Kingdom contributed to the relative intensity of public criticism. In this context, internment and interrogation in depth stimulated the first sustained public debate on counterinsurgency practices in Britain since the end of the Second World War. Criticism of British rights violations therefore had a greater effect on the Northern Ireland conflict than the wars in Cyprus and Aden.

From Civil Rights to Civil War: The Army's Deployment to Northern Ireland

After the 1919–21 Anglo-Irish War, in which the predominantly Catholic southern counties of Ireland obtained Dominion status, the six Protestant-majority counties of Northern Ireland remained a province within the United Kingdom in which Catholics faced systematic discrimination. The 1920 Government of Ireland Act established a devolved Parliament seated at Belfast's Stormont Castle. Catholics tended to oppose the Stormont regime and were labeled "nationalists" as a result. Commentators on the Troubles often distinguish between nationalists and republicans in that republicans were willing to use organized, deadly violence to achieve nationalist political aspirations. A similar distinction existed on the Protestant side, as unionists favored the existing arrangement. They dominated Stormont and wished to remain part of the United Kingdom. "Loyalists" were those unionists willing to resort to violence by targeting nationalists and republicans. Gerrymandering of electoral districts ensured that Protestants received greater per capita political representation than Catholics. Discrimination also occurred in the allocation of socialized council housing. Catholics often received smaller houses for larger families, whereas smaller Protestant families generally received larger or newer homes. Prejudicial employment practices meant that the civil service and police were overwhelmingly Protestant and large industrial employers tended to hire Protestants.[4] Such discrimination fueled a sense of disaffection among Catholics.

It was in this context of legalized political, social, and economic alienation that the Northern Irish civil rights movement emerged. During the 1960s, opposition to the Stormont regime coalesced among the political left. The primary organization formed to advance civil rights for Catholics was the Northern Ireland Civil Rights Association (NICRA). NICRA activists had close ties to a variety of left-wing organizations such as the Northern Ireland Labour Party, Communist Party of Northern Ireland, National Council for Civil Liberties, and Campaign for Social Justice. Inspired by the civil rights movement in the United States and the protest movements that swept across Europe and the world in the summer of 1968, these activists saw themselves as part of a global struggle against capitalism and imperialism.[5]

In August 1969, a confrontation over a march in Derry triggered the deployment of the British Army.[6] During the summer of 1969, local officials decreed that unionist groups were allowed to march, but Catholic marches were banned. Adding further insult to the Catholic community, authorities approved the march route for a unionist group called the Apprentice Boys—a route that would take fifteen thousand Protestant marchers through part of the Catholic Bogside neighborhood. But as the march began, Catholics barricaded the entrances to the Bogside. Catholic and Protestant factions clashed as the Royal Ulster Constabulary (RUC), Northern Ireland's police force, struggled to maintain order. Several RUC armored cars were firebombed. Both sides threw stones and bricks at each other and the police as RUC constables repeatedly charged with batons and shields to disperse the rioters. Catholic neighborhoods set up barricades, creating "no-go" areas for the police. Stormont's laws no longer applied in these areas as republican paramilitaries such as the Irish Republican Army enforced law and order. On the morning of August 14, RUC inspector general Anthony Peacocke officially requested that the army deploy to Londonderry. On the night of August 14, six people died as Protestants went on a rampage, burning entire streets in some Catholic areas. Attacks in Belfast increased as well, resulting in the August 15 decision to deploy troops to both Londonderry and Belfast.[7]

British officials were reluctant to get involved in Northern Ireland because many perceived the province as a backwater with a complex web of local problems that could easily turn into a quagmire. The Northern Ireland conflict posed a unique challenge for Britain. According to the historian Stephen Howe, the British presence in Ireland resulted in "a strange constitutional hybrid" that was neither a colony nor entirely integrated into the United Kingdom.[8] Formally, Northern Ireland was a constituent member of the United Kingdom, but this arrangement did not necessarily produce a shared identity. Republicans compared the province to a colony, perceiving themselves as freedom fighters struggling against imperial oppression.

Unionists were emotionally attached to the idea of being British, but other Britons did not necessarily share their sympathies. For many in Westminster, the idea of being British involved the demonstration of perceived British cultural values such as tolerance, respect for the rule of law, and moderation. To many in Britain, Northern Irish unionists appeared to have merely appropriated the symbols of this "Britishness." Unionists could therefore fall into the cultural category of "Irishness," which many Britons viewed as uncivilized, irrational, and dominated by emotions and passions. Ulster Protestants were therefore often regarded by their British countrymen as backward and foreign.[9] Direct involvement was not desirable. As then home secretary James Callaghan described it, the government's goal was to avoid being "sucked into the Irish bog."[10] Despite their preference for nonintervention, Westminster became increasingly involved in Northern Irish affairs once the decision was made to deploy the army.[11]

When the army was first ordered to intervene in August 1969, military leaders recognized the conflict's distinct circumstances and ensured that the army did not immediately and unthinkingly deploy its full repertoire of repressive "colonial" counterinsurgency methods.[12] As violence persisted into the summer of 1970, the army's approach toward the local population hardened.[13] The army's presence initially appeared to have calmed the situation, but officials at Stormont and Westminster had different expectations for what the army was supposed to achieve. Relations between the troops and civilians on both sides entered a honeymoon period. For Protestants, the army's presence indicated protection and security against Catholics. For Catholics, it meant that the overwhelmingly Protestant, and therefore biased, RUC was no longer patrolling the streets. Within government circles, however, the situation was more acrimonious as the army's deployment exposed Stormont's and Westminster's divergent objectives. Stormont officials wanted the army on the streets so that they could "beat the Micks," as the journalist Desmond Hamill described it, whereas Westminster wished to restore law and order rather than keeping the Micks down. These divergent goals led to confused and contradictory expectations. Soldiers were deployed to "aid the civil power," but military commanders soon came to see their mission as far more than simply restoring order. To many commanders, the army appeared to have walked into the middle of a civil war.[14]

The violence of 1969 roused old enemies while creating new ones. During the summer, the nationalist paramilitary Irish Republican Army (IRA) advocated political change but stopped short of ordering armed resistance. For many nationalists, this apparent failure to defend Catholic communities undermined the IRA's credibility. The IRA's shift toward political action bothered some of the organization's members. Tensions between these dissidents and existing commanders persisted into the winter, when the IRA Army Council voted to increase the organization's involvement in politics by allying with left-wing nationalist groups. This decision infuriated the dissident faction. On December 18, dissidents established the new Provisional wing (PIRA). The Provisionals believed that political action was meaningless without military force to back it up. In the future, the Provisionals would not back down as the Official IRA had.[15]

Nationalist violence resumed after a March 1970 commemoration of the 1916 Easter Rising—a failed revolt in which republicans seized several key buildings in Dublin—triggered three days of riots in Ballymurphy. These riots marked the first major confrontation between soldiers and Catholics. On June 27, an Orange Order parade passed near Belfast's Catholic Short Strand neighborhood. A loyalist mob threw petrol bombs at a Catholic church, but PIRA responded with a vigorous defense.[16] The ensuing five-hour gun battle, in which four Protestants were killed, achieved legendary status in republican circles. Many people fled the fighting. Working-class areas of both religions were hit hardest. In Belfast alone thirty thousand to forty thousand people left their homes to live in areas filled with their coreligionists. Areas of mixed religion declined, creating sharp divisions between Catholic and Protestant zones.[17]

Confrontation in the Short Strand soon led to an operation that transformed the conflict and ended the army's Northern Ireland honeymoon—the Falls Road curfew. After the Short Strand gun battle, British forces moved to capture a shipment of weapons believed to have been delivered to an Official IRA safe house in the Lower Falls. On July 3, soldiers moved into the area to seize the weapons. But as troops left the neighborhood, an incensed crowd gathered and began throwing stones. PIRA initiated gun battles in the Falls Road and Ardoyne, while the army deployed three thousand soldiers to the area and imposed a three-day curfew. During the curfew, troops searched house by house with little regard for civilian property. Homes and businesses were damaged, and in the rioting that followed, four Catholics were killed. Although PIRA had done the fighting in areas around the Lower Falls, the arms dump seized by the British army actually belonged to the Official IRA. In total, five people were killed, fifteen soldiers and sixty civilians injured. The curfew proved militarily successful in that the army found over a hundred guns and homemade bombs, 250 pounds of explosives, and 21,000 rounds of ammunition, but the operation failed politically. Desmond Hamill noted that after the curfew, relations between the Catholic community and the army changed from "sullen acceptance to open hostility."[18] PIRA recruitment soared and the officials were galvanized into action.

The army adopted harsher methods as violence escalated, including methods reminiscent of past colonial campaigns. By the end of June, the General Officer Commanding in Northern Ireland (GOC NI) relaxed restrictions on rules of engagement concerning the use of lethal force. The 1970 Conservative Party electoral victory also influenced army attitudes.

Catholics, the *Guardian* reported, insisted that "the Army attitude has toughened since the Conservatives came to power at Westminster" in July and that "soldiers are now going out of their way to provoke Catholic anger, and then responding harshly to it."[19] Efforts to improve security proved counterproductive as cordon-and-search operations, checkpoints and roadblocks, fortified army garrisons placed in disputed neighborhoods, and aggressive responses to riots further alienated many Catholics.[20]

The army's response to weekend riots in November 1970 was indicative of this get-tough approach. After rioters wounded forty-one soldiers and marines with petrol and nail bombs, commanders declared that in future confrontations where petrol or nail bombs were used, "soldiers will not wait to see what is thrown at them before responding with rifle fire." The journalist Simon Winchester, sitting in the audience at the press conference where the announcement was made, noted that "all the army's public relations staff at the conference were nodding in agreement with the CO's phrasing and it must be assumed that this is the army's latest attitude and one important aspect of its uncompromisingly tough policy."[21]

In March 1971, Northern Ireland's prime minister, James Chichester-Clark, further emphasized the new approach by insisting that he would station army units in all "riotous and subversive enclaves." The use of any lethal weapons by rioters—including guns, explosives, and petrol bombs—would result in what the *Guardian* described as "rigorously conducted house-to-house searches." The reporter Simon Winchester noted "the new tactics, which finally confirm that the army's role in Northern Ireland has changed, probably irreversibly, from its initial 'peace-keeping duties' to the more familiar colonial role of 'internal security.'" Inevitably, Winchester concluded, "massive security operations similar to the controversial Lower Falls 'curfew' of last July will follow any more disturbances."[22]

The army's adoption of stronger security measures played into republican paramilitaries' hands. As troops implemented tougher policies, Catholics grew increasingly suspicious of the army and therefore provided less intelligence and support to it than they had before. Many Catholics viewed the army's actions as repressive and turned against it as republican paramilitaries increased their hold on Catholic neighborhoods through intimidation campaigns of their own. The result was what the scholar Aaron Edwards termed "a negative equity" in which each side's actions reinforced antagonism.[23] Loyalist opinions hardened as well. In the July 1970 UK general election, the outspoken and controversial unionist Reverend Ian Paisley was elected to Westminster. On March 18, 1971, three thousand loyalists marched on Stormont demanding that Stormont leaders deal more effectively and vigorously with IRA terrorism. On March 31, Chichester-Clark resigned as Northern Ireland's prime minister.[24] A stronger crackdown was coming.

Internment and Interrogation

The violence convinced many unionist politicians that stronger security measures were necessary—particularly the authorization of internment without trial. On July 8, 1971, Stormont prime minister Brian Faulkner's tenuous attempt to compromise collapsed after British troops killed two rioters in Derry. Republican sympathizers demanded a public inquiry into the deaths, arguing that the men were unarmed when they were shot, but the government refused. In response, Stormont MPs from the moderate nationalist Social Democratic and Labour Party (SDLP) walked out of the assembly.[25] Faulkner faced severe political pressure from unionists, including many within his own cabinet, to order internment without trial.[26]

Military leaders were skeptical about the use of internment. Chief of the General Staff, General Sir Michael Carver, and GOC NI Lieutenant General Sir Harry Tuzo believed that internment would prove counterproductive. They thought it would merely antagonize nationalists. Faulkner also did not like the idea of internment for similar reasons but felt that he would lose unionist support if he did not adopt a tougher stance on security policy. Tuzo suggested that a large-scale, but limited, arrest operation of around a hundred key suspects would provide a useful alternative to internment. Such an operation would strike a strong blow against the IRA without appearing overly aggressive toward the Catholic community.[27]

On August 5, despite misgivings from army leaders, Faulkner asked Prime Minister Edward Heath for authorization to implement internment beginning on August 9. Heath acquiesced. Code-named Operation Demetrius, the internment plan involved large-scale battalion-sized sweeps of Catholic neighborhoods and targeted 464 IRA suspects. Troops searched houses with little regard for the occupants. The civil rights activist Michael Farrell recalled that soldiers beat up almost everyone who had been arrested. During the sweeps, the army captured 304 of the 464 individuals on their target list.[28]

The order to begin internment without trial was enough to antagonize the Catholic community, but the army's use of bellicose tactics exacerbated the situation. On August 17, the nationalist MP John Hume complained of soldiers' brutal treatment of civilians during searches of the Bogside in which three men were hospitalized with head injuries suffered during their arrest. One journalist concluded that "the army has tended to avoid confrontations, but it now appears to be adopting more aggressive tactics, charging and firing rubber bullets into the bystanders."[29] The army began dispatching larger patrols, but larger patrols led to more frequent and intrusive house searches, which created more confrontations with Catholics, therefore inflaming Catholic resentment. The IRA, particularly the Provisionals, also contributed to the army's increased "toughness." As they entered Catholic neighborhoods in Londonderry, soldiers faced petrol bomb attacks, stoning, and gunfire. On the day that Operation Demetrius began, five soldiers were shot and seven injured by stones or petrol bombs. One soldier was partially blinded after being hit in the face with a petrol bomb.[30] Over the next four months, thirty soldiers, eleven police, and seventy-three civilians died in gun battles, riots, or bombings. The army reacted by interning more suspects. Some were guilty, but many of those arrested were innocent—a fact that fueled the perception that, as one Catholic activist put it, the army was adopting "tougher and tougher methods of repression."[31]

To make matters worse, internment spread beyond the major cities of Belfast and Derry. Prior to the introduction of internment, paramilitary violence and civilian confrontations with security forces occurred regularly in Belfast and Londonderry, but midsize population centers such as Lurgan, Newry, Dungannon, and Enniskillen remained more peaceful. Tensions between nationalists and unionists existed in these towns, but Catholics were not alienated from the Stormont government to the extent that their coreligionists in Belfast and Londonderry were. Violence that had taken place prior to August 1971 occurred within confined areas. In Lurgan, for instance, preinternment clashes were limited to a five-mile radius. After internment was implemented in these areas, however, civil disobedience activities skyrocketed and nationalists flocked to join local civil rights organizations. Some neighborhoods went so far as to organize paramilitary groups to defend their communities from security force intrusions. The spread of internment policies to the Northern Irish countryside and smaller towns increased nationalist disaffection throughout the entire province.[32]

Internment without trial alienated the vast majority of Catholics because it appeared to herald a return to past discriminatory practices. The army did not target any Protestant areas, and no Protestant paramilitary suspects were interned until February 1972. On August 12, Oliver Napier of the cross-community Alliance Party told the Irish News that "every Northern Ireland Catholic sees the introduction of internment as the abandonment of the reform programme and the end of the principle of equal citizenship."[33] On August 16, the SDLP launched a civil disobedience campaign that linked protests against internment with the housing problems that had originally motivated the civil rights movement. The campaign's purpose, the Stormont MP and SLDP member John Hume explained, was to demonstrate that Stormont no longer governed with Catholic consent. Organizers planned to hold rent and rate strikes in which occupants of publicly owned homes and tenants who paid rates to local authorities would refuse to pay. Denying revenue to the government in this way was meant to demonstrate the Catholic community's rejection of Stormont's authority. In Derry, activists claimed that 90 percent of Catholic households participated in the strike. In Dungiven, only 2 of 850 tenants paid their August rent. The chant of "no freedom, no rent" became the strikers' rallying cry.[34]

Although internment stirred Catholic ire, the treatment of prisoners during interrogation aroused the nationalist community's deepest anger.[35] Although many of the 464 men on the army's initial arrest list were exposed to what the journalist Ian Cobain described as "systematic rough-handling," several internees had been identified for what MOD called "interrogation in depth." Security officials believed that those preselected for interrogation in depth possessed vital information about the IRA's organization and methods. Ultimately, RUC Special Branch, with military assistance, carried out these interrogations on 14 people through a special program code-named Operation Calaba.[36]

Operation Calaba was built on the edifice of previous interrogation programs such as those implemented in Cyprus and Aden. In 1956, the military reorganized interrogation with the creation of the Interrogation Branch—a Joint Service organization with direct access to the War Office's Director of Military Intelligence. Interrogation Branch primarily existed to conduct training courses. As a result of operational experiences in colonial conflicts such as Kenya and Cyprus, Interrogation Branch began to incorporate interrogation methods designed for antiterrorism and counterinsurgency operations. In 1965, Interrogation Branch was renamed the Joint Services Interrogation Wing (JSIW). In addition, the Joint Intelligence Committee codified a set of interrogation principles—but not specific practices or procedures—in the Joint Directive on Military Interrogation in Internal Security Operations Overseas, dated February 17, 1965. These principles included the imperative of undermining a prisoner's confidence and resilience through "psychological attack," although the directive also prohibited "outrage upon personal dignity" and "humiliating and degrading treatment." The joint directive was amended in 1967 after the release of the Bowen Report on interrogation in Aden, but the principle of psychological attack remained in effect.[37] Throughout the 1960s, the JSIW was the sole organization capable of conducting interrogation training for internal security operations. After the Bowen Report recommended that civilians conduct interrogation during internal security operations, the JSIW established a training program in which military interrogators taught other military personnel as well as police Special Branch officers.[38]

On March 17, 1971, RUC Special Branch requested interrogation training to improve its poor intelligence capabilities. The army was already aware of Special Branch's limitations. In 1969, General Sir Geoffrey Baker, chief of the General Staff, visited RUC Special Branch and wrote a report on his findings. He described Special Branch as "badly organised and run, with the result that speculation and guesswork largely replace intelligence."[39] Baker was experienced with the workings of intelligence organizations in colonial counterinsurgency campaigns as a result of his experience as chief of staff to the director of operations during the Cyprus Emergency. He was also author of the Baker Report on the Cyprus Emergency, the findings of which had influenced the colonial administration's response to the Aden Emergency of 1963–67. On March 24, 1971, MOD and MI5 representatives decided to send a member of the JSIW to Northern Ireland as an adviser and several others to provide training assistance. Between four and six officers as well as six to eight NCOs participated in the training and advisory mission. Under the terms of the arrangement, military personnel were not to participate in interrogations. They were only to advise and provide technical support to the RUC.[40]

To some senior officials, the introduction of internment provided an excellent opportunity to begin using interrogation in depth. The vice chief of the General Staff informed Defence Secretary Lord Carrington that internment, and the subsequent interrogation of interned prisoners, would yield vital intelligence. On August 10, Carrington and Home Secretary Maudling approved the military's advisory role in RUC interrogations. MOD arranged for twelve military interrogators to provide "technical support and advice on all aspects of the operation," in which twenty RUC Special Branch interrogators would conduct interrogations. An additional twenty-six constables from the RUC Special Patrol Group guarded the facilities.[41] In a prophetic gesture considering the criticism that soon followed, the GOC NI informed RUC Special Branch that as long as they conducted interrogation in depth using only techniques taught by the military, the army would try to prevent the RUC from being blamed if interrogations generated negative repercussions. The commander of the military interrogation unit advising Special Branch was informed that humiliating and degrading treatment, violence, and torture were prohibited. In addition, all detainees were to be treated humanely and in accord with the principles of Article 3 of the 1949 Geneva Convention concerning treatment of prisoners of war. These guidelines, however, were open to broad interpretation with minimal ministerial oversight.[42]

Interrogators used interrogation in depth to impose their will on detainees by controlling every aspect of their existence. The process relied upon five techniques designed to disorient and frighten the prisoner while also heightening his desire to communicate with other humans. The first of these was wall standing, in which detainees had to stand facing a wall with their arms raised. This method was supposed to reinforce discipline and control over the detainee while also protecting guards from any violence committed by the detainee. The second technique was hooding—the placement of a black hood over the detainee's head for prolonged periods—and was designed to limit his ability to interact with other prisoners or identify where he had been taken for questioning. The third technique, subjecting detainees to white noise, made communication between detainees more difficult, kept them psychologically disoriented, and increased their sense of isolation. Fourth, detainees were deprived of sleep to further disorient them. Fifth, interrogators imposed a bread-and-water diet. Bread and water were offered at six-hour intervals, which contributed to a detainee's disorientation—when they were fed more than three times a day, it would have been difficult for detainees to keep track of the time, therefore obscuring how long they had been in captivity.[43]

In addition to the five techniques, prisoners chosen for participation in Operation Calaba were often subjected to physical violence. Between questioning sessions, RUC officers forced detainees to stand at a wall, often in stressful positions. Those who failed to stand in the desired position were beaten. These sessions often lasted for hours. Documentation suggests that for eleven of the prisoners, time spent standing at the wall varied between nine and forty-three hours. During these standing sessions, detainees were prohibited from sleeping or speaking. When one man, James Auld, asked to use the toilet, he claimed that the guards denied permission and slammed his head against the wall as punishment for speaking. The detainee Patrick McClean said that he was never permitted to use a toilet. Prisoners, he said, simply had to "wet where we lay."[44]

The Interrogation Inquiries

An outcry ensued as details of these interrogation practices became public. Civil society groups such as the Association for Legal Justice spoke out about "new and disturbing elements" in the army's treatment of prisoners and recorded statements from several detainees for possible use in future legal proceedings. On August 12, Catholic clergymen such as Cardinal Conway, archbishop of Armagh, called for an investigation as well. A series of reports in the *Irish News* and *Irish Press* publicized specific allegations of brutal treatment related to the use of the five techniques. By August 20, press reports had convinced Prime Minister Heath to order an inquiry.[45] The Irish government also pressured Britain to take action. On August 25, the Republic of Ireland's ambassador formally requested a full and impartial inquiry. For the Irish government, no inquiry could qualify as "impartial" unless it included a non-British member. The Irish ambassador informed British officials that his government would also consider formal action at the European Court of Human Rights. Caught off guard by the Irish position, British officials asked to be informed prior to any Irish government public statements on the interrogation issue.[46]

Heath and Maudling responded to this uproar in a manner similar to that of their Cyprus and Aden counterparts: once scrutiny proved impossible to avoid, they ordered an inquiry that was limited in scope and consisted solely of British officials. On August 31, Home Secretary Maudling appointed a three-person committee of inquiry under Sir Edmund Compton, the ombudsman for Great Britain and a former Treasury official. The other two members were Edgar Fay—a judge—and Dr. Ronald Gibson, who was chair of the British Medical Association. The committee's terms of reference were to investigate allegations of physical brutality committed by security forces against prisoners arrested after internment, including allegations concerning detainees subjected to the five techniques and prisoners who had been arrested under internment but who had not faced interrogation in depth. These terms of reference, however, included only arrests conducted on August ninth—the first day of Operation Demetrius.[47]

The committee's composition, terms of reference, and findings led Northern Irish nationalists and many in the Republic of Ireland to view the Compton inquiry as nothing more than a whitewash. The Dublin government and nationalists in Northern Ireland opposed the committee on the grounds that the inquiry was not held in public, the committee members did not have full judicial powers, witnesses would not have legal representation, and the committee was composed solely of British officials. As a result of nationalist dissatisfaction, all but one of the prisoners subjected to interrogation in depth boycotted the committee by refusing to testify. The committee's equivocal findings, finalized on November 3, 1971, made matters worse. Compton did not address the legality of the five techniques but instead tried to differentiate between "brutality" and "ill treatment" by casting these terms as different degrees of physical abuse. The committee found no evidence of physical brutality but determined that physical ill treatment had occurred in the form of forced wall-standing, white noise, sleep deprivation, and the bread-and-water diet.[48] This determination was unsurprising considering that the committee defined "brutality" as "an inhuman or savage form of cruelty" that "implies a disposition to inflict suffering, coupled with indifference to, or pleasure in, the victim's pain."[49] This extreme definition of the term allowed the committee members to avoid labeling interrogators' actions brutality. The committee also determined that interrogations had followed the appropriate guidance regarding the treatment of detainees in a humane manner. The Compton report noted, however, that these rules were open to interpretation: "The precise application of these general rules is inevitably to some extent a matter of judgement on the part of those immediately responsible for the operations in question."[50] Ultimately, the report admitted that British forces had conducted physically violent interrogations through the use of the five techniques but simultaneously denied that these measures constituted brutality or torture.

Prime Minister Heath also criticized the report but from a different perspective—he believed that it went too far in accusing the security forces of ill treatment. Heath called it "one of the most unbalanced, ill-judged reports I have ever read" and considered the number of ill-treatment cases "trivial" considering that more than three hundred people had been arrested. He further complained that the report did not put these actions into the "context of the war against the IRA." In Heath's view, the allegations should have been dismissed because the prisoners had refused to testify before the committee. Finally, he believed that "the consequences of this report" would "infuriate Commanders in the Army, undermine the position of the soldiers and RUC in Northern Ireland, and produce grave international repercussions for us."[51] Heath felt that any admission of culpability would undermine the security effort. He saw the war as "not only a military war but a propaganda war."[52] To him, the Compton inquiry was supposed to shield the security forces from enemy propaganda, not expose them to it.

Hostile press coverage at home and abroad, the potential for a European Court of Human Rights case, and Heath's angry reaction to the Compton report resulted in Home Secretary Reginald Maudling's November 16, 1971, announcement of a second inquiry. Criticism of interrogation practices from Irish media—in both north and south—had commenced soon after the implementation of internment, but the British press largely ignored the stories. This situation changed in September 1971, when the *Sunday Times* "Insight" team began publishing articles critical of the government's internment and interrogation policies in Northern Ireland. Defending the decision, Maudling told the Commons that "the principles applied in the interrogation of suspects in Northern Ireland and the methods employed are the same as those which have been used in other struggles against armed terrorists in which Britain has been involved in recent years." Even so, he continued, "Her Majesty's Government consider, however, that it would be right now to review them." After Maudling's announcement, the Labour MP James Callaghan immediately compared the situation to Aden and pressed Maudling on whether the security forces in Northern Ireland had exceeded their authority by employing interrogation techniques that were not permitted under the 1965 Joint Directive on Military Interrogation, which had been amended in 1967 after the Bowen Report. Maudling assured Callaghan that "I am entirely satisfied that the methods used have not gone beyond the rules."[53] The person selected to chair the inquiry was Lord Parker, the recently retired Lord Chief Justice of England who was at times criticized during his tenure for demonstrating a tendency to side with the executive in criminal cases.[54] Parker was directed to examine the extent to which British forces' conduct in Northern Ireland conformed to established practices and whether such practices were legal.

As the Parker inquiry commenced, officials in the Ministry of Defence decided that the best way to convince commission members to allow interrogation in depth to remain in use was by casting the techniques as security measures rather than "softening up" procedures.[55] On November 23, Permanent Undersecretary of Defence Sir James Dunnett convened a meeting with the vice chief of the General Staff, Sir Cecil Blacker—who had commanded British forces in the 1964 Radfan campaign—as well as the director general of intelligence and intelligence coordinator Sir Dick White, a former head of MI5. At the meeting, they discussed the extent to which the five techniques formed an integral part of the interrogation process. Each official believed that interrogation in depth was vital to the collection of useful intelligence and had proven valuable in past conflicts such as Cyprus and Aden. They determined that the three primary techniques of wall-standing, hooding, and white noise were essential elements of the interrogation process because the measures both served security functions—so that a detainee could not identify other detainees or harm interrogators—and helped to soften up prisoners prior to questioning.[56] White described how the techniques satisfied the vital psychological attack aspect described in the Joint Directive on Military Interrogation. The prisoner, according to White, "must be brought to realise that he is now entirely alone, and above all, completely severed from connections with his former comrades who can neither help him further nor condemn him nor exact reprisals upon him." Despite their effectiveness for softening up prisoners prior to interrogation, White believed that techniques such as wall-standing, hooding, and white noise should be portrayed solely as security measures. MOD should not, in his view, present the procedures to the Parker commission as softening-up measures because using the techniques for reasons other than security could "lay us open to possible charges of physical assault."[57]

When published in March 1972, the Parker inquiry's results exposed a division within the committee over whether the five techniques were justifiable. In addition to Lord Parker, the commission also included two privy counselors: the Conservative MP John Boyd-Carpenter and Lord Gardiner, the reform-minded Amnesty International supporter and Labour peer. They were appointed to consider whether to amend interrogation procedures for terrorism suspects. After reviewing twenty-five written representations from the public and ten from organizations and hearing oral testimony from thirty-three witnesses, the committee members could not reach a consensus on their final recommendations. Instead, they submitted two reports—a majority report written by Parker and Boyd-Carpenter as well as a minority report authored by Lord Gardiner.[58]

In the majority report, Parker and Boyd-Carpenter asserted the legality of the five techniques and claimed them to be morally justified because they proved effective. Parker and Boyd-Carpenter concluded that interrogation was legally limited to the procedures authorized by the Joint Directive on Military Interrogation. They insisted that the directive "fairly set out the obligations under the Geneva Convention and those to whom it is addressed are enjoined to comply with them." In addition, the majority report excused the use of the five techniques because "there is no doubt that when used in the past these techniques have produced very valuable results in revealing rebel organisation, training and 'Battle Orders.'" The authors of the majority report claimed, "We do not subscribe to the principle that the end justifies the means," yet that was the position they adopted. Parker and Boyd-Carpenter implied that the techniques themselves were not the problem. Instead, they were morally questionable only if used improperly. According to the report, "There is of course a danger that, if the techniques are applied to an undue degree, the detainee will, either consciously or unconsciously, give false information." But, the authors argued, "subject to proper safeguards limiting the occasion on which and the degree to which they can be applied, [they] would be in conformity with the Directive." The morality of the issue lay in the "intensity with which these techniques are applied and on the provision of effective safeguards against excessive use." According to the majority report, as long as the techniques were effective in extracting information and used safely, their use was justifiable.[59]

Lord Gardiner's minority report highlighted the interrogation methods' illegality, thus undermining Heath and Maudling's attempts to justify interrogation in depth with the Compton and Parker inquiries' benign findings. Gardiner agreed with Parker and Boyd-Carpenter that the joint directive was the key document requiring interpretation, but he argued that "if any document or Minister had purported to authorise them [the interrogation procedures], it would have been invalid because the procedures were and are illegal by the domestic law and may also have been illegal by international law." Gardiner noted that the joint directive instructed interrogators "to follow the principles laid down in Article 3 of the Geneva Convention" of 1949, which prohibited "outrages upon personal dignity, in particular, humiliating and degrading treatment." Under domestic law, Gardiner continued, "where a man is in lawful custody it is lawful to do anything which is reasonably necessary to keep him in custody but it does not further or otherwise make lawful an assault." Wall-standing and forced hooding amounted to assault and were therefore "both a tort and a crime." Deprivation of sleep and food restrictions fell into the same category unless authorized as a punishment under prison rules. Gardiner surmised that "no Army Directive and no Minister could lawfully or validly have authorised the use of the procedures. Only Parliament can alter the law. The procedures were and are illegal."[60]

In addition to the legal considerations, Gardiner rejected the five techniques because of their effects on detainees' health and well-being. Regardless of the information obtained through the techniques, Gardiner argued, these methods created enduring, traumatic health problems. Eleven of the fourteen detainees subjected to the techniques reported physical injuries. Medical evidence indicated that at the noise level used during interrogation—eighty-five decibels—a temporary 8 percent loss of hearing was possible, as well as some permanent hearing loss. Mentally, medical research suggested that sensory isolation could induce artificial psychosis or episodes of insanity. Such psychological distress could last for months or years after interrogation. In addition, Gardiner noted, some of the men subjected to the five techniques had appeared cooperative from the beginning, suggesting that interrogation in depth was unnecessary. Information could have been obtained without resort to such harsh measures.[61]

Because he deemed the five techniques to be illegal, Gardiner concluded that the most pressing question was whether to recommend that Parliament pass legislation authorizing them. His answer was a resounding no because of the moral dilemma inherent in the authorization of a degree of physical violence against suspects who might or might not be guilty of a crime and because medical evidence indicated that the threshold at which physical or mental trauma could cause lasting harm varied tremendously from person to person. In essence, the techniques could not be used "safely," as the majority report suggested.[62]

The Parker inquiry majority report and the Compton report revealed the persistence in government of a predilection for avoiding accountability and denying wrongdoing. The Compton report called interrogation methods ill treatment but fell short of labeling them brutality or torture. The Parker majority report justified inflicting physical harm in the course of interrogation on the basis of doing it safely and within limits. This interpretation placed the onus of authority on lower levels of leadership, such as local commanders at the interrogation facility. By doing so, the majority report interpretation removed superior officers' responsibility for subordinates' actions. It absolved senior military and civilian leadership from accountability for possible "mistakes" that could result in serious injury to a prisoner or death. Similar attempts to justify British actions in Cyprus, in response to the Greek government's applications under the European Convention on Human Rights and the Famagusta and Geunyeli incidents, as well as the decision to deny Red Cross access to the Radfan and the Bowen report in Aden, demonstrated a distinct continuity in the way in which successive governments—from Whitehall to the colonies—responded to public criticism over wartime rights violations. The tendency to disguise brutality by denying wrongdoing, protecting members of the security forces from legal censure, and manipulating public perceptions was not limited to colonial counterinsurgencies.

Despite the Compton and Parker inquiries' limitations, the subsequent reports signaled a significant difference between the colonial wars of the 1950s and 1960s and the campaign in Northern Ireland. The Compton and Parker inquiries further stimulated public discussion of state violence. For the first time since the Second World War, soldiers, bureaucrats, elected officials, and informed members of the public engaged in a substantive and persistent public debate over counterinsurgency violence such as coercing civilians and torturing prisoners. When compared with past colonial campaigns, holding two parliamentary inquiries within six months on the same issue—especially one as sensitive as interrogation—was unprecedented. Nor did these reports end public debate. Instead, Lord Gardiner's minority report emboldened the government's critics. Lord Parker and Boyd-Carpenter argued in their majority report that as long as the techniques were used safely, they could continue. The minority report challenged the validity of those rules and the majority report's assumption of safety so vociferously that opponents of the government's interrogation practices launched renewed criticisms. In Northern Ireland, Gerry Fitt, of the nationalist SDLP, called the minority report a "damning indictment" and suggested that many of those interrogated would pursue legal action against the British government. In Ireland, "the Parker proposals were rather coldly received by members of all three parliamentary parties, who felt that condemnation of the in-depth interrogation techniques should be complete and unequivocal."[63]

Criticism from the Irish government and Northern Irish Catholics left far-reaching repercussions. Irish government officials believed that public opinion in the republic was such that people would not accept government inaction over internment and interrogation. Catholics in the north also wanted the Irish government to do something. The Compton and Parker reports had not improved this perception. On November 30, 1971, after the Compton report's release, the Irish cabinet resolved to take action against Britain for violating the European Convention on Human Rights. Such action, said Hugh McCann, secretary of the Republic of Ireland's Ministry of External Affairs, "would inevitably make the British much more careful in their handling of detainees" and "would make it more difficult for them to make progress in the direction of a military solution." If the British believed that a military solution was obtainable, McCann warned, "there would be less incentive for them to take unpalatable political action."[64] In December 1971, the Irish government lodged an interstate application against the United Kingdom with the European Commission of Human Rights. Application 5155/71, as the Irish complaint was known, alleged that by ordering internment, Britain had violated Articles 5, 6, and 14 of the convention, which protected an individual's rights to liberty, a fair trial, and to be free from discrimination.[65]

Faced with the prospect of proceedings before the European Commission of Human Rights and the deteriorating political situation in Northern Ireland, Heath spied the opportunity to appear cooperative by making a political concession on the use of the five techniques while retaining the option of employing harsh methods in the future. He believed that the situation in Northern Ireland was desperate and required drastic action to alleviate nationalist resentment over the internment and interrogation controversies. With the publication of the Parker reports, Heath admitted that the five techniques had been officially approved. Furthermore, he stated that the techniques would no longer be used. The Joint Directive on Military Interrogation was also updated, with a new version approved by the Joint Intelligence Committee in June 1972. Yet despite these admissions, Heath insisted that the five techniques had saved innocent lives. He refused to concede that the techniques were illegal or inappropriate.[66] In doing so, he had done what his forebears in Cyprus and Aden had not—placed specific legal restrictions on the use of force during interrogation operations.

Heath had multiple reasons for banning the five techniques.[67] One reason was the desire to prevent interrogators from facing domestic prosecution. The Parker Committee had concluded that at least some of the techniques amounted to common assault under English law. But in Northern Ireland—which was a separate jurisdiction—the techniques were the subject of a pending court case. Since they did not wish to prejudice the decision of a court, the Parker Committee did not offer a judgment on the techniques' legality in Northern Ireland.[68] Although the committee managed to sidestep the question of legality in Northern Ireland, Heath's government had to consider the potential consequences if the court case ended unfavorably. Cabinet Secretary Sir Burke Trend summarized the government's available options: "If the recommendation [of the majority report] is not accepted, those taking part in the [interrogation] operation would be legally at risk." Interrogators could therefore face civil claims and, possibly, criminal charges. If the government did not accept the majority report, ministers who wished to legally protect members of the security forces implicated in the interrogation controversy would have to justify their actions by overcoming Lord Gardiner's powerful moral objections. "The implication of this dilemma," Trend continued, "is that Ministers might well feel that they could not for some time . . . authorise the use of techniques of this kind in support of interrogation."[69] MOD and Home Office officials also sought to protect servicemen who could face civil or criminal charges. MOD and the Home Office agreed that in civil actions, the government would "continue to protect the identities of the individuals concerned and their costs and any damages would be paid by the Crown." In terms of criminal cases, "if the possibility of a more serious penalty such as imprisonment was involved we should resort to an Act of Indemnity on an individual basis."[70] Interrogation could continue, but to prevent potential legal action against individual interrogators, the five techniques would have to go.

A public repudiation of the techniques would undermine allegations at the European Commission of Human Rights that the British government had officially tolerated torture. By disassociating itself from the techniques, Britain could better defend its position at Strasbourg. According to the attorney general, "the risk that the Commission would, at the end of the day, make a finding, on the complaint of ill-treatment, which would seriously affect the reputation of Ministers or the Army would accordingly be substantially reduced." Disclosing sections of the joint directive, newly revised on the basis of the Parker report, to the European Commission would provide "substantial evidence of practical steps taken by the United Kingdom administration to prevent ill-treatment, which would rebut the allegation of official toleration."[71] When the Irish government's case was finally heard in 1976, British lawyers argued that the application should be terminated because Britain had already conducted an inquiry and Heath had already ordered an end to the five techniques.[72]

There was also the practical consideration that much useful intelligence had already been collected. Internment and interrogation in depth led to an intelligence boon as interrogators could now use the information they had received from questioning captured IRA operatives to identify Provisional and Official IRA organizational structures, operational plans, possible targets, and capabilities. One MOD assessment determined that approximately 75 percent of weapons found since the introduction of internment came from information gathered directly or indirectly through interrogation in depth and that "ten of these men provided large quantities of information of great value to the security forces."[73] In short, Operation Calaba was a massive military success. By the time the five techniques were abandoned, the security forces had developed a much stronger understanding of the threat they faced and could act against both the Provisional and Official IRA much more effectively than previously. The government had realized by December 1971 that a military solution was not sufficient—a political arrangement was necessary to end the violence. Heath had to accept the sectarian divide as a fact of life and find a political solution that incorporated sectarian politics into a mutually agreeable framework.[74] By acquiescing to nationalist sentiments on the issue of interrogation in depth, Heath could appear willing to compromise on political initiatives.

Heath's search for a political solution suffered a tragic setback when, on January 30, 1972, soldiers from the Parachute Regiment killed fourteen people during a Londonderry protest march in one of the most significant incidents of the Troubles—Bloody Sunday. After the introduction of internment, NICRA had planned a protest march in Derry. The march attracted thousands of participants. British troops expected that the march would descend into violence because IRA attacks had recently increased. Between January 28 and 30 alone, soldiers had encountered thirteen shooting incidents in Londonderry.[75] Early in the day, some protesters initiated violent confrontations with soldiers, including stone throwing and rifle fire. By late afternoon, the senior British commander, Brigadier MacLellan, authorized Lieutenant Colonel Derek Wilford of First Battalion, the Parachute Regiment, to mount an arrest operation targeting violent protestors. Wilford dispatched his support company to conduct the arrests, but the company went beyond the area in which MacLellan had authorized Wilford to make arrests. Upon entering Rossville Street, soldiers from the support company opened fire on several unarmed civilians who had not been involved in the earlier confrontations.[76]

Coming in close succession after internment and the interrogation controversies, Bloody Sunday further alienated Northern Irish nationalists, infuriated many in the south, and provoked paramilitary attacks from both factions of the IRA. Father Edward Daly, a Catholic priest in Derry, recalled that many Catholic youths grew increasingly militant as a result of Bloody Sunday.[77] In the words of Sean Collins, a ten-year-old boy who witnessed the events, "Bloody Sunday changed a lot of things for me. Up to that day I always believed that the British Army were the good guys. All my innocence in that regard was lost. I had no illusions about what the Brits were like and I had no sympathy when I heard subsequently about British soldiers being shot."[78] Another witness, Pauline Ferry, described her recollection of the events as "just the shock of it all—the shock that live gunfire was used at such a big crowd."[79] Shock and alienation could also describe the reactions of many in the republic. Jack Lynch, Taoiseach of the Republic of Ireland, declared a national day of mourning.[80] On February 2, nearly twenty thousand people gathered around the British embassy in Dublin. Some within the crowd firebombed the embassy.[81] In addition, both the Provisional and Official IRA launched offensives against British forces. An Official IRA attack on the Parachute Regiment's headquarters in Aldershot killed 7 people. Meanwhile, the Provisionals planted a car bomb on Donegall Street, in Belfast's city center, that killed 6 and wounded 150.[82]

The subsequent inquiry into the Bloody Sunday killings—the Widgery Tribunal—made matters worse. Intended to determine the sequence of events that led to the shootings and led by Baron Widgery, the Lord Chief Justice of England and Wales, the tribunal appeared to many nationalists as nothing but a whitewash. It took evidence from 117 witnesses but did not interview any of the victims who remained hospitalized and did not inspect the scene of the shootings. Such inquiries were supposed to ascertain the truth through an "inquisitorial" rather than "adversarial" investigation. But the Widgery Tribunal relied on army lawyers and attorneys representing the victims to gather and present sources of evidence for the tribunal members to consider. This procedure approximated the adversarial interactions of a courtroom trial rather than a supposedly objective inquiry into the facts. Many nationalists interpreted this procedural anomaly as a sign of the tribunal's bias in favor of the army. Furthermore, Widgery refused to consider some evidence offered by the victims' lawyers because the evidence did not meet the rules for the admissibility of evidence. For example, he rejected over 700 eyewitness statements from civil rights marchers because they had been submitted too late. Instead, he relied heavily on soldiers' testimony. Unsurprisingly, this favoritism toward the army infuriated nationalists. The location of the tribunal also fueled nationalist animosity because tribunal sessions were held in the predominantly unionist town of Coleraine—thirty-five miles from Derry.[83] The tribunal's final report exonerated the soldiers. Many mainstream British media outlets parroted the official line that the demonstrators and republican paramilitaries were to blame for the tragedy of Bloody Sunday.[84]

In March 1972, Heath imposed direct rule on Northern Ireland because Stormont leaders proved unwilling to make the reforms necessary to stop the fighting. In the aftermath of Bloody Sunday, Stormont prime minister Brian Faulkner told Heath that internment should continue as a means of promoting security. Faulkner also opposed political moves such as guaranteeing Catholic inclusion in government and did not want to pursue the option of a coalition unionist-nationalist government. When the SDLP refused to participate in any cross-party conference toward a political agreement, Heath lost confidence in the Stormont system. Stormont now lacked legitimacy not only in the eyes of the Catholic minority but also from the perspective of the British cabinet. On March 22, the cabinet voted to suspend Stormont's authority and placed a secretary of state for Northern Ireland in charge. Heath appointed William Whitelaw as the first Northern Ireland secretary. Whitelaw had a seat in the UK cabinet and ruled through the Northern Ireland office.[85]

Violent clashes throughout the months following Bloody Sunday, which culminated in the Provisional IRA's July 21 "Bloody Friday" bombings in central Belfast, elicited a large-scale military response from the British army. The following day, two thousand soldiers raided Catholic neighborhoods throughout Belfast. Two days after the bombing, General Sir Michael Carver, chief of the General Staff, decided that the Bloody Friday attacks amounted to a significant escalation. He decided to mount Operation Motorman—the reopening of no-go areas in nationalist neighborhoods. Motorman was the largest military operation since the 1956 Suez Canal intervention. It involved 22,000 regular army troops and 5,300 from the Ulster Defence Regiment (UDR).[86] The goal was to tear down barricades erected in Catholic no-go areas as well as Protestant neighborhoods, opening those areas to increased army patrolling and government control. Paramilitary resistance from both nationalist and unionist groups was minimal, although British troops had anticipated fierce firefights. Within days, Motorman had succeeded in its objective of reestablishing control over the no-go areas.[87]

Security operations throughout 1971–72 severely strained both factions of the IRA. Internment without trial provided British forces with the ability to arrest anyone they suspected of paramilitary sympathies. As in Cyprus and Aden, brutal interrogation methods in Northern Ireland generated a windfall of intelligence that security forces used against republican paramilitaries to good effect during Operation Motorman. Driven out of no-go areas in the cities, the IRA increased operations along the border with the Republic of Ireland.[88] But these British military gains came with significant political costs. Internment without trial, interrogation in depth, and the break-up of no-go areas during Operation Motorman contributed to the near-total alienation of nationalists and unleashed an unrelenting flood of public scrutiny—scrutiny that would grow throughout the 1970s.

Public Debate and the Troubles in Context

Cooperative manipulation was more contested during the Northern Ireland conflict than in previous wars in Cyprus and Aden because the Troubles occurred in a different historical context. Public debate over security operations in Northern Ireland generated a greater influence on the war for two reasons. First, international transformations in the field of civil society and human rights meant that many Europeans—Britons and Irish included—increasingly came to view human rights as an important political issue. Beginning in the late 1960s and accelerating during the 1970s, human rights concepts experienced a resurgence in Europe.[89] The historian Samuel Moyn described this process in Eastern Europe as a "moralization of dissent."[90] In Western Europe and the United States, left-wing activists and political parties embraced the moral language of human rights and used it to serve domestic or foreign policy purposes. Human rights issues achieved a particularly high profile in the United States during the second half of the 1970s under President Jimmy Carter.[91] Furthermore, formal human rights law gained prominence. The European Commission of Human Rights and the European Court of Human Rights had delivered few jurisprudential decisions during the 1950s and 1960s. These rulings, however, established important precedents for European human rights law and outlined the scope and responsibilities of the European Commission and European Court of Human Rights. By the 1970s, these institutions were established and began to expand the scope of their authority.[92] European institutions in general also grew increasingly important to British policymakers as Britain pursued and, in 1973, obtained membership in the European Communities.[93] This global revival and reappropriation of human rights ideas had a profound, transformative effect on international and British politics while inspiring greater support for ideas of universal individual rights.

The Northern Ireland war proved to be one of the British government's most pressing human rights concerns as politicians often found themselves on the receiving end of rights criticisms. Far from smothering criticism, the government's response to 1971–72 internment and interrogation controversies generated additional censure. Activists in Northern Ireland continued to denounce British security measures through pamphlets and reports documenting perceived abuses. NICRA complained about the army's persistent patrolling, claiming that "massive British Army presence in anti unionist areas is a harassment in itself" because "constant foot patrols and speeding army vehicles" conveyed the impression that soldiers behaved "like an army of occupation." The army was "not accepted as a peacekeeping force, and in the people's eyes they have taken the place of the hated Royal Ulster Constabulary."[94] One report recorded the events of a series of army searches from January 12 to 14, 1972, in the New Lodge Road community. According to NICRA, "everyone, men, women and children were searched without exception, many so frequently over the three days that they had forgotten how often houses were searched." The document included a statement from Gerrard McAttamney, who complained that he had been beaten by being "made to run a gauntlet of soldiers who pushed and hit as I ran." He was later handed over from army to RUC custody, where constables asked him whether he had any complaints against the army for his treatment. "I was so terrified," McAttamney said, "I said no and signed a document saying so."[95]

Other NGOs also contributed to the chorus of critics attacking British security practices. The Association for Legal Justice joined with NICRA to submit a report entitled *British Government Violations of Human Rights in N. Ireland*. The report was intended to present evidence indicating that British forces had committed a "consistent pattern of gross and reliably attested violations of human rights and fundamental freedoms." The authors argued that internment without trial violated the right to liberty and security of the person, unlawful killings routinely occurred in Catholic working-class neighborhoods, and prisoners were subjected to physical and psychological brutality during interrogation. The Association for Legal Justice insisted that the British government was applying a "military solution to a political problem" through persistent intimidation of the local population, the use of excessive force, discriminatory treatment of Catholics, and the absence of effective domestic legal remedies.[96] Judicial proceedings mattered little, as security forces were accused of rearresting individuals outside the courtroom after they had been acquitted. Under internment without trial, those arrested could be held indefinitely.[97]

In October 1973, Amnesty International's Irish section organized a conference on the abolition of torture. One speaker at the conference, Professor D. Russell Davis of the Department of Mental Health, Bristol University School of Medicine, criticized the Joint Directive on Military Interrogation. The *Irish Times* reported Davis as saying that "the official comments were confused, even if not contradictory." Davis described how the joint directive stated that "successful interrogation . . . calls for a psychological attack" yet simultaneously prohibited "outrage upon personal dignity, in particular, humiliating and degrading treatment." Such statements, Davis said, reflected "serious naivety and obtuseness in psychological matters on the part of the authors of the joint directive." More troubling, he noted, was that none of the directive's guidelines specified precise limits on the methods available to interrogators. The permissibility and appropriateness of one procedure or another would, by this standard, come down to a matter of opinion.[98]

Amnesty International's interest in torture allegations from Northern Ireland formed part of a broad initiative. On December 3, 1973, Amnesty published a 224-page *Report on Torture* addressing torture as a government-sponsored phenomenon around the world. The document was part of AI's global Campaign for the Abolition of Torture and preceded the organization's international Conference for the Abolition of Torture, held in Paris in December 1973. The *Report on Torture* exposed a lack of legal remedies for torture victims in several countries including Northern Ireland. Examining allegations made against more than sixty countries, the report amounted to a "world survey of torture" and an indictment of communist regimes, right-wing dictatorships, and democratic states alike.[99] In February 1974, building on its antitorture campaign, Amnesty announced its intention to adopt several prisoners held in Northern Ireland. Amnesty asked for the Association for Legal Justice and NICRA to submit a list of names for potential sponsorees. The *Guardian* reported that Amnesty would continue to support adopted prisoners until "the weight of public opinion forces the British Government to free the prisoner."[100]

In addition to civil society organizations, prominent government figures supported human rights through legal reform initiatives. The Labour Party peer Lord Brockway developed close relationships with Northern Irish civic organizations such as NICRA and the Campaign for Social Justice.[101] In 1971, Brockway chastised the government for adopting internment, demanded public trials for the internees, and called for "a constructive political plan for civil rights, no religious discrimination, proportional representation, and an urgent economic plan to end the appalling unemployment and housing difficulties."[102] Throughout the Northern Ireland conflict Brockway advocated the creation of a Bill of Rights for Northern Ireland to end discrimination. His Bill of Rights received support from the National Council for Civil Liberties and NICRA, among others.[103]

Lord Gardiner, who had authored the Parker inquiry minority report, chaired the 1975 Gardiner Committee, which was charged with recommending how the government could confront the insurgency while still ensuring "the preservation of civil liberties and human rights."[104] When the committee was established, violence had declined from the high levels of 1972, but political progress had stalled after the failed 1973 power-sharing agreement signed at Sunningdale by nationalists and unionists. In this context, the committee focused its recommendations on how to reduce nationalist alienation while maintaining order. With this in mind, the seven-member committee determined that internment should not be used as long-term solution, even though it was temporarily justifiable for imposing order. According to the Gardiner Committee, internment had tarnished the judicial process. The committee recommended several reforms, such as limiting the amount of time that suspects could be held without trial and appointing a detention advisory board to recommend on continuing or ending a suspect's imprisonment. Some of these recommendations were enacted in diluted form through the 1975 Emergency Provisions Act. For example, the act did not impose time limits for detention and established an adviser on detention rather than an advisory board. Although internment was phased out by the end of 1975, under the Emergency Provisions Act the government retained legal authority to reimpose it in the future. Ultimately, the Gardiner Committee recommendations highlighted the importance of human rights issues in the conflict but did not translate into an effective system of rights protections.[105]

In addition, allegations of British human rights violations routinely surfaced at the United Nations. UN Economic and Social Council Resolution 1503 of 1970 authorized the Sub-Commission on Prevention of Discrimination and Protection of Minorities to appoint a working group on issues that "appear to reveal a consistent pattern of gross and reliably attested violations of human rights." As the Northern Ireland conflict escalated through the early 1970s, human rights petitions began to arrive. In July 1973, NICRA and the Association for Legal Justice filed complaints against British forces for violating civilians' civil and political rights.[106] Officials at the FCO believed that British policy should promote Cold War aims by encouraging UN human rights bodies to more effectively investigate human rights violations in communist countries. According to the FCO, "such procedures are valuable in helping to ensure respect for the norms laid down in conventions and declarations in the human rights field." By strengthening UN human rights machinery over the long term, Britain could strike a blow at communist states. But Britain's short-term objective "to secure a satisfactory outcome" on discussions of human rights violations in Northern Ireland encouraged a different response. The FCO report concluded that "HMG is already under very considerable pressure at the European Commission on Human Rights as a result of the Irish State Case and many individual petitions, and adverse decisions in these cases would be to the detriment of HMG's overall policies in Northern Ireland." In this context, "discussion of human rights in Northern Ireland, particularly on 'torture', at the UN can only act as encouragement to those elements opposed to peaceful change in Northern Ireland to attempt to embarrass HMG further through international institutions." FCO officials concluded that on human rights issues in Northern Ireland, "the short-term objective must outweigh the longer-term considerations." British officials should therefore do their utmost to ensure that discussions of Northern Ireland at the UN were kept to "a bare minimum."[107] British policy at the UN attempted to reconcile the competing interests of promoting human rights internationally while simultaneously mitigating criticism of British actions in Northern Ireland.

Another significant difference between colonial counterinsurgencies and the Troubles was Northern Ireland's constitutional status. The fact that Northern Ireland was a constituent member of the United Kingdom bore significant consequences for public debate over the conflict because both Northern Irish nationalists and unionists could wield political influence in a way that Greek Cypriots or Arab nationalists in Aden never could—they could get elected. Gerry Fitt, the MP representing West Belfast, attended an October 5, 1968, civil rights rally in Derry and was famously beaten by the RUC in front of several television cameras. Images of blood streaming down his head were broadcast across Britain and Ireland.[108] Bernadette Devlin, a Catholic civil rights activist and leading member of the radical student group People's Democracy, routinely and energetically attacked British security policy in Northern Ireland.[109] The pressing need for political reform highlighted by Opposition MPs contributed to the government's 1973 *Northern Ireland Constitutional Proposals* white paper. The white paper advocated a system of proportional representation, devolved government, and formal relationships between Northern Ireland and the south. This path toward reform eventually came to fruition during the 1973 Sunningdale conference, although the resulting power-sharing executive collapsed because of unionist resistance. Most MPs from Northern Irish constituencies came from the majority unionist community. Ulster Unionist Party MPs often aligned with the Conservative Party in Westminster politics. This close relationship grew strained in March 1972, when the Conservative government imposed direct rule. But unionist MPs kept close relations with hard-line Tories such as Julian Amery and sympathetic backbenchers. Even so, dissension within unionist ranks over the future of political devolution meant that Ulster unionists' influence at Westminster declined during the 1970s.[110] Regardless of the degree to which Northern Irish MPs achieved their political objectives, their pronouncements shaped public debate and government policy.

The controversies over internment and interrogation in depth reveal the existence of divergent and nuanced opinions regarding the acceptability of counterinsurgency violence in Northern Ireland. For some activists and policymakers, their self-image of the United Kingdom as a paragon of democracy meant that the state should protect the rights of individuals within the political community. Critics of interrogation in depth such as Lord Gardiner adopted this perspective. But others thought differently. Many Britons supported tough security policies. In their view, however, such measures should be legitimized through changes to the law. Supporters of harsh measures proved willing to consider the legalization of tougher methods in part because republican paramilitaries were able to threaten Britain in a manner unlike any colonial insurgent group—they attacked the British homeland. These attacks began with the October 1971 IRA bombing of the London Post Office Tower. The most notorious of these attacks, such as the 1974 bombings of two Birmingham pubs that killed 21 people and the 1984 attack on the Conservative Party conference at the Brighton Grand Hotel, were committed by republican paramilitaries.[111]

Irish paramilitary violence in Britain often inspired politicians who sought to implement harsh security policies. The 1973 Diplock Commission resulted in new legislation establishing "scheduled offences" in which suspects could be tried without juries. The idea was to prevent paramilitary groups from intimidating jurors, but juryless trials also deviated from UK legal norms.[112] In the wake of PIRA's November 1974 Birmingham pub bombings, which killed 21 and injured 184, many within the British public worried about future violence or screamed for vengeance. The *Times* called the bombings an "Act of War." In this climate of fear and anger, then secretary of state Roy Jenkins introduced the Prevention of Terrorism Act, which would grant security officials broad authorities to counter republican paramilitary activities in the United Kingdom.[113] One MP justified the legislation on the grounds that "the nation as a whole is facing the gravest threat that it has faced since the end of the Second World War."[114]

In addition to the Prevention of Terrorism Act, some politicians and members of the public clamored for the reintroduction of capital punishment for terrorist offenses. The death penalty was suspended in Britain in 1965 and eliminated for Northern Ireland in 1973. But in June and July 1974, bombings at the Houses of Parliament and Tower of London led to an impassioned debate in the Commons. The Conservative MP Michael Ancram said that although he had supported abolishing the death penalty, "I have since been convinced . . . that while abolition was right for the crime dealt with then, we are now faced with a totally different sort of situation." Terrorism, Ancram continued, "is not a crime just against the person but a crime against humanity." Fellow Tory Sir Patrick Cormack argued that recent events had made many Britons wonder "whether the time has come for a change." The attorney general for Northern Ireland, Peter Rawlinson, also supported reintroducing the death penalty. In contrast, the Liberal MP Christopher Mayhew insisted that "there is no evidence that the execution of terrorists lessens terrorism or prevents it growing. On the contrary, we have many examples in history of precisely the opposite." Mayhew cited the executions of Irish nationalist James Connolly after the 1916 Easter Rising and American abolitionist John Brown on the eve of the American Civil War as evidence that capital punishment could create martyrs and "did nothing to stop the killing."[115]

The 1974 Birmingham pub bombings sparked further debate. On November 21, the day of the bombings, Conservative MPs Jill Knight and Hal Miller pressed their party to again consider introducing capital punishment. For another Tory, William Rees-Davis, "whatever view one takes of a death penalty, those who are enemies of the realm deserve to be dealt with swiftly and executed."[116] In December, both Houses of Parliament debated the death penalty. The Conservative Lord Bourne announced that "I have always backed the death penalty for war against the State" and categorized the IRA's activities as exactly that.[117] The government held firm and did not reinstate capital punishment during the 1974 death penalty debate. But the fact that the debate occurred at all revealed that republican terrorism at home had convinced some within British society to consider extraordinary measures.

Debates over counterinsurgency methods in Northern Ireland were therefore not a straightforward assertion of human rights norms as a means of restraining the conduct of the war but a give-and-take over the extent to which the protection of human rights and the imperative of preserving the state's ability to maintain order overlapped or conflicted. Many within government sought to strike a balance between ensuring security and preserving human rights. Lawmakers gave wide-ranging powers to security forces through measures such as the Prevention of Terrorism Act. The struggle to balance security with rights remained a key issue throughout the Troubles.

Government Responses to Public Scrutiny

In 1972, GOC NI Lieutenant General Sir Harry Tuzo dismissed complaints against the British army as "smoke without fire."[118] A later GOC NI, Lieutenant General Frank King, described allegations of army repression as "stories spread by propagandists." From the army's perspective, military success seemed to breed complaints against army conduct. Regardless of truth, members of the security forces often perceived allegations against them as nothing more than a propaganda campaign designed to undermine nationalist support for the government.[119] Indeed, the IRA did run a propaganda campaign designed to publicize—and embellish—security force brutality.[120] Although security force abuses continued, these actions coexisted alongside well-intentioned efforts designed to improve the security forces' image among the nationalist population and strengthen British claims to political legitimacy. These good-faith attempts, however, met with limited success because courts continued to protect soldiers from punishment, the government remained simultaneously cooperative and antagonistic toward the European Court of Human Rights, RUC constables resumed violent interrogations, and the policy shift toward Ulsterization exposed contradictions in the rule of law.

As in the Cyprus and Aden campaigns, officials who saw these allegations as propaganda often shielded soldiers from accountability before the law. When faced with criminal or civil claims filed against security forces, RUC investigators limited the number of cases that went to court. Few of these cases resulted in convictions. From March 1972 to September 1974, the RUC initiated 502 investigations into criminal allegations against the army and UDR. Prosecution occurred in 56 cases, but only 17 resulted in convictions. Sometimes claims would not even reach the Director of Public Prosecutions (DPP), who was responsible for prosecuting soldiers and police charged with breaking the law. Police officers conducting criminal investigations into fellow members of the security forces did not forward all the results of their investigations to the DPP. The DPP notified the chief of the General Staff that investigators had been "using their own discretion . . . very liberally." Most allegations concerned assault charges. In cases where soldiers were found guilty, the courts usually imposed fines and suspended sentences rather than prison time. Soldiers convicted for common assault usually paid fines in the range of £25–100.[121]

In civil cases, Ministry of Defence lawyers refused to admit that the government bore legal liability for injuries or deaths caused by the security forces. MOD attorneys contested cases that they were likely to win while settling out of court in cases the government would most likely lose. Between 1971 and 1974, aggrieved civilians filed an average of between 108 and 155 claims per month against the army. By January 1975, MOD had faced 6,000 claims, settling 410 out of court. Family members of those killed on Bloody Sunday submitted a total of 13 civil complaints. The attorney general assessed that of those 13 cases the government had "no prospect" of successfully defending 4 of them, was unlikely to succeed in defending 3 more, and had a "reasonable chance" of winning 4. The attorney general and secretary of state for Northern Ireland concurred that the best course of action was "to pay sums of money into Court, without admission of legal liability, in respect of the first seven cases, and to fight the remainder."[122] Out-of-court settlements minimized publicity by avoiding press coverage of drawn-out legal proceedings. The disadvantage of settlements, however, was that such payments implied that British forces were guilty of violations even though in point of law the government did not admit legal liability.[123]

The frequency with which soldiers had to appear in court led to several changes in tactics and training programs. Commanders understood that the army had a poor reputation among the nationalist population. This shortcoming was magnified by intense media coverage in the United Kingdom and abroad that was more pervasive—and critical—than previous colonial conflicts. According to then defense secretary Lord Carrington, "every action was carried out in the glare of television publicity."[124] Between August 1969 and December 1972 British television shows such as Granada's *World in Action* and Thames's *This Week*, as well as BBC1's *Panorama*, *Talkback*, and *24 Hours* broadcast more than thirty programs on specific aspects of the Troubles.[125] Although the government at times spread misinformation and pressured British media to conform to the official line, some journalists resisted. David Beresford and Peter Taylor, for example, proved unafraid of critiquing paramilitaries and politicians of all parties to the conflict. The BBC also developed an often-contentious relationship with government officials who sought to shape the war's public narrative.[126] According to one scholar of the conflict, such intense media attention meant that the "Northern Ireland conflict received more domestic and international press coverage than any of the emergencies in remote parts of the world."[127]

The army addressed its public relations problems by implementing new training programs. Training in how to interact with journalists and members of the public began with line battalions whose missions involved regular street patrolling and interaction with local civilians. But commanders soon realized that officers posted to HQ Northern Ireland did not receive the same public relations-oriented training as the line battalions. The headquarters therefore lacked officers capable of serving as media spokesmen. In September 1973, HQ Northern Ireland identified a need for twenty officers to complete "TV training." The RUC similarly lacked trained spokespersons and asked to send twenty officers of their own to army short courses.[128] By 1975, mandatory predeployment training for unit commanders at company and battalion level included "TV interview technique" courses, while all unit press officers and those serving as second in command at company level and above received public relations training.[129]

Beyond attempts to improve its relationship with broadcasters, the army developed new measures designed to minimize lawsuits over property damage resulting from house searches. Hundreds of house searches were conducted on a weekly basis. The numbers varied during the first half of the 1970s, but in 1974 the number of searches conducted by the army in Northern Ireland averaged six hundred to eight hundred per week.[130] The average in Belfast alone surpassed five hundred searches per week. British forces realized that slow, overly bureaucratic processes for compensating individuals who suffered property damage during the course of security operations engendered resentment from civilians. The army wanted to deploy "repair squads" to quickly fix any damage caused by army searches and empower local units to authorize small-claim settlement payments of up to £25.[131] To liaise with local communities and coordinate quick compensation schemes, Northern Ireland civil servants were seconded to the army. The first of these "civil representatives" was appointed in summer 1971. By 1973, every brigade in the province had a principal adviser and several deputies.[132] Through the civil representative program, civilians' wait time for receipt of settlement payments dropped from an average of ten to thirteen days to five days.[133] Military tactics also changed. Some units, such as the oft-criticized Paras, began filming searches with video cameras. Video footage could be used as evidence in court to counter false or exaggerated allegations. But the technique of filming house searches was also likely to prevent soldiers from smashing furniture or harassing locals because soldiers knew that their actions were on film too.[134]

Unlike the Cyprus and Aden conflicts, concern for human rights issues resulted in the establishment of government institutions designed to promote human rights. Created under the 1973 Sunningdale agreement, Northern Ireland's Standing Advisory Commission on Human Rights (SACHR) was the first government-appointed human rights body established in the United Kingdom. The Sunningdale system, which involved a power-sharing executive comprising unionist and nationalist parties, eventually collapsed because of unionist animosity, but SACHR continued to operate and released its first annual report in 1975. Although nationalist activist groups such as NICRA initially responded skeptically to the creation of SACHR and many right-wing politicians reacted with outright hostility, rights activists' opinions shifted as SACHR adopted political positions in line with their aspirations.[135] SACHR's 1977 annual report insisted that legislation was the best way to protect rights in Northern Ireland. Entitled *The Protection of Human Rights by Law in Northern Ireland*, the report suggested that the European Convention on Human Rights could form the basis of a domestic Bill of Rights. Advocacy for a Bill of Rights remained a core element of SACHR's platform for the next two decades.[136]

After the Labour Party's victory in the 1974 general election, the new government asked Lord Gardiner to lead a study of how to wage the Northern Ireland conflict with respect for civil liberties and human rights. The Gardiner Committee's subsequent report continued the argument Gardiner had put forth in the Parker minority report. He called for reinstating trial by jury, criticized the prison system's "appalling" conditions, and asserted that "detention cannot remain as a long-term policy." Gardiner also noted that "the prolonged effects of the use of detention are ultimately inimical to community life, fan a widespread sense of grievance and injustice, and obstruct those elements in Northern Ireland society which could lead to reconciliation." Yet Gardiner concluded that the degree of violence in the province meant that he could not recommend the immediate elimination of detention without trial. He held human rights in high esteem, but he was not blind to the grave threat that Northern Irish paramilitaries posed. After the Gardiner Committee report, the Labour government developed a new strategy for Northern Ireland.[137]

Convinced of the need to abandon many of the counterinsurgency methods employed since 1969, incoming secretary of state for Northern Ireland Merlyn Rees adopted a strategy of "Ulsterization." Basing the strategy on the 1976 report of a Home Office working group, Rees abandoned practices that had alienated the Catholic community, such as internment without trial and high-profile patrolling, in favor of "police primacy"—an approach that placed the RUC in the lead. The plan was to maintain law and order through policing and the legal system. Rather than drawing on colonial counterinsurgency experiences, this strategy was based on the West German and Italian governments' experiences countering European terrorist groups such as the Baader-Meinhof gang and the Red Brigades.[138] Under Ulsterization, the army largely redeployed to secure rural border areas, support the clandestine collection of intelligence, and conduct special operations against specific, known IRA targets. High-visibility daily patrols would fall to the RUC and Ulster Defence Regiment. Rees intended for this approach to contain the violence and reduce Catholic alienation, thus creating opportunities for a political settlement.[139]

Although the implementation of specific policies varied as British governments changed, the post-1976 strategic shift toward Ulsterization marked a conscious effort to bolster popular perceptions of the state's legitimacy through the rule of law. The problem with this rule-of-law approach was that British actions often proved inconsistent. Court decisions tended to protect security forces from punishment by establishing lenient legal precedents. Regarding murder and manslaughter charges, the House of Lords' verdict in the 1976 McElhone case appeared to legitimize the defense of "shot while trying to escape." In the view of Northern Irish human rights lawyers, this case established a precedent that permitted soldiers and police to use lethal force with little fear of judicial consequences. In County Tyrone, a soldier shot and killed Patrick McElhone, who had run away as the soldier tried to question him. The soldier believed that he could either allow the man to escape or shoot him to prevent his escape. At trial, the court found that the soldier had acted with "reasonable" force. After referral to the Court of Criminal Appeals, the case came before the House of Lords. Law Lords agreed that the use of force was reasonable and clarified the point of law that "if a plea of self-defence is put forward in answer to a charge of murder and fails because excessive force was used though some force was justifiable, as the law now stands the accused cannot be convicted of manslaughter."[140] The prominent Northern Irish defense attorney Tony Jennings wrote that the decision gave security forces "a licence to kill."[141] The Northern Irish human rights lawyer Brice Dickson assessed that this decision allowed security forces "to operate with virtual impunity when applying lethal force against suspected terrorists." The high standard necessary to obtain a murder conviction and the lack of any intermediate punishments for crimes such as manslaughter meant that few soldiers and police officers were convicted of the excessive use of lethal force.[142]

Whereas activists' appeals to human rights *norms* formed the basis of most complaints during the Cyprus and Aden conflicts, the strengthening of European human rights *law* occurred during the 1970s. Early cases such as the decisions of the European Commission of Human Rights on the two Cyprus applications of the 1950s suggested that European human rights institutions would allow member states wide latitude in emergency situations. This situation changed beginning in the 1970s. The European human rights system gained prestige as many prominent legal figures served on the commission or the European Court of Human Rights. Once legitimized in this way, the commission and court began asserting their newfound status. The result was a proliferation of European case law regarding human rights and internal conflict. As the commission and court began acting more aggressively on individuals' claims in the 1970s, the British government faced a flood of Troubles-related legal actions outside UK courts.[143] Between 1971 and 1998, the commission dealt with over sixty-five cases concerning the application of the European Convention on Human Rights to court proceedings, detention practices, police investigations, and the use of force in Northern Ireland.[144]

European human rights institutions grew increasingly proactive during and after the 1970s, but this change did not automatically result in an effective legal regime capable of restraining wartime violence. When the Irish government's 1971 application concerning the five techniques came before the European commission, Britain appeared to cooperate by allowing the commission to interview British officials but sought to prevent it from gathering key pieces of information. The British government refused to identify the locations where the five techniques were used—the commission and the public believed that Palace Barracks was the site of interrogation, but it was actually Ballykelly airfield. As the investigation continued into 1974, Britain also prohibited the commission from interviewing army and police witnesses in Strasbourg, citing security reasons. Instead, the government would permit commission representatives to question British officials only at a secure military airfield in Norway. British witnesses testified from behind a screen, where only the Commission delegates and lawyers could see them. To complicate matters further, the British government introduced its witnesses using alphanumeric ciphers rather than names. None of the witnesses admitted that any wrongdoing had occurred.[145] Furthermore, the government instructed witnesses not to answer questions about methods of interrogation despite the fact that detailed accounts of the five techniques had been published in many newspapers and books.[146] Through these limitations, the government resisted any semblance of guilt and controlled the commission's ability to gather testimony from British officials.

The commission later passed its investigation to the European Court of Human Rights, which ruled on the five-techniques case in 1978. The court determined that the five techniques constituted inhuman and degrading treatment but fell short of torture. This decision meant that Britain had violated the European Convention on Human Rights—which prohibited "inhuman and degrading treatment" as well as torture—but fell short of playing into paramilitaries' hands by labeling the five techniques torture.[147] In the same ruling, the court also supported the right of the state to impose order during times of unrest by determining that a public emergency threatening the life of the nation existed in Northern Ireland. The British government therefore had not exceeded its powers by implementing special security measures. Brice Dickson complained that the court's decision "sent a subliminal message to the UK government that it could continue to tolerate heavy-handed interrogation tactics without having to worry too much about international opprobrium."[148] Despite the court's partially critical verdict, Britain emerged relatively unscathed. The British government's apparent cooperation had masked its attempts to deflect scrutiny from the commission and court.

This façade of cooperation also persisted in response to human rights NGOs' efforts. In 1978, when Amnesty International again raised concerns over the resuscitation of brutal interrogation, officials masterfully evaded any acknowledgment of guilt. The Amnesty International investigation discovered evidence that from 1976 to 1979, members of the RUC had severely and systematically beaten prisoners at three prisons while police doctors covered up medical evidence of the abuse. Amnesty recommended a full public inquiry. Under pressure from human rights activists, Members of Parliament, as well as British and Irish journalists, then secretary of state for Northern Ireland Roy Mason instead ordered a private inquiry headed by Crown Court judge Harry Bennett. The Bennett committee proposed several interrogation and detention reforms, but none of the interrogators or doctors faced criminal charges.[149] The Bennett report did not explicitly state that RUC constables had abused prisoners, which allowed Mason to implement interrogation reforms while simultaneously claiming that the allegations had not been proven. Some within the RUC, such as Deputy Chief Constable Jack Hermon, supported initiatives to increase police accountability, but these initiatives had limited effect. The RUC was dominated by a Janus-faced culture in which police commanders publicly upheld official rules and regulations while privately accepting routine minor deviations from those regulations.[150] The Bennett report offered the appearance of cooperation with human rights groups while also demonstrating that senior ministers still refused to punish those responsible for the resurgence of brutal interrogation techniques.

Meanwhile, the adoption of police primacy proved problematic. At one level, police primacy placed the Protestant-dominated RUC and UDR in the forefront of security operations often oriented toward the Catholic minority—an image that served to reinforce nationalist alienation. The complementary policy of "criminalization" was intended to treat paramilitary violence as criminal rather than political and to punish offenders through the court system. This attempt to legitimize the justice system also failed to assuage nationalist resentment. One element of criminalization entailed the use of anonymous informants—"supergrasses"—to provide testimony in terrorism cases and led to numerous convictions in the 1980s, but there were claims that informers were offered immunity from prosecution for crimes they had committed in the past and had received cash payments to testify against suspected terrorists. Many informers were accused of having lied under oath. Convictions obtained through this system faced greater scrutiny at the appeals court. In one 1983 case, testimony by Christopher Black, an IRA informant, resulted in the convictions of eighteen IRA men, but by 1986 the appeals court had overturned their convictions. Similar cases further discredited the supergrass system. Rather than reinforcing British claims to political legitimacy, supergrass controversies undermined them.[151]

After 1972, government officials and military commanders responded to public scrutiny in a variety of ways. An aversion to scrutiny meant that government lawyers continued to shield troops from legal claims in court and deny legal liability for deaths or injuries caused by the security forces. The desire to mitigate further criticism and gain operational advantages by winning over the civilian population, however, resulted in the implementation of public relations training for soldiers, the assignment of civil representatives to army units, the creation of a government human rights body (SACHR), and the launch of Ulsterization. These efforts ultimately met with mixed success because courts continued to protect troops from legal punishments; Britain denied any semblance of guilt during proceedings before the European Commission and European Court of Human Rights while constraining the commission from gathering evidence in the case on interrogation in depth; the government under Prime Minister Harold Wilson ordered a private inquiry into Amnesty International's allegations that the RUC had resumed violent interrogations; and laws were enacted that seemed to contradict the basic principles of the justice system.

From 1969 to 1976 government bureaucrats and members of the security forces responded to human rights controversies in much the same way as they had during colonial campaigns in Cyprus and Aden. These measures took the form of government inquiries designed to shield violations from scrutiny while also involving the use of the law to facilitate counterinsurgency operations, protect members of the security forces from punishment, and deny legal liability for possible rights violations. But the Northern Ireland conflict differed from past colonial campaigns because British officials found their methods challenged on a consistent basis. Policies such as internment without trial and interrogation in depth drew particularly strong condemnation from rights groups, legal advocates, republican sympathizers, international organizations, foreign governments, and domestic political critics. To an unprecedented extent, criticism from journalists, clergy, civil society organizations, lawyers, and other activists generated substantive, persistent public discussions in Britain over counterinsurgency methods that continued throughout the Troubles.

The prevalence of human rights debates from the late 1960s onward placed the security forces under greater public pressure than they had faced during the Cyprus and Aden wars. The Heath government proved willing to order a series of formal inquiries into rights abuses, but these inquiries deflected criticism and sought to protect soldiers from scrutiny. The Compton committee on interrogation produced an equivocal finding that relied on legal semantics. The subsequent Parker committee majority report also failed to address the legality of the five techniques. Only Lord Gardiner's minority report asserted that British actions were illegal and immoral under all circumstances.

The minority report revealed that Northern Ireland was indeed "a more talkative place" than Cyprus and Aden. After this report, successive British governments were opened up to greater scrutiny than ever before. Activism during the Troubles consistently challenged the government's attempts to cloak brutal interrogation in the language of legality. But public criticism also reflected the variety of perspectives and lack of consensus within the government on how to handle human rights controversies. Some officials criticized security policies such as interrogation in depth and internment without trial, but others supported tough security measures. Proponents of strict punishments for terrorism-related offenses and looser restrictions on the security forces' conduct asserted the primacy of military considerations over law and rights at a time in which domestic and international publics grew increasingly aware of and interested in protecting human rights. Tension between human rights and security policies remained central to public debate throughout the Troubles.

These tensions were never resolved. Well-intentioned efforts to improve British political legitimacy were at times undermined by practices that contradicted the spirit of those efforts. As tough measures such as internment and interrogation in depth grew increasingly difficult to sustain under public pressure, illicit state violence appeared to go underground. Allegations that British troops, particularly the Special Air Service (SAS), sought to kill rather than capture dangerous paramilitary fighters surfaced during the 1970s. SAS ambushes eventually accounted for the deaths of thirty-six republican paramilitaries between 1976 and 1992. At a time when the government had publicly committed to upholding the rule of law, these killings aroused suspicions that the SAS had adopted a shoot-to-kill policy.[152] Government critics contended that this allowed security forces to avoid the judicial process by ensuring that paramilitaries never made it to trial.[153] The army and police also faced accusations of colluding with loyalist paramilitary groups to commit illegal murders. The most infamous collusion case was that of Pat Finucane, a Catholic Belfast human rights lawyer murdered by loyalist paramilitaries in 1989. Military personnel provided intelligence that loyalist paramilitaries used to plan Finucane's murder. When a police informant tried to warn his handlers of the impending murder, constables took no action to stop it.[154] Since the signing of the 1998 Good Friday Agreement ended the conflict, collusion—as well as the host of other human rights violations committed by both the state and its adversaries—have remained some of the Troubles' most sensitive and disturbing legacies.

From the Colonial to the Contemporary

Human rights issues have remained central to the legacy of the Troubles as the British government has only recently begun to seriously examine the conflict's most divisive and controversial events. A 2012 government inquiry implicated members of the security forces in the 1989 murder of Pat Finucane by loyalist paramilitaries. Prime Minister David Cameron subsequently described the degree of state collusion in Finucane's death as "shocking."[1] The extensive twelve-year Bloody Sunday Inquiry chaired by Lord Saville, which lasted from 1998 to 2010, conclusively determined that soldiers had fired on an unarmed, nonviolent crowd. As a result of these findings, the government opened a new investigation into soldiers' conduct.[2] In 2015, police arrested a former paratrooper for his role in the Bloody Sunday shootings.[3] In June 2014, Irish television aired a documentary in which journalists claimed to have found new evidence that the British government had purposely misled the European Court of Human Rights and that UK cabinet officials had authorized use of the five techniques despite claiming ignorance at the time. On the basis of the documentary report, several months later the Irish government requested that the European Court of Human Rights reconsider its 1978 judgment on Britain's use of the five techniques during interrogation.[4] The first step in this process began on June 4, 2015, when the Belfast High Court permitted the claimants in the original case to seek judicial review.[5]

These public inquiries and legal actions reveal the persistence of rights activism as well as the deep, lingering mistrust between loyalists, nationalists, and the British state. Since the end of widespread violence in 1998, activism has become entrenched in Northern Irish society and politics but not always in positive ways. According to one scholar, both unionists and nationalists have embraced human rights activism as a kind of "war by other means" in which each side attempts to cast itself as more legitimate than the other on moral grounds. In this sense, competition and confrontation over the future of Northern Ireland have endured but through activism rather than warfare. Activism therefore has exerted the contradictory influences of deepening mistrust while encouraging accountability.[6]

Government actions early in the conflict reinforced this sense of mistrust. In 1971, ministers responded to public criticism over interrogation methods in Northern Ireland by ordering inquiries into the use of the five techniques. In doing so, the government appeared to cooperate with public demands, but the resulting Compton and Parker inquiries cast the security forces' actions in a positive light. The results of these inquiries ultimately denied legal liability for British actions, upheld cabinet ministers' claims that they did not know about the techniques, and sought to prevent members of the security forces from being penalized. By the late 1970s, subsequent British governments had recognized the need to overcome nationalist alienation by abandoning repressive tactics. Many of these initiatives, however, were riddled with contradictions. Appeals to nationalists fell flat when courts operated without juries, anonymous informers provided court testimony after making secret deals with the government, and security forces colluded with loyalist paramilitaries to murder prominent or troublesome nationalists. Although republican and loyalist groups committed many atrocities as well, government attempts to deny official culpability for abuses proved a common trend during the Troubles but was also characteristic of past colonial wars.

During the Cyprus Emergency, colonial officials responded to rights activism by deflecting public scrutiny from counterinsurgency operations. When the European Commission of Human Rights sent investigators to Cyprus, British officials reacted by controlling what the investigators saw and heard during their visit to shape the narrative of events. In response to continued public criticism, the deputy governor and administrative secretary created the Special Investigation Group not to provide accountability but to prevent Greek Cypriot allegations from gaining traction. Furthermore, senior military commanders, Whitehall bureaucrats, and colonial officers in Cyprus censored portions of the Geunyeli inquiry report, while the coroner in the 1958 Famagusta inquest twisted the outcome of these investigations to shield security forces from possible legal liability. Through these efforts, British officials effectively obstructed Greek Cypriot human rights activism and hid abuses.

In Aden, authorities contained the unwanted involvement of the ICRC. With the 1964 Radfan campaign raging, High Commission officials hoped to keep the ICRC out of the conflict zone. Once this proved impossible, British officials tried to use the ICRC's presence as a public relations advantage. But after ICRC inspections found evidence of torture, pressure from Amnesty International resulted in the 1966 Bowen inquiry. In response, the Aden High Commission obscured the postinquiry resumption of torture and minimized the impact of subsequent reforms on the interrogation effort. Activists had succeeded in raising the issue of detainee abuse and had also succeeded in obtaining regular Red Cross access to prison and interrogation facilities, but the real consequence of these apparent victories was not the end of torture—colonial authorities simply became more proficient at hiding their abuses.

Although civil servants, ministers, and military commanders never used the term, they engaged in cooperative manipulation to stop activists' criticisms of brutal counterinsurgency practices. In doing so, officials sought to shield security forces from scrutiny and to protect Britain's reputation as a guardian of human rights. There were differences in the manner in which it was applied across the three cases examined in this book, but cooperative manipulation consistently emerged as the standard response to activism when the simple denial of allegations proved insufficient to smother activists' efforts. The regularity of this response is unsurprising considering the way in which many officials served in various colonial hotspots. From the 1950s to the 1970s, Geoffrey Baker, John Willoughby, Sir Richard Turnbull, Cecil Blacker, John Prendergast, and others like them gained expertise through participation in multiple counterinsurgencies. Cooperative manipulation continued in Northern Ireland, even as resistance to rights abuses reached a new level of intensity. Records of these techniques were not conveniently packaged and documented as counterinsurgency "best practices" like the more benign maxims of respect for the rule of law and use of minimum force. But the consistent pattern of thwarting activism and the frequent circulation of officials from one campaign to the next suggests that, like torture, experience with cooperative manipulation became one of the "dark arts" of British counterinsurgency.

But did these dark arts really prove effective, as many colonial officials seemed to believe? Tactics used by British security forces—such as collective punishments, forced relocation, an emphasis on intelligence collection, mass detention, and torture—were common techniques. Many of these methods were employed by other counterinsurgents such as the French in Algeria and the Americans in Vietnam. Yet nearly all colonial counterinsurgencies also involved political reforms and economic development initiatives designed to build popular support. Many factors shaped the outcome of these wars, and any retrospective assessment of "success" in counterinsurgency would require a multicausal explanation. Of the three wars discussed in this book, the Cyprus Emergency might be considered a British victory. This success, however, occurred only after the British government changed its strategic goal from retaining control over Cyprus to ensuring the use of airbases on Cyprus and settling the conflict between Greek and Turkish Cypriots, at least temporarily. In the end, all sides had to compromise. Aden, however, was an abject failure on at least two levels. After independence, the former colony descended into a civil war that was not settled until 1970. Moreover, the manner of Britain's departure from Aden stoked the domestic British sense that the country had fallen into decline as a great power. In contrast, the outcome in Northern Ireland could be perceived as a win for the British government (for preserving British rule) and the republican movement (for obtaining a power-sharing agreement), but a loss for unionists who had hoped to retain both British rule and local political dominance. Even so, success in Northern Ireland owed much to the recognition that heavy-handed methods such as internment were counterproductive and needed to be reversed. Britain's experience in these three conflicts therefore demonstrates that the mythologized "British Way" in counterinsurgency did not offer an infallible blueprint for success and brutal practices such as torture did not provide some sort of decisive advantage for achieving victory.[7]

If there was a peculiarly British Way in waging counterinsurgency, it was that Britain was unique in terms of how far officials would go to cover up frequent and systematic violence against noncombatants. Colonial officers and military commanders such as George Sinclair, Kenneth Darling, Richard Turnbull, and Lord Parker were so concerned with maintaining Britain's reputation that they went to great lengths to hide any appearance of officially sanctioned cruelty. Human rights activists' efforts to expose these abuses therefore posed a significant threat that had to be countered. This desire to hide evidence of brutality fueled the contemporary myth that British forces were exceptionally successful in fighting insurgencies because they obeyed the rule of law. Attempts to avoid public scrutiny shaped the memory of these wars: human rights abuses were forgotten and left out of the official narrative of decolonization because those abuses were often successfully covered up at the time. Those abuses that could not be hidden from view were described as aberrations in an otherwise sterling history of waging war according to liberal democratic notions such as the rule of law.

Yet, as this book has shown, British officials frequently used the rule of law to reinforce repression and regularly evaded allegations of torture. In the three conflicts examined here, the notable absence of international legal sanctions against Britain prior to the Troubles suggests that formal mechanisms of international law had little effect on the colonial counterinsurgencies of the 1950s and 1960s.[8] Even when activists pursued formal legal proceedings, such as the Cyprus ECHR cases, these efforts did not achieve their desired results. Activists therefore tried other options, bringing pressure to bear on the British government through public statements, private lobbying, and colonial courts. These overtures appealed to emerging rights norms rather than formal international law. This dynamic began to change during the Troubles as the European Court of Human Rights heard an increasing number of cases involving British human rights violations in Northern Ireland. But the influence of human rights activism on warfare in each of the conflicts studied in this book should therefore be seen as a consequence of the weakness, rather than the strength, of international law.

With little recourse to international law, anticolonial nationalists and international organizations mobilized concepts of human rights as one way to achieve their objectives. By embracing human rights as a means to undermine Britain's intelligence program and challenge the moral legitimacy of British rule, Greek Cypriot human rights lawyers pursued their primary objective of self-determination. International organizations such as the ICRC and Amnesty International, however, viewed the humane treatment of prisoners and civilians as an end in itself. The ICRC asserted the dignity of the individual by alleviating the suffering of refugees and detainees. Amnesty International sought to end torture because torture violated the notion that all individuals should be treated with respect and dignity. In contrast, the insurgents and their Arab League supporters who actively encouraged ICRC and AI involvement in Aden saw those organizations as beneficial for undermining British counterinsurgency policies and practices through moral and legal appeals. Regardless of motivation, human rights activists added another dimension to the counterinsurgency battlefield by challenging British officials with moral and legal arguments.

Human Rights and Contemporary Counterinsurgency

The relationship between human rights ideas and the conduct of war has changed since the 1970s as formal legal mechanisms have grown increasingly influential.[9] This process began as human rights law overlapped with international humanitarian law through a series of revisions to the Geneva Conventions, largely as wars of decolonization wound down during the late 1960s. In 1968 the UN General Assembly passed Resolution 2444 calling for the revision of international humanitarian law to ensure "respect for human rights in armed conflicts."[10] Protracted discussions between state parties to the Geneva Conventions and the ICRC eventually produced the 1977 Additional Protocols to the Geneva Conventions. Reflecting the experience of anticolonial wars, the first protocol applied international humanitarian law to "armed conflicts in which peoples are fighting against colonial domination and alien occupation and against racist regimes in the exercise of the right of self-determination."[11] The second protocol expanded protections for combatants and civilians in noninternational armed conflicts, but states refused to include more specific language in the protocol that would have extended the same protections to all forms of noninternational armed conflict such as colonial emergencies.[12]

In Britain, new domestic laws such as the UK Human Rights Act have strengthened the judiciary's power to enforce human rights legislation. Passed in 1998, the act came into force two years later. It was in part the product of lobbying by civil society organizations such as Charter 88, which believed that the British government held too many unchecked powers and that limiting the government's power required a formal enumeration of basic rights.[13] But the act's origins can also be found in the Northern Ireland peace process.[14] Both nationalist and unionist communities perceived comprehensive protections of fundamental rights as a means of protecting their interests. In 1995, the British government committed to establishing a legal guarantee to protect each community's civil, social, and cultural rights. As part of the 1998 Belfast agreement that ended the Troubles, the British government pledged to incorporate the European Convention into UK domestic law. Under the Human Rights Act, the protections of the convention applied not only to army and police conduct in Northern Ireland but throughout the United Kingdom.[15]

Despite these changes, abuses have persisted. After the 9/11 terrorist attacks on the United States, Britain's involvement in the Iraq and Afghanistan wars raised further questions about the role of human rights in wartime.[16] In 2003, British forces detained an Iraqi hotel worker named Baha Mousa, who later died in custody after suffering ninety-three separate injuries. In January 2004—in a manner reminiscent of the way that they handled civil cases in Northern Ireland—the MOD announced that it had paid compensation to Baha Mousa's family, but it did not admit legal liability for his death. The 2011 Baha Mousa inquiry later confirmed that soldiers had beaten Baha Mousa, placed him in stress positions, deprived him of sleep, and kept him hooded for twenty-four of the thirty-six hours during which he was in custody—all methods that had been used previously in Northern Ireland. Soldiers had also used these practices on several other detainees at the prison.[17] One scholar concluded that "substantial, systemic flaws existed" that resulted in "non-combatants being harmed."[18] The victims' family members also asked for the court to review the MOD's failure to investigate the deaths.[19]

When Baha Mousa's family brought the case to trial, a series of court proceedings and appeals brought the case to the Supreme Court in the House of Lords. The legal point at issue concerned the extraterritoriality of the 1998 UK Human Rights Act and, by extension, the European Convention on Human Rights—that is, whether this legislation applied to the conduct of British soldiers outside British territory. According to Article 1 of the ECHR, member states must respect the rights and freedoms described in the convention and apply those rights "to everyone within their jurisdiction."[20] Ultimately, the House of Lords determined that under the terms of the UK Human Rights Act, the ECHR applied to the actions of British soldiers on military bases in Iraq. On the basis of this judgment, the jurisdiction of European human rights law extended to the conduct of British forces beyond Europe.[21]

The role of the ECHR and the UK Human Rights Act are once again in question as a result of the June 2016 "Brexit" vote to leave the European Union.[22] One of the key arguments for the pro-Brexit camp was the desire to exert greater control over British sovereignty than permitted under EU membership. Much of the debate concerned the introduction of stricter immigration laws. Any new limitations on immigration, however, would raise the issue of whether such measures would restrict the free movement of

UK and Irish citizens along the border between the Republic of Ireland and Northern Ireland—a key stipulation of the 1998 Good Friday Agreement that ended the Troubles.[23] In a similar vein, many Britons have grown frustrated with the influence of EU law on domestic issues and see this issue as yet more evidence of EU intrusions on British sovereignty. Several prominent politicians, including Prime Minister Theresa May, have called for removing the United Kingdom from the ECHR.[24] The future of human rights law in the United Kingdom is therefore very much in flux.

Unrestrained by European human rights law, the United States adopted a different approach during the early 2000s. The Bush administration's refusal to apply the Geneva Conventions to captured enemy combatants after 9/11, the use of indefinite detention at Guantanamo Bay, and the approval of so-called enhanced interrogation techniques—which were similar to Britain's five techniques—contributed to the emergence of an interrogation and detention system that legalized methods now widely regarded as torture.[25] In this instance, American lawyers used the same trick as their British counterparts had used in Northern Ireland—they defined "torture" in narrow terms to permit the use of coercive and traumatic techniques. When health professionals from the Central Intelligence Agency criticized the interrogation program on medical grounds, psychologists from the American Psychological Association's ethics committee coordinated with CIA and Defense Department officials to ensure that the APA's code of ethics did not preclude psychologists from participating in enhanced interrogation programs. Such distortion of professional ethical guidelines and collusion with official institutions are reminiscent of colonial officers' efforts to manipulate regulations and provide an air of legitimacy to their actions.[26]

These legalistic justifications of torture and detention ignore the important role of moral appeals in contemporary conflict. Emile Simpson, a strategic studies scholar and former British army officer, links the tension between physical and moral victories to the production of strategic narratives. Simpson argues that in a world defined by contemporary globalization, in which communication across continents has become easier than ever before, no belligerent wages war without a public explanation of why it is fighting and what it hopes to achieve—this is the strategic narrative. Such a narrative must appeal to its intended audience rationally, emotionally, and morally. Wartime objectives must appear logical and the reason for fighting must elicit supporters' passions or neutrals' sympathies. But reason and emotion can sometimes justify extreme measures. Moral concerns, according to Simpson, act as a check against excessive brutality. In contemporary conflicts, international human rights norms and laws help to define the moral boundaries of military action. An effective strategic narrative therefore requires a moral explanation of the conflict. For Simpson, moral arguments are part of strategy.[27]

Simpson describes how fighting in a morally unacceptable manner can prove counterproductive by examining the Russian army's actions in Chechnya during the 1990s and the Sri Lankan Army's 2006–9 campaign against the separatist Tamil Tigers. Both the Russians and Sri Lankans employed brutal methods against their adversaries and largely succeeded in establishing an acceptable level of security. But human rights violations committed in the process of achieving security objectives undermined those victories in the eyes of much of the international community while also fomenting resentment among defeated populations. According to Simpson, "the moral high ground, once evacuated, is very hard to regain."[28] Moral choices therefore generate military and political consequences on the battlefield and beyond.

In contemporary British and American wars, such moral and political consequences have not been limited to interrogation and detention; new technologies have also raised concerns. Employing guided missiles capable of precision strikes, American drone attacks increased dramatically during the first years of the Obama administration. In 2009, President Obama's first year in office, an estimated 298 people were killed by drone strikes—more than the total killed by drones during the last four years of the George W. Bush administration combined. The number of deaths from U.S. drone attacks peaked in 2010, when 849 people were estimated to have been killed.[29] Drone strikes may have degraded the operational capabilities of violent extremist groups like Al Qaeda, but American reliance on airstrikes has generated a moral backlash.[30] Such attacks have killed many insurgents but have also resulted in the deaths of civilians and, in some cases, American hostages.[31] The apparent injustice of civilian deaths and lack of redress for victims' families have contributed to bitterness and anger toward American security policy in places such as Pakistan, Afghanistan, and Yemen. These sentiments have the potential to inflame opposition toward American interests and increase support for violent extremists.[32]

In Britain and the United States, debates over interrogation, detention, and drone strikes highlight the centrality of moral issues in contemporary warfare, but such questions are not solely a twenty-first-century phenomenon. Although they are not simply a set of pure and impartial ideals, human rights concepts influenced military operations during the end of the British Empire and beyond. From the decolonization era to the post-9/11 War on Terror, such choices have played an important role in the conduct of war. The Cyprus, Aden, and Northern Ireland examples demonstrate that during the wars of decolonization and after, adversaries and third-party actors routinely mobilized human rights to serve their own purposes. These objectives may be self-serving or altruistic or may form some combination of the two. Regardless of how or why they were mobilized, human rights became part of the topography of war—the terrain of the battlefield. And like terrain, human rights may be used to one's advantage or ignored to one's peril.

Notes

Archival Abbreviations

AI	Amnesty International
AIR	Air Ministry
CAB	Cabinet
CAIN	Conflict Archive on the Internet
CO	Colonial Office
CJ 4	Home Office and Northern Ireland Office
CSA	Cyprus State Archives
DEFE	Ministry of Defence
DO	Dominions Office
FCO	Foreign and Commonwealth Office
FO	Foreign Office
HC Deb	House of Commons, Hansard Parliamentary Debates
HL Deb	House of Lords, Hansard Parliamentary Debates
ICRC	International Committee of the Red Cross
IOR	India Office Records
LCO	Lord Chancellor's Office
LO	Law Officers' Department
PREM	Prime Minister's Office
PRONI	Public Record Office of Northern Ireland, Belfast
NIPC	Northern Ireland Political Collection
U DJU	JUSTICE Papers
WO	War Office

Introduction

1. Brian Knowlton, "Top U.S. General in Iraq Sees 'Classical Guerrilla-Type' War," *New York Times*, July 16, 2003.

2. See Marnia Lazreg, *Torture and the Twilight of Empire: From Algiers to Baghdad* (Princeton: Princeton University Press, 2008). On torture more broadly, see Darius Rejali, *Torture and Democracy* (Princeton: Princeton University Press, 2009).

3. Robert M. Cassidy, *Counterinsurgency and the Global War on Terror: Military Culture and Irregular War* (Stanford: Stanford University Press, 2008); John Nagl, *Learning to Eat Soup with a Knife: Counterinsurgency Lessons from Malaya and Vietnam* (Chicago: University of Chicago Press, 2005).

4. See Michelle Gordon, "Army, Marine Corps Unveil Counterinsurgency Field Manual," U.S. Army News Archives, December 15, 2006, http://www.army.mil/article/1005; and Sarah Sewall, introduction to *Counterinsurgency Field Manual*, by U.S. Army and Marine Corps (Chicago: University of Chicago Press, 2007), xxxv.

5. Sewall, introduction, xxiv. Sewall does, however, recognize that "Britain sanctioned tactics that would not pass moral muster today" such as the limitation of food rations (starvation) and torture. See xxxiv.

6. Samantha Power, "Our War on Terror," *New York Times*, July 29, 2007. Also see Tom Hayden, "Samantha Power Goes to War," *Nation*, March 30, 2011.

7. See Cassidy, *Counterinsurgency and the Global War on Terror*, and Nagl, *Learning to Eat Soup with a Knife*. For criticism of the "British approach" from within the U.S. defense establishment, see Gian Gentile, *Wrong Turn: America's Deadly Embrace of Counterinsurgency* (New York: New Press, 2013), and Douglas Porch, *Counterinsurgency: Exposing the Myths of the New Way of War* (Cambridge: Cambridge University Press, 2013).

8. See David H. Ucko and Robert Egnell, *Counterinsurgency in Crisis: Britain and the Challenges of Modern Warfare* (New York: Columbia University Press, 2013), for a critique of the British army's contemporary, mythologized views of its counterinsurgency expertise.

9. Caroline Elkins, "Archives, Intelligence and Secrecy: The Cold War and the End of the British Empire," in *Decolonization and the Cold War: Negotiating Independence* (London: Bloomsbury, 2015); David French, *The British Way in Counter-Insurgency, 1945–1967* (Oxford: Oxford University Press, 2011); John Newsinger, *British Counterinsurgency: From Palestine to Northern Ireland*, 2nd ed. (Basingstoke: Palgrave Macmillan, 2015); and Martin Thomas and Gareth Curless, eds., *Decolonization and Conflict: Colonial Comparisons and Legacies* (London: Bloomsbury, 2017).

10. Christopher Bayly and Tim Harper, *Forgotten Wars: Freedom and Revolution in Southeast Asia* (Cambridge, MA: Belknap Press, 2010), 407–56, and Karl Hack, "Everyone Lived in Fear: Malaya and the British Way of Counter-Insurgency," *Small Wars & Insurgencies* 23, nos. 4–5 (October–December 2012): 671–99.

11. David Anderson, *Histories of the Hanged: Britain's Dirty War in Kenya and the End of Empire* (New York: Norton, 2005); Huw Bennett, *Fighting the Mau Mau: The British Army and Counter-Insurgency in the Kenya Emergency* (Cambridge: Cambridge University Press, 2012); Caroline Elkins, *Imperial Reckoning: The Untold Story of Britain's Gulag in Kenya* (New York: Henry Holt, 2005); and Fabian Klose, *Human Rights in the Shadow of Colonial Violence: The Wars of Independence in Kenya and Algeria*, trans. Dona Geyer (Philadelphia: University of Pennsylvania Press, 2013).

12. On the Lari massacre in Kenya see David Anderson, "Making the Loyalist Bargain: Surrender, Amnesty, and Impunity in Kenya's Decolonization, 1952–63," *International History Review* 39, no. 1 (2017): 50–1. On the plight of informers in Cyprus, see David French, "Toads and Informers: How the British Treated Their Collaborators during the Cyprus Emergency, 1955–9," *International History Review* 39, no. 1 (2017): 71–88.

13. For discussion of the many varieties of "internationalisms" on offer during the twentieth century, see Erez Manela, *The Wilsonian Moment: Self-Determination and the International Origins of Anticolonial Nationalism* (New York: Oxford University Press, 2007), and Mark Mazower, *No Enchanted Palace: The End of Empire and the Ideological Origins of the United Nations* (Princeton: Princeton University Press, 2009). For a sharp critique of the post-1945 international rights regime's effectiveness, see Samuel Moyn, *The Last Utopia: Human Rights in History* (Cambridge, MA: Harvard University Press, 2010).

14. This contradiction was an inherent feature of colonialism. See Dipesh Chakrabarty, *Provincializing Europe: Postcolonial Thought and Historical Difference* (Princeton: Princeton Univer-

sity Press, 2000), and Andrew Sartori, "The British Empire and Its Liberal Mission," *Journal of Modern History* 78, no. 3 (2005): 623–42.

15. It was only after the wars of decolonization that European powers supported the ICRC's attempts to introduce stronger protections for "irregular fighters." See Sibylle Scheipers, " 'Unlawful Combatants': The West's Treatment of Irregular Fighters in the 'War on Terror,' " *Orbis* 58, no. 4 (2014): 575–76.

16. For example, see how the colonial state responded to Eileen Fletcher's 1956 allegations of widespread abuse in Mau Mau detention camps. John Stuart, "Overseas Mission, Voluntary Service and Aid to Africa: Max Warren, the Church Missionary Society and Kenya, 1945–63," in *Ambiguities of Empire: Essays in Honour of Andrew Porter,* ed. Robert Holland and Sarah Stockwell (New York: Routledge, 2009), 191.

17. Caroline Elkins, "The Re-assertion of the British Empire in Southeast Asia," *Journal of Interdisciplinary History* 39, no. 3 (Winter 2009): 378.

18. Aoife Duffy, "Legacies of British Colonial Violence: Viewing Kenyan Detention Camps through the Hanslope Disclosure," *Law & History Review* 33, no. 3 (2015): 489–542. The apparent lack of activism in campaigns such as those in Malaya and Kenya stands in marked contrast to Britain's wars in Cyprus and Aden as well as the public discourse concerning French experiences during the 1954–62 Algerian War, in which Algerian anticolonial nationalists used public forums to expose the contradictions inherent in French colonial rule and to undermine European ideals of progress and civilization, which implicitly embraced some notion of human rights. See Matthew Connelly, *A Diplomatic Revolution: Algeria's Fight for Independence and the Origins of the Post-Cold War Era* (New York: Oxford University Press, 2002), 26–27.

19. For the purposes of this book, I include the ICRC as an "activist" organization because ICRC representatives lobbied the British government on behalf of refugees and detainees.

20. For recent studies on the violent end of empire, see Christopher Bayly and Tim Harper, *Forgotten Wars,* and Martin Thomas, *Fight or Flight: Britain, France, and Their Roads from Empire* (Oxford: Oxford University Press, 2014).

21. On imperial powers' moves toward federation, see Michael Collins, "Decolonization and the 'Federal' Moment," *Diplomacy & Statecraft* 24 (2013): 21–40, and Fred Cooper, *Citizenship between Empire and Nation: Remaking France and French Africa, 1945–1960* (Princeton: Princeton University Press, 2014).

22. Scholars have traditionally marked the Aden conflict as Britain's last war for empire and the late 1960s as the supposed "end" of the empire. See John Darwin, *The Empire Project: The Rise and Fall of the British World-System, 1830–1970* (Cambridge: Cambridge University Press, 2009), and Bernard Porter, *The Lion's Share: A Short History of British Imperialism, 1850–1970* (New York: Longman, 1975). David French follows this approach in his comprehensive study of post-1945 colonial counterinsurgency campaigns. See French, *The British Way in Counter-Insurgency.*

23. For example, see Jordanna Bailkin, *The Afterlife of Empire* (Berkeley: University of California Press, 2012); Paul Gilroy, *Postcolonial Melancholia* (New York: Columbia University Press, 2006); Wm. Roger Louis and Robert Robinson, "The Imperialism of Decolonization," *Journal of Imperial and Commonwealth History* 22, no. 3 (1994): 462–511; Sarah Stockwell, "Ends of Empire," in *The British Empire: Themes and Perspectives,* ed. Sarah Stockwell (Oxford: Blackwell, 2008), and Andrew S. Thompson, *The Empire Strikes Back? The Impact of Imperialism on Britain from the Mid-Nineteenth Century* (New York: Routledge, 2005).

24. Robert Thompson, *Defeating Communist Insurgency: The Lessons of Malaya and Vietnam* (New York: Praeger, 1966).

25. Director of Operations, Malaya, *The Conduct of Anti-Terrorist Operations in Malaya,* 3rd ed. (London: HMSO, 1958), IV-3–IV-4.

26. Historians understand colonial legal systems as pluralistic spaces in which law often applied to different groups in different ways. See Lauren Benton, *Law and Colonial Cultures: Legal Regimes in World History, 1400–1900* (Cambridge: Cambridge University Press, 2001), and Jane Burbank and Frederick Cooper, *Empires in World History: Power and the Politics of Difference* (Princeton: Princeton University Press, 2011).

27. Thompson, *Defeating Communist Insurgency*, 52–54.

28. Studies that contributed to this mythologized interpretation include Ian F. W. Beckett and John Pimlott, eds., *Armed Forces and Modern Counter-Insurgency* (New York: St. Martin's, 1985), and Thomas Mockaitis, *British Counterinsurgency, 1919–60* (Basingstoke: Macmillan, 1990). This view met with criticism from other scholars at the time, however. One reviewer of Mockaitis's book called it nothing more than "an academic retelling of the British army's version of events." See John Newsinger, "Review of Thomas Mockaitis, *British Counterinsurgency, 1919–60*," *Race & Class* 34, no. 2 (1992): 96. On Beckett and Pimlott, see Annette Seegers, "If Only . . . The Ongoing Search for Method in Counter Insurgency," *Journal of Contemporary African Studies* 9, no. 2 (1990): 203–24.

29. Nasser Hussain, *The Jurisprudence of Emergency: Colonialism and the Rule of Law* (Ann Arbor: University of Michigan Press, 2003), 6, 136, and Diane Kirby and Catharine Colebourne, eds., *Law, History, Colonialism: The Reach of Empire* (Manchester, UK: Manchester University Press, 2010).

30. French, *The British Way in Counter-Insurgency*; A. W. B. Simpson, *Human Rights and the End of Empire: Britain and the Genesis of the European Convention* (Oxford: Oxford University Press, 2001). For the argument that the growth of state power through such pragmatic moves as emergency legislation has been a central aspect of twentieth-century government, see Giorgio Agamben, *State of Exception*, trans. Kevin Attell (Chicago: University of Chicago Press, 2005).

31. David Anderson, "Mau Mau in the High Court and the 'Lost' British Empire Archives: Colonial Conspiracy, or Bureaucratic Bungle?," *Journal of Imperial and Commonwealth History* 39, no. 5 (2011): 699–716, and Caroline Elkins, "Alchemy of Evidence: Mau Mau, the British Empire, and the High Court of Justice," *Journal of Imperial and Commonwealth History* 39, no. 5 (2011): 731–48.

32. BBC News, "Mau Mau Uprising: Kenyans Win UK Torture Ruling," October 5, 2012, http://www.bbc.co.uk/news/uk-19843719; and "Mau Mau Torture Victims to Receive Compensation," June 6, 2013, http://www.bbc.com/news/uk-22790037.

33. Richard Drayton, "The Foreign Office Secretly Hoarded 1.2m Files. It's Historical Narcissism," *Guardian*, October 27, 2013.

34. For recent studies of the migrated archive see David Anderson, "Guilty Secrets: Deceit, Denial, and the Discovery of Kenya's 'Migrated Archive,'" *History Workshop Journal* 80, no. 1 (2015): 142–60, and Caroline Elkins, "Looking beyond Mau Mau: Archiving Violence in the Era of Decolonization," *American Historical Review* 120, no. 3 (2015): 852–68.

35. On the importance of private collections and oral testimonies, see Elkins, "Re-assertion of the British Empire," 383–84. Many key figures are no longer alive, but scholars can rely on prerecorded interviews held in collections such as the archives of Amnesty International's International Secretariat and the Imperial War Museum's accessions. In June 2015, the International Committee of the Red Cross publicly released archival material from 1966 through 1975. Several underutilized collections of personal papers also provide valuable insight. I did not conduct new interviews for chapter 5 because of the abundance of contemporary reporting, first-person testimonies, recent public inquiries, and historical literature on the Troubles means that a significant amount of this material is already available. The Northern Ireland case is included to demonstrate the persistence of cooperative manipulation beyond the traditional colonial context. Although a full-fledged investigation of human rights and counterinsurgency in Northern Ireland warrants deeper study in its own right, such an exploration is beyond the scope of this book.

36. On war, law, and empire, see Geoffrey Best, *Humanity in Warfare* (London: Wiedenfeld and Nicolson, 1980); Stephen Neff, *War and the Law of Nations: A General History* (Cambridge: Cambridge University Press, 2008); and Martti Koskenniemi, *The Gentle Civilizer of Nations: The Rise and Fall of International Law, 1870–1960* (Cambridge: Cambridge University Press, 2002).

37. For this interpretation, see Elizabeth Borgwardt, *A New Deal for the World: America's Vision for Human Rights* (Cambridge, MA: Harvard University Press, 2007); Micheline Ishay, *The History of Human Rights: From Ancient Times to the Globalization Era* (Berkeley: University of California Press, 2004); and Paul Gordon Lauren, *The Evolution of International Human Rights: Visions Seen* (Philadelphia: University of Pennsylvania Press, 1998). These scholars view the

idea of human rights as broadly inclusive of state-derived civil and political rights, self-determination sought by anticolonial nationalists, economic and social rights, and individual rights that belong to all human beings by virtue of their common humanity.

38. See Barbara Keys, *Reclaiming American Virtue: The Human Rights Revolution of the 1970s* (Cambridge, MA: Harvard University Press, 2014); Moyn, *The Last Utopia*, 166. See also Jan Eckel and Samuel Moyn, eds., *The Breakthrough: Human Rights in the 1970s* (Philadelphia: University of Pennsylvania Press, 2014).

39. Stefan-Ludwig Hoffmann, "Human Rights in History," *Past & Present* 232 (August 2016): 279–310. For a broad study of human rights genealogies, see Stefan-Ludwig Hoffmann, ed., *Human Rights in the Twentieth Century* (Cambridge: Cambridge University Press, 2010).

40. On minority rights, see Carole Fink, *Defending the Rights of Others: The Great Powers, the Jews, and International Minority Protection, 1878–1938* (Cambridge: Cambridge University Press, 2004).

41. Moyn, *The Last Utopia*, 106–9.

42. Bruno Cabanes, *The Great War and the Origins of Humanitarianism, 1918–1924* (Cambridge: Cambridge University Press, 2014).

43. On the role of non-Western states, see Roland Burke, *Decolonization and the Evolution of International Human Rights* (Philadelphia: University of Pennsylvania Press, 2011); Steven L. B. Jensen, *The Making of International Human Rights: The 1960s, Decolonization, and the Reconstruction of Global Values* (Cambridge: Cambridge University Press, 2016); and Brad Simpson, "'The First Right': The Carter Administration, Indonesia, and the Transnational Human Rights Politics of the 1970s," in *The Human Rights Revolution: An International History*, ed. Akira Iriye, Petra Goedde, and William Hitchcock (Oxford: Oxford University Press, 2012).

44. Universal Declaration of Human Rights, http://www.un.org/en/documents/udhr.

45. Other scholars have also employed this definition when examining human rights during the post-1945 era. See Sarah B. Snyder, *Human Rights Activism and the End of the Cold War: A Transnational History of the Helsinki Network* (New York: Cambridge University Press, 2011), 4–5.

46. See George J. Andreopolous, "The Age of National Liberation Movements," in *The Laws of War: Constraints on Warfare in the Western World*, ed. Michael Howard, George Andreopoulos, and Mark Shulman (New Haven: Yale University Press, 1994), 191–213; William Hitchcock, "Human Rights and the Laws of War: The Geneva Conventions of 1949," in Iriye et al., *Human Rights Revolution*, 93–112; and Michael Howard, "Constraints on Warfare," in Iriye at al., *Human Rights Revolution*; and Best, *Humanity in Warfare*, 33–53.

47. Charles Dunlap, "Lawfare Today: A Perspective," *Yale Journal of International Affairs*, Winter 2008, 146.

48. For example, David Frakt, "Lawfare and Counterlawfare: The Demonization of the Gitmo Bar and Other Legal Strategies in the War on Terror," *Case Western Reserve Journal of International Law* 43 (2010): 335, and Orde F. Kittrie, *Lawfare: Law as a Weapon of War* (New York: Oxford University Press, 2016). On the older history of lawfare, see Erika Myers, "Conquering Peace: Military Commissions as a Lawfare Strategy in the Mexican War," *American Journal of Criminal Law* 35 (2007): 201.

49. George Andreopoulos, "The Age of National Liberation Movements," in Howard et al., *Laws of War*, 191–213; and Neff, *War and the Law of Nations*, 314–56.

50. Andreas Eckert, "African Nationalists and Human Rights, 1940s-1970s," in Hoffmann, *Human Rights in the Twentieth Century*, 283–300.

51. See Connelly, *A Diplomatic Revolution*; Fabian Klose, "The Colonial Testing Ground: The International Committee of the Red Cross and the Violent End of Empire," *Humanity: An International Journal of Human Rights, Humanitarianism, and Development* 2, no. 1 (Spring 2011): 107–27. In Algeria, the insurgent Front de Libération Nationale (FLN) ordered its fighters to obey the 1949 Geneva Conventions at a time when France refused to accept that the Geneva Conventions applied to colonial wars.

52. Geoffrey Best, *War and Law since 1945* (Oxford: Clarendon Press, 1994).

53. There were three interrelated ECHRs—the European Convention on Human Rights, the European Commission of Human Rights, and the European Court of Human Rights. For the sake of clarity, I use the abbreviation ECHR to refer only to the convention.

54. Mikael Rask Madsen, " 'Legal Diplomacy'—Law, Politics and the Genesis of Postwar European Human Rights," in Hoffmann, *Human Rights in the Twentieth Century*, and Marco Duranti, "Conservatism, Christian Democracy and the European Human Rights Project: 1945–1950" (PhD diss., Yale University, 2009).

55. Madsen, "Legal Diplomacy," 62–81.

56. Simpson, *Human Rights and the End of Empire*, 824–44. Despite the decision to support what Simpson calls an "export trade" in human rights, Colonial Office officials largely opposed the ECHR. On the origins of the ECHR, see Marco Duranti, "Curbing Labour's Totalitarian Temptation: European Human Rights Law and British Postwar Politics," *Humanity: An International Journal of Human Rights, Humanitarianism, and Development* 3, no. 3 (2012): 361–83; Marco Duranti, *The Conservative Human Rights Revolution: European Identity, Transnational Politics, and the Origins of the European Convention* (Oxford: Oxford University Press, 2017); Andrew Moravcsik, "The Origins of Human Rights Regimes: Democratic Delegation in Postwar Europe," *International Organization* 54, no. 2 (2000): 217–52; Charles O. H. Parkinson, *Bills of Rights and Decolonization: The Emergence of Domestic Human Rights Instruments in Britain's Overseas Territories* (Oxford: Oxford University Press, 2007); and A. W. B. Simpson, "Round Up the Usual Suspects: The Legacy of British Colonialism and the European Convention on Human Rights," *Loyola Law Review* 41, no. 4 (1996): 629–711.

57. French, *The British Way in Counter-Insurgency*, 74–138.

58. Koskenniemi, *The Gentle Civilizer of Nations*, 130.

59. Hussain, *The Jurisprudence of Emergency*, 136.

60. For the post–World War II context, see Mazower, *No Enchanted Palace*, 28–65. Such racism also generated domestic opposition to empire from organizations such as the Movement for Colonial Freedom. See Stephen Howe, *Anticolonialism in British Politics: The Left and the End of Empire, 1918–1964* (Oxford: Clarendon Press, 1993).

61. Roger Heacock, "The Framing of Empire: Cyprus and Cypriots through British Eyes, 1878–1960," *Cyprus Review* 23, no. 2 (Fall 2011): 21–37.

62. Peter Neumann, *Britain's Long War: British Strategy in the Northern Ireland Conflict, 1969–98* (Basingstoke: Palgrave Macmillan, 2003), 17–21.

63. French, *The British Way in Counter-Insurgency*.

64. Simpson, *Human Rights and the End of Empire*, 870. See also Frank Heinlein, *British Government Policy and Decolonisation, 1945–1963: Scrutinising the Official Mind* (London: Frank Cass, 2002).

65. DO 35/3776, Creech-Jones Circular 25102/2/49, March 28, 1949, as quoted in Fabian Klose, " 'Source of Embarrassment': Human Rights, State of Emergency, and the Wars of Decolonization," in Hoffmann, *Human Rights in the Twentieth Century*, 242.

66. ICRC, B AG 202-049-001, De Traz [ICRC representative] to ICRC headquarters, Geneva, March 27, 1957.

67. David Vincent, *The Culture of Secrecy: Britain, 1832–1998* (Oxford: Oxford University Press, 1998), 12–17. Vincent calls government secrecy "the natural guardian of embarrassment," 315. For more on secrecy, see Ian Cobain, *The History Thieves: Secrets, Lies and the Shaping of a Modern Nation* (London: Portobello Books, 2016), and Christopher Moran, *Classified: Secrecy and the State in Modern Britain* (Cambridge: Cambridge University Press, 2013).

68. Political scientists Margaret Keck and Kathryn Sikkink argue that activists seek to achieve their goals by publicizing their cause, using rhetorical symbols to influence public opinions, gaining support from strong external allies, and publicly criticizing politicians who fail to take action against abuses. See Keck and Sikkink, *Activists beyond Borders: Advocacy Networks in International Politics* (Ithaca: Cornell University Press, 1998).

1. A Lawyers' War

1. Hansard, HL Deb., February 27, 1957, vol. 202, cols. 98–99.

2. On the use of emergency regulations during British campaigns, see French, *The British Way in Counter-Insurgency*, 74–104.

3. See Nancy Crawshaw, *The Cyprus Revolt: An Account of the Struggle for Union with Greece* (London: George Allen & Unwin, 1978); Robert Holland, *Britain and the Revolt in Cyprus, 1954–1959* (Oxford: Clarendon Press, 1998); and Mockaitis, *British Counterinsurgency, 1919–60*.

4. See Ian Cobain, *Cruel Britannia: A Secret History of Torture* (London: Portobello Books, 2012); Tabitha Morgan, *Sweet and Bitter Island: A History of the British in Cyprus* (London: I.B. Tauris, 2010); John Newsinger, *British Counterinsurgency: From Palestine to Northern Ireland*, 2nd ed. (Basingstoke: Palgrave Macmillan, 2015); and Calder Walton, *Empire of Secrets: British Intelligence, the Cold War, and the Twilight of Empire* (New York: Overlook Press, 2013).

5. David French, *Fighting EOKA: The British Counter-Insurgency Campaign on Cyprus, 1955–1959* (Oxford: Oxford University Press, 2015).

6. In Cyprus, as in other legal systems based on the British tradition, the legal profession was divided between barristers, who conducted courtroom advocacy, and solicitors, who were not authorized to argue cases before a court. The lawyers mentioned in this book are barristers—I use the term interchangeably with "lawyers" and "attorneys."

7. Holland, *Britain and the Revolt in Cyprus*, 11–19; Simpson, *Human Rights and the End of Empire*, 884–87; Thomas, *Fight or Flight*, 269–70; Anastasia Yiangou, *Cyprus in World War II: Politics and Conflict in the Eastern Mediterranean* (London: I.B. Tauris, 2012), 15–17.

8. For an overview of the conflict, see Holland, *Britain and the Revolt in Cyprus*.

9. On the international dimension of the conflict, see Evanthis Hatzivassiliou, *Britain and the International Status of Cyprus, 1955–1959* (Minneapolis: University of Minnesota Press, 1997); Edward Johnson, "Britain and the Cyprus Problem at the United Nations," *Journal of Imperial and Commonwealth History* 28, no. 3 (2000): 113–30.

10. For a thorough military history, see French, *Fighting EOKA*. Grivas's memoirs are an interesting, if biased, perspective on the insurgents' side of the war. See George Grivas, *The Memoirs of General Grivas*, ed. Charles Foley (New York: Praeger, 1964).

11. Holland, *Britain and the Revolt in Cyprus*, 55–57.

12. Ibid., 60–76.

13. French, *Fighting EOKA*, 92.

14. Ibid., 130–31. See also CO 926/549, Harding to Colonial Secretary, April 5, 1956.

15. CO 926/562, Colonial Secretary to Harding, November 25, 1955, and Harding to Colonial Secretary, November 26, 1955.

16. Simpson, *Human Rights and the End of Empire*, 80–90.

17. WO 106/6020, Report on the Cyprus Emergency, 1959, pp. 91–94.

18. FCO 141/4320, Governor, Cyprus to Colonial Office, May 3, 1956, and FCO 141/3795, *Cyprus Gazette*, no. 3891, Emergency Powers (Public Safety and Order) Regulations, November 26, 1955.

19. French, *Fighting EOKA*, 95.

20. FCO 141/3795, *Cyprus Gazette*, no. 3891.

21. FCO 141/3665, undersecretary (internal security) to all commissioners, December 28, 1955.

22. FCO 141/3665, Commissioner of Police to Chief of Staff, April 27, 1956.

23. WO 106/6020, Report on the Cyprus Emergency, 1959, p. 50.

24. David French, *The British Way in Counter-Insurgency*, 107–9.

25. FCO 141/3795, Assistant Commissioner of Police, CID, to Faiz, Secretariat Nicosia, November 3, 1956.

26. FCO 141/3795, *Cyprus Gazette*, no. 3891.

27. As quoted Simpson, *Human Rights and the End of Empire*, 931.

28. French, *Fighting EOKA*, 130–31. See also CO 926/549, Harding to Colonial Secretary, April 5, 1956.

29. Jim Herlihy, correspondence with author, July 18–19, 2013.

30. French, *Fighting EOKA*, 145–49.

31. FCO 141/4314, Harding to Chief of Staff, His Excellency the Governor, April 10, 1956.

32. In at least two cases in which interrogators left physical evidence of their brutal interrogation methods, the interrogators were prosecuted and convicted. See chapter 2.

33. CO 926/458, Colonial Secretary to Harding, September 8, 1956; French, *Fighting EOKA*, 205–7.

34. FCO 141/4310, Governor, Cyprus to Colonial Secretary, March 2, 1957.

35. David French, "Toads and Informers: How the British Treated Their Collaborators during the Cyprus Emergency, 1955–9," *International History Review* 39, no. 1 (2017): 71–88.

36. French, *Fighting EOKA*, 145–49.

37. Benton, *Law and Colonial Cultures*; Burbank and Cooper, *Empires in World History*; and Bonny Ibhawoh, *Imperial Justice: Africans in Empire's Court* (Oxford: Oxford University Press, 2013).

38. On "imperial intermediaries," see Burbank and Cooper, *Empires in World History*.

39. Dimitrios H. Taliadoros, *An Album of Lawyers Who Defended EOKA Fighters, 1955–1959* (Nicosia: Department of Education and Culture, 2002), 45–46.

40. Ibid., 47–50.

41. Law Office of the Republic of Cyprus website, Former Attorneys General, http://www.law.gov.cy/law/lawoffice.nsf/dmlformerattorneygenerals_bn/dmlformerattorneygenerals_bn?OpenDocument.

42. Author interview with Renos Lyssiotis, January 8, 2014.

43. Author interview with Lellos Demetriades, February 25, 2014.

44. Nancy Crawshaw, "Justice in Cyprus: In the Special Courts," *Manchester Guardian*, July 2, 1957.

45. Simpson, *Human Rights and the End of Empire*, 920.

46. CSA, SA1/1096/1956, Petition for Special Leave to Appeal, Case of Karaolis and the Queen, December 9, 1955.

47. FCO 141/4305, Colonial Secretary to Harding, April 4, 1956; Harding to Colonial Secretary, April 10, 1956; Colonial Secretary to Harding, April 13, 1956.

48. FCO 141/4305, Harding to Colonial Secretary, April 20, 1956.

49. CSA, SA1/1297/1957, Clerides and Triantafyllides to the Governor, October 7, 1957, and Acting Administrative Secretary to Triantafyllides, October 16, 1957.

50. FO 371/123904/RG 1081/1436, sample dated May 25, 1956.

51. Simpson, *Human Rights and the End of Empire*, 921.

52. Hansard, HC Deb., March 12, 1956, vol. 550, col. 36. Eventually, the domestic debate over capital punishment resulted in the 1957 Homicide Act, which limited the death penalty to five categories of murder. See Lizzie Seal, *Capital Punishment in Twentieth-Century Britain: Audience, Justice, Memory* (New York: Routledge, 2014).

53. FCO 141/4305, Karaolis case talking points, not dated. During the course of the emergency, thirty-eight EOKA suspects were condemned to death. Nine were executed. All others either saw their punishments reduced on appeal or were granted clemency by the governor. Of the nine men hanged, all were convicted on murder or attempted murder charges except for one, who was convicted of violating the law that prohibited the carrying or possession of firearms or explosives—as opposed to laws proscribing the actual use of these weapons. See French, *Fighting EOKA, 97–99*, and FCO 141/4458, Impressions of Mr. Lockley, Head of the CID, August 27, 1957, p. 21.

54. Shaw made this statement during the trial of Charalambos Christodoulides, but he had applied the same logic during the Sampson case. See CO 926/879, Case No. 466/57, February 17, 1957, p. 5.

55. FCO 141/4458, Impressions of Mr. Lockley, p. 20.

56. Crawshaw, *The Cyprus Revolt*, 247 and Holland, *Britain and the Revolt in Cyprus*, 191. In June 1956, Shaw was wounded in an EOKA attack. Security force commanders suspected that after the attack, he went out of his way to demonstrate his impartiality so that he could not be accused of seeking revenge on EOKA defendants. In contrast, Greek Cypriot barristers perceived Shaw as strict but fair. See Glafkos Clerides, *Cyprus: My Deposition*, vol. 1 (Nicosia: Alithia Publishing, 1989), 111.

57. For example, see the case of Charalambos Christodoulides, CO 926/879, Case No. 466/57, February 18, 1957, pp. 3–4, 6, and the case of George Sfongaras, CO 926/880, Cyprus—Appeal, telegram numbered H-531, May 21, 1957.

58. As quoted in Simpson, *Human Rights and the End of Empire*, 910, from FO 371/136286/RG1019/3.

59. FCO 141/4590, Elected Members of the Bar Council, not dated.

60. FCO 141/3951, Cassels to Harding, January 23, 1958.

61. FCO 141/3400, Kutchuk to Armitage, September 19, 1955.

62. FCO 141/3951, Cassels to Harding, January 23, 1958; French, *Fighting EOKA*, 257; and "Rauf Denktash," *Daily Telegraph*, January 15, 2012, http://www.telegraph.co.uk/news/obituaries/politics-obituaries/9016548/Rauf-Denktash.html.

63. FCO 141/4593, Notes from Meeting at Government House with Representatives of the Bar Council, December 17, 1958.

64. FCO 141/4360, Notes of a Meeting Held at Government House at 4 P.M. on Thursday, the 3rd of January, 1957.

65. French, *Fighting EOKA*, 140–41.

66. FCO 141/4591, Munir to Chief of Staff, February 15, 1956.

67. FCO 141/4591, Chief of Staff Memorandum, "Arrest & Detention without Warrant," February 18, 1956.

68. FCO 141/4591, Munir to Chief of Staff.

69. On British colonial legal systems, see Nasser Hussain, *The Jurisprudence of Emergency: Colonialism and the Rule of Law* (Ann Arbor: University of Michigan Press, 2003); Ibhawoh, *Imperial Justice*; Diane Kirby and Catharine Colebourne, eds., *Law, History, Colonialism: The Reach of Empire* (Manchester, UK: Manchester University Press, 2010); and Elizabeth Kolsky, *Colonial Justice in British India: White Violence and the Rule of Law* (Cambridge: Cambridge University Press, 2010).

70. FCO 141/4591, Administrative Secretary Memorandum, August 17, 1956.

71. FCO 141/4458, Impressions of Mr. Lockley, p. 27, 17–20.

72. French, *Fighting EOKA*, 144.

73. FCO 141/4590, telegram, Demetriades to Henry, October 17, 1956, and telegram, October 18, 1956.

74. FCO 141/4590, Pavlides and Triantafyllides to Henry, October 18, 1956.

75. FCO 141/4591, Henry to Staff Officer-in-Charge, Nicosia, December 10, 1958.

76. French, *Fighting EOKA*, 140–45. For a selection on the Suez Crisis generally, see Wm. Roger Louis, *Ends of British Imperialism: The Scramble for Empire, Suez, and Decolonization* (London: I.B.Tauris, 2006), 589–638; Wm. Roger Louis and Roger Owen, *Suez 1956: The Crisis and Its Consequences* (Oxford: Clarendon Press, 1989); Simon C. Smith, ed., *Reassessing Suez 1956: New Perspectives on the Crisis and its Aftermath* (Aldershot, UK: Ashgate, 2008); and Thomas, *Fight or Flight*, 165–87.

77. FCO 141/3795, Supplement no. 3 to *Cyprus Gazette,* no. 4002, November 23, 1956, and no. 3891, November 26, 1956, p. 728.

78. As quoted in French, *The British Way in Counter-Insurgency*. See also WO 106/6020, Report on the Cyprus Emergency, 1959, Annex "T," Emergency Legislation, p. 95.

79. FCO 141/3795, *Cyprus Gazette,* no. 4001, Emergency Powers (Public Safety and Order) Regulations, November 22, 1956; WO 106/6020, Report on the Cyprus Emergency, 1959, p. 95.

80. French, *Fighting EOKA*, 145–49.

81. FCO 141/4593, Cyprus Bar Council Resolution, December 8, 1956, and accompanying cover letter, Pavlides to the governor, December 11, 1956.

82. FCO 141/4593, Pavlides to the governor, December 11, 1956; duplicate in FCO 141/4590.

83. FCO 141/4360, Governor to Colonial Secretary, December 21, 1956.

84. Charles Foley, *Island in Revolt* (London: Longman's, 1962), 125.

85. Eric Baker Papers, EB1/H2, "Notes on Conversation with Peter Benenson after Meeting with Sir Hugh Foot, 1.12.57"; AI-982, Benenson essay, August 1983, pp. 4–6, and Benenson interview, November 12, 1983, pp. 55–56.

86. "New Regulations in Cyprus: 'Ruthless Severity,'" *Manchester Guardian*, December 5, 1956.

87. See Hansard, HL Deb., December 6, 1956, vol. 200, cols. 813–25. For press reporting on the debate, see "Press Decree to End 'Slander,'" November 29, 1956; "Cyprus Editor in Court" and "Press Decree in Cyprus: Mr. Grimond Horrified," December 1, 1956; and "New Emergency Regulations in Cyprus Attacked," December 7, 1956, all in the *Manchester Guardian*.

88. Hansard, HC Deb., December 21, 1956, vol. 562, cols. 1610–1611, 1622.

89. Benenson later traveled to Cyprus with Labour MP Barbara Castle, who also maintained strong interest in the Cyprus conflict and met with Cyprus Bar Council representatives. See Castle Papers 10, diary entries September 18–21, 1958, and Castle Papers 252.

90. FCO 141/4361, Clerides to Benenson, December 17, 1956.

91. Hansard, HC Deb., December 21, 1956, vol. 562, cols. 1622–1631.

92. Ibid.

93. Ibid.

94. FCO 141/4360, note by the Attorney General on matters raised by the Bar Council of Cyprus.

95. FCO 141/4360, Harding to Deputy Governor, December 22, 1956.

96. FCO 141/4320, Governor, Cyprus, to Colonial Secretary, December 21, 1956.

97. On Eden's role in the Suez Crisis, see Ronald Hyam, *Britain's Declining Empire: The Road to Decolonisation, 1918–1968* (Cambridge: Cambridge University Press, 2006), 221–40; Jonathan Pearson, *Sir Anthony Eden and the Suez Crisis: Reluctant Gamble* (New York: Palgrave Macmillan, 2003); and David Reynolds, "Eden the Diplomatist, 1931–1956: Suezide of a Statesman?" *History* 74, no. 1 (1989): 64–84. On the aftermath of Suez more broadly, see G. C. Peden, "Suez and Britain's Decline as a World Power," *Historical Journal* 55, no. 4 (December 2012): 1073–96.

98. Hansard, HC Deb., February 19, 1957 vol. 565, col. 322.

99. "Cyprus Policy in 'Blind Alley,'" *Manchester Guardian*, February 20, 1957.

100. FCO 141/4360, Colonial Office to Harding, telegram 383, March 8, 1957.

101. FCO 141/4360, Colonial Office to Harding, telegram 376, March 8, 1957.

102. French, *Fighting EOKA*, 237–38.

103. Ibid., 154–57. On the Cyprus issue at the UN, see Hatzivassiliou, *Britain and the International Status of Cyprus, 1955–1959*, and Johnson, "Britain and the Cyprus Problem."

104. Council of Europe, European Convention on Human Rights, p. 6, 13, http://www.echr.coe.int/Documents/Convention_BNG.pdf.

105. Simpson, *Human Rights and the End of Empire*, 2–4.

106. Simpson believes that Greek officials agreed to a limited investigation of emergency legislation because they sought a quick decision before discussing Cyprus again at the next UN General Assembly meeting; see ibid., 937–39.

107. Author interview with Renos Lyssiotis, January 8, 2014; and Taliadoros, *An Album of Lawyers*.

108. FCO 141/4310, Governor, Cyprus, to Colonial Secretary, February 19, 1957. Lambrou's situation was documented upon her October 13, 1956, arrest. She was pregnant but unmarried, aborted while in custody, and was taken to a hospital. A Cypriot doctor stated that she had had a septic abortion and that her genital organs were dirty and infected. The doctor was unable to say what had caused the abortion.

109. FCO 141/4592, Memorandum of Evidence Prepared by the Bar of Cyprus, discussed at Government House on January 9, 1957.

110. U DJU 11–15, extract from *Times of Cyprus*, June 29, 1957.

111. The officers in question were Lieutenant Robin Linzee and Captain Gerald O'Driscoll. See WO 71/1231, and Simpson, *Human Rights and the End of Empire*, 896–97.

112. FCO 141/4310, Governor, Cyprus, to Colonial Secretary, March 2, 1957; see also French, *Fighting EOKA*, 203–4.

113. FO 371/130145, Cyprus to Colonial Secretary, October 2, 1957.

114. Simpson, *Human Rights and the End of Empire*, 932–35, quote on 934, originally CO 936/294, Minute by Marnham, May 22, 1956. Simpson indicated that in personal correspondence between himself and Vallat, Vallat described the "consternation" that the Greek application had caused in Whitehall.

115. Ibid., 962, quoting CO 936/297, Vallat to McPetrie, December 21, 1956.

116. French, *Fighting EOKA*, 216. This new constitution was devised by a committee headed by Lord Radcliffe. Greek Cypriots opposed the recommendations because Cyprus would remain under British rule and Radcliffe had presided over the border commission that partitioned India and Pakistan in 1947. Greek Cypriots and Turkish Cypriots alike feared a similar fate.

117. FCO 141/4320, Governor, Cyprus, to Colonial Office, January 30, 1957.
118. Simpson, *Human Rights and the End of Empire*, 931.
119. FCO 141/4320, Governor, Cyprus, to Colonial Secretary, January 31, 1957.
120. French, *Fighting EOKA*, 154–57.
121. Simpson, *Human Rights and the End of Empire*, 971–73.

2. The Shadow of Strasbourg

1. Simpson, *Human Rights and the End of Empire*, 1020–26. For details on the forty-nine cases, see CO 926/881–7, 504–30. The second Greek application was formally registered as Application No. 299/57.
2. Stanley Mayes, *Makarios: A Biography* (New York: St. Martin's, 1981), 46–61, and Holland, *Britain and the Revolt in Cyprus*, 28.
3. Hatzivassiliou, *Britain and the International Status of Cyprus*, 10–12, and Holland, *Britain and the Revolt in Cyprus*, 32.
4. Edward Johnson, "Britain and the Cyprus Problem," 113–16. On British great power politics in the Mediterranean, including Cyprus's role, see Robert Holland, *Blue-Water Empire: The British in the Mediterranean since 1800* (New York: Penguin, 2012).
5. Holland, *Britain and the Revolt in Cyprus*, 290.
6. FCO 141/4592, Memorandum of Evidence Prepared by the Bar of Cyprus, discussed at Government House, January 9, 1957.
7. French, *The British Way in Counter-Insurgency*, 230.
8. Bennett, *Fighting the Mau Mau*, 77–80. Bennett provides an excellent discussion of Common Article 3; a formal definition for "noninternational armed conflict" was not established until a 1997 ruling by the International Criminal Tribunal for the former Yugoslavia.
9. FCO 141/4673, Nicosia Central Prison report on de Traz's second visit, March 22, 1957.
10. ICRC, B AG-202-049-001, de Traz to ICRC, August 21, 1957.
11. ICRC, B AG-202-049-003.01, de Traz to ICRC, August 23, 1957.
12. ICRC, B AG 225-049-002, de Preux, ICRC headquarters, to de Traz, November 26, 1958.
13. It is not clear whether this water torture was the same technique as contemporary waterboarding. Regarding genital twisting, Simpson notes that "given the fragility of the male anatomy this technique is effective and need leave no obvious traces even though considerable pain has been caused. It was, I recall, not an unknown practice in my public school." See Simpson, *Human Rights and the End of Empire*, 1025.
14. Ibid., 1020–26.
15. CO 926/880, loose minute, May 31, 1957, and CO 926/881, Kirkness to Morris, June 19, 1957. On the atrocity campaign, see Crawshaw, *The Cyprus Revolt*, 244–55.
16. French, *Fighting EOKA*, 196, quoting CO 926/672/CIC (57) 22 (Final), July 14, 1957.
17. FCO 141/4495, Governor, Cyprus, to Colonial Office, May 7, 58.
18. Simpson, *Human Rights and the End of Empire*, 1025.
19. Ibid., 1023–27.
20. FCO 141/4361, Clerides to Benenson, December 17, 1956.
21. Taliadoros, *An Album of Lawyers,* and author interview with Renos Lyssiotis, January 8, 2014.
22. Crawshaw, *The Cyprus Revolt*, 251.
23. French, *Fighting EOKA*, 198–99.
24. CO 926/880, Governor, Cyprus, to Colonial Secretary, telegram no. 1162, June 10, 1957.
25. CO 926/880, Foreword by the Governor, "Allegations of Brutality" white paper, June 1957.
26. Crawshaw, *The Cyprus Revolt*, 250–51.
27. CO 926/880, Foreword, "Allegations of Brutality."
28. CO 926/879; there were six convictions for abuse by March 1957; also see FO 371/123885/808; "Archbishop Makarios Repeats His Torture Allegations," *Manchester Guardian*, July 20, 1957. The following year, a former soldier wrote to the editor of the *Manchester*

Guardian, claiming that during his intelligence training course, he and his colleagues were taught that "it would probably be necessary for us to use various forms of physical torture. The tortures that were described to us had the advantage of leaving none of the visible traces which might be noticed by members of the International Red Cross." See WO 32/17501, "Training in Torture," and letter from *Manchester Guardian* editor Alastair Hetherington to Secretary of State for War Christopher Soames, December 3, 1958. After receiving a strident denial from the Ministry of Defence, the *Manchester Guardian* did not publish the soldier's letter.

29. "Inquiry into Cypriot Prison Charges Refused: Complaints 'Timed with Archbishop,'" *Manchester Guardian,* June 28, 1957.

30. CO 926/881, Kirkness to Morris, June 19, 1957.

31. Ibid.

32. CO 926/881, Lennox-Boyd to Harding, June 26, 1957.

33. Simpson, *Human Rights and the End of Empire,* 977–78, quoting FO 371/130144/1073/5A.

34. "'Human Rights' Probe Begins on Jan. 13th," *Times of Cyprus,* December 9, 1957.

35. Quoted in Simpson, *Human Rights and the End of Empire,* 986.

36. Ibid., 981, quoting CO 936/487 telegram, February 12, 1957.

37. Ibid., 985. See CAB 129/90 C. (57) 258.

38. Holland, *Britain and the Revolt in Cyprus,* 206–9.

39. Simpson, *Human Rights and the End of Empire,* 983–86.

40. Harding Papers 5, Sinclair to Harding, November 12, 1957.

41. During the investigation, many Greek Cypriot interviewees raised the issue of ill treatment even though it was beyond the subcommission's terms of reference. British officials were livid that the subcommission indulged witnesses by allowing them to describe and discuss ill treatment, but they could not raise this issue with the investigators because, in Neale's words, "much of the material was culled from very delicate sources." The Cyprus government had spied on the investigators' confidential interview sessions. Simpson, *Human Rights and the End of Empire,* 989–991, quoting CO 936/489; also see CO 936/488—Neale's report indicates that there were secret sources of information. Simpson believes that MI5 bugged subcommission facilities.

42. Simpson, *Human Rights and the End of Empire,* 1049. Simpson writes that commissioners disagreed over the justification of a state of emergency, although the majority supported Britain. He notes that the dissenting opinion offered more convincing arguments than the majority opinion. According to Simpson, if the report had been publicly released at the time (it was held secret until 1997), it would have brought the commission into disrepute and could have opened a public dialogue on the role of human rights in colonial insurgencies.

43. Ibid., 959, 1018–19.

44. For an insightful legal analysis of these developments, see ibid., 996–1019.

45. CO 926/888, Report on the Cyprus Police Force by Chief Inspector Butler, Metropolitan Police, November 21, 1958.

46. Quoted in Simpson, *Human Rights and the End of Empire,* 986 and 995.

47. FO 371/136400, Sinclair to Higham, March 19, 1958.

48. Simpson, *Human Rights and the End of Empire,* 1030.

49. LO 2/503, Joint Memorandum by Foreign Office and Colonial Office Officials—Cyprus: Human Rights.

50. FCO 141/4495, Governor, Cyprus to Colonial Office, May 7, 1958.

51. FCO 141/4495, Sinclair to Reddaway, May 6, 1958.

52. Foley, *Island in Revolt,* 127. In 1960, Michael reentered Parliament and later led Labour in opposition to Margaret Thatcher.

53. Foot recorded his preference for clemency in capital cases in his correspondence with the prime minister. See Foot Papers 7/2, Prime Minister to Foot, December 18, 1958, and Foot's response, December 20, 1958.

54. FCO 141/4609, Munir to Foot, December 31, 1958.

55. FCO 141/4493, Governor, Cyprus to Colonial Office, November 1, 1958.

56. Holland, *Britain and the Revolt in Cyprus,* 209. Also see Foot Papers 1/4, Sinclair to Foot, January 1, 1958.

57. John Reddaway, Imperial War Museum accession 9173, reel 8.

58. FCO 141/4495, Copy Minute by Deputy Governor: Allegations against the Security Forces, May 27, 1958.

59. Ibid., Cyprus to Colonial Office, May 10, 1958.

60. Ibid., SIG Quarterly Progress Report, June to September 30, 1958.

61. Ibid., SIG Quarterly Progress Report, October 1 to December 31, 1958.

62. Ibid., Sinclair to Reddaway, May 6, 1958.

63. Ibid., Cyprus to Colonial Office, May 10, 1958.

64. Ibid., Complaints and Allegations against Security Forces, June 12, 1958.

65. Ibid., Foot to Mayor of Kyrenia, September 20, 1958.

66. Ibid., Foot to Neale, September 2, 1958.

67. Ibid., SIG Quarterly Progress Report, January to March 1959, app. A, March 11, 1959.

68. Ibid., SIG Quarterly Progress Report, June to September 30, 1958.

69. Ibid.

70. FCO 141/4495, SIG Quarterly Progress Report, October 1 to December 31, 1958.

71. FCO 141/4642, Covering Report: Allegations against SF by villagers of Pano Panayia, August 7, 1958; investigation on August 13, 1958.

72. Ibid.

73. FCO 141/4495, SIG Final Quarterly Progress Report, January 1to March 1959.

74. FCO 141/4495, SIG Quarterly Progress Report, October 1 to December 31, 1958, p. 6.

75. Ibid.

76. FCO 141/4495, SIG Quarterly Progress Report, June to September 30, 1958.

77. Holland, *Britain and the Revolt in Cyprus*, 246–53, and Johnson, "Britain and the Cyprus Problem," 120–21.

78. FCO 141/4615, Findings of the Commission of Inquiry into the Incidents at Geunyeli, Cyprus on 12th June 1958, pp. 6–15, 18–20 (Geunyeli Commission Report).

79. FCO 141/4615, Appointment of Commissioner of Inquiry, June 16, 1958.

80. Holland, *Britain and the Revolt in Cyprus*, 255.

81. FCO 141/4615, Geunyeli Commission Report.

82. Simpson, *Human Rights and the End of Empire*, 896.

83. FCO 141/4615, Geunyeli Commission Report, pp. 13–14.

84. Ibid.

85. Ibid., p. 16.

86. FCO 141/4615, Foot to Martin, quoting Bower's comments, July 16, 1958.

87. FCO 141/4487, Foot to Bower, October 19, 1958.

88. FCO 141/4487, Kendrew to Bower, July 8, 1958.

89. FCO 141/4615, Governor, Cyprus, to Colonial Office, July 19, 1958.

90. FCO 141/4487, Minute by Deputy Governor, Geunyeli Report, July 17, 1958.

91. FCO 141/4615, Governor, Cyprus, to Colonial Office, July 29, 1958.

92. FCO 141/4615, Governor, Cyprus, to Colonial Office, November 1, 1958.

93. FCO 141/4615, Higham to Foot, August 30, 1958.

94. FCO 141/4487, Record of a Meeting Held in the Colonial Office at 11 A.M. on Friday, 5th September, 1958.

95. Ibid. See also FCO 141/4615, Colonial Office to Governor, Cyprus, September 2, 1958.

96. FCO 141/4615, Munir to Administrative Secretary, September 16, 1958.

97. Ibid., Governor, Cyprus, to Colonial Office, November 4, 1958.

98. Ibid., Governor, Cyprus, to Colonial Office, November 1, 1958.

99. Ibid., Governor, Cyprus, to Colonial Office, November 7, 1958.

100. Ibid., Colonial Office to Governor, Cyprus, November 22, 1958.

101. Ibid., Colonial Office to Governor, Cyprus, December 1, 1958.

102. Ibid., Governor, Cyprus, to Colonial Office, December 6, 1958; Hansard, HC Deb., December 10, 1958, vol. 597, col. 345.

103. FCO 141/4493, SIG Report on Famagusta Allegations: Murder of British Serviceman's Wife, October 10, 1958.

104. Some were released and rearrested; a conservative estimate of total individuals was one thousand—see ibid.

105. FCO 141/4495, SIG Quarterly Progress Report, October 1 to December 31, 1958.

106. FCO 141/4493, SIG Report on Famagusta Allegations.

107. Harry Slater, "Re: Photo—Karaolos Camp, Cyprus," *42 Regiment Royal Artillery Message Forum* (blog), October 11, 2012, http://pub2.bravenet.com/forum/static/show.php?usernum=140248687&frmid=12&msgid=866080&cmd=show. Accessed June 29, 2014.

108. David Carter, *Aphrodite's Killers: Cyprus, the EOKA Conflict and the Road to Partition* (London: Downlow Publications, 2010), 404–45. This work draws heavily on former British servicemen's firsthand accounts.

109. Ibid., 406.

110. FCO 141/4493, SIG Report on Famagusta Allegations.

111. FCO 141/4493, Foot to Colonial Office, October 4, 1958.

112. As quoted in Carter, *Aphrodite's Killers*, 405. Carter interviewed Baily years after the event.

113. FCO 141/4495, SIG Quarterly Progress Report, October 1 to December 31, 1958.

114. FCO 141/4493, SIG Report on Famagusta Allegations.

115. FCO 141/4495, SIG Quarterly Progress Report, October 1 to December 31, 1958.

116. FCO 141/4610, Munir to Henry, October 17, 1958.

117. FCO 141/4493, Foot to Deputy Governor, October 14, 1958.

118. Darling Papers 5, Darling to Stockwell, November 5, 1958.

119. Darling Papers 7, "The British Counter-Insurgency Experience," Kermit Roosevelt Lecture Series at the U.S. Army Command and General Staff College, May 1964.

120. For information on inquests, see Jonathan Law and Elizabeth A. Martin, "Inquest," in *A Dictionary of Law*, 7th ed. (Oxford University Press, 2014), http://www.oxfordreference.com.

121. FCO 141/4610, Munir to Henry, October 17, 1958.

122. FCO 141/4610, Henry to Foot, October 22, 1958; here Henry relates Darling's points to the governor.

123. FCO 141/4403, Bourke to Henry, November 28, 1958.

124. FCO 141/4610, Bourke to Henry, October 11, 1958.

125. Ibid., Munir to Henry, October 17, 1958.

126. Ibid., Henry to Foot, October 22, 1958.

127. Ibid., Henry to Foot, October 22, 1958; on Avgorou, see FCO 141/4610, Coroner's Verdict, Inquest Nos. 10/58 and 11/58, August 8, 1958. The debate over inquests proved far more controversial than officials would have liked. Local doctors from the Cyprus Medical Association established a human rights committee based on that of the Cyprus Bar Council. On October 29, the committee requested permission from the government to allow a member of the association to observe postmortem examinations of individuals killed by security forces. Their request was denied, but the timing of the doctors' involvement—weeks after the Cutliffe murder—suggests that they wanted to observe the autopsies of the three Greek Cypriots who died during the wave of British reprisals. Foot and Brigadier Gleadell, the chief of staff, dismissed the doctors' motives as "of course primarily political." See FCO 141/4610, Minute by Chief of Staff, October 29, 1958; Minute by Chief of Staff, October 31, 1958; Governor to Colonial Office, November 1, 1958.

128. FCO 141/4403, Governor to Colonial Office, November 9, 1958.

129. FCO 141/4610, Foot to Melville, November 27, 1958.

130. FCO 141/4495, SIG Quarterly Progress Report, October 1 to December 31, 1958; FCO 141/4493, Governor to Colonial Office, November 24, 1958.

131. FCO 141/4495, SIG Quarterly Progress Report, October 1 to December 31, 1958.

132. FCO 141/4493, Governor to Colonial Office, December 4, 1958.

133. FCO 141/4493, Governor to Colonial Office, November 1, 1958.

134. FCO 141/4493, Governor to Colonial Office, December 1, 1958.

135. The diagnosis is no longer used in twenty-first-century medical practice. See Ann Dally, "*Status Lymphaticus*: Sudden Death in Children from 'Visitation of God' to Cot Death," *Medical History* 41 (1997): 70–85.

136. FCO 141/4493, Foot to Sinclair, November 17, 1958, and Sinclair to Foot, November 18, 1958.

137. LO 2/503, Vallat to Hylton-Foster, Solicitor General, January 22, 1959.

138. Holland, *Britain and the Revolt in Cyprus*, 304–18, and Simpson, *Human Rights and the End of Empire*, 1050–51.

139. FCO 141/4459, Baker Report, p. 64.

3. "Hunger War"

1. FCO 141/4458, Luce to Sinclair, May 31, 1958; Sinclair to Churchill, June 5, 1958; and Harding Papers, AFH 5, Sinclair to Baker, April 24, 1959.

2. On the mid- and late1960s as a major transition point, see P. J. Cain and A. G. Hopkins, *British Imperialism: 1688–2000*, 2nd ed. (New York: Routledge, 2001), 632–44; Darwin, *The Empire Project*, 638–48; Louis, "The Withdrawal from the Gulf," in *Ends of British Imperialism*, 877–903; Porter, *The Lion's Share*, 275–79; Thomas, *Fight or Flight*, 281–84; and Thompson, *The Empire Strikes Back?*, 209–16.

3. For a general history, see Paul Dresch, *A History of Modern Yemen* (Cambridge: Cambridge University Press, 2000). For a detailed military account, see Jonathan Walker, *Aden Insurgency: The Savage War in South Arabia, 1962–1967* (Staplehurst, UK: Spellmount, 2005).

4. Cabanes, *The Great War*, 3–8.

5. Klose, "The Colonial Testing Ground," 107–26.

6. Spencer Mawby, *British Policy in Aden and the Protectorates 1955–67: Last Outpost of a Middle East Empire* (London: Routledge, 2005), 3–5. Also see CAB 131/28, D 3 (63), Future Defence Policy: Cabinet Defence Committee meeting minutes, February 9, 1963; and CAB 130/190, The implications of withdrawal from the Middle and Far East: minutes of a Cabinet (official) Committee on Defence meeting, May 21, 1963, in ed. Ronald Hyam and Wm. Roger Louis, *The Conservative Government and the End of Empire 1957–1964 Part I* (London: HMSO, 2000).

7. FO 371/174488, "No. 13 Policy and Strategy in the Gulf: Aden and Kuwait," June 17, 1964, in ed. Hyam and Louis, *The Conservative Government*, 289.

8. Mawby, *British Policy in Aden and the Protectorates*, 4–5, 31–34, and Thomas, *Fight or Flight*, 279–81.

9. Dresch, *A History of Modern Yemen*, 10, and Mawby, *British Policy in Aden and the Protectorates*, 65–75.

10. Adeed Dawisha, *Arab Nationalism in the Twentieth Century: From Triumph to Despair* (Princeton: Princeton University Press, 2003), 138.

11. Mawby, *British Policy in Aden and the Protectorates*, 32, and Dawisha, *Arab Nationalism*, 139. On Nasser's relations with the United States, see Salim Yaqub, *Containing Arab Nationalism: The Eisenhower Doctrine and the Middle East* (Chapel Hill: University of North Carolina Press, 2004). On Nasser in general, see Said K. Aburish, *Nasser: The Last Arab* (New York: St. Martin's, 2004).

12. On the confrontation between Britain and Egypt, see Nigel Ashton, "Macmillan and the Middle East" in *Harold Macmillan and Britain's World Role*, ed. Richard Aldous and Sabine Lee (New York: Macmillan, 1996); Louis, *Ends of British Imperialism*, 589–638, and Robert McNamara, *Britain, Nasser and the Balance of Power in the Middle East, 1952–1977: From the Egyptian Revolution to the Six Day War* (London: Frank Cass, 2003).

13. Malcolm H. Kerr, *The Arab Cold War, 1958–1966: A Study of Ideology in Politics* (New York: Oxford University Press, 1965). On integrating diplomatic history and postcolonial studies, see Matthew Connelly, "Taking Off the Cold War Lens: Visions of North-South Conflict during the Algerian War for Independence," *American Historical Review* 105, no. 3 (June 2000): 739–69.

14. On the Aden Group, see Andrew Mumford, *The Counter-Insurgency Myth: The British Experience of Irregular Warfare* (London: Routledge, 2012), 74, and Clive Jones, *Britain and the Yemen Civil War, 1962–1965: Ministers, Mercenaries and Mandarins : Foreign Policy and the Limits of Covert Action* (Brighton: Sussex Academic Press, 2010).

15. Mawby, *British Policy in Aden and the Protectorates*, quote on 107.

16. Spencer Mawby, "The Clandestine Defence of Empire: British Special Operations in Yemen, 1951–64," *Intelligence and National Security* 17, no. 3 (2002): 109–14.

17. On covert action, see Jones, *Britain and the Yemen Civil War*. Scholars debate the extent and nature of Israeli involvement in the operation; see 148–49. For an analysis of the Egyptian perspective, see Jesse Ferris, *Nasser's Gamble: How Intervention in Yemen Caused the Six-Day War and the Decline of Egyptian Power* (Princeton: Princeton University Press, 2013).

18. Kennedy Trevaskis, *Shades of Amber: A South Arabian Episode* (London: Hutchinson, 1968), 68.

19. Julian Amery Papers 1/7/7, Amery to Douglas-Home, December 10, 1964.

20. Mawby, *British Policy in Aden and the Protectorates*, 78–81; Trevaskis Papers, part 1, 3/3, p. 4; and CO 1055/154, "The People's Socialist Party" memorandum, August 17, 1962.

21. Trevaskis Papers, part 1, 3/3, pp. 1–13.

22. CO 859/1784, General Secretariat, ATUC to Director General, International Labour Organization (ILO), December 15, 1962; Secretary of the World Federation of Trade Unions to Director General, ILO, December 11, 1962.

23. Hickling Papers 2, pp. 165–69.

24. WO 386/22, Report on Operations in Radfan, August 1, 1964, p. 1 and 75, 80–81. Although the NLF received Egyptian support, they were not simply pawns of Egyptian interests. See Spencer Mawby, "Orientalism and the Failure of British Policy in the Middle East: The Case of Aden," *History* 95 (July 2010): 342–43.

25. Dresch, *A History of Modern Yemen*, 97.

26. Mawby, *British Policy in Aden and the Protectorates*, 102.

27. On radio in the Middle East, see Connelly, *A Diplomatic Revolution*, 28. The British government also recognized the value of radio as a tool of influence. See James Vaughan, "Propaganda by Proxy? Britain, America, and Arab Radio Broadcasting, 1953–1957," *Historical Journal of Film, Radio and Television* 22, no. 2 (2002): 157–72. Post-1945 British propaganda efforts failed not because of a lack of trying; instead, propagandists misunderstood the nature of Arab nationalism. See James Vaughan, "'A Certain Idea of Britain': British Cultural Diplomacy in the Middle East, 1945–57," *Contemporary British History* 19, no. 2 (2005): 151–68.

28. As quoted in Dresch, *A History of Modern Yemen*, 96.

29. Victoria Clark, *Yemen: Dancing on the Heads of Snakes* (New Haven: Yale University Press, 2010), 80–81; Mawby, *British Policy in Aden and the Protectorates*, 102–3 (as quoted on 102); and Trevaskis, *Shades of Amber*, 207.

30. Dresch, *A History of Modern Yemen*, 76–78 and 98.

31. Walker, *Aden Insurgency*, 79–84; DO 174/19, Trevaskis to Colonial Secretary, January 16, 1964, and January 30, 1964; and WO 386/22, p. 76.

32. DO 174/19, Trevaskis to Colonial Secretary, April 9, 1964.

33. CO 1055/216, annex, Aden and the Federation of South Arabia, April 21, 1964.

34. WO 386/22, Political Directive to British forces, April 29, 1964, p. 70.

35. Ibid., 71.

36. Trevaskis Papers, part 1, 6/1, Trevaskis to Harington, April 5, 1964, pp. 7–8.

37. DO 174/19, Trevaskis to Sandys, April 5, 1964.

38. IOR, R/20/D/63, Cairo to Political Officer, Middle East Command [POMEC], June 1, 1964.

39. Charles Townshend, "Civilization and 'Frightfulness': Air Control in the Middle East between the Wars" in *Warfare, Diplomacy, and Politics: Essays in Honour of A. J. P. Taylor*, ed. Chris Wrigley (London: H. Hamilton, 1986).

40. C. F. A. Portal, "Air Force Co-Operation in Policing the Empire," *RUSI Journal* 82 (November 1937): 343–58, quote on 353.

41. Priya Satia, *Spies in Arabia: The Great War and the Cultural Foundations of Britain's Covert Empire in the Middle East* (Oxford: Oxford University Press, 2008), 256.

42. David E. Omissi, *Air Power and Colonial Control: The Royal Air Force, 1919–1939* (Manchester, UK: Manchester University Press, 1990), 18–38, and Robert Mackey, "Policing the Empire: How the Royal Air Force Won Its Wings in the Middle East," *Journal of Military History* 24, no. 7 (2007): 26–36.

43. James Corum, "The Myth of Air Control," *Aerospace Power Journal*, Winter 2000, 70–72.

44. Dresch, *A History of Modern Yemen*, 60–61.

45. Bennett, *Fighting the Mau Mau*, 93.

46. "Why We Shot Up the Yemen Fortress," *Sunday Times*, April 5, 1964.

47. DO 174/19, Dean to Foreign Office, April 7, 1964.

48. Ibid., Colonial Secretary to Trevaskis, April 5, 1964; annex to Minute 3, part 1 to Chief of Staff, 29th meeting, April 1964.

49. Ibid., Dean to Foreign Office, April 7, 1964.

50. Ibid., Sandys to Trevaskis, April 5, 1964.

51. Ibid., Annex to Minute 3.

52. CO 1055/122, Trevaskis to Colonial Secretary, April 16, 1964.

53. DO 174/19, FO telegram. 271, April 24, 1964. DO 174/19 COS (64), 33rd meeting, Minute 6, May 5, 1964, references a previous decision that air proscription should not be used. See DO 174/19 COS (64), 18th meeting, Minute 1. The commander in chief, Middle East, and chief of the defence staff urged civilian leaders to authorize close air support when ground forces were under enemy fire. See DO 174/19, annex to Minute 3.

54. Walker, *Aden Insurgency*, 97, 104–6.

55. Trevaskis Papers, part 1, 6/1, Trevaskis to Sandys, April 30, 1964.

56. DO 174/19, Trevaskis to Sandys, May 2, 1964.

57. Ibid., Commander-in-Chief, Middle East to Ministry of Defence UK, May 7, 1964.

58. Ibid., Sandys to Trevaskis, May 3, 1964.

59. Ibid., Trevaskis to Sandys, May 7, 1964.

60. Ibid., Trevaskis to Sandys, May 4, 1964.

61. Ibid., Sandys to Trevaskis, May 8, 1964.

62. Ibid., Aden to Colonial Office; from Sandys to Prime Minister and Defence Secretary, May 11, 1964.

63. Ibid., Sandys (from Aden) to the Colonial Office, May 11, 1964.

64. Ibid.

65. WO 386/22, p. 73.

66. DO 174/19, Sandys (from Aden) to the Colonial Office, May 11, 1964.

67. AIR 20/12115, Radfan Operations—1964, page 8, Mission Nos. 3/202 and 3/201, May 31, 1964.

68. AIR 20/12115, Radfan Operations—1964, page 6, Mission Nos. 209 and 281, May 23, 1964.

69. AIR 20/12115, Radfan Operations—1964, page 16, Mission No. 3/226, June 4, 1964.

70. IOR, R/20/D/63, HC Office to Air Officer Commander, May 31, 1964.

71. Walker, *Aden Insurgency*, 110.

72. Hickling Papers 2, p. 134.

73. WO 386/22, p. 39.

74. IOR, R/20/D/63, Baillie to Trevaskis, May 12, 1964.

75. Ibid.

76. WO 386/22, p. 39.

77. DO 174/19, Oates (Acting High Commissioner) to Sandys, September 9, 1964.

78. CO 1055/201, Aden to Colonial Secretary, June 21, 1964.

79. R. Beeston, "'Hunger War' on Radfan Tribes," *Sunday Telegraph*, June 1, 1964.

80. Waring Papers, manuscript by Harry Cockerill, "The Tribes of the Radfan and Haiman Hills," September 1967.

81. CO 1055/260, letter from the League of Red Cross Societies to Renison, January 7, 1965. The British estimated that between twenty and twenty-seven thousand people lived in the Radfan. See WO 386/22, Operations in Radfan, August 1, 1964, pp. 80–81.

82. "1,000 Refugees Ask South Arabia's Aid," *New York Times*, May 25, 1964.

83. David Holden, "British Troops Burn Arab Food Stocks," *Guardian*, June 1, 1964; "Aden Rebels Give Up Guns in Bid for Peace," *Los Angeles Times*, May 25, 1964.

84. Hickling Papers 2, p. 134.

85. CO 1055/201, POMEC to Foreign Office, November 10, 1964.

86. CO 1055/154, Cairo to Foreign Office, June 29, 1964.

87. CO 1055/155, translation of letter from the South Yemen Liberation Movement, November 29, 1964.

88. CO 1055/260, Radio Monitoring Report, December 19, 1964.

89. IOR, R/20/D/62, Radio Monitoring Service report, June 29, 1964.

90. DO 174/22, Delhi to CRO, June 2, 1964.

91. DO 174/22, Acting HC India to CRO, May 25, 1964.

92. PREM 11/5184, Memorandum "UN Committee of 24," May 8, 1964.

93. DO 174/22, Huijsman to Garner, May 11, 1964.

94. DO 174/22, CRO telegram "Security Operation in Federation of Southern Arabia," May 12, 1964.

95. DO 174/22, Foreign Office to Cairo, June 3, 1964.

96. IOR, R/20/D/63, Commander-in-Chief, Middle East to Ministry of Defence, UK, June 8, 1964.

97. IOR, R/20/D/63, Baillie to Harington, June 2, 1964.

98. CO 1055/260, draft, Monson to Trevaskis, March 24, 1964. The telegram describes a conversation between Benenson and Nigel Fisher, minister of state for the colonies, in which Benenson told Fisher of the Amnesty-ICRC arrangement.

99. Michael Barnett, *Empire of Humanity: A History of Humanitarianism* (Ithaca: Cornell University Press, 2011), 76–80. For histories of the ICRC, see David P. Forsythe, *The Humanitarians: The International Committee of the Red Cross* (Cambridge: Cambridge University Press, 2005), and Caroline Moorehead, *Dunant's Dream: War, Switzerland and the History of the Red Cross* (New York: HarperCollins, 1999).

100. Barnett, *Empire of Humanity*, 13.

101. Cabanes, *The Great War*, 3–8.

102. J. D. Armstrong, "The International Committee of the Red Cross and Political Prisoners," *International Organization* 39, no. 4 (1985): 624.

103. Bennett, *Fighting the Mau Mau*, 78; French, *The British Way in Counter-Insurgency*, 139; and Klose, *Human Rights*, 38.

104. Katharine Fortin, "Complementarity between the ICRC and the United Nations and International Humanitarian Law and International Human Rights Law, 1948–1968," *International Review of the Red Cross* 94, no. 888 (Winter 2012): 1433–54.

105. French, *The British Way in Counter-Insurgency*, 136–37; Moorehead, *Dunant's Dream*, 544–49. On the Red Cross during the Holocaust, see Jean-Claude Favez, *The Red Cross and the Holocaust* (Cambridge: Cambridge University Press, 1999).

106. Leopold Boissier, "The Silence of the International Committee of the Red Cross," *International Review of the Red Cross*, April 1968, 179.

107. Klose, *Human Rights*, 128–32.

108. Benenson's Cyprus experiences have often been overlooked in histories of AI's establishment. According to the traditional narrative, Benenson was inspired to form AI after he read a newspaper article about two students in authoritarian Portugal who were imprisoned for making a toast to freedom in a local bar. In addition, the Soviet crackdown during the 1956 Hungarian uprising and the general suppression of Catholicism in the Eastern Bloc outraged Benenson. See Ann Marie Clark, *Diplomacy of Conscience: Amnesty International and Changing Human Rights Norms* (Princeton: Princeton University Press, 2001); Stephen Hopgood, *Keepers of the Flame: Understanding Amnesty International* (Ithaca: Cornell University Press, 2013); Egon Larsen, *A Flame in Barbed Wire: The Story of Amnesty International* (London: Frederick Muller, 1978); and Jonathan Power, *Like Water on Stone: The Story of Amnesty International* (Boston: Northeastern University Press, 2001). For a critical analysis of Amnesty's origins, see Buchanan, " 'The Truth Will Set You Free': The Making of Amnesty International," *Journal of Contemporary History* 37, no. 4 (October 2002): 575–97.

109. AI-982, Benenson essay, August 83, pp. 4–6; Benenson interview, November 12, 1983, pp. 55–56. *Gangrene* appeared first in French, then in English translation. Benenson authored the foreword to the English translation. See *Gangrene* (London: Calder Books, 1960).

110. Although AI espoused impartiality by advocating on behalf of prisoners on both sides of the Cold War as well as the emerging Third World, the organization was staunchly anticommunist. This attitude stemmed from its leaders' intellectual origins in Christian peace movements and their aversion to official Soviet atheism. See Moyn, *The Last Utopia*, 130.

111. Baker Papers 2/1, Benenson to Baker, January 13, 1961.

112. AI-982, Benenson interview, November 12, 1983, p. 77.

113. Buchanan, " 'The Truth Will Set You Free,' " 575–79.

114. Peter Benenson, "The Forgotten Prisoners," *Observer*, May 28, 1961.

115. Baker Papers 2/1, AI, n.d., but likely composed in January 1961.

116. Baker Papers 2/1, Benenson, "Appeal for Amnesty: A Report on the First 6 Months," n.d.

117. Mawby, *British Policy in Aden and the Protectorates*, 95.

118. CO 859/1784, Zakaria to Morse, January 24, 1964.

119. FCO 859/1785, Dewar to Director-General, ILO, April 7, 1964.

120. Hansard, HC Deb., December 19, 1963, vol. 686, col. 1446.

121. CO 1055/260, Benenson to Colonial Secretary, December 19, 1963.

122. Ibid., Reid to Formoy, December 20, 1963.

123. Ibid., Colonial Office to Aden, December 20, 1963.

124. Ibid., Aden to Colonial Office, December 27, 1963; Gilmore to Benenson, January 7, 1964; the chief justice's findings were released in February 1964. See CO 1055/266, report by the chief justice on the treatment of detainees, February 9, 1964.

125. Ibid., Benenson to Gilmore, January 9, 1964.

126. Ibid., Benenson to Doble, March 9, 1964.

127. Ibid., draft, Assistant Undersecretary of State Monson to Trevaskis, March 24, 1964.

128. Ibid., Geneva to Foreign Office, July 6, 1964.

129. Ibid., Foreign Office to Geneva, May 29, 1964.

130. Ibid., Aden to Colonial Secretary, June 4, 1964.

131. Ibid., Boissier to Butler, July 14, 1964.

132. Ibid., Colonial Secretary to Aden, July 16, 1964.

133. Ibid. and CO 1055/260, Foreign Office to Jedda, July 28, 1964.

134. Ibid., Acting High Commissioner (Oates) to Monson, August 20, 1964.

135. Ibid., Colonial Office to Aden, August 21, 1964.

136. Ibid., Aden to Colonial Office, August 29, 1964.

137. Ibid.

138. CO 1055/260, Posnett, Colonial Office, to Shegog, Foreign Office, September 10, 1964.

139. See ibid., Aden to Colonial Office, September 12, 1964, and September 24, 1964; Posnett to Formoy, September 28, 1964.

140. Ibid., Aden to Colonial Office, October 13, 1964.

141. Ibid., Renison to Shegog, December 29, 1964.

142. IOR, R/20/D/62, Renison to Shegog, January 26, 1965.

143. CO 1055/260, Colonial Office to Aden, February 19, 1965.

144. CO 1055/260, Aden to CO, February 27, 1965.

145. IOR, R/20/D/62, McCarthy to Turnbull, February 18, 1965. See also *The Diplomatic Service List 1966* (London: HMSO, 1966), p. 237.

146. Klose, "The Colonial Testing Ground," 107–26. Colonial officials applied a similar logic after the 1959 Hola camp massacre in Kenya. The government allowed ICRC representatives to visit detention camps in an effort to convince its critics that conditions in the camps were not as deplorable as the Hola incident made them appear. ICRC delegates, however, found widespread torture and other forms of physical punishment.

147. CO 1055/260, "Note for the Secretary of State: Recent Visit of M. Rochat, I.C.R.C. Delegate in the Yemen, to Aden," March 9, 1965.

148. Greenwood Papers 6311, correspondence with J.W. Stacpoole, December 11 and 14, 1964; and interview in the *Tribune*, April 23, 1965.

149. CO 1055/261, Benenson to Greenwood, October 29, 1965.

150. CO 1055/261, Greenwood to Turnbull, November 10, 1965.
151. IOR, R/20/D/62, Assistant High Commissioner to Turnbull, November 11, 1965.
152. CO 1055/261, Greenwood to Turnbull, November 10, 1965.
153. CO 1055/261, Wiltshire to Posnett, June 16, 1965.
154. CO 1055/260, South Arabian Press Service, "International Red Cross Delegate Visits Federation," No. 406/65.
155. CO 1055/261, Mullin to Watts, August 24, 1965.
156. As quoted in French, *The British Way in Counter-Insurgency*, 198–99.
157. CO 1055/261, Turnbull to Greenwood, November 19, 1965.
158. Ibid., Greenwood to Turnbull, November 25, 1965.
159. Ibid., Mullin to Goulding, November 26, 1965.
160. Ibid., Goulding to Mullin, December 2, 1965.
161. WO 32/20987, Baker memorandum on Aden, October 1966.
162. WO 386/22, p. 74.
163. PREM 13/1294, Aden to Foreign Office, September 25, 1966.

4. "This Unhappy Affair"

1. Amnesty International, "Aden Report by S. Rastgeldi," December 1966, p. 7. Most studies of Rastgeldi's visit place it in the context of Amnesty International's organizational history as a human rights nongovernmental organization (NGO). See Tom Buchanan, "Amnesty International in Crisis, 1966–7," *Twentieth Century British History* 15, no.3 (2004): 267–89; Hopgood, *Keepers of the Flame*; Power, *Like Water on Stone*; and Kirsten Sellars, *The Rise and Rise of Human Rights* (Stroud: Sutton Publishing, 2002).
2. On torture in Aden, see Huw Bennett, " 'Detainees Are Always One's Achilles Heel': Detention, Interrogation and Its External Scrutiny in Aden, 1963–67," *War in History* 23, no. 4 (2016): 457–88; Cobain, *Cruel Britannia*, 106; Sellars, *The Rise and Rise of Human Rights*, 105; and Simpson, "Round Up the Usual Suspects," 676–77. Sellars argues that the Bowen inquiry was a whitewash; Bennett believes that the inquiry resulted in reform but did not end harsh interrogation. Furthermore, Bennett argues that British forces sought to protect the interrogation system from external scrutiny so that they could continue employing torture to collect intelligence. Sophia Dingli and Caroline Kennedy argue that the strengthening of an international human rights discourse during the 1960s meant that public criticism of the government's abusive practices in Aden—especially AI's activism—caused a "pivot" in which British security forces moved away from coercive counterinsurgency practices. See Dingli and Kennedy, "The Aden Pivot? British Counter-Insurgency after Aden," *Civil Wars* 16, no.1 (2014): 86–104. Although I agree with Dingli and Kennedy that AI's activism led to the Bowen inquiry, my conclusion that torture resumed in the months following the Bowen inquiry supports Bennett's analysis.
3. Bennett, " 'Detainees Are Always One's Achilles Heel,' " 463; Spencer Mawby, "Orientalism and the Failure of British Policy in the Middle East: The Case of Aden," *History* 95, no. 319 (July 2010): 341.
4. Dunbar Papers 2/5, lecture notes—II, not dated.
5. Willoughby Papers, diary entry, July 10, 1965. On the difficulties that Special Branch faced up to the spring of 1965, see the CO 1035/178 collection.
6. Willoughby Papers, diary entry, August 29, 1965.
7. Ibid., September 14, 1965.
8. CO 1035/178, Strong to DGI (MOD), February 1, 1965. See also Aaron Edwards, *Mad Mitch's Tribal Law: Aden and the End of Empire* (Edinburgh: Mainstream Publishing, 2014), 88–90.
9. Jim Herlihy, correspondence with author, July 22–23, 2013.
10. Bennett, " 'Detainees Are Always One's Achilles Heel,' " 463–65.
11. Ibid., 10.
12. DEFE 11/505, Turnbull to Foreign Office, October 5, 1966. Emergency laws in Aden authorized holding an individual for interrogation for up to seven days, which could be ex-

tended to twenty-eight days. The High Commissioner could sign a detention order to approve detention beyond twenty-eight days.

13. Hickling Papers 2, pp. 114–16.

14. Ibid., 117, 126.

15. Ibid., 2, and "Professor Hugh Hickling," obituary, *Daily Telegraph*, April 17, 2007.

16. Hickling Papers 2, pp. 114–15.

17. The newly constructed Mansoura Detention Centre opened in September 1965. It was more secure than the older Aden prisons. Ibid., 114–15, 118.

18. DEFE 13/529, Bowen Report, November 14, 1966. Bowen's findings corroborate the version of events that Hickling describes in his manuscript.

19. On South Asian migrations, see Sugata Bose, *A Hundred Horizons: The Indian Ocean in the Age of Global Empire* (Cambridge, MA: Harvard University Press, 2006), and Thomas Metcalf, *Imperial Connections: India in the Indian Ocean Arena, 1860–1920* (Berkeley: University of California Press, 2007). On African lawyers in Kenya, see Anderson, *Histories of the Hanged*, 156, 160, 327.

20. Saeed Hassan Sohbi, correspondence with author, May 26, 2015.

21. On the ILO's concern with trades union rights in Aden during the 1960s, see the following collections: CO 859/1784, CO 859/1785, CO 859/1786, FCO 61/120, FCO 61/121, and LAB 13/933.

22. CO 1055/276, Greenwood to Turnbull, November 3, 1965.

23. CO 1055/276, Lord Beswick: Visit to South Arabia, 5th–23rd November 1965, annex III (itinerary).

24. Willoughby Papers, diary entry, November 17, 1965.

25. CO 1055/276, report by Lord Beswick, November 30, 1965, p. 8.

26. Hickling Papers 2, pp. 119–20.

27. Ibid., 121.

28. Willoughby Papers, diary entry, November 28, 1965.

29. Willoughby Papers 7.2, Willoughby to Major General Freeland, Ministry of Defence, December 4, 1965.

30. CO 1055/286, Roberts, Colonial Office to Turnbull, December 2, 1965.

31. CO 1055/286, Healey to Greenwood, December 9, 1965.

32. Willoughby Papers, diaries for October 1955–October 1956.

33. Willoughby Papers 7.2, Thorburn to Willoughby, December 15, 1965.

34. Beating, especially with open-hand slaps, has been a common torture practice. See Rejali, *Torture and Democracy*, 337–40 and 554. Unsurprisingly, victims often suffer perforated eardrums. The injury can occur from a blow to the ear, which rapidly increases pressure in the ear canal, rupturing the tympanic membrane. See Physicians for Human Rights, "PHR Toolkits Module 4: Torture Methods and Their Medical Consequences," http://phrtoolkits.org/tool kits/istanbul-protocol-model-medical-curriculum/module-4-torture-methods-and-their-medical-consequences/torture-methods/ear-trauma.

35. Hickling Papers 2, p. 121.

36. DEFE 13/529, Bowen Report, p. 19.

37. Hickling Papers 2, pp. 124–25.

38. Dunbar Papers 2/4, "Casualties and Incidents—Aden State—1964–1967," not dated, but likely July 1967.

39. Spencer Mawby, "From Tribal Rebellions to Revolution: British Counter-Insurgency Operations in Southwest Arabia 1955–67," *Electronic Journal of International History* 5 (2000), http://sas-space.sas.ac.uk/3392/1/Journal_of_International_History_2000_n5_Mawby.pdf.

40. Edwards, *Mad Mitch's Tribal Law*, 102–4; Mawby, *British Policy in Aden and the Protectorates*, 134; and Walker, *Aden Insurgency*, 181–85.

41. Ibid., McCarthy to Turnbull, March 24, 1966.

42. Ibid., Willoughby to Oates, March 24, 1966.

43. ICRC, B AG 225-001-004, Rochat Report No.1, March 22, 1966.

44. ICRC, B AG 202-001-001, Rochat Report No.2, May 28, 1966.

45. Willoughby Papers 7.2, Willoughby to Oates, March 24, 1966.

46. Ibid., McCarthy to Turnbull, March 24, 1966.

47. Ibid.

48. Willoughby Papers 7.2, McCarthy to Willoughby, April 14, 1966.

49. Ibid.

50. DEFE 13/529, Bowen Report, pp. 20–21.

51. DEFE 24/252, Hewetson to Minister (Army), April 27, 1967.

52. Caroline Elkins, "Archives, Intelligence and Secrecy: The Cold War and the End of the British Empire," in *Decolonization and the Cold War: Negotiating Independence,* ed. Leslie James and Elisabeth Leake (London: Bloomsbury, 2015), 257–84.

53. Edwards, *Mad Mitch's Tribal Law,* 120–21, and Jim Herlihy, correspondence with author, July 22–23, 2013.

54. ICRC, B AG 225-001-004, Rochat Report No. 4, September 1966, pp. 10–18.

55. Willoughby Papers 7.2, Turnbull to Marnham, April 24, 1966.

56. WO 32/20987, Baker memorandum on Aden, October 1966.

57. Sellars, *The Rise and Rise of Human Rights,* 98–103.

58. Power, *Like Water on Stone,* 127.

59. WO 32/20987, Swann to Padley, July 20, 1966.

60. Ibid., Baker memorandum on Aden, October 1966.

61. Ibid., "Letters from Mr. Walter Padley to Amnesty International," June 22, 1966. This letter references Swann's June 9, 1966, correspondence.

62. Ibid., Swann to Padley, July 1, 1966.

63. Ibid., "Letters from Mr. Walter Padley to Amnesty International," June 22, 1966.

64. Ibid., July 18, 1966.

65. Ibid.

66. WO 32/20987, Baker memorandum on Aden, October 1966.

67. Hansard, HC Deb., July 18, 1966, vol. 732, col. 24–25.

68. WO 32/20987, Swann to Padley, July 20, 1966.

69. PREM 13/1294, "Memorandum from the Civil Service Association of South Arabia on the Torture of Civil Servants Detained by the British Military Authorities in Aden," n.d. The document was included in a letter from AI to the prime minister.

70. PREM 13/1294, Managing Committee, Graduates' Congress to Rastgeldi, August 2, 1966.

71. PREM 13/1294, "Memorandum on the Torture of Civil Servants."

72. WO 32/20987, Baker memorandum on Aden, October 1966.

73. Ibid.

74. PREM 13/1294, Turnbull to Foreign Office, September 25, 1966.

75. PREM 13/1294, Turnbull to Deputy Undersecretary of State Allen, Foreign Office, September 28, 1966.

76. DEFE 11/505, Le Fanu to Hull, September 29, 1966.

77. DEFE 11/505, Cooper to Private Secretary to the Defence Secretary, September 29, 1966.

78. "Rhodesia Refuses to Free Lecturers," *Times,* July 30, 1966.

79. "Rhodesia Uses Emergency Powers for Detention," *Times,* September 3, 1966.

80. Sellars, *The Rise and Rise of Human Rights,* 108.

81. PREM 13/1294, Marnham to Aden, September 28, 1966.

82. Ibid.

83. DEFE 11/505, Foreign Office to Aden, October 1, 1966.

84. DEFE 11/505, Turnbull to Foreign Office, October 5, 1966.

85. The Foreign and Colonial Offices merged on August 1, 1966.

86. DEFE 13/529, O'Neill to Allen, October 10, 1966.

87. AI-1293, Benenson to Franck, November 17, 1966. Benenson wrote to the head of Amnesty's Swedish section in November and summarized the events leading to publication of Rastgeldi's report.

88. WO 32/20987, Baker memorandum on Aden, October 1966.

89. AI-1293, Benenson to Franck, November 17, 1966.

90. FO 953/2506, Press Release No. 92, October 13, 1966.

91. WO 32/20987, Amnesty International Press Release, October 17, 1966, and "Amnesty Discloses Aden Torture Allegations," *Times*, October 19, 1966. AI released Rastgeldi's report in full on December 19. See "Amnesty Publish Text of Rastgeldi Allegations," *Times*, December 20, 1966.

92. Buchanan, "Amnesty International in Crisis, 1966–7," 277.

93. PREM 13/1294, letter from Franck to Wilson, October 18, 1966.

94. "Government Is Criticized by Amnesty," *Times*, October 21, 1966.

95. "Torture Charged to British in Aden," *New York Times*, October 20, 1966.

96. "Inquiries on Suspects in Aden," *Times*, October 14, 1966.

97. FO 953/2506, Press Release No. 92. The news brief lists the statement that appeared in the *Times* under "unattributable" comments. The *Times* reproduced the statement almost verbatim.

98. Willoughby Papers 7.2, Ministry of Defence to Commander-in-Chief, Middle East Command, October 13, 1966.

99. Buchanan, "Amnesty International in Crisis, 1966–7," 277.

100. "Allegations of Torture 'Not Corroborated,'" *Guardian*, October 19, 1966.

101. Buchanan, "Amnesty International in Crisis, 1966–7," 277–78.

102. Sellars, *The Rise and Rise of Human Rights*, 107.

103. "'Nothing to Be Ashamed of in Aden': Minister's Letter to Amnesty Official." *Times*, October 20, 1966.

104. Judith Listowel, "Amnesty Report: Letters to the Editor." *Times*, October 22, 1966. Robert Swann corrected Lady Listowel's error in Robert Swann, "Amnesty Report: Letters to the Editor." *Times*, October 26, 1966.

105. WO 32/20987, Turnbull to Roberts, October 1, 1966, and PREM 13/1294, Turnbull to Foreign Office, September 25, 1966.

106. Willoughby Papers, diary entry, November 5, 1966.

107. Willoughby Papers 7.2, McCarthy draft telegram to Foreign Office, December 2, 1966.

108. John Graham Jones, "Bowen, Evan Roderic," Welsh Biography Online, National Library of Wales, http://wbo.llgc.org.uk/en/s8-BOWE-ROD-1913.html.

109. DEFE 13/529, Bowen Report, p. 1.

110. Willoughby Papers, diary entry, November 5, 1966.

111. DEFE 13/529, Lennox to C. D. Hamilton, Editor, *Sunday Times*, October 25, 1966; Hamilton forwarded Lennox's letter to Bowen. See DEFE 13/529, Ellis-Rees to AG, November 24, 1966.

112. DEFE 13/529, Bowen Report, p. 13.

113. Ibid., 13–14.

114. Ibid., 11.

115. Ibid., 17–18, 21.

116. Ibid., 22–23. See also WO 32/20987, Brown to Turnbull, November 14, 1966; Brown conveyed Bowen's recommendations to Turnbull immediately upon receipt of Bowen's report.

117. DEFE 13/529, FO to Aden, November 15, 1966, and WO 32/20987, Batstone, Foreign Office to Legal Adviser Vallat, Foreign Office, November 17, 1966.

118. DEFE 13/529, Minister (Army) to Defence Secretary, November 23, 1966.

119. Willoughby Papers, diary entry, November 5, 1966.

120. Ibid., November 7, 1966.

121. Ibid., November 16, 1966.

122. DEFE 13/529, CINC MIDEAST to MOD UK, November 16, 1966.

123. Ibid., Nairne to Private Secretary/Minister (Army), November 24, 1966.

124. Ibid., Cooper to Private Secretary/Secretary of State, November 16, 1966.

125. Ibid., memorandum by the Foreign Secretary, "South Arabia: Bowen Report on the Handling of Detainees in Aden," November 29, 1966.

126. WO 32/20987, Turnbull to Brown, November 11, 1966.

127. DEFE 24/252, Oates to Brenchley, Foreign Office, January 17, 1967.

128. DEFE 24/252, "Return of Complaints—31st December, 1966." See DEFE 24/252, Oates to McCarthy, April 11, 1967, and DEFE 24/252, Ollquist to McCarthy, April 27, 1967, for additional reports.

129. FCO 8/180, Turnbull to Foreign Office, February 9, 1967.

130. FCO 8/226, Turnbull to Brenchley, March 22, 1967.

131. Turnbull did not implement all of Bowen's recommendations: He did not relocate the interrogation center and did not replace military interrogators with civilians because these measures were deemed impractical. See DEFE 13/529, Turnbull to Foreign Office, November 16, 1966, and WO 32/20987 POMEC (Chairman LIC) to Foreign Office, November 15, 1966.

132. DEFE 24/252, Proposals for procedure to be adopted on the occasion of M. Rochat's visit to Aden in January 1967, December 15, 1966.

133. FCO 8/226, McCarthy to Brenchley, April 29, 1967.

134. DEFE 24/252, Proposals for procedure to be adopted on the occasion of M. Rochat's visit.

135. Boissier, "The Silence of the International Committee of the Red Cross."

136. DEFE 24/252, March Return, Complaints by Detainees 234 and 1/67, April 27, 1967.

137. DEFE 24/252, February Return, Complaint by Detainee 240, March 1967; the individual case sheets are dated March 1967, but the return was filed with the Foreign Office on April 11.

138. DEFE 13/529, Minister (Army) to Defence Secretary, November 23, 1966.

139. DEFE 24/252, Hewetson to Minister (Army), April 4, 1967.

140. Some scrutiny fell on Cowper and the interrogation center commander. DEFE 13/529, Assistant Secretary, Adjutant General Secretariat to Private Secretary/Minister (Army), November 28, 1966.

141. FCO 8/238, Turnbull to Foreign Office, April 24, 1967.

142. FCO 8/238, McCarthy to Brenchley, April 25, 1967, p. 3.

143. FCO 8/238, "Black-Eye Case Envoy Cleared," Daily Express, May 12, 1967.

144. DEFE 24/252, Turnbull to Foreign Office, April 22, 1967.

145. FCO 8/238, McCarthy to Turnbull, April 29, 1967.

146. FCO 8/238, Shackleton to Foreign Office, April 22, 1967.

147. FCO 8/238, Thomson, Foreign Office to Swann, May 12, 1967.

148. Cobain, Cruel Britannia, and Edwards, Mad Mitch's Tribal Law, 130.

149. Joe Starling, Soldier On! The Testament of a Tom (Staplehurst, UK: Spellmount, 1992), 50–52.

150. "Aden—Mad Mitch and His Tribal Law," Empire Warriors, BBC, London, 2004.

151. John Baxter, Imperial War Museum accession 13145, reel 3.

152. When the battalion returned home, the drummers recalled that they "had a very interesting and exciting tour, thanks to the clandestine nature of our work," but "now it's back to drumming!" Dunbar Papers 2/1, Supplement—The Regimental Magazine of the Lancashire Regiment, Autumn 1967.

153. ICRC, B AG 225-001-002, Gaillard to Rochat, January 13, 1967, p. 3.

154. Walker, Aden Insurgency, 219–24. See also Dunbar Papers 2/4, "Casualties and Incidents—Aden State."

155. ICRC, B AG 225-001-005, Rochat Report No.7, April–May 1967, pp. 6–7.

156. FO 8/494, Maynard to McCarthy, June 10, 1967.

157. FO 8/494, Trevelyan to Allen, June 10, 1967.

158. AI-1294, Baker letter, "The Bowen Report on Aden," December 1966.

159. AI-1295 Amnesty International Bulletin, no. 18, February 1967.

160. For an in-depth study of AI's internal crisis, see Buchanan, "Amnesty International in Crisis, 1966–7."

161. AI-1295, Benenson to Baker, January 9, 1967.

162. "50 Aden Deaths Kept Secret," Times, February 27, 1967; "Amnesty Head Accuses the FO," Guardian, February 27, 1967.

163. For MacBride's discussion of CIA funding see AI-1295, Comment by the Secretary-General of the ICJ, February 20, 1967.

164. AI-1295, Benenson to Chairman, Hoare's Bank, January 9, 1967. AI was also implicated in a scandal over secretly accepting government funds for supporting the families of political prisoners in Rhodesia. See Sellars, The Rise and Rise of Human Rights, 108–9.

165. AI-1295, An Investigation into the Operations of the International Secretariat, February 28, 1967.

166. AI-1296, "Private and Confidential Letter to All Members" by Eric Baker, March 20, 1967.

167. Edwards, *Mad Mitch's Tribal Law*, 135.

168. Mawby, *British Policy in Aden and the Protectorates*, 146–65 and Walker, *Aden Insurgency*, 219–35.

169. Ibid., 167–76.

170. Hickling Papers 2, p. 119.

5. "A More Talkative Place"

1. For general historiography on the Troubles and the primary belligerents, see Tim Pat Coogan, *The Troubles: Ireland's Ordeal and the Search for Peace* (Basingstoke, UK: Palgrave Macmillan, 2002); Paul Dixon, *Northern Ireland: The Politics of War and Peace*, 2nd ed. (Basingstoke, UK: Palgrave Macmillan, 2008); Marc Mulholland, *The Longest War: Northern Ireland's Troubled History* (Oxford: Oxford University Press, 2002); Richard English, *Armed Struggle: The History of the IRA* (New York: Oxford University Press, 2003); Ed Moloney, *A Secret History of the IRA* (New York: Norton, 2003); Ian Wood, *Crimes of Loyalty: A History of the UDA* (Edinburgh: Edinburgh University Press, 2006); Steve Bruce, *The Red Hand: Protestant Paramilitaries in Northern Ireland* (Oxford: Oxford University Press, 1992); Andrew Sanders and Ian S. Wood, *Times of Troubles: Britain's War in Northern Ireland* (Edinburgh: Edinburgh University Press, 2012); Ken Wharton, *A Long Long War: Voices from the British Army in Northern Ireland, 1969–98* (Solihull, UK: Helion, 2008); and Brendan O'Leary and John McGarry, *The Politics of Antagonism: Understanding Northern Ireland* (London: Athlone Press, 1993).

2. For a chronology including many of the inquiries, investigations, and reports conducted during the Troubles, see CAIN Web Service, "A Chronology of the Conflict—1968 to the Present," http://cain.ulst.ac.uk/othelem/ chron.htm.

3. As quoted in Desmond Hamill, *Pig in the Middle: The Army in Northern Ireland 1969–1984* (London: Methuen, 1985), 67.

4. Paul Bew, *Ireland: The Politics of Enmity 1789–2006* (Oxford: Oxford University Press, 2007), 488–95; Brice Dickson, *The European Convention on Human Rights and the Conflict in Northern Ireland* (Oxford: Oxford University Press, 2010), 7–11; Christine Kinealy, *War and Peace: Ireland since the 1960s* (London: Reaktion Books, 2010), 33–40.

5. Simon Prince, *Northern Ireland's '68: Civil Rights, Global Revolt and the Origins of the Troubles* (Dublin: Irish Academic Press, 2007), 1–5, 69.

6. Sectarian symbolism was so prevalent in Northern Ireland that even the names of cities reveal political sentiments. Derry/Londonderry provides the best example—nationalists preferred to call the city Derry, whereas unionists favored Londonderry. I use the terms interchangeably without seeking to privilege one political persuasion over another.

7. Hamill, *Pig in the Middle*, 3–7.

8. Stephen Howe, *Ireland and Empire: Colonial Legacies in Irish History and Culture* (Oxford: Oxford University Press, 2000), 69.

9. Peter Neumann, *Britain's Long War: British Strategy in the Northern Ireland Conflict, 1969–98* (Basingstoke, UK: Palgrave Macmillan, 2003), 17–21.

10. As quoted ibid., 16.

11. David McKittrick and David McVea, *Making Sense of the Troubles: A History of the Northern Ireland Conflict* (Chicago: New Amsterdam Books, 2002), 57–59.

12. On the army's transplanting colonial methods into Northern Ireland, see David Benest, "Aden to Northern Ireland, 1966–1976," in *Big Wars and Small Wars: The British Army and the Lessons of War in the Twentieth Century*, ed. Hew Strachan, (London: Routledge, 2006), 115–44; Aaron Edwards, "Misapplying Lessons Learned? Analysing the Utility of British Counterinsurgency Strategy in Northern Ireland, 1971–76," *Small Wars & Insurgencies* 21, no. 2 (June 2010): 303–30; Keith Jeffery, "Security Policy in Northern Ireland: Some Reflections on the Manage-

ment of Violent Conflict," *Terrorism and Political Violence* 2, no. 1 (Spring 1990): 21–35; John Newsinger, "From Counter-Insurgency to Internal Security: Northern Ireland 1969–1992," *Small Wars & Insurgencies* 6, no. 1 (March 1995): 88–111; Christopher Tuck, "Northern Ireland and the British Approach to Counter-Insurgency," *Defense & Security Analysis* 23, no. 2 (June 2007): 165–83; and Paul Dixon, "'Hearts and Minds'? British Counter-Insurgency Strategy in Northern Ireland," *Journal of Strategic Studies* 32, no. 3 (June 2009): 445–74.

13. This "get tough" attitude did not permeate all British operations and did not mark a linear progression of constantly increasing state violence against insurgents and civilians. British strategy and tactics remained flexible throughout the war. See Huw Bennett, "From Direct Rule to Motorman: Adjusting British Military Strategy for Northern Ireland in 1972," *Studies in Conflict and Terrorism* 33, no. 6 (June 2010): 511–32; Neumann, *Britain's Long War*; and M. L. R. Smith and Peter Neumann, "Motorman's Long Journey: Changing the Strategic Setting in Northern Ireland," *Contemporary British History* 19, no. 4 (December 2005): 413–35.

14. Hamill, *Pig in the Middle*, 13.

15. Moloney, *A Secret History of the IRA*, 198, and English, *Armed Struggle*, 88–108.

16. English, *Armed Struggle*, 134–35.

17. Hamill, *Pig in the Middle*, 35–36.

18. As quoted ibid., 36. Also see Moloney, *A Secret History of the IRA*, 89–92, and Thomas Hennessey, *The Evolution of the Troubles 1970–72* (Dublin: Irish Academic Press, 2007), 37–46.

19. "The Army and the Mob," *Guardian*, August 5, 1970.

20. Douglas Porch, *Counterinsurgency: Exposing the Myths of the New Way of War* (Cambridge: Cambridge University Press, 2013), 274–75.

21. Simon Winchester, "Army Told to Open Fire on Nail-Bombers," *Guardian*, November 2, 1970.

22. Simon Winchester, "Tough New Measures for Ulster Riot Areas," *Guardian*, March 3, 1971.

23. Edwards, "Misapplying Lessons Learned?," 308–12.

24. Hennessey, *The Evolution of the Troubles 1970–72*, 76–77.

25. BBC, "1971: British Troops Shoot Londonderry Rioters," *On This Day*, http://news.bbc.co.uk/onthisday/hi/dates/stories/july/8/newsid_2496000/2496479.stm.

26. Hamill, *Pig in the Middle*, 53–55.

27. Ibid., 55–57.

28. Hennessey, *The Evolution of the Troubles 1970–72*, 120–32.

29. Peter Hildrew, "MP Alleges Brutality by Army in Bogside," *Guardian*, August 18, 1971.

30. Harold Jackson, "Troops Wounded in Derry Gunfire," *Guardian*, August 10, 1971.

31. As quoted in Hamill, *Pig in the Middle*, 77. Also see 61–65.

32. See chapters 4 and 5 in Martin McCleery, *Operation Demetrius and Its Aftermath: A New History of the Use of Internment without Trial in Northern Ireland 1971–75* (Manchester: Manchester University Press, 2015).

33. As quoted in Hennessey, *The Evolution of the Troubles 1970–72*, 144.

34. Ibid., 146–47.

35. On coercive interrogation, see Samantha Newbery, "Intelligence and Controversial British Interrogation Techniques: The Northern Ireland Case, 1971–2," *Irish Studies in International Affairs* 20 (January 2009): 103–19; Samantha Newbery et al., "Interrogation, Intelligence and the Issue of Human Rights," *Intelligence & National Security* 24, no. 5 (October 2009): 631–43; Cobain, *Cruel Britannia*, 135–203; and Peter Taylor, *Beating the Terrorists?: Interrogation at Omagh, Gough, and Castlereagh* (New York: Penguin Books, 1980).

36. Cobain, *Cruel Britannia*, 140; Newbery et al., "Interrogation, Intelligence and the Issue of Human Rights," 631; Newbery, "Intelligence and Controversial British Interrogation Techniques," 103–5.

37. Hennessey, *The Evolution of the Troubles 1970–72*, 152–53; Newbery, "Intelligence and Controversial British Interrogation Techniques," 106–7. See also PREM 15/485, Trend, Cabinet Secretary to the Prime Minister, November 10, 1971, and Dunnett, Ministry of Defence, to Trend, November 15, 1971.

38. PREM 15/485, Robertson, Cabinet Office to Armstrong, Principal Private Secretary to the Prime Minister, enclosure on interrogation training, October 19, 1971.

39. BBC, "Papers Reveal Government 'in Dark' over IRA," January 1, 2000, http://news. bbc.co.uk/2/hi/uk_news/northern_ireland/585080.stm.

40. Hamill, *Pig in the Middle*, 66–67, and Hennessey, *The Evolution of the Troubles 1970–72*, 153–54.

41. PREM 15/485, Robertson to Armstrong, enclosure: Operation Calaba, October 19, 1971.

42. Hennessey, *The Evolution of the Troubles 1970–72*, 154–55.

43. Ibid., 156; Newbery, "Intelligence and Controversial British Interrogation Techniques" 110–12.

44. As quoted in Hennessey, *The Evolution of the Troubles 1970–72*, 159.

45. PREM 15/485, Woodfield, Home Office to Gregson, Prime Minister's Office, August 20, 1971.

46. Hennessey, *The Evolution of the Troubles 1970–72*, 157–60. Writing in 2001, the journalist Peter Taylor noted that on the subject of interrogation in depth, "even thirty years after the event, it is extraordinarily difficult to pin down who was responsible for making the decision and then carrying it out. Those I spoke to either said they did not know it was happening, or, if they did, they were not responsible for it. The buck is passed with alacrity." Peter Taylor, *Brits: The War Against the IRA* (London: Bloomsbury, 2001), 68.

47. Samantha Newbery, *Interrogation, Intelligence and Security: Controversial British Techniques* (Manchester, UK: Manchester University Press, 2015), 86–88.

48. Hennessey, *The Evolution of the Troubles 1970–72*, 160–63.

49. Edmund Compton, *Report of the Enquiry into Allegations against the Security Forces of Physical Brutality in Northern Ireland Arising Out of Events on the 9th August, 1971* (London: HMSO, 1971), 23 (Compton Report).

50. Taylor, *Brits*, 69. Also see Compton Report, 12.

51. PREM 15/485, letter to Cabinet Secretary, PM Minute No. M66/71, November 8, 1971.

52. As quoted in Hennessey, *The Evolution of the Troubles 1970–72*, 299. Heath made this remark in the aftermath of the January 1972 Bloody Sunday shootings, but it is an accurate reflection of his view of the conflict in 1971 as well.

53. Hansard, HC Deb., November 16, 1971 vol. 826, cols. 216–18.

54. D. A. S. Cairns, "Parker, Hubert Lister, Baron Parker of Waddington (1900–1972)," rev. Robert Stevens, *Oxford Dictionary of National Biography* (Oxford: Oxford University Press, 2004), 684–85.

55. This analysis draws heavily from Newbery, "Intelligence and Controversial British Interrogation Techniques." Reference materials and evidence provided by the army to the Parker committee can be found in DEFE 23/111.

56. WO 32/21776, note of a meeting held by permanent undersecretary on November 23, 1971, to discuss a draft historical paper, November 25, 1971.

57. DEFE 13 /918, Privy Councillor's Enquiry: Note by the Intelligence Coordinator, undated.

58. WO 296/25, Report of the Committee on Interrogation Procedures (Parker Report), January 31, 1972, p. 2.

59. WO 296/25, Parker Report, 3–11.

60. Ibid., 17–19.

61. Ibid., 21–23.

62. Ibid., 26–27.

63. Simon Hoggart, "Gardiner Report 'an Indictment,'" *Guardian*, March 3, 1972.

64. As quoted in Hennessey, *The Evolution of the Troubles 1970–72*, 163–64. Original from National Archives of Ireland, D/T 2002/8/495 NcCann, Secretary of External Affairs, Note, November 18, 1971.

65. Dickson, *The European Convention on Human Rights*, 61–68.

66. McKittrick and McVea, *Making Sense of the Troubles*, 74–79, and Newbery, "Intelligence and Controversial British Interrogation Techniques," 118.

67. Commentators are divided over the implications of Heath's ban on the techniques. Samantha Newbery argues that "the decision to issue new interrogation guidelines, decisions on their form and the pressure caused by the case before the European Commission of Human Rights were between them some of the most tangible effects" on the British government. See Newbery, "Intelligence and Controversial British Interrogation Techniques," 118. In contrast, Ian Cobain calls Heath's ban a bureaucratic "sleight of hand" because the joint directive was split into two parts. Part 1 was published and included the ban on the five techniques. Part 2, however, existed in draft form so that it could permit the techniques unofficially. Part 2 was concealed from the public and from the European Commission of Human Rights when the commission heard evidence on the Irish government's application. Cobain insists that Heath knew of these omissions. Cobain, *Cruel Britannia*, 163–64.

68. PREM 15/1035, Private Secretary to Prime Minister, February 17, 1972.

69. PREM 15/1035, Private Secretary to Prime Minister, February 8, 1972.

70. PREM 15/1035, Jeffs to Roberts, March 1, 1972.

71. PREM 15/1709, Attorney General to Prime Minister, February 23, 1973.

72. Dickson, *The European Convention on Human Rights*, 150.

73. DEFE 23/110, "Interrogation in Northern Ireland: An Assessment of Local Factors Affecting its Operation and a Record of Its Value in Security Force Activities," not dated.

74. Hennessey, *The Evolution of the Troubles 1970–72*, 214–19, and Neumann, *Britain's Long War*, 58–63.

75. Lord Saville, *Report of the Bloody Sunday Inquiry*, vol. 1 (London: TSO, 2010), 9.27 (BSI Report), http://webarchive.nationalarchives.gov.uk/20101103103930/http:/report.bloody-sunday-inquiry.org.

76. Ibid., 3.1–3.42.

77. McKittrick and McVea, *Making Sense of the Troubles*, 77.

78. BSI Report, AC74 Sean Collins statement.

79. BSI Report, AF15, Pauline Ferry statement.

80. Taoiseach is the Republic of Ireland's head of government.

81. Hamill, *Pig in the Middle*, 93–94, and Simon Hoggart, "Rioters and Police Clash after Embassy Burns," *Guardian*, February 3, 1972.

82. Tony Geraghty, *The Irish War: The Hidden Conflict between the IRA and British Intelligence* (Baltimore: Johns Hopkins University Press, 2000), 66–68, and McKittrick and McVea, *Making Sense of the Troubles*, 78.

83. Dermot P. J. Walsh, *Bloody Sunday and the Rule of Law in Northern Ireland* (Basingstoke, UK: Macmillan, 2000), 54–84.

84. On the media's reluctance to challenge the official interpretation, see Greg McLaughlin and Stephen Baker, *The British Media and Bloody Sunday* (Bristol, UK: Intellect, 2015).

85. Hennessey, *The Evolution of the Troubles 1970–72*, 320–34; McKittrick and McVea, *Making Sense of the Troubles*, 82; and Mulholland, *The Longest War*, 104–5.

86. Smith and Neumann, "Motorman's Long Journey," 414.

87. Andrew Sanders, "Operation Motorman (1972) and the Search for a Coherent British Counterinsurgency Strategy in Northern Ireland," *Small Wars & Insurgencies* 24, no. 3 (July 2013): 479–82.

88. Hennessey, *The Evolution of the Troubles 1970–72*, 345–47.

89. On populist and radical politics during the global protests of 1968, see Martin Klimke, *The Other Alliance: Student Protest in West Germany and the United States in the Global Sixties* (Princeton: Princeton University Press, 2010), and Jeremi Suri, *Power and Protest: Global Revolution in the Age of Detente* (Cambridge, MA: Harvard University Press, 2003).

90. Moyn, *The Last Utopia*, 166.

91. Keys, *Reclaiming American Virtue*, 214–68.

92. Madsen, " 'Legal Diplomacy,' " 75–79.

93. James E. Cronin, *Global Rules: America, Britain and a Disordered World* (New Haven: Yale University Press, 2014), 65–69.

94. NIPC, P1076-NICRA, dossier on harassment and brutality by the British army, 1972.

95. NIPC, P2116-NICRA, Behaviour of the British Army in North Belfast, January 1972.

96. CJ, 4/605 NICRA, "British Government Violations of Human Rights in N. Ireland," 1973, p. 3, and CJ, 4/605 NICRA and Association for Legal Justice, "Communication Concerning Violations of Human Rights in Northern Ireland," July 25, 1973.

97. CJ, 4/605 McCann to Farrington, Home Office, February 11, 1974.

98. Dick Grogan, "Damage Caused by Torture Studied by Amnesty Group," *Irish Times*, October 8, 1973.

99. CJ, 4/603, Amnesty International News Release, December 3, 1973.

100. "Ulster Prisoners Adopted," *Guardian*, February 4, 1974, and "Amnesty to Adopt N.I. prisoners," *Irish Times*, February 4, 1974.

101. CAIN Web Service, NICRA, *"We Shall Overcome"* . . . *The History of the Struggle for Civil Rights in Northern Ireland 1968–1978* (1978), http://cain.ulst.ac.uk/events/crights/nicra/nicra781.htm. For Brockway's 1970s correspondence with many groups regarding Northern Ireland, see Brockway Papers, 47-220a-g.

102. Hansard, HL Deb. October 11, 1971, vol. 324, cols. 197–200.

103. For Lord Brockway's correspondence on this matter, see Brockway Papers 47-220a-b. See PRONI, D/3159/4/1 and D/3816/12 for NICRA and Ulster Unionist Party views on a bill of rights prior to direct rule.

104. Lord Gardiner, *Report of a Committee to Consider, in the Context of Civil Liberties and Human Rights, Measures to Deal with Terrorism in Northern Ireland* (London: HMSO, 1975). For excerpts and a summary of key points, see CAIN Web Service, "Gardiner Committee Report," http://cain.ulst.ac.uk/hmso/gardiner.htm#1.

105. Dickson, *The European Convention on Human Rights*, 57–58, and Kevin Boyle, "Human Rights and the Northern Ireland Emergency," in *Human Rights in Criminal Procedure: A Comparative Study*, ed. John A. Andrews (The Hague: Martinus Nijhoff Publishers, 1982), 153–54.

106. CJ, 4/605 "Violations of Human Rights: Agenda Item No. 12(b)," UN Documents Section, FCO, February 14, 1974.

107. Ibid.

108. Coogan, *The Troubles*, 73.

109. Hansard, HC Deb., April 22, 1969, vol. 782, cols. 281–88.

110. McKittrick and McVea, *Making Sense of the Troubles*, 87–114; Alvin Jackson, "Tame Tory Hacks? The Ulster Party at Westminster, 1922–72," *Historical Journal* 54, no. 2 (2011): 453–75; and Graham Walker, *A History of the Ulster Unionist Party: Protest, Pragmatism, and Pessimism* (Manchester, UK: Manchester University Press, 2004), 212–85.

111. English, *Armed Struggle*, 169–70 and 248.

112. Dickson, *The European Convention on Human Rights*, 55–60, and Neumann, *Britain's Long War*, 109. For in-depth analysis of the Diplock courts, see John Jackson, "Vicious and Virtuous Cycles in Prosecuting Terrorism: The Diplock Court Experience," in *Guantanamo Bay and Beyond: Exceptional Courts and Military Commissions in Comparative Perspective* (New York: Cambridge University Press, 2013), 225–44; and John D. Jackson and Seán Doran, *Judge without Jury: Diplock Trials in the Adversary System* (Oxford: Clarendon Press, 1995).

113. Clive Walker, *The Prevention of Terrorism in British Law*, 2nd ed. (Manchester, UK: Manchester University Press, 1992), 31.

114. Hansard, HC Deb., November 28, 1974, vol. 882, col. 743.

115. Hansard, HC Deb., July 25, 1974, vol. 877, cols. 1844–71.

116. Hansard, HC Deb., November 28, 1974, vol. 882, cols. 692–93.

117. Hansard, HL Deb., December 12, 1974, vol. 355, col. 843.

118. As quoted in Huw Bennett, " 'Smoke Without Fire'? Allegations against the British Army in Northern Ireland, 1972–5," *Twentieth Century British History* 24, no. 2 (June 2013): 276.

119. Ibid., 277–81.

120. For example, see English, *Armed Struggle*, 122, 170.

121. Bennett, " 'Smoke without Fire'?," 287–88 (quote on p. 287).

122. CJ, 4/969, Cox, Northern Ireland Office to Prime Minister, March 23, 1973.

123. Bennett, " 'Smoke Without Fire'?," 290–94.

124. Peter Carrington, *Reflecting on Things Past: The Memoirs of Peter Lord Carrington* (New York: Harper & Row, 1988), 247.

125. CAIN Web Service, "A List of British Television Programmes about the Conflict (1968 to 1978)," http://cain.ulst.ac.uk/othelem/media/tv10yrs.htm.

126. On the role of the media in the war, see David Miller, *Don't Mention the War: Northern Ireland, Propaganda and the Media* (London: Pluto Press, 1994), and Robert J. Savage, *The BBC's "Irish Troubles": Television, Conflict and Northern Ireland* (Manchester: Manchester University Press, 2015).

127. Neumann, *Britain's Long War*, 22.

128. DEFE, 24/838, W. H. Sillitoe, Ministry of Defence, memorandum, Television Training, September 13, 1973.

129. DEFE 24/838, Summary of Pre-Northern Ireland Specialist Training, 3rd Revise, April 1975.

130. CJ, 4/1169, Webster, Northern Ireland Office to England, October 3, 1975.

131. Ibid., Hill, Northern Ireland Office to Webster, October 3, 1975.

132. Ibid., Staff in Confidence Memorandum, Civil Representatives, n.d.

133. Ibid., Morrison to England, January 28, 1976.

134. Bennett, "'Smoke without Fire'?," 284–85.

135. For NICRA's initial objections, see Linen Hall Library (LHL), NIPC P1051, "The Feather Commission . . . Obstruction to Justice?," NICRA, 1975. For Conservative MPs' opposition, see John Biggs-Davison and Enoch Powell's statements in Hansard, HC Deb., June 20, 1973, vol. 858, cols. 800–801.

136. CJ, 4/3572, "SACHR Proposal for a Bill of Rights in NI," background note, 1980. SACHR's proposals for incorporating the European Convention on Human Rights into UK domestic law later formed the basis for the 2000 UK Human Rights Act.

137. Gardiner, *Report of a Committee*.

138. John Newsinger, *British Counterinsurgency: From Palestine to Northern Ireland*, 2nd ed. (Basingstoke, UK: Palgrave Macmillan, 2015), 185.

139. Porch, *Counterinsurgency*, 280. The UDR was a locally recruited army regiment that replaced the all-Protestant police reserve, the "B-Specials," in 1969.

140. Dickson, *The European Convention on Human Rights*, 250–252 (quote on 251).

141. Anthony Jennings, *Justice Under Fire: The Abuse of Civil Liberties in Northern Ireland* (London: Pluto Press, 1988), 109.

142. The first conviction of a soldier for murder did not come until 1984. The soldier in question—Private Lee Clegg—was released under orders from the home secretary after serving less than two years of his life sentence. He was later acquitted of murder and returned to the army. See Dickson, *The European Convention on Human Rights*, 252–53.

143. Madsen, "'Legal Diplomacy,'" 75–79.

144. Dickson, *The European Convention on Human Rights*, 377–95.

145. Cobain, *Cruel Britannia*, 159–60, and Taylor, *Beating the Terrorists?*, 23–26.

146. See, for example, John McGuffin, *The Guineapigs* (London: Penguin, 1974).

147. A 2014 documentary asserted that recently released evidence indicated that Britain had purposely misrepresented its interrogation activities before the European Court. See *The Torture Files*, RTÉ Investigations Unit, RTÉ One (Dublin), June 4, 2014.

148. Dickson, *The European Convention on Human Rights*, 150–152, as quoted on 167.

149. Taylor, *Beating the Terrorists?*, 270–302 and 324–42.

150. Aogan Mulcahy, *Policing Northern Ireland: Conflict, Legitimacy and Reform* (Cullompton, UK: Willan, 2005), 61–63.

151. Geraghty, *The Irish War*, 101, and Neumann, *Britain's Long War*, 97. On supergrasses, see Steven Greer, *Supergrasses: A Study in Anti-Terrorist Law Enforcement in Northern Ireland* (Oxford: Clarendon Press, 1995).

152. Taylor, *Brits*, 278–85, and Geraghty, *The Irish War*, 116–27.

153. Bill Rolston, "'An Effective Mask for Terror': Democracy, Death Squads and Northern Ireland," *Crime, Law & Social Change* 44, no. 2 (2005): 192.

154. For an extensive treatment of collusion allegations, see Anne Cadwallader, *Lethal Allies: British Collusion in Ireland* (Cork, Ire.: Mercier Press, 2013), and Maurice Punch, *State Violence, Collusion and the Troubles: Counter Insurgency, Government Deviance and Northern Ireland* (London: Pluto Press, 2012).

Conclusion

1. "Pat Finucane Murder: 'Shocking State Collusion,' Says PM," BBC News, December 12, 2012, http://www.bbc.com/ news/uk-northern-ireland-20662412.

2. Lord Saville, *Report of the Bloody Sunday Inquiry* (London: HMSO, 2010), http://web archive.nationalarchives.gov.uk/20101103103930/http:/report.bloody-sunday-inquiry.org/.

3. "Bloody Sunday: Ex-Soldier Arrested over Londonderry Shootings," BBC News, November 10, 2015, http://www.bbc.com/news/uk-northern-ireland-34775466.

4. Evidence came to light in the RTÉ television documentary *The Torture Files*. See "Hooded Men: Irish Government Bid to Reopen 'Torture' Case," BBC News, December 2, 2014, http://www.bbc.com/news/uk-northern-ireland-30296397; and Susan McKay, "The Torture Centre: Northern Ireland's 'Hooded Men,'" *Irish Times*, July 25, 2015.

5. Alan Erwin, "'Hooded Men' Granted Judicial Review as They Clear First Stage in Legal Battle," *Belfast Telegraph*, June 4, 2015.

6. Jennifer Curtis, *Human Rights as War by Other Means: Peace Politics in Northern Ireland* (Philadelphia: University of Pennsylvania Press, 2014), 4.

7. Scholars have also convincingly challenged the notion that the British army's organizational culture as a relatively decentralized and innovative "learning organization" explains British success against insurgencies. See Austin Long, *The Soul of Armies: Counterinsurgency Doctrine and Military Culture in the US and UK* (Ithaca: Cornell University Press, 2016).

8. For example, Common Article 3 of the 1949 Geneva Conventions included a provision that protections for noncombatants applied during "non-international armed conflict" as well as international wars. But British legal officers simply insisted that agreements such as the Geneva Conventions—the cornerstone of international humanitarian law—did not apply to colonial emergencies. ICRC, *1949 Conventions and Additional Protocols, and Their Commentaries*, https://www.icrc.org/applic/ihl/ihl.nsf/vwTreaties1949.xsp. See also Fabian Klose, "Human Rights for and against Empire: Legal and Public Discourses in the Age of Decolonization," *Journal of the History of International Law* 18, no. 1 (2016): 317–38.

9. Robert Jennings and Arthur Watts, *Oppenheim's International Law*, 9th ed. (London: Longman's, 1992), 12, and Emily Crawford, *The Treatment of Combatants and Insurgents under the Law of Armed Conflict* (Oxford: Oxford University Press, 2010), 37.

10. UN GAOR Res. A/RES/2444 (XXIII), "Declaration on Respect for Human Rights in Armed Conflict," December 19, 1968, as quoted in Klose, "Human Rights for and against Empire," 318.

11. ICRC, Protocols Additional to the Geneva Conventions of 12 August 1949, June 8, 1977, https://www.icrc.org/applic/ihl/ihl.nsf/Treaty.xsp?documentId=D9E6B6264D7723C3C1256 3CD002D6CE4&action=openDocument.

12. Klose, "Human Rights for and against Empire," 317–20.

13. Charter 88, box 1, "Add Your Name to Ours" and "Twenty-One Questions Answered by Charter 88," not dated.

14. Charter 88, box 13, executive meeting minutes, February 27, 1996.

15. CAIN Web Service, "The Framework Documents 22 Feb 1995," University of Ulster, http://cain.ulst.ac.uk/ events/ peace/docs/fd22295.htm; and "The Agreement: The Agreement Reached in the Multi-Party Negotiations, 10 April 1998," http://cain.ulst.ac.uk/events/ peace/ docs/agreement.htm.

16. See Peter Rowe, *Legal Accountability in Britain's Wars, 2000–2015* (London: Routledge, 2016), and Peter Rowe, *The Impact of Human Rights Law on Armed Forces* (Cambridge: Cambridge University Press, 2005).

17. Sir William Gage, *The Report of the Baha Mousa Inquiry* (London: TSO, 2011), 263–409.

18. Huw Bennett, "Baha Mousa and the British Army in Iraq," in *The British Approach to Counterinsurgency: From Malaya and Northern Ireland to Iraq and Afghanistan*, ed. Paul Dixon (Basingstoke: Palgrave Macmillan, 2012), 201.

19. See *R (Al-Skeini) v. Secretary of State for Defence* [2008], 1 AC 153, and Andrew Williams, *A Very British Killing: The Death of Baha Mousa* (London: Jonathan Cape, 2012). The Baha Mousa proceedings are formally known in the courts under the name Al-Skeini.

20. Article 1, *European Convention for the Protection of Human Rights and Fundamental Freedoms,* Council of Europe, http://www.echr.coe.int/Documents/Convention_BNG.pdf.

21. The European Court of Human Rights also heard the case and ruled that the European Convention applied to British forces not just when they were on British bases in Iraq but also while on patrol. See *Al-Skeini v. UK* (2011), 53 EHRR 18, Section H8(c), p. 3. On the Baha Mousa case, see Rachel Stevenson and Matthew Weaver, "Timeline: Baha Mousa Case," *Guardian,* September 8, 2011, http://www.theguardian.com /uk/2008/may/14/mousa.timeline; and Melina Padron, "*Al-Skeini* May Open Door to More War Claims," *UK Human Rights Blog,* http:// ukhumanrightsblog.com/2011/08/15/al-skeini-may-open-door-to-more-war-claims.

22. Nigel Farage, the leader of the UK Independence Party, was one politician who questioned this role. See UK Independence Party, "Let's get it straight on human rights," http:// www.ukip.org/let_s_get_it_straight_on_human_rights. The Conservative home secretary Theresa May, who did not publicly support leaving the EU, also favored leaving the European Convention. See Christopher Hope and Peter Dominiczak, "Chaos as Theresa May Demands UK Quits European Convention on Human Rights in Challenge to David Cameron as Price of Staying in EU," *Daily Telegraph,* April 25, 2016.

23. Fintan O'Toole, "The English Have Placed a Bomb under the Irish Peace Process," *Guardian,* June 24, 2016, and "Brexit Is Being Driven by English Nationalism. And It Will End in Self-Rule," *Guardian,* June 19, 2016.

24. Christopher Hope, "Theresa May to Fight 2020 Election on Plans to Take Britain Out of European Convention on Human Rights after Brexit Is Completed," *Telegraph,* December 28, 2016, http://www.telegraph.co.uk/news/2016/12/28/theresa-may-fight-2020-election-plans-take-britain-european/.

25. National Security Archive, George Washington University, "The Interrogation Documents: Debating U.S. Policy and Methods," July 13, 2004, http://nsarchive.gwu.edu/ NSAEBB/NSAEBB127/index.htm.

26. James Risen, "Outside Psychologists Shielded U.S. Torture Program, Report Finds," *New York Times,* July 10, 2015, and David Hoffman et al., "Report to the Special Committee of the Board of Directors of the American Psychological Association: Independent Review Relating to APA Ethics Guidelines, National Security Interrogations, and Torture," Sidley Austin LLP, July 2, 2015.

27. Emile Simpson, *War from the Ground Up: Twenty-First Century Combat as Politics* (New York: Oxford University Press, 2013), 208–13.

28. Ibid., 209.

29. Wayne E. Lee, *Waging War: Conflict, Culture, and Innovation in World History* (New York: Oxford University Press, 2015), 507–15.

30. Micah Zenko and Sarah Kreps, "Limiting Armed Drone Proliferation" (New York: Council on Foreign Relations Press, 2014).

31. David Rohde, "What the United States Owes Warren Weinstein," *Atlantic,* April 28, 2015.

32. Steve Coll, "The Unblinking Stare: The Drone War in Pakistan," *New Yorker,* November 24, 2014.

Bibliography

Archives and Private Papers

Cyprus

Cyprus State Archives, Nicosia (CSA)

The Netherlands

International Institute of Social History, Amsterdam
   Amnesty International (AI) International Secretariat Archive and Oral History
   Project

Switzerland

International Committee of the Red Cross, Geneva (ICRC)

United Kingdom

Bodleian Library and Rhodes House, Oxford University, Oxford
   Barbara Castle, Baroness Castle of Blackburn
   Hugh Foot, Baron Caradon
   Anthony Greenwood, Lord Greenwood of Rossendale
   Sir Kennedy Trevaskis
British Library, London
   India Office Records—Aden (IOR)
Churchill Archives Centre, Cambridge University, Cambridge

Julian Amery, Lord Amery
Fenner Brockway, Lord Brockway
Gerald Gardiner, Lord Gardiner
Hugh Hickling
Duncan Sandys, Baron Duncan-Sandys
Hansard Parliamentary Debates
  House of Commons (HC)
  House of Lords (HL)
Hull Archives Centre, Kingston-upon-Hull
  JUSTICE Papers (U DJU)
Imperial War Museum, London
  John P. Baxter
  General Sir Kenneth Darling
  Field Marshal Lord Harding
  John Reddaway
  Sir Richard Turnbull
  Colonel H. B. H. Waring
  Major General Sir John Willoughby
Liddell Hart Centre for Military Archives, King's College London
  Major General Charles Dunbar
Linen Hall Library, Belfast
  Northern Ireland Political Collection (NIPC)
  Public Record Office of Northern Ireland, Belfast (PRONI)
The National Archives, Kew
  Air Ministry (AIR)
  Cabinet (CAB)
  Colonial Office (CO)
  Ministry of Defence (DEFE)
  Dominions Office (DO)
  Foreign and Commonwealth Office (FCO)
  Foreign Office (FO)
  Home Office and Northern Ireland Office (CJ 4)
  Law Officers' Department (LO)
  Lord Chancellor's Office (LCO)
  Prime Minister's Office (PREM)
  War Office (WO)
University of Bradford, Bradford
  Eric Baker
University of Essex, Colchester
  Charter 88
University of Ulster
  Conflict Archive on the Internet (CAIN)

Interviews and Correspondence

Lellos Demetriades, Cyprus Bar Council
James Herlihy, Special Branch (Cyprus and Aden)

Renos Lyssiotis, Cyprus Bar Council
Saeed Hassan Sobhi, Aden Bar Council

Newspapers and Media

BBC
Belfast Telegraph
Daily Telegraph and *Sunday Telegraph*
Los Angeles Times
Manchester Guardian and *The Guardian*
New York Times
Irish News
Irish Times
The Observer
RTÉ
The Times
The Tribune

Published Primary Sources

Carrington, Peter. *Reflecting on Things Past: The Memoirs of Peter Lord Carrington*. New York: Harper & Row, 1988.
Castle, Barbara. *Fighting All the Way*. London: Macmillan, 1993.
Clerides, Glafkos. *Cyprus: My Deposition*. Vol. 1. Nicosia: Alithia Publishing, 1989.
Foley, Charles. *Island in Revolt*. London: Longman's, 1962.
Foot, Hugh (Baron Caradon). *A Start in Freedom*. New York: Harper & Row, 1964.
Gangrene. London: Calder Books, 1960.
Grivas, George. *The Memoirs of General Grivas*. Edited by Charles Foley. New York: Praeger, 1964.
Reddaway, John. *Burdened with Cyprus: The British Connection*. London: Weidenfeld & Nicolson, 1986.
Trevaskis, Kennedy. *Shades of Amber: A South Arabian Episode*. London: Hutchinson, 1968.

Document Collections

Ashton, S. R., and Wm. Roger Louis, eds. *East of Suez and the Commonwealth 1964–1971*. British Documents on the End of Empire. London: HMSO, 2004.
Coughlan, Reed, ed. *Enosis and the British: British Official Documents 1878–1950*. Sources for the History of Cyprus. Exeter: Greece and Cyprus Research Center, 2004.
Goldsworthy, David, ed. *The Conservative Government and the End of Empire 1951–1957*. British Documents on the End of Empire. London: HMSO, 1994.
Hyam, Ronald, and Wm. Roger Louis, eds. *The Conservative Government and the End of Empire 1957–1964*. British Documents on the End of Empire. London: HMSO, 2000.

229

Soulioti, Stella, ed. *Fettered Independence: Cyprus, 1878–1964*. Vol. 2, *The Documents*. Minnesota Mediterranean and East European Monographs. Minneapolis: University of Minnesota Press,2006.

Stockwell, A. J., ed. *Malaya*. Part 2, *The Communist Insurrection, 1948–53*. British Documents on the End of Empire. London: HMSO, 1995.

Index

CPSIA information can be obtained
at www.ICGtesting.com
Printed in the USA
LVOW07*1108151217

559833LV00003B/139/P